INTERNATIONAL COOPERATION ON WMD NONPROLIFERATION

STUDIES IN SECURITY AND INTERNATIONAL AFFAIRS

SERIES EDITORS

William W. Keller
*Professor of International Affairs,
Center for International Trade and
Security, University of Georgia*

Scott A. Jones
*Director of Export Control Programs,
Center for International Trade and
Security, University of Georgia*

SERIES ADVISORY BOARD

Pauline H. Baker
The Fund for Peace

Eliot Cohen
*Paul H. Nitze School of Advanced International
Studies, Johns Hopkins University*

Eric Einhorn
*Center for Public Policy and Administration,
University of Massachusetts, Amherst*

John J. Hamre
*The Center for Strategic and International
Studies*

Josef Joffe
*Hoover Institution, Institute for International
Studies, Stanford University*

Lawrence J. Korb
Center for American Progress

William J. Long
*Sam Nunn School of International Affairs,
Georgia Institute of Technology*

Jessica Tuchman Mathews
Carnegie Endowment for International Peace

Scott D. Sagan
*Center for International Security and
Cooperation, Stanford University*

Lawrence Scheinman
*Middlebury Institute of International Studies at
Monterey, CNS-WDC*

David Shambaugh
*The Elliott School of International Affairs,
George Washington University*

Jessica Stern
FXB Center, Harvard School of Public Health

International Cooperation on WMD Nonproliferation

Edited by Jeffrey W. Knopf

The University of Georgia Press
Athens

Paperback edition, 2018
© 2016 by the University of Georgia Press
Athens, Georgia 30602
www.ugapress.org
All rights reserved
Set in Minion Pro by Graphic Composition, Inc., Bogart, Georgia

Most University of Georgia Press titles are
available from popular e-book vendors.

Printed digitally

The Library of Congress has cataloged the
hardcover edition of this book as follows:

International cooperation on WMD nonproliferation / edited
by Jeffrey W. Knopf.
xiii, 333 pages ; 24 cm
Includes bibliographical references and index.
ISBN 978-0-8203-4891-9 (ebook) — ISBN 978-0-8203-4527-7 (hardcover : alk. paper)
1. Nuclear nonproliferation.   2. National security.
3. Security, International.   I. Knopf, Jeffrey W.

JZ5675.I687 2016
327.1'745—dc23

2015012856

Paperback ISBN 978-0-8203-5381-4

CONTENTS

Preface   ix

List of Abbreviations   xi

CHAPTER ONE. International Cooperation on Nonproliferation: The Growth and Diversity of Cooperative Efforts   1
  Jeffrey W. Knopf

CHAPTER TWO. The Multilateral Export Control Regimes: Informality Begets Collaboration   23
  Scott A. Jones

CHAPTER THREE. Nuclear Nonproliferation via Coercion and Consensus: The Success and Limits of the RERTR Program (1978–2004)   46
  Alan J. Kuperman

CHAPTER FOUR. Implementing Nonproliferation Programs: The Cooperative Threat Reduction Process in the Former Soviet Union   72
  Togzhan Kassenova

CHAPTER FIVE. The G8 Global Partnership: A Glass Half Full   97
  Wyn Q. Bowen and Alan Heyes

CHAPTER SIX. The Proliferation Security Initiative: The Achievements and Limits of an Informal Approach to Cooperation   116
  Emma Belcher

CHAPTER SEVEN. UN Security Council Resolution 1540: Origins, Status, and Future Prospects   140
  Tanya Ogilvie-White

CHAPTER EIGHT. Formal and Informal Mechanisms for Countering Nuclear Terrorism: The ICSANT and the GICNT   163
  Gavin Cameron

CHAPTER NINE. The Nuclear Security Summit Experiment: Has It Been a Catalyst for Action?   182
  Elizabeth Turpen

CHAPTER TEN. Cooperating Regionally, Denuclearizing Globally: Multilateral Nuclear-Weapon-Free-Zone Initiatives   206
  Michael Hamel-Green

CHAPTER ELEVEN. Bilateral Cooperation on Nonproliferation: The Role of an Epistemic Community in Argentina and Brazil's Creation of a Joint Safeguards Arrangement   229
  Sara Z. Kutchesfahani

CHAPTER TWELVE. Understanding the "Proliferation" of Nuclear Cooperation: An Alternative Theoretical Framework and Its Implications for Regional Efforts   250
  Francesca Giovannini

CHAPTER THIRTEEN. European and P5 Responses to Iran's Nuclear Program   271
  David Santoro

CHAPTER FOURTEEN. Conclusions   294
  Jeffrey W. Knopf

Contributors   317

Index   321

PREFACE

This book is a testament to the value of hallway conversations. The idea for this project grew out of a series of conversations I had with Michael Malley, a former colleague at the Naval Postgraduate School. Mike is a specialist on Southeast Asia who had begun to do work on initiatives within the region dealing with nuclear proliferation. He asked me about theoretical literature on international cooperation that might help him understand cooperation in the nonproliferation domain. Our discussions led to the realization that the leading existing frameworks fall short of capturing the kinds of dynamics we were both observing empirically. The seeds of suggestion for a new research project had been planted, and I thank Mike for providing the intellectual stimulus to embark on this line of research.

Funding to support this research was provided by the U.S. Defense Threat Reduction Agency, through its Project on Advanced Systems and Concepts for Countering WMD (PASCC). I am grateful to PASCC for the support. The views expressed in this book, however, are entirely those of the authors and are not intended to represent U.S. government policy.

After a canvass of the existing literature, I developed a preliminary theoretical framework that could guide further exploration of the sources and impact of international cooperation intended to counter the proliferation of nuclear, biological, and chemical weapons. I then invited a group of subject-matter experts to apply this framework to case studies of cooperative initiatives in support of nonproliferation. We came together to discuss first drafts of the case studies at a workshop at the Portola Hotel in Monterey, California, in March 2012. Since then, two additional authors who focus on regional efforts joined the project, and all the chapters have been revised and updated to reflect further developments, in most cases through about mid-2014.

Many people helped make this book possible and gave valuable suggestions to improve its contents. I give special thanks to Angela Archambault, whose administrative assistance ensured our authors' workshop ran smoothly. In addition to most of the authors whose chapters appear in this volume, several other people participated in the workshop and gave feedback on the individual papers and the project as a whole. This book benefitted from the valuable comments provided by Christine Wing, Wade Huntley, Bill Potter, Clay Moltz, Jeffrey Fields, Arturo Sotomayor, Bryan Lee, Anne Clunan, and Mike Malley. I also thank the anonymous reviewers of the book proposal and manuscript for their helpful suggestions. From start to finish, it has been a pleasure to work with the people at the University of Georgia Press, including Nancy Grayson, Walter Biggins, Jon Davies, and Bethany Snead. In addition, I am grateful to Joseph Dahm for his careful copyediting and to Kate Lucitt and Crystal Wilhite for preparing the index. Finally, I learned more than I can convey from the other contributors to this volume, and I thank each of them for accepting my invitation to be part of this project.

ABBREVIATIONS

ABACC	Brazilian-Argentine Agency for Accounting and Control of Nuclear Materials
AFA	Argentine Physics Association (Asociación Física Argentina)
AFNWFZ	African Nuclear-Weapon-Free Zone
AG	Australia Group
ANZUS	Australia, New Zealand, and United States Security Treaty
AP	Additional Protocol
ASEAN	Association of Southeast Asian Nations
BJP	Bharatiya Janata Party
BOG	Board of Governors (of the IAEA)
BWC	Biological and Toxin Weapons Convention
CANWFZ	Central Asia Nuclear-Weapon-Free Zone
CBRN	chemical, biological, radiological, and nuclear
CISAC	Center for International Security and Cooperation
CITS	Center for International Trade and Security
CMSS	Centre for Military and Strategic Studies
CNEA	Argentina's National Atomic Energy Commission
CNEN	Brazil's National Nuclear Energy Commission
COCOM	Coordinating Committee on Multilateral Export Controls
COE	Center of Excellence
CPPNM	Convention on the Physical Protection of Nuclear Material
CSCAP	Council on Security Cooperation in the Asia-Pacific
CTBT	Comprehensive Nuclear Test Ban Treaty
CTR	Cooperative Threat Reduction
CWC	Chemical Weapons Convention
DG	director-general (of the IAEA)
DOE	U.S. Department of Energy
DPRK	Democratic People's Republic of Korea
EBRD	European Bank for Reconstruction and Development
EEZ	Exclusive Economic Zone
ENR	enrichment and reprocessing
EU	European Union
FATF	Financial Action Task Force
FMCT	fissile material cutoff treaty

FSU	Former Soviet Union
GAO	Government Accountability Office (formerly General Accounting Office)
GICNT	Global Initiative to Combat Nuclear Terrorism
GP	Global Partnership
GRIT	graduated reciprocation in tension reduction
G7/G8	Group of 7 / Group of 8
GTRI	Global Threat Reduction Initiative
HCOC	Hague Code of Conduct
HEU	highly enriched uranium
IAEA	International Atomic Energy Agency
IAG	Implementation and Assessment Group (of the GICNT)
ICSANT	International Convention for the Suppression of Acts of Nuclear Terrorism
INFCIRC	International Atomic Energy Agency Information Circular
IPP	Initiatives for Proliferation Prevention
IPPAS	International Physical Protection Advisory Service
IR	international relations
ISIS	Institute for Science and International Security
ISTC	International Science and Technology Center
JWG	Joint Working Group on Nuclear Affairs
LANL	Los Alamos National Laboratory
LANWFZ	Latin American Nuclear-Weapon-Free Zone
LEU	low-enriched uranium
MECR	multilateral export control regime
MOX	mixed oxide
MPC&A	material protection, control, and accounting
MTCR	Missile Technology Control Regime
NAM	Non-Aligned Movement
NATO	North Atlantic Treaty Organization
NBC	nuclear, biological, and chemical
NCI	Nuclear Cities Initiative
NFZ	nuclear-free zone
NGO	nongovernmental organization
NIE	National Intelligence Estimate
NPT	Treaty on the Non-Proliferation of Nuclear Weapons
NRC	U.S. Nuclear Regulatory Commission
NSF	Nuclear Security Fund
NSG	Nuclear Suppliers Group
NSS	Nuclear Security Summit
NTI	Nuclear Threat Initiative

ABBREVIATIONS [xiii]

NWFZ	nuclear-weapon-free zone
NWS	nuclear weapon states
OAU	Organization of African Unity
OEG	Operational Experts Group (of the PSI)
OPANAL	Agency for the Prohibition of Nuclear Weapons in Latin America and the Caribbean
OPCW	Organization for the Prohibition of Chemical Weapons
PASCC	Project on Advanced Systems and Concepts for Countering WMD
PCNA	Permanent Committee on Nuclear Affairs
PD	prisoner's dilemma
P5	five permanent members of the UN Security Council
PMDA	Plutonium Management and Disposition Agreement
PSI	Proliferation Security Initiative
RERTR	Reduced Enrichment for Research and Test Reactors
ROK	Republic of Korea
SBF	Brazilian Physics Society (Sociedade Brasileira de Fisica)
SBPC	Brazilian Society for the Advancement of Science (Sociedade Brasileira para o Progresso da Ciência)
SCCC	Common System of Accounting and Control
SEANWFZ	Southeast Asian Nuclear-Weapon-Free Zone
SPNFZ	South Pacific Nuclear Free Zone
SQ	significant quantity
START	Strategic Arms Reduction Treaty
STCU	Science and Technology Center Ukraine
SUA	Suppression of Unlawful Acts
TRR	Tehran Research Reactor
UNCLOS	United Nations Convention on the Law of the Sea
UNDC	United Nations Disarmament Commission
UNODA	United Nations Office for Disarmament Affairs
UNSCR 1540	United Nations Security Council Resolution 1540
USEC	U.S. Enrichment Corporation
USIC	U.S. Industry Coalition
WA	Wassenaar Arrangement
WINS	World Institute for Nuclear Security
WMD	weapons of mass destruction

INTERNATIONAL COOPERATION ON
WMD NONPROLIFERATION

CHAPTER ONE

International Cooperation on Nonproliferation

The Growth and Diversity of Cooperative Efforts

JEFFREY W. KNOPF

GLOBAL EFFORTS TO PREVENT the spread of weapons of mass destruction (WMD) have given rise to international regimes that cover nuclear, biological, and chemical (NBC) weapons, respectively. These regimes each have at their core a global treaty: the Treaty on the Non-Proliferation of Nuclear Weapons (NPT), the Biological and Toxin Weapons Convention (BWC), and the Chemical Weapons Convention (CWC). These core treaties have been complemented by other global treaties, such as the Comprehensive Nuclear Test Ban Treaty (CTBT), and by formal international organizations, such as the International Atomic Energy Agency (IAEA) and the Organization for the Prohibition of Chemical Weapons (OPCW). Reflecting the centrality of these treaties and their associated international organizations, many discussions of nonproliferation focus on these instruments. Analyses of nonproliferation devote considerable effort to assessing the health and effectiveness of these treaties, analyzing why states join them, or finding ways to bring about greater compliance with them.

These issues are important, but they do not address the full range of international nonproliferation efforts. A number of other initiatives have sprung up alongside the core nonproliferation treaties and organizations. This volume explores the nature and sources of these other cooperative arrangements for combating proliferation and seeks to draw lessons for how to make cooperative nonproliferation measures as effective as possible.

Beyond the major treaties, the range of cooperative nonproliferation efforts has become quite extensive and diverse. Initiatives parallel to the core nonproliferation treaties began to emerge while the Cold War was still in full swing. For example, a 1974 nuclear test by India prompted a group of states involved in civil nuclear trade to establish the Nuclear Suppliers Group (NSG) with the goal of controlling exports of items that could be used in nuclear weapons development. The end of the Cold War ushered in a new set of initiatives. When the Soviet Union disintegrated, the United States launched the Cooperative Threat

Reduction (CTR) program to help former Soviet republics secure NBC weapons, materials, and know-how so these would not "leak" and facilitate WMD acquisition by new actors.

The 9/11 attacks and the discovery of the A. Q. Khan network stimulated further efforts. In 2003, the George W. Bush administration inaugurated the Proliferation Security Initiative (PSI), which seeks to promote international cooperation to interdict potential WMD-related shipments. The following year, UN Security Council Resolution (UNSCR) 1540 mandated that states enact laws and regulations to help keep NBC weapons out of the hands of terrorist actors. In an attempt to reinforce efforts to make it harder for terrorists to obtain nuclear materials, in 2010 President Barack Obama launched a series of nuclear security summits.

There have also been regional initiatives, in some cases established outside the NPT regime. In 1991, for example, Argentina and Brazil created the Brazilian-Argentine Agency for Accounting and Control of Nuclear Materials (ABACC) to verify, at a time when neither country had yet signed the NPT, that each was complying with full-scope safeguards on its nuclear activities. Indicators that certain countries are pursuing WMD have also led to ad hoc cooperative efforts to turn these potential proliferators away from this path. There have been Six-Party Talks on the issue of North Korea's nuclear program. The five permanent members of the UN Security Council (the P5) plus Germany have also engaged in negotiations with Iran about its nuclear activities.

In short, there is a tremendous amount of cooperative activity beyond the core nonproliferation treaties. Many of these initiatives have attracted the attention of analysts, and there are now multiple studies of several of them, such as CTR, PSI, and UNSCR 1540.[1] Each initiative, however, is typically studied in isolation. Until very recently, there have been no published studies dedicated to a comparative analysis, and those that do discuss multiple examples from among the newer initiatives are usually far from comprehensive.[2]

Among recent studies, Oliver Meier and Christopher Daase have edited an interesting volume concerned with recent patterns in arms control and nonproliferation.[3] They argue that recent initiatives have been more informal and coercive in nature than past efforts, and they interpret this as a move away from cooperation. With the lone exception of PSI, however, the volume does not contain case studies of individual initiatives. Moreover, even coercive measures often require cooperation. Efforts to interdict WMD shipments or to impose sanctions on treaty violators typically work only if relevant countries cooperate in their implementation. The need to assess and explain the level of cooperation hence remains.

Another project, led by Harald Müller and Carmen Wunderlich, emphasizes the importance of norms in multilateral arms control.[4] Their focus is hence on demonstrating the importance of a particular variable, rather than on examining a range of factors that could explain the development of cooperation on nonproliferation. In a follow-up study, they and other colleagues compare six multilateral initiatives with respect to how widely each effort is perceived as legitimate.[5] They conclude that states are more likely to embrace initiatives if those efforts are inclusive in membership, emphasize persuasion and capacity-building over coercion, and are framed as nuclear security measures (to reduce the threat of nuclear terrorism by non-state actors) enabling them to bypass existing cleavages in the nuclear nonproliferation regime. Their report is the one study with similar motivations to the current volume, but this volume considers a wider range of case studies and delves deeper into the sources of cooperation. In short, although recent research has begun to take account of the newer strands of nonproliferation activity, no existing study systematically examines the origins, nature, and accomplishments of the different initiatives that seek to promote cooperation against WMD proliferation.

Scott Sagan has called for the scholarly community to devote more attention to nonproliferation efforts besides the NPT. He observes, "We have strong studies of the origins of the NPT itself. But there are no equivalent studies of the origins or effectiveness of the NSG, or UN Security Council Resolution 1540, or the Proliferation Security Initiative. These newer institutions are crucial elements of the nonproliferation regime and should not be ignored."[6] This project addresses the gap identified by Sagan and provides the first systematic comparative analysis of cooperative nonproliferation activities beyond the core nonproliferation treaties.

The volume contains case studies of a wide range of nonproliferation initiatives that involve interstate cooperation. Each case study has been guided by a common analytical framework. This chapter summarizes the analytical framework that guided the study. The concluding chapter provides the lessons identified through comparative analysis of the cases. It suggests that we are witnessing a process of "building cooperation" through the gradual addition of new measures and participating states.

GOALS OF THIS VOLUME

This project has two main goals: to identify sources of cooperative nonproliferation activities and to assess the effectiveness of such endeavors. First, this project deepens our understanding of the origins of these efforts and why key states either do or do not participate in the various initiatives. Subsequent sections of this introductory chapter review existing literature on international cooperation and mine it to identify factors that could prove relevant in explaining cooperation on nonproliferation. The case study chapters that follow consider the relevance of those factors in the cases examined.

The following review shows that reality has moved beyond existing theory. Some of the activities taking place in the nonproliferation realm are not easy to describe and explain within the existing analytical frameworks for discussing cooperation. Since the NPT was signed, cooperation in practice has gradually become less about negotiating new formal international agreements and more about building new forms of cooperation, many of which are operationally oriented. Treaties have not ceased to be a goal—the BWC, CWC, and CTBT followed the NPT, and many states remain interested in negotiating a fissile material cutoff treaty (FMCT) or additional regional measures. Because of the global treaties that have already been established, however, the range of what could be addressed through new global treaties has shrunk. Chemical and biological weapons are already outlawed, so the biggest remaining question involves whether a nuclear disarmament treaty might be added to the measures prohibiting chemical and biological arms. Prospects for new treaties, and especially a nuclear weapons convention, are dim however, and the existing treaties provide strong legal and normative foundations for WMD nonproliferation efforts. As a result, cooperation increasingly involves taking steps that cannot necessarily be accomplished through a signature on a treaty.

International cooperation theory has focused mainly on whether states reach or comply with agreements or create or sustain international organizations. Much of nonproliferation activity today does not look like this. As a broad, starting hypothesis for the project, I propose that important elements of nonproliferation involve building and expanding cooperative arrangements, perhaps through working-level relationships, and that sometimes though not always this does not require reaching new formal agreements. If so, the literature needs to consider not only how agreements to cooperate are reached but also how they are made operational.

The range of cooperative nonproliferation arrangements presents a puzzle, because this cooperation is both more and less robust than various observers might expect. It is more extensive than literature in the field of international relations (IR) might lead one to predict. IR theorists, especially those of a realist bent, have long argued that international cooperation is hard to achieve and sustain. Particularly on security issues, the argument goes, states will be reluctant to cooperate because of fears either that the other side may cheat (i.e., "defect") or that it will achieve relative gains from the terms of cooperation, putting the first state at a disadvantage if there is a future conflict.[7] In the case of multilateral efforts, collective action problems create the additional risk of free riding, which again would reduce the scale of cooperation observed.[8]

Other scholars, especially those dubbed neoliberals, argue international cooperation is nevertheless possible and might even increase over time.[9] Yet such cooperation theorists do not predict that cooperation will automatically grow over time, so even neoliberals do not lead one to expect that cooperation will necessarily be extensive, and cooperation theorists have also largely ignored the nonproliferation realm.[10] As a result, cooperation on nonproliferation has largely flown under the radar of the IR literature. There is much more going on than those in the IR field seem to have expected, and as a result the field has devoted little attention to considering the implications of the many cooperative nonproliferation initiatives that have emerged.

If cooperation on nonproliferation is more extensive than some seem to have anticipated, it is in other ways less than some might expect. We live in an era of globalization, interdependence, and transnational problems associated with those trends. It has become an article of faith that, in such a world, global problems cannot be solved by any one state acting on its own, not even the United States as the sole global superpower. WMD proliferation and global terrorism are transnational problems par excellence, and if the rhetoric about common global interests is accepted at face value we should expect there to be considerable multilateral cooperation on nonproliferation as a matter of necessity. Yet the reality seems to fall short of this vision. States—including the United States—do not always agree to join the various cooperative initiatives that are proposed, and when they do their participation is sometimes grudging and halfhearted. Because cooperation is not always forthcoming when it would seem to be in the interests of states to contribute to the public good of nonproliferation, the sources of cooperation need to be explored and not simply assumed. In short, because cooperation on nonproliferation is both more and less extensive than different observers might expect, it is important to describe the patterns of cooperation that have actually developed and consider how to explain them.

As a second goal, this volume evaluates how effective various cooperative measures have been in contributing to nonproliferation. Given the difficulty of this task, the project offers only a rough, preliminary assessment of each initiative examined here. For most, there will be some observable indicators of whether the initiative has performed well or poorly with respect to its own goals. As long as it is possible to make reasonable estimates, it should be possible to use a comparison across the cases to draw some policy-relevant lessons about factors that make international cooperation more or less effective in achieving its objectives.

COOPERATION: GETTING FROM THEORY TO PRACTICE

One goal of this project is to gain better understanding of the sources of cooperation on nonproliferation. This involves exploring both the origins of cooperative initiatives and the reasons why individual states do or do not participate in them. This section briefly summarizes alternative theories in IR concerning international cooperation. In its current state, cooperation theory offers useful pointers for identifying potential sources of cooperation on nonproliferation, but it does not fully capture the types of cooperation involved. In particular, cooperation theory does not devote adequate attention to what might broadly be construed as the implementation side, or the steps involved in getting from a policy objective to an operating enterprise.[11] After a review of cooperation theory, therefore, this section describes more concretely the nature of the cooperation that has been developing in the nonproliferation arena. Following that, the next section in this chapter uses the review of cooperation theory to identify specific factors that might be relevant for explaining cooperation in the case studies in the rest of this volume.

In the field of IR, theories of cooperation became a central issue in a larger interparadigm debate between neorealists and neoliberals.[12] The emergence of social constructivism subsequently added another potential perspective for explaining cooperation. In addition, work emphasizing domestic and bureaucratic politics or human psychology could provide insights into the sources of cooperation. In this project, potentially relevant factors for explaining patterns of cooperation have been drawn from each of these approaches.

The research that focused most on cooperation emerged with neoliberalism. Neoliberal cooperation theory contained two overlapping strands. One strand focused on international regimes; these are arrangements to govern a particular issue area based on a shared understanding of the underlying principles and norms that should guide state behavior in that issue area.[13] The other strand drew inspiration from game theory and examined how cooperation could emerge in bilateral interactions. It focused especially on the game of prisoner's dilemma (PD). In this game, both players would attain a higher payoff from mutual cooperation than from mutual defection, but in a single play of the game the only rational strategy for each player is to defect, resulting in both players obtaining a suboptimal payoff. The key insight of cooperation theorists was that, if PD is iterated, strategies of reciprocity such as tit-for-tat could make stable cooperation possible.[14]

Neoliberal cooperation theory was concerned above all with demonstrating the possibility of cooperation even in an anarchic system (i.e., one lacking a central authority to enforce agreements).[15] The leading works in cooperation theory helped identify the circumstances when cooperation is possible, but the theories said less about how and when cooperation would actually emerge. Ironically, the critique by neorealists reinforced this feature of cooperation theory. Neorealists charged that neoliberals had overlooked the problem of concern about relative gains. After further research, however, it became clear that relative gains concerns vary with the situation and that there are ways for states to address those concerns, meaning cooperation can still emerge.[16] In the end, both neorealists and neoliberals devote much of their attention to identifying background conditions that shape whether or not cooperation is possible, but say less about the factors and processes involved in bringing about cooperation in practice.

Some other work has pointed to factors that might play a role in actualizing cooperation. This work is reviewed here to identify candidate factors that are subsequently explored in the case studies in this volume. The review starts with neorealist approaches and then works its way through other paradigms and levels of analysis.

Neorealism draws attention to the issue of power, leading some realists to stress the potentially critical role of a hegemonic state. According to hegemonic stability theory, only a hegemonic power has the incentives and capacity to provide public goods for the international system.[17] Hegemonic leadership has often been provided by the United States, although it is worth noting that cooperation has sometimes been established without an active U.S. role and even despite U.S. resistance.[18] Still, given U.S. concerns about WMD proliferation, hegemonic leadership by the United States will clearly be a relevant factor to consider.

Neoliberalism is primarily a theory based on interests. Neoliberalism posits that interdependence creates a rational self-interest for states to engage in cooperation.[19] When states are interdependent, uncoordinated behavior can leave all states with a suboptimal outcome, creating incentives to coordinate through cooperative arrangements such as international regimes. State interests are hence also an important factor to consider.

Not all states might share the same interests, however, or those interests might not be self-evident. One critique of neoliberalism suggested that theorists should not simply assume that states will perceive an interest in cooperation. Instead, critics argued, the sources of state preferences need to be examined, because state leaders might not see their situation as one in which mutual cooperation is desirable.[20] This opens the door to theories based on ideas, domestic politics, or psychology.

Theories that emphasize the role of knowledge and ideas, and that belong more or less to the social constructivist camp, have become an important element of the cooperation literature. Haas and Adler, for example, have drawn attention to the possible role of epistemic communities.[21] These are transnational networks of technical or scientific experts in a particular field who largely agree on the nature of and appropriate solutions to some problem. If they gain government advisory roles, members of epistemic communities facilitate a process of states perceiving a common interest in a cooperative approach to some problem, such as reducing pollution in a shared waterway. Others have pointed to the significance of collective or transnational identities and shared values as providing a foundation for norms of cooperation.[22]

Domestic politics are another potential source of state preferences.[23] In Robert Putnam's two-level game model, for example, domestic constituencies play a large role in determining whether or not a state will ratify and therefore participate in an agreement to cooperate.[24] In addition to acting as veto players who block cooperation, domestic actors can also be a source of pressures to pursue cooperation.[25] Hence, domestic politics can be a relevant factor both when states support and when they decline to participate in cooperative arrangements.

Strategy is another variable that has received attention. Axelrod's work drew attention to the potential effectiveness of tit-for-tat in eliciting long-term cooperation. Other theorists have argued that Charles Osgood's graduated reciprocation in tension reduction (GRIT) strategy is more effective.[26] GRIT also demonstrates the value of considering psychological factors. Its effects are aimed at the individual level, based on the idea GRIT will change the other side's image of the first side, thereby overcoming cognitive barriers to cooperation.[27]

Experimental research on collective action problems points to another important factor. Cooperation levels are substantially increased when players can engage in face-to-face communication. Direct communication has significant effects even in situations like one-shot PD where rational choice models predict mutual defection.[28] Empirical research has similarly found that personal ties and interpersonal communication affect the speed with which international organizations are able to act.[29]

The literature discussed so far tends to assume a single, binary outcome of interest: either there is cooperation or there is not. In the realm of nonproliferation, however, it will also be relevant to consider the form that cooperation takes and the various steps through which cooperation is built up. After discussing these issues, this chapter uses the research described above to identify factors that the case study chapters consider as potentially relevant for explaining cooperation in support of nonproliferation.

The Increasingly Collaborative Nature of Cooperation

In relation to international cooperation, Art Stein introduced an important distinction between "coordination" and "collaboration" scenarios.[30] Coordination is required when actors seek to avoid a particular bad outcome, such as the car crash outcome in a game of chicken, but need not align their actions beyond that. Collaboration, in contrast, is needed when states have to specify more concretely the actions they will take to ensure a particular good outcome, such as how to achieve the mutual cooperation payoff in PD.

This distinction is reflected in different definitions of cooperation. In a widely embraced definition, Keohane depicted international cooperation as involving "policy coordination."[31] Others, such as Zartman and Touval, define cooperation as involving "working together."[32] This would seem to be a synonym for collaboration, whose root terms suggest "co-laboring" as the essence of cooperation. An examination of nonproliferation activities shows the value of working with both terms and thinking in terms of a spectrum along which cooperation can fall, ranging from minimal coordination to robust forms of collaboration. I also suggest departing from Stein's definitions, to use the terms as they would be applied in everyday speech. Coordination is hence defined as an aligning of otherwise separate actions, while collaboration implies working jointly on a common task.

Treaties to control WMD are frequently interpreted as cases of collaboration,[33] but in some respects they more closely resemble a coordination scenario. To avoid unwanted outcomes such as an arms race or proliferation, both Cold War nuclear arms control and the NPT required mutual restraint—they rested upon each signatory agreeing not to do certain things conditional on other signatories also not doing those things.[34] Although IR theorists include both Cold War arms control and the NPT under the rubric of collaboration games, this language seems a misnomer. Negotiating the treaties required some working together, but thereafter implementation was largely carried out separately by the relevant nations acting on their own. For example, under the NPT, each non-nuclear state party agrees not to have a nuclear weapons program, but either not starting such an effort or dismantling an existing program is something it can do on its own without the involvement of other states. Verification requires cooperating with an international organization, the IAEA, but again does not require working directly with other states. Because they are basically agreements to exercise mutual restraint, both nuclear arms control and the main WMD nonproliferation treaties seem closer to coordination, as the dictionary would define that term. They require states to act separately to align their policies around common objectives, but do not require states to work side by side in a shared endeavor. Rather than a sharp dichotomy between coordination and collaboration, this suggests, it is more useful to think in terms of a continuum in which traditional arms control and nonproliferation measures—though perhaps involving modest collaboration—fall closer to the coordination end.

The various nonproliferation activities beyond the NPT are to varying degrees more collaborative in nature, in the sense that many of them require actually working together. Some, like UNSCR 1540, still remain closer to the coordination end of the spectrum; states can enact the domestic legislation mandated by 1540 on their own without outside help. Other activities, like the export control regimes, are slightly more collaborative in nature. They require periodic meetings to discuss what should be included on "trigger lists" of items that should not be exported freely and also sharing of information about export denials. Other activities are intensely collaborative. Efforts to secure WMD materials or convert nuclear reactors, for instance, can require personnel from different states to work together, sometimes in an ongoing manner. The interdiction activities called for by PSI also involve collaboration, as they can require intelligence agencies to share information or navies to carry out joint operations. In short, although the trend is not linear or unidirectional, there has been a shift over time in the nature of nonproliferation cooperation. *Since the NPT entered into force, additional nonproliferation activities have tended to move from simple coordination to involve greater elements of collaboration.*

Not all observers interpret recent trends in this way. Meier and Daase, for example, argue that recent initiatives no longer require mutual restraint. These initiatives instead involve unidirectional efforts to enforce nonproliferation obligations on others. Meier and Daase describe this as a move away from cooperation and toward coercion.[35] As noted above, however, efforts to prevent proliferation or enforce nonproliferation norms still require groups of states to cooperate. It is hence relevant to study how the nature of cooperation has changed and why some states have supported these changes. In addition, even controversial programs such as PSI have been promoted as being in support of agreed-upon nonproliferation goals, and can hence be seen as part of the larger fabric of international cooperation to prevent the spread of WMD. That said, however, the fact that some initiatives appear more coercive and unilateral in nature, and less based on reciprocity, can help account for why some states have been reluctant to cooperate with some of the more recent initiatives.

Where nonproliferation activities fall on the spectrum from coordination to ever more demanding forms of collaboration seems likely to have important implications. On the one hand, in theory, coordination should be easier to achieve than collaboration. It enables states to implement the actions they have agreed to and adjust their policies to the behavior of others entirely on their own, without having to figure out how to make a working relationship work in practice. Collaboration, in contrast, increases the potential for friction, as states have to find common ground on the details of carrying out a joint enterprise.

On the other hand, if the role of collaboration is in fact growing over time, this might also be helpful for explaining the patterns of cooperation observed in the nonproliferation arena. Because collaboration requires working together, it might serve as a conduit or a catalyst for the expansion of cooperation. Certainly some working relationships turn sour and harm cooperation. But when working relationships go well, they might have a multiplier effect on cooperation. Collaboration at the working level can lead to increasing levels of trust, the sharing of information or know-how, the discovery of new problems that require the further development of cooperation, or the emergence or strengthening of transnational identities. Or the process might simply result in a greater comfort level with collaboration, as the various parties learn how to work together.[36] Whether or not this turns out to be the case, the key point here is that cooperation in the nonproliferation area seems to involve the increasing use of active collaboration and not just policy coordination.

The Stages of Cooperation

Many of the leading works treat cooperation as binary: states choose either to cooperate or to defect; mutual cooperation either emerges or does not. Other theorists recognize that there can be different stages in the cooperation process, but much of this work focuses on treaty ratification or compliance, rather than on how cooperation itself develops over time.[37] For purposes of this study, four steps in the cooperation process seem most likely to be relevant: proposal making, establishment, enlargement, and implementation.

First, although regimes can develop organically from custom, nonproliferation initiatives do not emerge in this way. Instead, an actor suggests them. Identifying who first proposes an initiative and why can hence be an important step to examine in an attempt to understand the origins of cooperation.

The second step involves negotiations or some other mechanism to bring a cooperative activity into being. Why do other states come to the table, and what accounts for the parties eventually reaching an agreement? The second stage is labeled "establishment" rather than "negotiation" because some of the activities being considered in this study did not emerge from formal negotiations. In some cases, such as PSI, a state decided unilaterally to launch an initiative and invited others to join in. In such cases, the states that first respond affirmatively to a unilateral initiative effectively establish that program as a going enterprise.

Sometimes, new states join cooperative arrangements after they have been established. This process of recruiting additional participants can be called "enlargement." Examining why these latecomers decide to come on board may prove instructive. States that hang back at first and then change their minds may have different motivational profiles from those who sign on to cooperative arrangements from the beginning. In addition, enlargement can be an important goal in its own right. Some cooperative arrangements become more effective when new participants join in, so it is worth examining enlargement as a separate phase in the building of cooperation.

Finally, it may be important to pay attention to implementation as a distinct step. Many of the cooperative activities in the nonproliferation realm require something other than pure self-restraint (i.e., other than not starting a nuclear or biological or chemical weapons program). They require states to take active steps; in some cases, these steps include working together in an operational way to secure or interdict WMD materials. Implementation, in this sense, includes but goes beyond compliance. Dismantling chemical weapons is a form of compliance with the CWC. But if a state lacks the capacity to do this on its own, it may require help via a supplemental cooperative arrangement. Implementing this supplemental arrangement is more a matter of finding an effective way to carry it out than a question of compliance. Even if a state has every intention of complying with the CWC, chemical disarmament may fail if these other cooperative arrangements do not work. Conversely, these more collaborative arrangements are emerging in part because the goals of the WMD nonproliferation regimes may not be achievable without them. Implementation is a distinct phase in international cooperation, and in the nonproliferation realm it is giving rise to efforts to make collaborative activities operational. Because success in this regard is not automatic, it is important both to consider what factors lead to efforts at cooperation and to assess the effectiveness of such efforts in accomplishing their goals. The next two sections provide suggestions for how to address these two questions in turn.

EXPLAINING COOPERATION: POTENTIALLY RELEVANT FACTORS

The case studies in this project examine different cooperative nonproliferation activities. Reflecting the different stages of cooperation discussed above, the following questions were provided to the case study authors to consider:

- Who first proposed the cooperative activity and why?
- How did the activity come to be established as a functioning arrangement?
- Which key actors joined in the activity and why? Have any critical actors refrained from participating and, if so, why?
- To the extent implementation is necessary, how has the activity been made operational in practice? How has it evolved over time, and why has it evolved in this way?

Each of these questions is concerned with factors that lead to or impede cooperation. Based on the review of cooperation theory presented above, case study authors were asked to consider the relevance of the following seven factors for explaining the case in question. In the absence of well-established hypotheses in the existing literature that predict when cooperation will actually develop, this study took an exploratory approach. The goal was to consider a wide range of factors that might help us understand the number and diversity of cooperative nonproliferation arrangements that have emerged. The factors listed here are hence suggested as possible raw materials for explaining the cases in this project, but it is anticipated that there will also be idiosyncratic elements in each case.

1. *Self-interest*: State interests are the strongest explanatory factor in neoliberal cooperation theory; national interests also have a long pedigree as a core variable in realism. This makes self-interest the obvious place to start in considering possible explanations for nonproliferation cooperation. In some cases, participation will be a result of a rather obvious, direct national interest. Desire to strengthen nonproliferation might be especially likely to result from perceived security threats, for example in the case of a country that fears WMD acquisition by a regional rival. An absence of a perceived threat, such as a belief a state is not likely to be a target for WMD terrorism, could likewise explain a choice not to cooperate with a new nonproliferation effort. Alternative interests could also be an explanation for noncooperation. A state might see a strategic advantage in fostering proliferation or have an economic interest in exporting nuclear materials or technology, and these interests could account for nonparticipation in nonproliferation efforts.[38]
2. *U.S. leadership*: Neorealism views cooperation as unlikely except, according to hegemonic stability theory, when it is promoted by a hegemonic power. In the period covered by the cases in this volume, only the United States could be considered a hegemonic state. This makes it important to examine whether U.S. leadership helps explain nonproliferation cooperation. Where U.S. leadership is a major factor, it will also be important to consider U.S. motivations for promoting cooperation in the form that it did.[39]
3. *Norms and identity*: The ideational factors emphasized by social constructivism are also potentially relevant. In some cases, decisions may flow more from national leaders' feelings about what is right or wrong rather than rational cost-benefit calculations. If so, cooperation might reflect a normative understanding, for example that WMD proliferation is bad or that joining multilateral institutions is good.[40] States that prioritize other norms, such as the NPT's promise of access to peaceful nuclear technology, might instead resist certain post-NPT nonproliferation initiatives in the belief they conflict with these other norms. In other cases, decisions about cooperation might be more a function of identity, for example a desire to show solidarity with the United States or "the international community" or alternatively a motivation to express defiance toward the existing international order.[41]
4. *Ideas, learning, and transnational networks*: In some cases, it will not be immediately obvious what best serves a state's interests, or the question of whether an activity serves the national interest might be a subject of debate. In some of these cases, the way a state's decision makers come to think about the relevant problem or activity could be important. Especially in cases where a state changes course—from being a holdout to a participant, for instance—a process of "learning" or the embrace of "new thinking" might be a key factor.[42] In some of these cases, the relevant ideas may be transmitted through transnational networks—such as an epistemic community—to which certain officials or experts in a state belong.[43] This

might be especially likely when nonproliferation cooperation involves working-level relationships that can add to the transnational networks connecting states.

5. *Outside inducements or persuasion*: In some cases, states that are initially reluctant to join a nonproliferation initiative might be persuaded by outside actors to do so. Although the cooperation literature emphasizes strategies like tit-for-tat and GRIT, these are less likely to be relevant here. Such strategies are largely geared to changing the minds of rivals or adversaries. Cooperative nonproliferation is about recruiting states that are more or less on the same side of the issue to work together to keep various third parties from acquiring WMD. If essentially like-minded states are refraining from acting—perhaps because of free riding—the available strategies to change their behavior could include the use of carrots and/or sticks. As Lisa Martin has noted with respect to economic sanctions, cooperation in applying multilateral sanctions is sometimes achieved through coercive measures.[44] In addition to threats, bribes and suasive messages can also be used to influence states.[45] In cases where states change their policies in a cooperative direction, it is worth examining whether they were provided with negative incentives (i.e., coercive threats or pressures), positive incentives (i.e., economic aid or other side payments), or communications that contained persuasive information or analysis.

6. *Domestic politics*: In the cooperation literature, it is now widely acknowledged that domestic politics can be an important factor. In some cases, whether or not to cooperate can be a subject of internal disagreement or debate. In these cases, it may be possible to relate a decision about whether to participate to the outcome of domestic debate or to a change in governmental leadership. It is also possible that joining or defying a multilateral nonproliferation effort is a useful ploy for a leadership seeking to rally domestic support or legitimize itself domestically.[46]

7. *Capabilities*: The first six factors all have to do with state preferences, that is, whether or not states think it worthwhile to cooperate with a nonproliferation measure. In some cases, a policy may be less a function of preferences than of capabilities. A state may lack the necessary resources—money, technology, know-how—to be able to participate in some activities. In such cases, it might have an interest in or a preference for participating, but still not be able to cooperate in practice. It is also possible that states that initially stay out of an activity and later join might do so because of a change in capabilities rather than preferences, that is, because they developed or were provided with the necessary capabilities. Hence, capabilities are another factor to consider in explaining nonproliferation cooperation or its absence.[47]

These seven possible explanatory factors are not mutually exclusive and some also overlap. For example, it might be the role of hegemonic leadership to provide outside inducements in the form of aid that builds up technical capabilities.⁴⁸ Or the ties that certain government officials enjoy with transnational networks might help tilt an internal debate, leading to a domestic decision in favor of cooperation. In short, these seven factors are not alternative hypotheses to be tested against each other; the agenda here is not to show that one factor or theory is best. Rather, these factors are potential raw ingredients for an explanation of individual cases, and it may be necessary to combine them—perhaps even in different ways—to explain different cases.

ASSESSING EFFECTIVENESS

In addition to seeking greater understanding of the sources of cooperation on nonproliferation, this project also seeks to evaluate the effectiveness of cooperative nonproliferation activities. Due to both data and time limitations, the cases here are not intended to supply the kind of detailed program evaluation that might be carried out by a government oversight office. Rather, the goal in each case is to make an informed estimate of how successful each initiative has been in achieving its ostensible objectives.

Broadly speaking, three aspects of each activity are likely to be relevant: the degree of cooperation achieved, the extent to which that cooperation generated the intended activity or product (e.g., secure nuclear facilities or a common negotiating position on Iran), and the degree to which that product contributed to the successful prevention of proliferation. To start with, each initiative was intended to elicit cooperation, and each can be assessed by how much cooperation occurred. That cooperation, in turn, was meant to be instrumental in developing some mechanism or process for limiting the spread of WMD, so each activity can also be assessed in terms of how well it did in creating the intended nonproliferation mechanism or work product. The acid test, however, is whether the cooperative endeavor actually contributes to nonproliferation, so this will be the most important part of each assessment.

This is also likely to be the hardest question to answer. As is often the case, failure may be easier to identify than success. If Iran eventually develops nuclear weapons, for example, the P5+1 negotiations with Iran will not have achieved their ultimate objective. Even so, failure might not be so clear-cut. One must also consider the counterfactual question of whether, in this example, Iran's progress toward a nuclear weapon might have been even more rapid in the absence of outside diplomatic efforts (and there will also be the question of the role of other factors, such as sanctions).⁴⁹ In contrast, if a feared outcome does not happen—for example, if no terrorist group acquires a nuclear device—it may be hard to judge how much any particular effort, such as CTR or UNSCR 1540, contributed to that outcome. Some informed speculation may be possible, but where it is not, evaluation will have to focus on how successfully the program achieved its intermediate objective, such as dismantling weapons or convincing states to pass new domestic legislation.

To help case study authors in assessing cooperative activities, the following questions were suggested:

- What were the primary objectives of the program(s) being studied?
- How much cooperation was achieved, and how did this compare to the amount of cooperation that was sought?
- To what extent did each program succeed in implementing the activity or activities it was intended to promote? What are the program's most visible accomplishments? What are its most visible failures?
- How successfully did the activity contribute to the goal of nonproliferation?

Even if the evaluations in some individual cases are necessarily rough or incomplete, it should still be possible to gain insights from the exercise of going through a systematic assessment. In addition, it should also be possible to draw lessons from a comparison across cases. This study will not be the final word on the subject. But, because no comparative analysis of cooperative nonproliferation activities has ever been carried out previously, the comparative assessment that follows in this study should provide insights that can help improve the effectiveness of international nonproliferation efforts.

SCOPE OF THE VOLUME

The following chapters apply the questions and analytical framework described above to a set of case studies. The goal was to be as comprehensive as possible in capturing the range of cooperative nonproliferation activities that have developed beyond the global nonproliferation treaties and associated international organizations, with the caveat that the cases involve states as the main actors and do not involve adding new elements or activities to existing treaties or organizations. Hence, the study does not consider, for example, state adoption of the Additional Protocol (AP), as this is a device for supplementing preexisting safeguards associated with the NPT rather than a separate new initiative.

Within the universe of cases involving new initiatives for interstate cooperation, the cases in this volume were selected to be representative of different ways of categorizing the cases. They have their origins in different time periods, from the Cold War through the Obama administration. Some represent global efforts initiated by the United States, while others involve regional initiatives. Some of the initiatives studied take legally binding forms, while others are rather informal. And some reflect the traditional nonproliferation goal of preventing states from acquiring NBC weapons, while others reflect concerns about terrorism and the goal of securing nuclear and other WMD-related materials so they do not fall into the hands of non-state actors.

The case study chapters begin with globally oriented efforts presented more or less in chronological order of their origins. These are followed by examples of regional efforts, and the case studies conclude with one case of ad hoc diplomatic cooperation to enforce the NPT. The first empirical chapter, by Scott Jones, examines the four major multilateral export control regimes, with a primary focus on the Nuclear Suppliers Group. In the next chapter, Alan Kuperman reviews the Reduced Enrichment for Research and Test Reactors (RERTR) program. This U.S.-based program has sought to reduce the use of highly enriched uranium (HEU) in nuclear reactors because of the fact that HEU can also be used as the explosive material in a nuclear bomb.

Next, Togzhan Kassenova examines the signature post–Cold War effort, the Cooperative Threat Reduction (CTR) program. Thereafter, Wyn Bowen and Alan Heyes discuss the G8 Global Partnership (GP) against the Spread of Weapons and Materials of Mass Destruction, initiated in 2002. The GP built on the U.S. CTR effort, but also reflected the heightened concern about WMD terrorism that developed after 9/11. The next case study, by Emma Belcher, addresses the most original effort to emerge from the George W. Bush administration, the Proliferation Security Initiative. Tanya Ogilvie-White follows this with an analysis of UN Security Council Resolution 1540. Continuing the focus on efforts at the intersection of nonproliferation and counterterrorism, Gavin Cameron discusses two initiatives, the International Convention for the Suppression of Acts of Nuclear Terrorism and the Global Initiative to Combat Nuclear Terrorism. The nuclear security summit process initiated by President Obama forms the next case study, by Libby Turpen.

The three subsequent chapters focus on regional efforts. Michael Hamel-Green provides an overview of the various regional nuclear-weapon-free-zone treaties. Next, Sara Kutchesfahani describes the role of an epistemic community in the creation of the ABACC. Then, Francesca Giovannini proposes an alternative theory of regional nonproliferation cooperation, which she illustrates with examples drawn from Europe and Southeast Asia. The final case study is by David Santoro, who discusses the efforts of the EU-3 and later the P5+1 to coordinate with each other in efforts to achieve a diplomatic resolution of concerns about Iran's nuclear activities.

The case studies were completed before events in Ukraine in 2014 led to a significant rupture in Russia's relations with the United States and other countries. Where possible, the cases have been updated to account for the impact of these events, an issue that I return to in the concluding chapter.

The diversity of the cases considered in this volume also raises an obvious question: How well do the different nonproliferation activities fit together?[50]

Do they work more or less in harmony as elements of a coherent nonproliferation regime? Or do they represent competing arrangements that might work at cross-purposes? The concluding chapter considers the question of coherence versus fragmentation or contestation within nonproliferation arrangements. It suggests that there are real elements of tension in what is best described as a nonproliferation "regime complex,"[51] but despite this there is a discernible trend toward support for nonproliferation norms and cooperative efforts to promote nonproliferation.

CONCLUSION

The international regimes that seek to prevent WMD proliferation rest upon foundations provided by global treaties: the NPT, BWC, and CWC. These treaties have not by themselves, however, removed every possible risk of proliferation. As a result, states have launched a variety of other efforts to address some of the remaining proliferation problems as well as new problems, such as possible WMD acquisition by terrorist groups, that have grown in salience since the key nonproliferation treaties were concluded. Many of these newer efforts require cooperation, and often multilateral cooperation, to achieve their objectives.

No existing study has focused on and sought to compare these additional cooperative endeavors beyond the core nonproliferation treaties. The goals of this study are to examine the sources of cooperation on nonproliferation and assess the effectiveness of cooperative nonproliferation activities. As an overarching hypothesis to be considered in the following case study chapters, this introductory essay has put forward one broad observation concerning an evolution of nonproliferation cooperation from simple coordination toward more active collaboration. The core treaties all involve a commitment to self-restraint by each signatory. As such, they are primarily about policy coordination. In contrast, many of the cooperative efforts that have emerged since involve greater degrees of working together collaboratively. To the extent this is true, implementation is likely to involve carrying out operational activities. This, in turn, is likely to put a greater premium on working-level relationships than was necessary when the key treaties were being negotiated.

Existing theories of cooperation do not entirely capture the type of cooperative nonproliferation activity that has developed in practice. Cooperation theory has generally focused on agreements to cooperate, such as whether negotiations result in an agreement or individual states agree to comply with cooperative arrangements. This study, in contrast, identifies a need to also take into account what might be called "building cooperation." In the nonproliferation realm, cooperation is being built by adding on new initiatives, new participants, and new working-level relationships.

In addition to a broad starting hypothesis, this chapter has presented a framework that guides the case studies in this volume. Drawing on a range of theories, it has identified seven factors that might prove relevant to explaining cooperation on different nonproliferation initiatives. This chapter has also presented a list of questions to consider when assessing the effectiveness of cooperative activities. Across the chapters that follow, the ultimate goal is to identify lessons for how to build upon and improve the effectiveness of cooperative nonproliferation efforts.

Notes

1. On CTR, see John M. Shields and William C. Potter, eds., *Dismantling the Cold War: U.S. and NIS Perspectives on the Nunn-Lugar Cooperative Threat Reduction Program* (Cambridge, Mass.: MIT Press, 1997); Jason D. Ellis, *Defense by Other Means: The Politics of U.S.-NIS Threat Reduction and Nuclear Security Cooperation* (Westport, Conn.: Praeger, 2001); Togzhan Kassenova, *From Antagonism to Partnership: The Uneasy Path of the U.S.-Russian Cooperative Threat Reduction* (Stuttgart: Ibidem-Verlag, 2007); Sharon K. Weiner, *Our Own Worst Enemy? Institutional Interests and the Proliferation of Nuclear Weapons Expertise* (Cambridge, Mass.: MIT Press, 2011). On PSI, see Andrew C. Winner, "The Proliferation Security Initiative: The New Face of Interdiction," *Washington Quarterly* 28, no. 2 (Spring 2005): 129–43; Mark R. Shulman, "The Proliferation Security Initiative as a New Paradigm for Peace and Security" (Strategic Studies Institute, U.S. Army War College, April 2006); David A. Cooper, "Challenging Contemporary Notions of Middle Power Influence: Implications of the Proliferation Security Initiative for 'Middle Power Theory,'" *Foreign Policy Analysis* 7, no. 3 (July 2011): 317–36. On 1540, see Olivia Bosch and Peter van Ham, eds., *Global Non-proliferation and Counterterrorism: The Impact of UNSCR 1540* (London: Chatham House, 2007); Lawrence Scheinman, ed., *Implementing Resolution 1540: The Role of Regional Organizations* (Geneva: UNIDIR, 2008).

2. Works that discuss the nontreaty measures include Paul I. Bernstein, "Combating WMD Collaboratively," *Joint Forces Quarterly*, no. 51 (4th Quarter 2008): 37–45; Nathan E. Busch and Daniel H. Joyner, eds., *Combating Weapons of Mass Destruction: The Future of International Nonproliferation Policy* (Athens: University of Georgia Press, 2009); and Christine Wing, "The Evolution of Nuclear Nonproliferation Institutions," 122–42, and Fiona Simpson, "Biological and Chemical Weapons," 166–84, both in *Cooperating for Peace and Security: Evolving Institutions and Arrangements in a Context of Changing U.S. Security Policy*, ed. Bruce D. Jones, Shepard Forman, and Richard Gowan (Cambridge: Cambridge University Press, 2010).

3. Oliver Meier and Christopher Daase, eds., *Arms Control in the 21st Century: Between Coercion and Cooperation* (New York: Routledge, 2013).

4. Harald Müller and Carmen Wunderlich, eds., *Norm Dynamics in Multilateral Arms Control: Interests, Conflicts, and Justice* (Athens: University of Georgia Press, 2013).

5. Harald Müller et al., *Non-proliferation "Clubs" vs. the NPT* (Swedish Radiation Safety Authority, report 2014:04, January 2014).

6. Scott D. Sagan, "The Causes of Nuclear Weapons Proliferation," *Annual Review of Political Science* 14 (2011): 239.

7. Charles Lipson, "International Cooperation in Security and Economic Affairs," *World Politics* 37, no. 1 (October 1984): 1–23; Joseph M. Grieco, "Anarchy and the Limits of Cooper-

ation: A Realist Critique of the Newest Liberal Institutionalism," *International Organization* 42, no. 3 (August 1988): 485–507.

8. Mitchell B. Reiss, "Foreword," in Busch and Joyner, *Combating Weapons of Mass Destruction*, xi.

9. Robert Axelrod, *The Evolution of Cooperation* (New York: Basic Books, 1984); Robert O. Keohane, *After Hegemony: Cooperation and Discord in the World Political Economy* (Princeton: Princeton University Press, 1984).

10. But for an exception, see Roger K. Smith, "Explaining the Non-proliferation Regime: Anomalies for Contemporary International Relations Theory," *International Organization* 41, no. 2 (Spring 1987): 253–81.

11. The same point can be made about literature on proliferation. It has traditionally focused on explaining state decisions to either seek or renounce nuclear weapons. A recent book by Jacques E. C. Hymans points out, however, that implementation is a crucial part of proliferation. Some states that want nuclear weapons nevertheless fail to develop them due to problems they encounter in implementing their nuclear programs. See *Achieving Nuclear Ambitions: Scientists, Politicians, and Proliferation* (Cambridge: Cambridge University Press, 2012).

12. David A. Baldwin, ed., *Neorealism and Neoliberalism: The Contemporary Debate* (New York: Columbia University Press, 1993).

13. Stephen D. Krasner, ed., *International Regimes* (Ithaca, N.Y.: Cornell University Press, 1983).

14. Axelrod, *Evolution of Cooperation*.

15. Kenneth A. Oye, ed., *Cooperation under Anarchy* (Princeton: Princeton University Press, 1986).

16. See the essays in Baldwin, *Neorealism and Neoliberalism*.

17. Stephen D. Krasner, "State Power and the Structure of International Trade," *World Politics* 28, no. 3 (April 1976): 317–47; Robert O. Keohane, "The Theory of Hegemonic Stability and Changes in International Economic Regimes, 1967–1977," in *Change in the International System*, ed. O. R. Holsti, R. M. Siverson, and A. L. George (Boulder, Colo.: Westview, 1980), 131–62. For a discussion of different pathways by which states might cooperate to provide global public goods, see Scott Barrett, *Why Cooperate? The Incentive to Supply Global Public Goods* (Oxford: Oxford University Press, 2007).

18. Stefan Brem and Kendall Stiles, eds., *Cooperating without America: Theories and Case Studies of Non-hegemonic Regimes* (London: Routledge, 2009); Bruce D. Jones and Shepard Forman, "Introduction: 'Two Worlds' of International Security," in Jones, Forman, and Gowan, *Cooperating for Peace and Security*, 3–19.

19. Robert O. Keohane and Joseph S. Nye, *Power and Interdependence* (Boston: Little, Brown, 1977); Ernst B. Haas, "Why Collaborate? Issue-Linkage and International Regimes," *World Politics* 32, no. 3 (April 1980): 357–405.

20. Robert Jervis, "Realism, Game Theory, and Cooperation," *World Politics* 40, no. 3 (April 1988): 317–49; Matthew Evangelista, "Cooperation Theory and Disarmament Negotiations in the 1950s," *World Politics* 42, no. 4 (July 1990): 502–28.

21. See the essays in "Knowledge, Power, and International Policy Coordination," ed. Peter M. Haas, special issue, *International Organization* 46, no. 1 (Winter 1992).

22. Thomas Risse-Kappen, *Cooperation among Democracies: The European Influence on U.S. Foreign Policy* (Princeton: Princeton University Press, 1995); Bruce Cronin, *Community under Anarchy: Transnational Identity and the Evolution of Cooperation* (New York: Columbia University Press, 1999).

23. Andrew Moravcsik, "Taking Preferences Seriously: A Liberal Theory of International Politics," *International Organization* 51, no. 4 (Autumn 1997): 513–53.

24. Robert D. Putnam, "Diplomacy and Domestic Politics: The Logic of Two-Level Games," *International Organization* 42, no. 3 (Summer 1988): 427–60. Xinyuan Dai and Duncan Snidal cite Putnam's work as an example of cooperation theory in their review essay, "International Cooperation Theory," in *The International Studies Encyclopedia*, ed. Robert A. Denemark (Cambridge: Blackwell, 2010).

25. Jeffrey W. Knopf, *Domestic Society and International Cooperation: The Impact of Protest on U.S. Arms Control Policy* (Cambridge: Cambridge University Press, 1998).

26. Deborah Welch Larson, "Crisis Prevention and the Austrian State Treaty," *International Organization* 41, no. 1 (Winter 1987): 27–60.

27. Drawing on a different branch of social psychology, Brian C. Rathbun argues that whether individual leaders have a general tendency to be trusting is an important determinant of whether or not they prefer international cooperation. "Before Hegemony: Generalized Trust and the Creation and Design of International Security Organizations," *International Organization* 65, no. 2 (Spring 2011): 243–73.

28. Elinor Ostrom, "A Behavioral Approach to the Rational Choice Theory of Collective Action," *American Political Science Review* 92, no. 1 (March 1998): 6–7.

29. Heidi Hardt, *Time to React: The Efficiency of International Organizations in Crisis Response* (New York: Oxford University Press, 2014).

30. Arthur A. Stein, "Coordination and Collaboration: Regimes in an Anarchic World," in Krasner, *International Regimes*, 115–40.

31. Keohane, *After Hegemony*, 51–52. This is described as a consensus definition by Helen Milner, "International Theories of Cooperation among Nations: Strengths and Weaknesses," *World Politics* 44, no. 3 (April 1992): 467.

32. I. William Zartman and Saadia Touval, eds., *International Cooperation: The Extents and Limits of Multilateralism* (Cambridge: Cambridge University Press, 2010), 1.

33. For example, Steve Weber, *Cooperation and Discord in U.S.-Soviet Arms Control* (Princeton: Princeton University Press, 1991).

34. Barrett, *Why Cooperate?*, chap. 5.

35. Meier and Daase, *Arms Control in the 21st Century*.

36. This perspective on collaboration has some similarities to social constructivist discussions of pluralistic security communities. Security communities are sets of states that believe war against other members of the community has become unthinkable; as a result, states develop expectations that disputes involving other states in the community will be resolved through peaceful means. In a social constructivist account of security communities, practical interests in cooperation are reinforced by the development of trust, learning, and shared identities. The same processes might also bolster collaboration on behalf of nonproliferation, but without necessarily leading to development of a security community. For constructivist research on security communities, see Emanuel Adler and Michael Barnett, eds., *Security Communities* (Cambridge: Cambridge University Press, 1998).

37. For example, Srini Sitaraman, *State Participation in International Treaty Regimes* (Farnham, U.K.: Ashgate, 2009).

38. For an attempt to test strategic versus economic motivations for sensitive nuclear exports, see Matthew Kroenig, "Exporting the Bomb: Why States Provide Sensitive Nuclear Assistance," *American Political Science Review* 103, no. 1 (February 2009): 113–33.

39. For a study that asks this question but focuses on a different issue area, see Sarah E. Kreps, *Coalitions of Convenience: United States Military Interventions after the Cold War* (Ox-

ford: Oxford University Press, 2011). She argues the United States often chooses a multilateral approach based on the instrumental calculation that a multilateral format will give U.S. action greater international legitimacy and increase burden sharing by others.

40. Maria Rost Rublee, *Nonproliferation Norms: Why States Choose Nuclear Restraint* (Athens: University of Georgia Press, 2009); Müller and Wunderlich, *Norm Dynamics in Multilateral Arms Control*.

41. Jacques Hymans contends that an identity based on "oppositional nationalism" is often a motivation for state efforts to acquire nuclear weapons. Jacques E. C. Hymans, *The Psychology of Nuclear Proliferation: Identity, Emotions, and Foreign Policy* (Cambridge: Cambridge University Press, 2006).

42. For an argument that joint learning was important in the case of Argentine-Brazilian denuclearization, see Jeffrey W. Knopf, "The Importance of International Learning," *Review of International Studies* 29, no. 2 (April 2003): 187–209.

43. Emanuel Adler claims a U.S.-based epistemic community transmitted the mainstream theory of nuclear arms control to its Soviet counterparts. "The Emergence of Cooperation: National Epistemic Communities and the International Evolution of the Idea of Nuclear Arms Control," *International Organization* 46, no. 1 (Winter 1992): 101–45.

44. Lisa L. Martin, *Coercive Cooperation: Explaining Multilateral Economic Sanctions* (Princeton: Princeton University Press, 1992).

45. On the use of positive incentives in nonproliferation, see Thomas Bernauer and Dieter Ruloff, eds., *The Politics of Positive Incentives in Arms Control* (Columbia: University of South Carolina Press, 1999); Miroslav Nincic, "Getting What You Want: Positive Inducements in International Relations," *International Security* 35, no. 1 (Summer 2010): 138–83.

46. Michael Barletta argues some decisions to join nonproliferation treaties are a form of "diversionary peace" to remove potential sources of opposition to ruling regimes. Michael Barletta, "Democratic Security and Diversionary Peace: Nuclear Confidence-Building in Argentina and Brazil," *National Security Studies Quarterly* 5, no. 3 (Summer 1999): 19–38.

47. One study of compliance with UNSCR 1540 concludes that state compliance is driven more by state capacities than by interests. See Douglas M. Stinnett, Bryan R. Early, Cale Horne, and Johannes Karreth, "Complying by Denying: Explaining Why States Develop Nonproliferation Export Controls," *International Studies Perspectives* 12, no. 3 (August 2011): 308–26.

48. U.S. security assistance efforts are often described as being intended for "capacity building" in U.S. partners.

49. I thank Wade Huntley for suggesting the importance of counterfactuals in assessments of effectiveness.

50. I thank Christine Wing for drawing attention to this question at the authors' workshop at which we discussed first drafts of the theory framework and case study chapters.

51. I thank Scott Jones for drawing my attention to the regime complex literature. A regime complex is a set of loosely linked, partially overlapping, and partially separate regimes that regulate a particular issue area in global politics. See Kal Raustiala and David Victor, "The Regime Complex for Plant Genetic Resources," *International Organization* 58, no. 2 (Spring 2004): 277–310; Robert O. Keohane and David G. Victor, "The Regime Complex for Climate Change," *Perspectives on Politics* 9, no. 1 (March 2011): 7–23; Amandine Orsini, Jean-Frédéric Morin, and Oran Young, "Regime Complexes: A Buzz, a Boom, or a Boost for Global Governance?," *Global Governance* 19, no. 1 (January–March 2013): 27–39.

CHAPTER TWO

The Multilateral Export Control Regimes
Informality Begets Collaboration

SCOTT A. JONES

EFFORTS TO PREVENT proliferation can be characterized in terms of whether they address the demand side or the supply side. Demand-side measures seek to reduce the motivations that lead states to seek weapons of mass destruction (WMD). Supply-side measures, in contrast, seek to make it harder for development efforts to succeed by restricting access to items useful to weapons programs, including dual-use items that can be applied to either commercial or military purposes. One way to limit supply is through export controls.

As part of their efforts to inhibit states and terrorist organizations from acquiring nuclear, chemical, biological, and advanced conventional weapons, the United States and other countries have taken steps to coordinate export controls that monitor and restrict the flow of dual-use equipment, materials, and technologies. They have established four informal multilateral export control regimes (MECR) that complement and support broader international nonproliferation objectives and nonproliferation treaties. These are the Nuclear Suppliers Group, the Australia Group, the Missile Technology Control Regime, and the Wassenaar Arrangement. To assist member states to bolster and harmonize their respective national export control systems, the regimes typically develop broad guidelines about the circumstances when states should exercise restraint combined with more specific lists of items to which controls should be applied. These normative guidelines and technology control lists provide public goods, including, for example, much of the practical content for UN Security Council resolutions such as 1540 and those targeting Iran and North Korea.

Originally conceived as informal consultative forums for relatively small groups of like-minded supplier countries, the regimes have evolved into semiformal international organizations with greatly expanded memberships and regular meetings. The current MECR contain an average of forty members and one international organization (the European Union) and conduct annual plenaries, multiple intersessional working group meetings, and numerous outreach seminars. An important part of their work involves making regular, significant changes to update their respective control lists and guidelines. This welter of activity, it should be emphasized, is conducted under the auspices of voluntary, nonbinding institutions that are not officially part of the nonproliferation treaties. Decisions made within the regimes are predicated upon consensus.

Prior analyses of the regimes have focused almost exclusively on the apparent disjuncture between procedural aspects of the regimes and their increasingly large and diverse memberships. Critics claim, for example, that consensus decision-making rules will not work in organizations with large memberships housed in informal structures.[1] The critical treatments of the regimes have not, however, focused on the pattern or "dynamic density" of cooperation over time.[2] This chapter offers a contrary interpretation. It suggests that the regimes have been remarkably robust in not only sustaining, but advancing multilateral export control cooperation both within and outside the regimes. Moreover, a key source of this cooperation arises from what has often been cited as a critical liability of the regimes: their informality. To substantiate this assertion, I focus on developing measures of cooperation for the MECR, an exercise otherwise lacking in the MECR literature.

After a review of the nature of the arrangements in general, I provide a brief background on the origins and operations of each individual export control regime.[3] Subsequent sections identify two categories of multilateral export control cooperation, and then assess the evidence in the case of the Nuclear Suppliers Group for these two categories of cooperation. I find that multilateral cooperation has persisted and deepened despite changes in membership. I then briefly consider candidate explanations for not only the persistence but depth of cooperation within the MECR. I conclude that the fit between the necessarily collaborative nature of the MECR functions—the construction and continuous revision of guidelines and control lists—and the informal procedural setup of the regimes explains this outcome most convincingly. In terms of factors proposed by Knopf, a combination of norms and learning, in the form of social learning, is involved in this explanation. But it also involves a factor not included in Knopf's framework: the design of the regimes themselves.

THE NATURE OF THE MULTILATERAL EXPORT CONTROL REGIMES

The multilateral export control system currently comprises four separate supplier-state regimes: the Australia Group (AG), the Missile Technology Control Regime (MTCR), the Nuclear Suppliers Group (NSG), and the Wassenaar Arrangement (WA). Although the MECR are not the product of any treaty, participants generally see them as a way to supplement the provisions of binding, multilateral treaties primarily focused on the development and possession of weapons technologies, including the 1968 Nuclear Non-Proliferation Treaty (NPT), the 1972 Biological Weapons Convention (BWC), and the 1993 Chemical Weapons Convention (CWC).[4] While certain differences exist in the particulars of the regimes, their essential attributes share a great deal of similarity.

All four MECR are informal, nonbinding political arrangements. However, the extant literature on international regimes (such as on environmental regimes) primarily focuses on formal institutions, which can create misleading expectations with respect to the MECR.[5] In contrast to formally negotiated, treaty-based multilateral institutions, the export control regimes lack official institutions. They operate instead through annual and semiannual meetings. The most fundamental components of these regimes are their guidelines and control lists. While some regimes, such as the WA, have secretariats, the de facto regime-specific bodies are purely coordinative in function. Nevertheless, the tasks of creating and revising guidelines and control lists require a high degree of collaboration among members as decision-making procedures are based exclusively on consensus. This informal structure need not be a barrier to effectiveness. Research has found that institutions with an informal character, such as ASEAN for example, can be productive in other environments involving interest heterogeneity.[6]

The informal, consultative nature of the export control arrangements, this suggests, does not necessarily circumscribe the degree and type of cooperation among members. Even modest, less formal mediums of cooperation or coordination can produce significant results in international affairs.[7] After a brief historical review of each regime, I examine the patterns of cooperation within the NSG in greater detail. Because the four regimes are similar, patterns observed in the NSG should be typical of those in the other MECR. The review demonstrates that multilateral export control cooperation has increased despite increases in membership and environmental challenges faced by the regimes.

THE EVOLUTION OF SUPPLY-SIDE CONTROLS

Following World War II and the commencement of the Cold War, the United States and a number of its allies formed the Coordinating Committee on Multilateral Export Controls (COCOM), with the intention of ensuring that trade with the Soviet Union and its allies did not enable the Soviet bloc to gain access to militarily relevant technology.[8] In many respects, COCOM served as the model for the subsequent dual-use supplier regimes. Tensions sometimes arose between Western European countries and the United States, for example regarding whether to relax controls to pursue the political benefits that might follow from expanded trade with Eastern Europe, but COCOM members were able to adapt the organization so it kept functioning. These periodic tensions and COCOM's singular focus on the Soviet bloc explain in part why the United States pushed for the creation of new WMD-focused MECR, separate from COCOM.[9]

The predominant nonproliferation approach of the 1960s involved multilateral treaty negotiations, the overarching achievement of which was the NPT. The NPT contained provisions intended to address both the supply and demand sides of proliferation. The challenges of dealing with the supply dimensions of proliferation, however, were only starting to become clear in the late 1960s and early 1970s. When India detonated a so-called peaceful nuclear explosion in 1974, using plutonium obtained from a Canadian-supplied nuclear reactor, the shock shifted global nonproliferation attention to the problem of supply.

Prior to the Indian test, in 1971, a group of seven NPT nuclear supplier nations formed the Nuclear Exporters Committee, known as the Zangger Committee (after its first chair), to flesh out how to implement certain rules for nuclear trade contained in Article III of the NPT. India's 1974 test, along with efforts among other non-nuclear-weapon states such as Argentina and Brazil to develop a complete nuclear fuel cycle, led to heightened concern among supplier states regarding nuclear proliferation. Moreover, the nuclear supplier states within the NPT were also concerned that although they themselves were bound by their NPT commitments, and could coordinate stricter regulations on nuclear trade within the Zangger Committee, non-NPT nuclear suppliers—which at that time still included countries such as France and Japan—faced no such constraints on their nuclear exports.[10]

In 1975, a group of nuclear supplier states (Canada, France, Japan, West Germany, the Soviet Union, the United Kingdom, and the United States) met in London with the purpose of supplementing the Zangger Committee's work in the field of nuclear export controls. Over successive meetings, this group became known unofficially as the "London Club" and, in 1978, officially as the NSG. In 1974, the Zangger Committee had innovated the idea of a trigger list of items that, if used contrary to the exporter's intentions, could contribute to a nuclear weapons program; export of those items would "trigger" a requirement they be placed under International Atomic Energy Agency (IAEA) safeguards. Consistent with NPT language, the Zangger list included only certain kinds of nuclear materials and equipment specifically designed to use or produce those materials. Building on this approach, the NSG adopted more restrictive export control guidelines that included some dual-use items.[11] In particular, because uranium enrichment and spent-fuel reprocessing to extract plutonium can be used to make both nuclear fuel for reactors and nuclear materials for a bomb, the NSG guidelines called for suppliers to exercise restraint regarding transfers of enrichment and reprocessing (ENR) technology.[12] The guidelines also required the provision of physical security for transferred nuclear facilities and materials, acceptance of safeguards on replicated facilities, and prohibitions against retransfer of nuclear exports to third parties. Importantly, in contrast to the Zangger Committee, the NSG guidelines would apply to potential exports to members of the NPT and not only to nonparties. The NSG guidelines on nuclear exports were published in 1978, when the group submitted them to the IAEA, which published them as INFCIRC/254.

From its inception, the NSG sought to emphasize its informal, nonbinding nature. While clearly a result of perceived imperfections in the nonproliferation regime to date, the NSG was at pains to minimize the appearance of excessive controls on nuclear technology that could undermine the right to develop peaceful uses of nuclear energy established in Article IV of the NPT or reduce the prospects for economic development and free trade.[13] After formulating the guidelines on nuclear transfers, the members of the NSG did not openly institutionalize cooperation among themselves and did not convene again as a group until 1991, when they met in response to the exposure of Iraq's clandestine efforts to acquire WMD. Because Iraq had built much of its nuclear program through imports of dual-use items not covered on existing trigger lists, the NSG in 1992 adopted a new, second set of *Guidelines for Transfers of Nuclear-Related Dual-Use Equipment, Material and Related Technology*.[14] These were added to INFCIRC/254 as part II, with the original guidelines and their subsequent revisions now being contained in part I.

During the NSG's interregnum, two more supplier regimes emerged: the AG and MTCR. Largely in response to the use of chemical weapons during the Iran-Iraq War, the AG was established in 1985 to prevent any contribution to chemical and biological weapons programs through the inadvertent supply of chemical precursors, biological agents, and related dual-use equipment.[15] The participating governments in this regime agree to common guidelines for chemical and biological export licensing. Although the AG is concerned with regulating trade in chemical and biological weapon articles, it also seeks to ensure that legitimate trade is not inhibited.[16]

U.S. concerns regarding the proliferation of space-launch capabilities and a series of events in the late 1970s and early 1980s, including a South Korean ballistic missile test in 1978 and India's July 1980 launch of its Satellite Launch Vehicle-3, prompted negotiations on a missile control consortium. These culminated in the establishment in April 1987 of the MTCR and the release of its guidelines. The United States had been the first to conceive of missiles as a proliferation problem and had unilaterally implemented some export controls in the early 1980s.[17] Until this point, efforts to limit delivery means for WMD had been confined to arms control negotiations between the United States and the Soviet Union. The concern that other states—particularly in the developing world—could wed the growing availability of ballistic missile technology with nuclear weapons prompted U.S.-led efforts to coordinate supply-side controls. In 2002, a group of states sought to supplement missile nonproliferation efforts by adopting an International Code of Conduct, later renamed the Hague Code of Conduct (HCOC). The HCOC primarily involves voluntary confidence-building measures, and the MTCR remains the primary vehicle for missile-related export controls.

The NSG, AG, and MTCR were, like COCOM, creations of the Cold War, albeit without the dedicated targeting of export controls on the Soviet bloc. With the dissolution of the Soviet Union, COCOM's raison d'être disappeared. Most members, particularly European Union member states, were eager to expand trade, with some former COCOM members pressing for its full termination.[18] However, the United States sought to create a successor regime, but with the recognition that a new regime would have to accommodate the economic concerns of the majority of member states.[19] The resulting Wassenaar Arrangement was, as noted by Michael Lipson, "created with greater concern for its effect on commerce than had characterized CoCom."[20] The Wassenaar guidelines and control lists were designed to promote transparency, an exchange of views and information, and greater responsibility in preventing "destabilizing accumulations" of advanced conventional weapons and related technologies.[21]

Beyond the WA, states have attempted to put some restraints on conventional arms transfers into legally binding form with the UN adoption of the Arms Trade Treaty in 2013. The WA continues to function, however, as a body that can flexibly adapt to new developments in a way a treaty-based mechanism may not be able to. Having summarized the emergence of the four MECRs, this chapter's next section starts to develop a new interpretation of how effective the regimes have been in achieving cooperation.

COOPERATION IN CONTEXT: ASSESSING MECR COOPERATION IN SITU

Most prior studies of the MECR have emphasized what they see as basic limitations of the regimes, including their informality, consensus decision-making rules, lack of enforcement capability, vague membership criteria and provisions,[22] and inadequate transparency.[23] However, these studies have not adequately specified their concept of regime effectiveness. Gahlaut and Zaborsky, for example, argued that the effectiveness of the MTCR and NSG was being undermined by the inclusion of more, increasingly diverse states.[24] The study adopted a fairly narrow definition of regime effectiveness, essentially conflating regime form with function. It argued that cartel-like informal organizations, as illustrated by the initial membership of the AG, NSG, and MTCR, are inappropriate for larger, politically diverse memberships, especially given that some of the newer members are not actually supplier states. In a similar vein, the U.S. General Accounting Office argued that the regimes were limited in their nonproliferation missions by limited information sharing, slow and uneven adoption of control list changes, and disparate levels of export control capabilities among regime members.[25]

Studies of the regimes so far have, implicitly or explicitly, adopted metrics that focus on listing ways in which the regimes are ineffective. In these studies, effectiveness is seen to be inversely correlated with the degree to which the regimes have departed from their initial conditions. However, the studies have not included patterns of cooperation in their measures of effectiveness, meaning the level of cooperation in the MECR has not been examined.

Cooperation Metrics

Although few studies attempt to measure the degree of multilateral cooperation on export controls, an analysis by Cupitt and Grillot of the transition from COCOM to the WA provides a welcome exception. The following analysis uses a modified version of their measure of cooperation, which is defined here as the adjustment of policies to the preferences and actions of others, contingent on others altering their behavior, through a voluntary process of coordination.[26] I do not, however, seek to differentiate coordination from collaboration in this context. In practice, the process of policy adjustment more closely resembles coordination rather than collaboration because operational implementation of export controls still occurs largely at the national level, rather than jointly. As described below, however, policy adjustment has taken on an increasingly collaborative aspect.

Despite having only rudimentary organizational structures, the MECR seek to coordinate collective action among members so as to avoid exports that contribute to WMD proliferation. In the absence of treaties that give rules legal force or an official adjudicating body, states have to orchestrate this type of collective action through procedural norms and mutually agreed-upon rules. In this regard, the extent of international cooperation on export controls expresses itself through various measures, including the frequency and depth of information sharing, the extent of harmonization among national export control regimes, the adaptation of the lists of controlled items to changes in the environment, the use of compromise policy tools (such as persuasion and incentives) rather than sanctions, and changes in membership to broaden participation in cooperative arrangements.[27] Within a regime, whether formal or not, at least two kinds of policy adjustments exist: changes in substantive rules and in procedural norms.[28]

Cupitt and Grillot developed a regime-specific measure of cooperation in order to assess levels of cooperation among COCOM members. A modified form of their measures suggests that MECR members engage in substantive policy construction and adjustment in two areas: adding, deleting, or modifying items on the control lists and amending the guidelines. Regarding procedural norms adjustments, there are also two measures: inducting new members and following compromise decision strategies. Together, these provide four measures of cooperation that can be observed over time.

The actual decision-making procedures (e.g., the requirement for consensus) across the regimes have not changed since their inception; however, the *procedural norms* across the regimes have changed significantly from compliance to compromise scenarios.[29] Rather than using coercive measures to uphold compliance with existing rules, members of the regimes increasingly engage in give-and-take over whether and how to update the rules. As will be discussed, the NSG's endorsement of the U.S.-India nuclear deal and simultaneous inability of the United States to gain wider acceptance of comprehensive ENR control criteria in the NSG illustrate the range of compromise within the regime.[30]

Each measure generates a series of expectations with respect to whether there will be increased or decreased cooperation. For example, within the substantive policy adjustment measure, we would expect decreased cooperation if member states failed consistently to modify the control list, since this would likely indicate the inability of a large membership to reach consensus. As noted in chapter 1, there are four distinct phases of cooperation: proposal making, establishment, enlargement, and implementation. In the following analysis, the measures of cooperation are applied to the implementation stage as affected by enlargement following the establishment of the NSG in 1978, since the critical question is whether enlargement has hindered implementation.

Choice of Case Study

The four export control regimes all have a nearly identical structure: guidelines, control lists, and various technical and policy forums at which regime issues are deliberated. While some variation exists in, for example, membership and information sharing systems, the functional equivalencies are consistent across regimes.[31] Over time and despite membership changes, the regimes have continued to adjust their guidelines and control lists. Furthermore, they have also sought to expand their institutional capabilities through the establishment of intersessional technical and policy working groups, an indication of increasing cooperation density.

To assess the level of cooperation density, I review the evolution of the NSG by employing the measures noted in the previous section. Because space does not permit a comprehensive review of all the regimes, the NSG case is chosen as it is one of the first export control regimes and representative of regime

Table 2.1   Regime Measures of Cooperation in the NSG Case

	Substantive Policy Adjustments		Procedural Norms Adjustments	
	Control List	Guidelines	Membership Expansion	Compromise Strategies
NSG	Annual and Semiannual	Annual	7 to 48 (1978–2014)	China, India, Safeguards, ENR

challenges cited in critical reviews of the MECR. I expect the findings to pertain to the other regimes, particularly given the official participant overlap and structural-functional similarities. Unlike previous studies of the regimes, it is not my intent to assess regime "effectiveness," but, rather, to measure and explain the density of cooperation within the regimes. Hence, the focus is not the national implementation of regime provisions, but the functioning of the regime itself.

NSG CASE STUDY

As of mid-2014, there are forty-eight members of the NSG, up from a founding group of seven countries. With the exception of a roughly ten-year hiatus during the 1980s, the NSG has extensively revised its guidelines and control lists every year since the early 1990s. With a larger and more diverse membership, the regime has migrated to a more collaborative, as opposed to coordinative, form of cooperation—that is, the group's work involves more frequent meetings and active discussions than it used to.

Regarding the first area for measuring cooperation, substantive policy adjustments, both the guidelines and control lists of the NSG have undergone extensive revisions. As in the other regimes, the NSG guidelines are amended to reflect changes in the international technology and/or security environment. Likewise, all guideline revisions are made on the basis of consensus decision-making rules. In 1994, for example, the NSG added a provision, the nonproliferation principle, to part I of the guidelines. The NSG included this principle in an attempt to inhibit transfers that might assist proliferation even if those transfers are not explicitly proscribed by the guidelines. The provision states that "notwithstanding other provisions of these Guidelines, suppliers should authorize transfer of items or related technology identified in the trigger list only when they are satisfied that the transfers would not contribute to the proliferation of nuclear weapons or other nuclear explosive devices or be diverted to acts of nuclear terrorism." The guidelines were amended again in 2003 in response to concerns about nuclear terrorism. Other subjects included in the guidelines revisions process over time include controls over intangible transfers of technology (i.e., transfers involving knowledge or design information), brokering, catch-all, outreach, and information sharing.[32] The catch-all provision has goals similar to the nonproliferation principle. If an exporter has a reasonable suspicion that an end user intends to use an item in a nuclear weapons program, it should deny the export even if the item does not appear on a control list. The brokering provision, meanwhile, covers efforts to broker deals between other parties that would lead to exports that should be restricted.

Adjustments of procedural norms, the second area in which cooperation is measured, have also been much in evidence in the NSG. Compared to its early years, when the group went more than a decade without meeting, the collective activities of the NSG today consist of an annual plenary meeting, a Consultative Group, information exchange meetings, and ad hoc working groups (e.g., the Licensing and Enforcement Experts Meeting) organized to examine particular issues. The country acting as the rotating NSG chair organizes the plenary meeting and coordinates activities for one calendar year. The chair can also be mandated to carry out activities on behalf of the group, such as outreach to particular countries to promote adherence to the NSG guidelines. Information on denials and working-group-related information can be shared electronically via the Nuclear Information Sharing System. The practical effect of this evolving structure is to facilitate iterative learning as states gain experience with cooperation based upon consensus rules.

As noted, all substantive and normative adjustments in the regime are predicated upon consensus decision-making rules. With a larger and more diverse membership, we would expect cooperation to decrease or, at a minimum, regress. Arguably, the inclusion of a de facto target of the regime, China, as a member would likewise decrease cooperation.[33] However, two important cases show the ability of NSG members to reach a compromise. The first came in response to the controversial U.S.-India nuclear deal, in which the United States made India's commercial nuclear energy sector eligible for trade and assistance even though India is a nonparty to the NPT with a nuclear weapons program. To keep the deal from running afoul of NSG guidelines, in 2008, at the NSG meeting in Vienna, India was granted a waiver from the NSG guidelines that require comprehensive international safeguards as a condition of nuclear trade. Consensus was achieved only after overcoming concerns expressed by a number of countries, especially Austria, Ireland, and New Zealand. Before granting the waiver, the NSG required several minor changes to the waiver text proposed by the United States.[34] Critics of the India deal suggest that the NSG, and, by extension, the NPT, has been irreparably compromised.[35] While I am sympathetic to this assertion, the point here is to illustrate the internal patterns of cooperation in the NSG, not assess the impact of its decisions. The India case shows the degree to which compromise, rather than defection when there is disagreement, prevails in the decision making among a large and diverse membership. And even though the United States mostly got its way, it did not have unlimited influence, as it had to accept some changes to the waiver.

A second case shows the limits of U.S. influence more clearly. When the United States sought to amend the guidelines to require Additional Protocol (AP) safeguards as a condition of supply, it found its influence checked by less powerful members.[36] While not voted down, a provision to make the AP a condition of supply was modified to apply only to transfers related to enrichment and reprocessing. Many states view peaceful nuclear energy programs as an inherent right enshrined in the NPT. As such, any effort to increase controls over transfers of ENR equipment and technology is highly controversial. The deliberations on this issue began in 2008, culminating in a 2011 decision to revise the guidelines. Specifically, the NSG reached agreement on revisions of paragraphs 6 and 7 of the group's guidelines, those that cover ENR transfers. The new guidelines ban ENR exports to states that have not signed or are not in compliance with the NPT, have not implemented comprehensive IAEA safeguards, or have not brought into force the AP or an alternative to permit more extensive monitoring, among other criteria.[37]

The ENR issue illustrates the NSG's evolution from informal coordination to compromise-based cooperation. As the NSG membership has grown from a small, relatively like-minded set of states into a large, diverse group, critics have predicted that, with the group's consensus decision-making structure, a greater divergence in member interests would lead to stalled updates to the control lists or revisions to the guidelines. On the contrary, levels of cooperation within the regime have remained high over time. Key suppliers and former critics of the regimes, such as China and India, have also petitioned to join the regime.[38] In the following section, I explain the robust nature of cooperation within the NSG and, by extension, across the MECR.

MECR COOPERATION EXPLAINED

Throughout the evolution of the various MECR, the degree and type of export control cooperation have largely been a function of regime design, characterized by a mix of fixed and changing features. For example, while membership has increased in both number and political-economic diversity, decision-making procedures (i.e., consensus rules) remain unchanged. The above analysis determined, in the case of the NSG, that cooperation remains robust, a finding that can likely be extrapolated from the NSG across the MECR.

A Focus on Implementation

In assessing possible explanations for this cooperation, it is important to distinguish between stages. As the measures used focused on implementation, so too must the explanation for cooperation. In other words, the decision to seek membership in a regime is not here being treated as the final indicator of cooperation. Multilateral export control cooperation is, precisely, implementation—in the means by which adherents discuss export controls on a regular basis, adjust interpretations of control policies, turn unilateral into multilateral practices, and share sensitive information on end users.

In the case of the MECR, the more revealing question is why cooperation persists, as evidenced in the continuous adjustments of substantive policies and procedural norms. With regard to the candidate explanations of cooperation outlined by Knopf, there are insufficient data to determine the explanations for individual countries given the opacity of governmental deliberations and the number of member states. Instead, to explain the durability and deepening of cooperation requires looking at the impact of the iterative interaction of member states through informally arranged institutions. These features of the regimes increase the likelihood of continued cooperation by facilitating the reduction of uncertainty and encouraging compromise.

Before outlining the primary explanation for cooperation, it is worth noting some other factors that are relevant. Self-interest plays a role, but its implications are complicated. States have set up and joined the MECR because they have an interest in preventing proliferation and perhaps hope for side benefits from being "part of the club." As suppliers, however, they also have economic interests in promoting exports governed by the regimes. Given these cross-cutting interests, it becomes hard to make a clear prediction about whether self-interest will increase or decrease cooperation. A more clearly important factor has been U.S. leadership. This factor mattered most in the creation of the regimes. When we turn to implementation, U.S. leadership still plays a role, but it is not the only factor involved given the increasingly compromise nature of decision making in the regimes over time.

Two other sets of factors on Knopf's list—norms and identity, and learning—loom larger in the implementation stage. The combination of these factors, or learning about norms, is called "social learning" and is central in my explanation of cooperation in the MECR. The opportunity for social learning, however, has been affected by another factor not included on Knopf's list, namely regime design. The next section describes how these factors have combined to support cooperation.

Iterative Cooperation and Social Learning

Any decision taken in the regimes requires consensus. Currently, there is an average of forty countries per regime, including some that were formerly vehement critics of the MECR.[39] Yet, on a regular basis, the various guidelines and control lists get revised. As noted in the case of the NSG, changing the guidelines and control lists regarding ENR proved highly contentious given the mix of economic and security interests involved. Nevertheless, through compromise, NSG members were able to develop a common approach and thereby establish a global norm on the supply of critical nuclear technology.

Unfortunately, most regime discussions are truly black boxes. For example, in a 2011 interview, NSG chair Ambassador Piet de Klerk responded that "how far you can go in discussing sensitive issues like the Chinese supplies and whether India should become a member remains to be seen. You can't be too specific about debates that are still under way and are not finished yet."[40] Even though information on internal deliberations remains scarce, we can, however, examine outcomes.

Although informal arrangements, the regimes require a high degree of semi-regular and intensely technical cooperation in order to produce results. Despite a fairly high degree of interest heterogeneity, cooperation has remained consistent, if not robust, over time even with the absence of enforcement capabilities. This has been possible because, through oftentimes highly technical interactions, member states have evolved a capacity to compromise as a result of iteration in their interactions. In most cases, regime participants are usually the same individuals across regime meetings. They have learned that if they make a concession on one issue in one regime context today, they are likely to receive a concession on some other issue in some other context later. The scope of compromise is further enhanced precisely because of the lack of an enforcement capability: members implement the guidelines and control lists at their discretion. Some analysts have cited this absence as a weakness of the MECR structure, citing, for example, the Russian decision to supply nuclear fuel to India's Tarapur reactor.[41] However, national discretion creates more room for compromise as members know that they have flexibility in how they subsequently align their interests with the guidelines. Furthermore, national discretion does not obviate group or bilateral censure, as the Russia-Tarapur case also indicates.[42]

To claim that the regimes produce suboptimal outcomes is to project a more formal and confrontational role for the regimes than the sovereign states that created them would be comfortable with. The regimes exist primarily to coordinate guidelines and control lists. The hope is that states will mostly choose to follow the associated norms and rules. To expect perfect compliance is not realistic. If the regimes lead to increasing agreement on the appropriate norms and the trend is for more states follow these norms more of the time, this is evidence of social learning, and it means the regimes are being about as effective as one could hope for. That there are consistent, measurable outcomes in the MECR over time suggests a high degree of compromise facilitated through iterative exchanges and procedural flexibility.

The informal, consensus nature of the regimes also makes it less risky for new states to consider joining, as they are less likely to find themselves forced to act contrary to their interests. As more states join and consolidate the regime norms, participating becomes more attractive to other states as a way to demonstrate good international citizenship. India's petition to join the NSG, for example, arguably represents an attempt to demonstrate an identity as a "responsible" steward of nuclear weapons despite its nonmembership in the NPT. This process of social learning of export control norms, facilitated by the largely informal regime design, fosters an expansion of cooperation that helps explain the patterns observed in the MECR.

GLOBAL EXPORT CONTROL NORMS AND BEST PRACTICES

Despite the rudimentary nature of their cooperation, the members in the multilateral arrangements have made considerable progress in several areas. Though open-source evidence is scarce, it seems likely that multilateral cooperation on export controls has made the acquisition of WMD more difficult and may have helped deter some governments from even attempting to acquire such weapons. The MTCR, for example, played a critical role in ending sensitive ballistic missile programs in Argentina, Brazil, Egypt, South Africa, and Taiwan, while it helped curtail developments in India, Iran, Israel, North Korea, and Pakistan.[43] The effects of the barriers erected by the MECR are also reflected in the fact that contemporary proliferation efforts are predicated upon defeating export controls, as evidenced in, for instance, the A. Q. Khan network.[44] The MECR are effective to the extent that they establish the global standards for technology transfers (i.e., guidelines) and provide the practicable means by which to focus these standards (i.e., control lists). Progress in the regimes is also evidenced in the following characteristics, most of which can also be considered lessons learned about best practices in multilateral export controls.

Most Major Suppliers Participate in the Regimes

By 2012, thirty governments had joined all four of the regimes, with forty-six participating in at least one arrangement. Given the ever more global flow of goods and services, some states have joined that are not themselves major suppliers, such as Cyprus, which participates due to its EU membership and role as a transshipment state.[45] Moreover the EU Commission is a member of the AG and NSG and an MTCR observer. India has also expressed its desire to join all four regimes.[46]

Getting major supplier countries to join the regimes, particularly former critics, is necessary to the continued functioning of the regimes. Expansion should be seen as an indicator of the regimes' ongoing relevance, not a sign the regimes are being diluted. Inducting major suppliers often requires compromise. In the case of the MTCR, for example, bringing countries into the regime has often involved negotiations to adapt MTCR standards to permit smaller missile projects, typically within MTCR thresholds, or allowing continued progress on civilian space launch projects. For instance, Brazil joined in 1995 after winning access to U.S. technical assistance for its space launch program.[47] As noted by Aaron Karp, "Every new country that joins the MTCR brings change in the form of its own agenda and priorities. The great strength of the regime is its ability to accommodate this diversity while enhancing progress toward basic goals."[48]

The Arrangements Serve as a Regular Forum for Discussion and Information Exchange

In all four arrangements, members conduct regular plenary sessions, have technical meetings, and maintain working groups. The arrangements provide a means by which adherents can discuss export controls on a regular basis, adjust interpretations of control policies, turn unilateral into multilateral practices, and share sensitive information on end users.

Given the relative lack of intelligence resources available to most governments, the regimes have a critical impact on the effectiveness of national export controls through the sharing of information on projects of proliferation concern, suspect end users and companies, and acquisition methods. Annual rotation of chair assignments for plenary sessions and other groups and a practice of giving new members responsibility for holding meetings have helped raise export controls higher on the political agenda of many members, as well as facilitated the transfer of knowledge leading to practical enhancements of national controls. Most important, the arrangements play a key role in norm development. Through guideline revisions, the regimes have sought to address emerging risks. For example, all of the regimes have adopted provisions incorporating catch-all, intangible transfers of technology, brokering, and transit controls in an effort to keep pace with the proliferation threat.[49]

The export control norms and practices of the MECR have provided underpinnings for other multilateral nonproliferation efforts, which in turn help disseminate and reinforce the export control norms. UN Security Council Resolution 1540 (adopted in 2004) requires all member states to develop effective laws and procedures to control WMD-related transfers. Resolution 1540's approach is clearly based on the regimes, as it calls for national control lists as well as laws that include brokering, transit, transshipment, and re-export control provisions.[50] The regimes also provide the normative and practical substance for UN resolutions targeting Iranian and North Korean proliferation activities. At

Table 2.2 Organizational Features of the MECR (as of mid-2014)

Group	Members	Information Exchange System	Governance	Plenaries	Technical Meetings	Working Groups
AG	41	Dedicated e-system (AG Information System)	Point of Contact (POC) (Australia)	Yearly	As needed (Technical Advisory Group and Synthetic Biology Advisory Body)	Yearly
MTCR	34	Bilateral	POC (France)	Yearly	Yearly (Technical Experts Meetings [TEM])	As needed (Information Exchange [IE] and Licensing and Enforcement Experts Meeting [LEEM]); also conducts Reinforced Point of Contact (RPOC) and Monthly Point of Contact (POC)
NSG	48	Dedicated e-system (NISS)	POC (Japan)	Semiannual	As needed (Dedicated Meeting of Technical Experts [DMTE])	As needed (Consultative Group [CG]; Information Exchange Meeting [IEM]; and Licensing and Enforcement Experts Meeting [LEEM])
WA	41	Dedicated e-system	Secretariat (in Vienna)	Yearly	As needed (Experts Group [EG])	As needed (General Working Group [GWG]; Licensing and Enforcement Officers Meeting [LEOM]; and Vienna Points of Contact [VPOC])*

* VPOC meetings are called-for periodic meetings under the Plenary Chair to facilitate intersessional information flow and communications between/among participating states and the secretariat.

the regional level, the EU has, in essence, codified the regime control lists and guidelines into a binding Regulation.⁵¹

Participants Share Common Lists of Items of Concern

All of the arrangements have lists of controlled items. Unlike the strictly illustrative categories in the original trigger list, dual-use lists present very detailed parameter descriptions of the goods and technologies subject to control. The coverage of relevant items varies from the NSG, which controls most nuclear items of concern, to the AG lists, where advances in biotechnology have challenging implications for identifying items for control. Interestingly, the EU consolidated the MECR control lists and required all EU member states to implement this list at the national level. The resulting EU dual-use control list is becoming the de facto global standard for national control lists.⁵² Likewise, the EU Common Military List mirrors the WA Military List.

Revisions to control lists require a high degree of political, economic, and technical collaboration, particularly as the revision process is also subject to consensus decision-making rules. Individual participant state interest in list changes can be motivated by both economic and security considerations. As such, the process of list revisions requires significant compromise strategies. The informal nature of the regimes facilitates progress in what might otherwise become a deadlocked process in cases where there is pronounced interest heterogeneity.

The Arrangements Have "No Undercut" Policies to Reduce Opportunities to Abuse Multilateral Cooperation for National Commercial Advantage

Nonproliferation efforts in general, and multilateral export controls in particular, are a public good. As with the provision of public goods generally, the prospect of free riding and related transaction costs can suppress cooperation. In COCOM, participants could veto another participant's prospective strategic exports, thereby establishing a "no undercut" provision in practice. However, in the absence of joint licensing, three of the four regimes have established an explicit no undercut provision. In the AG, MTCR, and NSG, states share information on denials and undertake obligations not to export items denied by another member, usually for three years, except through prior consultation and agreement with that member. One of the major critiques of the WA is that it lacks a prior notification requirement and members do not have an obligation not to export items denied by other parties; however, participants are expected to inform other members after they undercut another's denial.⁵³

WMD Acquisition Tactics Are Predicated upon Evading Export Controls

Finally, and ironically, perhaps the best indicator of the impact of these arrangements comes from the fact that some states and non-state actors seeking to acquire WMD capabilities continually look for new means to evade export controls.[54] While export controls cannot prevent proliferation, they delay and frustrate acquisition efforts, thereby allowing other nonproliferation activities and policies to work. In some instances, they may even deter countries from starting WMD projects by raising their costs of developing WMD or by increasing the chance of detection and potential for international opprobrium.

By including most major suppliers, providing forums for regular discussion and information exchange, facilitating agreement on common lists of items to control, and incorporating no undercut provisions, the export control regimes work in tandem with other elements of the nonproliferation regime to make WMD acquisition harder. These factors that contribute to the impact of the regimes also provide lessons about best practices that can be built upon in future export control efforts.

CONCLUSION

The history of proliferation strongly suggests that proliferant states and, increasingly, non-state actors seek WMD production capability through commercial acquisition. These acquisition strategies are predicated upon evading national export control systems. The collective action problem involved in getting all supplier states to uphold export controls is compounded by the inherent complexity of the relevant technologies and the evolving nature of the proliferation threat. In this context, the multilateral export control regimes have helped to develop and disseminate export control norms and practices through information sharing and collaboration.

Critiques of the regimes focus on their informal nature, consensus rules, discretionary implementation (i.e., lack of enforcement), and disparate membership. These critiques fail, however, to explicate clear metrics of effectiveness. In this chapter, I have developed a proxy indicator of cooperation based on measures involving adjustments to substantive policies and procedural norms. By these measures, the regimes, since their inception, have continued to perform consistently the work of the regimes: the promulgation of guidelines and control lists. Furthermore, the iterative process of interaction involved in developing, revising, and clarifying export control lists and guidelines has evolved into a mechanism for compromise through social learning, despite the increased number and diversity of the participants. In this regard, the informality cited by critics as a liability is actually an underlying strength of the regime structure.

The stated objective of the regimes is targeted coordination. Realistically, we hope that export control coordination will decrease, though it cannot end, the likelihood of proliferation, while advancing legitimate trade. To expect more asks too much of these informal arrangements. However, when they are understood to be just part of the overall nonproliferation regime "complex," the MECR are unburdened of these performance expectations.[55] In many respects the MECR are "innovations" of the nonproliferation regime complex, emerging in response to critical international events for which the treaties were necessary but insufficient solutions to WMD proliferation.[56]

According to Arthur Stein, "regimes are maintained as long as the patterns of interest that gave rise to them remain."[57] In the case of the MECR, export control cooperation has not only increased but deepened despite significant environmental and membership changes. While an examination of individual participant motivations is beyond the scope of this chapter, the outcomes of regime activity suggest a robust adaptive mechanism inherent in certain features of the regimes. Created initially in large part due to the exercise of U.S. leadership, the export control regimes have sustained cooperation mainly due to social learning and compromise decision making facilitated by iterative interactions within relatively informal regime structures. The MECR cases show that norms, learning, regime design, and working relationships among the participants are key factors in explaining cooperation.

Notes

1. See, for example, Seema Gahlaut, "Multilateral Export Control Regimes: Operations, Successes, Failures and the Challenges Ahead," in *Non-proliferation Export Controls: Origins, Challenges, and Proposals for Strengthening*, ed. Daniel J. Joyner (London: Ashgate, 2006), 7–29.

2. Dynamic density, a term John Ruggie adapted from Emile Durkheim, refers to the amount and intensity of interaction among actors in a system, and is expected by him to change the character of outcomes in the system. This suggests that having more members interacting more frequently in the regimes might not necessarily complicate cooperation but instead encourage it. See John Gerard Ruggie, "Continuity and Transformation in the World Polity: Toward a Neorealist Synthesis," in *Neorealism and Its Critics*, ed. Robert O. Keohane (New York: Columbia University Press, 1986), 131–57.

3. This chapter does not include a comprehensive examination of national perspectives on the four multilateral arrangements. With thirty-seven governments participating as of 2012 in at least one of the arrangements and several more adhering to some of the multilateral guidelines, a thorough investigation of all relevant states would demand a research effort well beyond any conducted in the field so far. For a representative example of national export

control system analyses, see Michael D. Beck, Richard T. Cupitt, Seema Gahlaut, and Scott A. Jones, *To Supply or to Deny: Comparing Nonproliferation Export Controls in Five Key Countries* (Amsterdam: Kluwer, 2006).

4. Nonmembers have been more critical. For an example of criticisms of the regimes by nonmembers, which charge them with acting like cartels, see a working paper submitted by members of the Group of Non-Aligned States Parties to the Treaty on the Non-Proliferation of Nuclear Weapons (NPT/CONF.2000/WP.8), available at cns.miis.edu/nam/index.php/site/documents?forum_id=3&forum_name=NPT&doctype_id=6&doctype_name=Meeting+Summaries.

5. As noted by Michael Byers, "Regime theorists have not written much about informal rules and procedures. Regime theorists have instead focused on multilateral treaties and international organizations, around or within which informal rules or procedures may develop, but, if they do develop, will fulfill only supplementary roles." Michael Byers, *Custom, Power and the Power of Rules: International Relations and Customary International Law* (Cambridge: Cambridge University Press, 1999), 26.

6. In their study of the Association of Southeast Asian Nations (ASEAN), Acharya and Johnston note that "institutions can still help attain their original goals and induce preference change with informal rules and deliberative mandate[s].... More informal groups such as ASEAN have had a discernible impact in changing the preferences and norms of their members." Amitav Acharya and Alastair Iain Johnston, "Conclusion: Institutional Features, Cooperation Effects and the Agenda for Further Research on Comparative Regionalism," in *Crafting Cooperation: Regional International Institutions in Comparative Perspective*, ed. Amitav Acharya and Alastair Iain Johnston (Cambridge: Cambridge University Press, 2007), 269.

7. Kenneth W. Abbott and Duncan Snidal, "Why States Act through Formal International Organizations," *Journal of Conflict Resolution* 42, no. 1 (February 1998): 11.

8. For a good history and evaluation of COCOM's impact, see Gary K. Bertsch, *East-West Strategic Trade, COCOM and the Atlantic Alliance* (Paris: Atlantic Institute for International Affairs, 1983).

9. Frank M. Cevasco, "Survey and Assessment: Alternative Multilateral Export Control Structures" (Working Paper 3, Study Group on Enhancing Multilateral Export Controls for U.S. National Security, Henry L. Stimson Center/Center for Strategic and International Studies, Washington, D.C., 2001).

10. Japan and France did not ratify the NPT until 1976 and 1992, respectively.

11. Because the discussions in the NSG were not directly associated with the text of the NPT, participating states were able to take a more flexible and extensive approach to developing a list of items subject to agreed guidelines. See David Fischer, "The London Club and the Zangger Committee: How Effective?," in *Proliferation and Export Controls*, ed. Kathleen Bailey and Robert Rudney (Lanham, Md.: University Press of America, 1993), 39–48.

12. The Zangger list also covered some ENR technology, but the Zangger guidelines did not call on suppliers to exercise restraint in exporting such items.

13. Critics have charged that preventing development and economic competition is actually the goal of the export control regimes. Indian scholar Brahma Chellaney, for example, has argued that "the non-proliferation policies of Western powers are founded on a strategy of preventing Third World development of technologies that might impinge on the Western powers' military and economic interests." See Brahma Chellaney, "An Indian Critique of U.S. Export Controls," *Orbis* 38, no. 3 (Summer 1994): 439–56.

14. In 1992, the NSG participants also issued a statement in which they declared that full-scope safeguards would be required as a condition for future transfers. See Carlton E. Thorne,

ed., *A Guide to Nuclear Export Controls 1999-2000*, 2nd ed. (Burke, Va.: Proliferation Data Services, 1999).

15. The AG focused initially just on chemical weapons but later expanded its scope to include biological weapons. After the ratification of the Chemical Weapons Convention (CWC) in 1995, the Organization for Prohibition on Chemical Weapons (OPCW) was established. It is charged with the implementation of export control and verification protocols of the CWC. AG members now view the institution as aiding their efforts to meet their obligations under the CWC, although some CWC members who are not in the AG are more critical and argue that export controls should be managed by the OPCW. This would not cover biological weapons, however, which are also part of the AG mandate.

16. Amy E. Smithson, "Separating Fact from Fiction: The Australia Group and the Chemical Weapons Convention" (Occasional Paper 34, Henry L. Stimson Center, Washington, D.C., March 1997).

17. Scott A. Jones, "Emptying the Haunted Air: Delivery Means and the Post-modern MTCR," in Joyner, *Non-proliferation Export Controls*, 75-100.

18. Ron Smith and Bernard Udis, "New Challenges to Arms Export Control: Whither Wassenaar?," *Nonproliferation Review* 8, no. 2 (Summer 2001): 81-92.

19. Kenneth A. Dursht, "From Containment to Cooperation: Collective Action and the Wassenaar Arrangement," *Cardozo Law Review* 19, no. 3 (December 1997): 1079-1123.

20. Michael Lipson, "The Reincarnation of CoCom: Explaining Post-Cold War Export Controls," *Nonproliferation Review* 6, no. 2 (Winter 2009): 33-51.

21. Richard T. Cupitt and Suzette R. Grillot, "COCOM Is Dead, Long Live COCOM: Persistence and Change in Multilateral Security Institutions," *British Journal of Political Science* 27, no. 3 (July 1997): 361-89.

22. For instance, members of the Wassenaar Arrangement, which seeks to prevent "destabilizing accumulations" of arms by regulating transfers by suppliers have been unable to define, to the satisfaction of all parties, what the term "destabilizing accumulation" means. See Dursht, "From Containment to Cooperation."

23. While not an exhaustive list, the above-noted limitations represent a consensus view across MECR studies. See, in particular, Michael Beck and Seema Gahlaut, "Creating a New Multilateral Export Control Regime," *Arms Control Today* 33, no. 3 (April 2003).

24. Seema Gahlaut and Victor Zaborsky, "Do Export Control Regimes Have Members They Really Need?," *Comparative Strategy* 23, no. 1 (Summer 2004): 73-91.

25. U.S. General Accounting Office (GAO), "Strategy Needed to Strengthen Multilateral Export Control Regimes" (GAO-03-43, October 2002).

26. Cupitt and Grillot, "COCOM Is Dead," 365.

27. Methodologically, we cannot assess levels of export control cooperation by examining the state of WMD proliferation or the status of national implementation of that cooperation at any given time. These other variables start to get at the effects of cooperation. The measure of cooperation itself, however, must be confined to the scope and internal activities of the regime.

28. Stephen D. Krasner, "Structural Causes and Regime Consequences: Regimes as Intervening Variables," in *International Regimes*, ed. Stephen D. Krasner (Ithaca, N.Y.: Cornell University Press, 1983), 3. See also Cupitt and Grillot, "COCOM Is Dead," 366.

29. Beverly Crawford and Stephanie Lenway, "Decision Modes and International Regime Change: Western Collaboration on East-West Trade," *World Politics* 37, no. 3 (April 1985): 375-402. They argue that over time both compliance and problem-solving decision-making modes give way to compromise as the key decision-making mode in international institutions.

30. On these NSG decisions, see Daniel Horner, "NSG Revises Rules on Sensitive Exports," *Arms Control Today* 41, no. 6 (July–August 2011).

31. The organizational consistency is by both design and effect, the latter owing to a tendency for the same officials to participate in each of the four regimes. This tendency is a source of both stability and complaint among smaller member states, which find their resources stretched by the effort to participate in activities of four regimes. See Michael Beck, Seema Gahlaut, Scott Jones, and Dan Joyner, "Roadmap to Reform: Creating a New Multilateral Export Control Regime" (Center for International Trade and Security working paper, University of Georgia, Athens, 2004).

32. Ian Anthony, Christer Ahlström, and Vitaly Fedchenko, *Reforming Nuclear Export Controls: The Future of the Nuclear Suppliers Group* (Stockholm International Peace Research Institute Research Report No. 22; New York: Oxford University Press, 2007), 123.

33. On the evolution of China's nonproliferation policy, see J. D. Yuan, "The New Player in the Game: China, Arms Control, and Multilateralism," in *China Turns to Multilateralism: Foreign Policy and Regional Security*, ed. Guoguang Wu and Helen Lansdowne (London: Routledge, 2008), 51–72, and Taek Goo Kang, "Assessing China's Approach to Regional Multilateral Security Cooperation," *Australian Journal of International Affairs* 64, no. 4 (August 2010): 406–31.

34. Wade Boese, "NSG, Congress Approve Nuclear Trade with India," *Arms Control Today* 38, no. 8 (October 2008).

35. For a critique of the India deal, see Daryl Kimball, "Indian Membership in the NSG? A Bad Idea Whose Time Has Not Come," *Arms Control Now*, June 23, 2011, http://armscontrolnow.org/2011/06/23/indian-membership-iin-the-nsg-a-bad-idea-whose-time-has-not-come/.

36. Wade Boese, "U.S. Nuclear Trade Restriction Initiatives Still on Hold," *Arms Control Today* 34, no. 10 (December 2004).

37. The proposed November 2008 version of the NSG guidelines also included a fairly specific list of so-called subjective criteria a potential nuclear supplier should consider. The final text dispensed with that list and replaced it with more general language saying that suppliers should "tak[e] into account at their national discretion, any relevant factors as may be applicable." Horner, "NSG Revises Rules," 30.

38. China became an NSG member in 2004. Initially, China's membership was not universally supported. India expressed its intention to join the NSG in 2008, but as of this writing objections from key states have prevented India from gaining membership. For some of the earlier thinking on Chinese MECR membership, see Victor Zaborsky, "Does China Belong in the Missile Technology Control Regime?," *Arms Control Today* 34, no. 8 (October 2004).

39. For example, regarding the evolution of China's nonproliferation policy, see Evan Madeiros, *Reluctant Restraint: The Evolution of China's Nonproliferation Policies and Practices, 1980–2004* (Stanford: Stanford University Press, 2007).

40. "The NSG in a Time of Change: An Interview with NSG Chairman Piet de Klerk," *Arms Control Today* 41, no. 8 (October 2011).

41. See, for example, Beck and Gahlaut, "Creating a New Multilateral Export Control Regime."

42. On how the Russian decision to supply fuel to India apparently conflicted with then NSG guidelines, see V. Fedchenko and R. Timerbaev, "Russian-Indian Nuclear Relations and Export Control Issues" (PIR Study Paper 17), in *The Problem of Proliferation and Nonproliferation in South Asia: Current Situation and Perspectives* (Moscow: PIR Center, 2001), 62–84.

43. Dennis M. Gormley, *Missile Contagion: Cruise Missile Proliferation and the Threat to International Security* (Annapolis, Md.: Naval Institute Press, 2008); and Dinshaw Mistry,

Containing Missile Proliferation: Strategic Technology, Security Regimes, and International Cooperation in Arms Control (Seattle: University of Washington Press, 2003).

44. The research on proliferation networks suggests that proliferators use them in an effort to foil export controls in order to acquire dual-use goods and materials necessary for WMD production. See, for example, David Albright, *Peddling Peril: How the Secret Nuclear Trade Arms America's Enemies* (New York: Free Press, 2010). For a review of non-state acquisition methods, see Gavin Cameron, "Multitrack Microproliferation: Lessons from Aum Shinrikyo and Al Qaeda," *Studies in Conflict and Terrorism* 22, no. 4 (October–December 1999): 277–309.

45. The EU has enacted a dual-use export control regime, in the form of a regulation, since 2000. In many respects, the EU regulation, which consists of a guideline and control list, mirrors the form and function of the regimes. In fact, the EU dual-use control list is a compilation of the MECR control lists. For more on the EU system, see Anna Wetter, "Enforcing European Union Law on Exports of Dual-Use Goods" (Stockholm International Peace Research Institute Research Paper No. 24, Stockholm, 2009).

46. Following India's bid, Pakistan is also seeking membership in the NSG and other MECRs.

47. Wyn Q. Bowen, "Brazil's Accession to the MTCR," *Nonproliferation Review* 3, no. 3 (Spring–Summer 1996): 86–91.

48. Aaron Karp, "Stemming the Spread of Missiles: Hits, Misses, and Hard Cases," *Arms Control Today* 42, no. 3 (April 2012).

49. Scott A. Jones, Michael D. Beck, and Seema Gahlaut, "Trade Controls and International Security," in *Combating Weapons of Mass Destruction: The Future of International Nonproliferation Policy*, ed. Nathan E. Busch and Daniel H. Joyner (Athens: University of Georgia Press, 2009), 118–38.

50. Scott A. Jones, "Resolution 1540: Universalizing Export Control Standards?," *Arms Control Today* 36, no. 4 (May 2006).

51. Scott Jones, "EU Enlargement: Implications for EU and Multilateral Export Controls," *Nonproliferation Review* 10, no. 2 (Summer 2003): 80–89.

52. The United States, for example, adopted the EU control list structure in 1996.

53. In practice, however, the member states rarely undercut other regime members. See Michael Lipson, "The Wassenaar Arrangement: Transparency and Restraint through Transgovernmental Cooperation," in Joyner, *Non-proliferation Export Controls*, 56.

54. Ian Anthony et al., "Controls on Security-Related International Transfers," in *SIPRI Yearbook, 2009: Armaments, Disarmament, and International Security* (Stockholm: Stockholm International Peace Research Institute, 2008), 459–81.

55. Where interests and power are fragmented, incentives for cooperation often lead to what Raustiala and Victor have called "regime complexes." In their terms, a regime complex is "an array of partially overlapping and nonhierarchical institutions governing a particular issue area." Kal Raustiala and David Victor, "The Regime Complex for Plant Genetic Resources," *International Organization* 58, no. 2 (Spring 2004): 277–310.

56. Colgan, Keohane, and Van der Graaf describe the process of regime complex innovation as resulting from dissatisfaction with the status quo in an issue area, such that new regimes may emerge within a complex to address emerging problems. Jeff D. Colgan, Robert O. Keohane, and Thijs Van de Graaf, "Punctuated Equilibrium in the Energy Regime Complex," *Review of International Organizations* 7, no. 2 (June 2012): 117–43.

57. Arthur A. Stein, "Coordination and Collaboration: Regimes in an Anarchic World," *International Organization* 36, no. 2 (Spring 1982): 321.

CHAPTER THREE

Nuclear Nonproliferation via Coercion and Consensus

The Success and Limits of the RERTR Program (1978–2004)

ALAN J. KUPERMAN

ALTHOUGH LESS WELL KNOWN than some other nonproliferation initiatives, the U.S.-based Reduced Enrichment for Research and Test Reactors (RERTR) Program greatly improved worldwide nuclear security at remarkably little cost, during its initial phase from 1978 to 2004. Averaging only two dozen employees and an annual budget of four million dollars,[1] the program substantially reduced international civilian commerce in bomb-grade, highly enriched uranium (HEU), and thereby lowered global risks of nuclear proliferation and nuclear terrorism. This chapter explores the factors that enabled, and constrained, the achievements of the RERTR program during its first quarter century, when it was a relatively obscure and low-budget affair. Following that initial phase, in the wake of the terror attacks of September 11, 2001, the RERTR program in 2004 was subsumed by the U.S. Department of Energy (DOE) into the Global Threat Reduction Initiative (GTRI), where it benefited from substantially greater funding and political support. That second phase may offer additional lessons that are worthy of a separate inquiry.

One unusual feature of RERTR, among nonproliferation programs, is that its foreign participants were mainly the operators of nuclear facilities, rather than representatives of national governments. Accordingly, this chapter addresses two main questions. First, why did so many of these foreign actors cooperate with the program, despite the fact that doing so imposed costs on them? Second, what determined the limits of that cooperation? In terms of the framework set out by Jeffrey Knopf in chapter 1, cooperation was shaped strongly by the interaction between U.S. leadership and the self-interest of facility operators. To identify precisely the causal mechanisms, this chapter utilizes the case study methodology of "process tracing" to investigate seven potential explanations for foreign cooperation:

1. *Coercion*—The United States threatened otherwise to impose some punishment, in the form of a financial penalty or other inconvenience regarding fuel supply or disposition.
2. *Perceived costs reduced*—The United States convinced foreign partners that the costs of cooperation were lower than originally perceived.
3. *Norms*—Despite the costs of cooperation, foreign actors internalized a norm that it was the right thing to do, thereby valuing the common interest above self-interest.
4. *Side payments*—The United States purchased cooperation by providing additional inducements, in the form of either financial reward or other benefit.
5. *Diplomacy*—Foreign governments cooperated, and compelled their private enterprises to do so, because the United States applied diplomatic pressure and the foreign governments expected that their concessions would be diffusely reciprocated over time.
6. *Inherent benefit*—Foreign actors cooperated because they perceived that the cost of doing so would be more than offset by some inherent benefit of cooperating, such as improving the performance of their nuclear facilities.
7. *Other factors*—Although the preceding six possibilities may be exhaustive, the chapter also looks for other explanations of foreign cooperation.

The remainder of this chapter is organized as follows. First, it summarizes the RERTR program's rationale, objectives, achievements, and limitations. Second, it investigates the causes of cooperation and noncooperation, assessing each of the above seven hypotheses. Third, it draws lessons for promoting cooperation on nuclear nonproliferation, including but not limited to further efforts to reduce international commerce in bomb-grade uranium.

RERTR OVERVIEW

Starting in the 1950s, the United States and the Soviet Union exported dozens of nuclear research reactors. At the beginning, developing countries mainly received fuel of low-enriched uranium (LEU) that is deemed unsuitable for nuclear weapons because it contains less than 20 percent of the fissile isotope U-235 that sustains a nuclear chain reaction. But after some technical difficulties with that fuel, the United States switched to exporting HEU fuel enriched to 93 percent U-235—the same material used in U.S. nuclear weapons—to almost all of the research reactors it supplied.[2]

Experts typically assume that twenty-five kilograms of such HEU is sufficient for a nuclear weapon. In that light, it is remarkable that in the mid-1960s, annual U.S. HEU exports for research reactors approached three metric tons, enough for more than one hundred nuclear weapons each year (see figure 3.3). As late as 1978, when the RERTR program was created, 141 reactors around the world annually required thirteen hundred kilograms of HEU from the United States, equivalent to more than fifty nuclear weapons per year.[3]

ORIGINS AND ACHIEVEMENTS OF RERTR

The RERTR program, based at Argonne National Laboratory, aimed to reduce HEU commerce by converting research reactors to use 19.8 percent enriched LEU fuel, which significantly raises the technical barriers to proliferation. As indicated in figure 3.1, reducing enrichment from 93 to 19.8 percent can increase by nearly twenty times the critical mass required for a nuclear weapon, depending on various assumptions. The main technical challenge for the RERTR program was to increase the density of the uranium in LEU fuel so that it would contain at least as much U-235 in the same space as lower-density HEU fuel, even though the LEU itself has less than one-quarter as much U-235 by weight. Maximizing the amount of U-235 per unit volume (see figure 3.2) was necessary to sustain the lifetime of the fuel with only a marginal loss of the neutron flux that is the key output of most research reactors.

FIGURE 3.1   Switch to LEU Fuel Inhibits Misuse for Weapons by Increasing Critical Mass

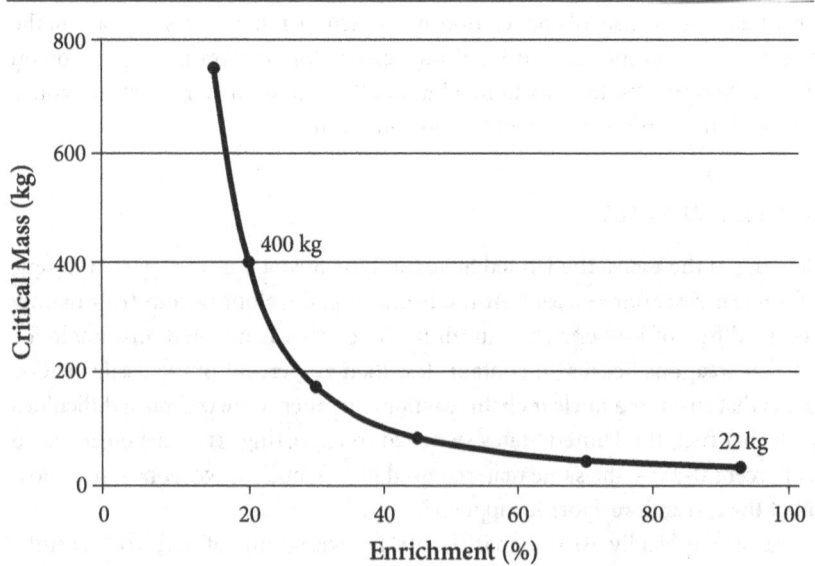

Note: Critical mass of a uranium sphere surrounded by a 5-cm beryllium reflector.

Source: Alexander Glaser and Frank N. von Hippel, "Global Cleanout: Reducing the Threat of HEU-Fueled Nuclear Terrorism," *Arms Control Today* (January–February 2006): 19.

FIGURE 3.2   Higher Uranium Density Enables Lower Enrichment

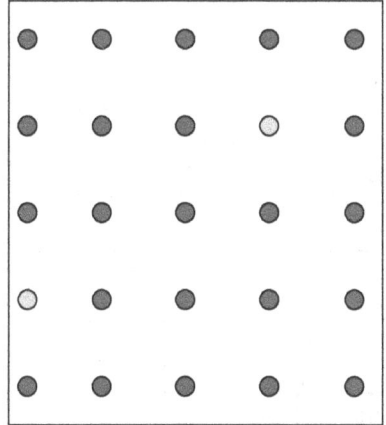
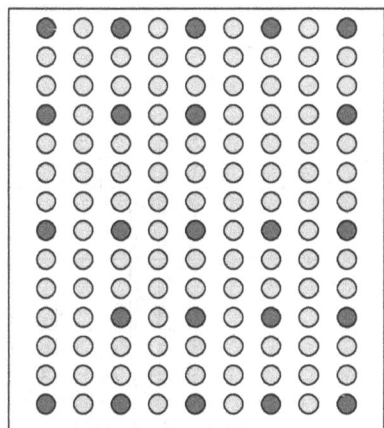

HEU: 93.3%-enriched   LEU: 19.9%-enriched

Key: ● = U-235
       ○ = U-238

Source: Alan J. Kuperman, "Global HEU Phase-Out: Prospects & Challenges," in *Nuclear Terrorism and Global Security: The Challenge of Phasing Out Highly Enriched Uranium*, ed. Alan J. Kuperman (New York: Routledge, 2013), 7.

In essence, the RERTR program sought ways to cram much more of the nonfissile isotope U-238 into the fuel, such that the uranium would be transformed from HEU to LEU. This reduced the proliferation and terrorism risks, but without significantly affecting four key aspects of the reactor: design, performance, fuel lifetime, and safety licensing.[4] In practice, LEU fuel typically requires approximately 15 percent more U-235 by volume than HEU fuel, because the extra U-238 absorbs some neutrons. When the uranium density of the fuel cannot be increased sufficiently, other adjustments can be made to compensate: increasing the thickness of the fuel meat by thinning the fuel's cladding, redesigning the fuel element to have fewer but thicker plates, and/or optimizing the pattern in which fuel is shuffled in and out of the reactor core. During the 1980s, the RERTR program developed progressively higher density fuel to enable conversion of higher performance research reactors. The program also conducted neutronic and safety analyses, as well as the tests necessary to persuade operators of reactors—and the regulatory bodies in the United States and abroad—that the higher density LEU fuels were safe and effective substitutes for HEU fuel.

In this manner, the RERTR program facilitated a gradual reduction of global

FIGURE 3.3   RERTR Program Facilitates Sharp Decline in U.S. Exports of Civil HEU

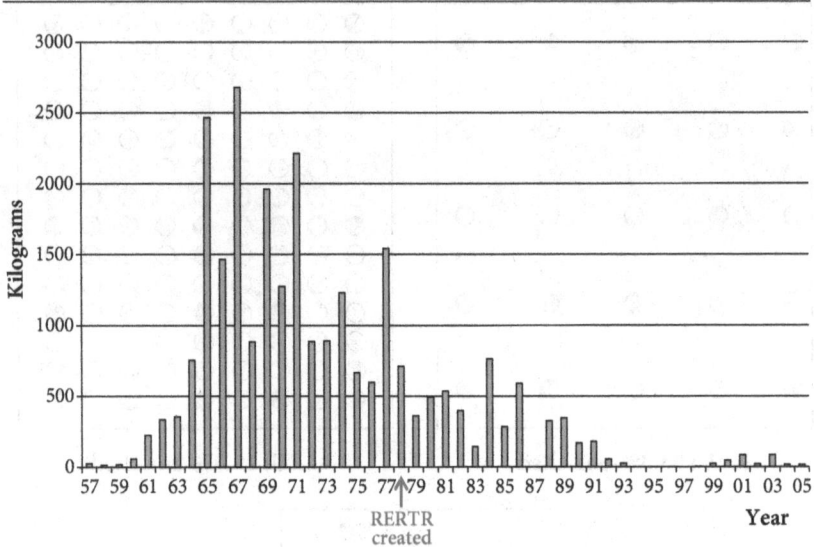

Source: Adapted from Alan J. Kuperman, "Civilian Highly Enriched Uranium and the Fissile Material Convention," in *Nuclear Power & the Spread of Nuclear Weapons*, ed. Paul L. Leventhal (Dulles, Va.: Brassey's, 2002), 252.

commerce in HEU for nonweapons purposes (see figure 3.3). The program initially focused mainly on converting U.S.-supplied reactors in foreign countries. By the early 1980s, however, the Soviet Union had established an analogous program to convert to lower enriched fuel the reactors it supplied. In 1986, the U.S. Nuclear Regulatory Commission (NRC) ordered the conversion to LEU fuel of the research reactors that it licensed, which included all in the United States except those of the DOE and the Defense Department. At the same time, the RERTR program began developing LEU "targets" to replace the HEU targets that were irradiated to produce most of the world's medical isotopes. In 1993, the program initiated formal collaboration with Russian laboratories to reduce further the enrichment of the fuel in Soviet-supplied reactors.[5] Finally, in 2004, the United States committed also to convert all DOE reactors to LEU fuel.[6]

By 2004, as a result of these efforts, thirty-nine foreign and domestic research reactors had been converted from HEU to LEU fuel, or were in the process of converting, or had purchased LEU fuel in anticipation of converting,[7] yielding an annual reduction in HEU commerce of about 250 kilograms. Outside the United States, this included twenty reactors that had been fully converted,[8] and seven more that had been partially converted,[9] in twenty-one countries. In addition, from 1980 to 2004, at least twenty-one new research reactors in sixteen countries were designed to use LEU fuel,[10] while only one reactor that started construction after 1986 used HEU fuel.[11] In 2002, Argentina converted to LEU targets for producing medical isotopes.[12] By 2004, Russia had successfully developed one higher-density LEU fuel and was conducting conversion studies for seven Soviet-supplied reactors in six countries.[13] Together these achievements reduced annual worldwide HEU commerce by hundreds of kilograms, diminishing the risk that such fissile material could be stolen or diverted to make nuclear weapons.

On that basis, the RERTR program's first quarter century qualifies as a success. Yet, significant amounts of civilian HEU commerce persisted. As of 2004, some sixty-seven reactors within the program's scope still used about 830 kilograms of HEU annually, more than had been eliminated by converting thirty-nine reactors and designing twenty-one new reactors to use LEU fuel. In addition, HEU fuel continued to be used at fifty-six facilities outside the scope of the RERTR program, including critical assemblies, pulsed reactors, and Russian research reactors.[14] Thus, according to a 2004 program assessment, 123 reactors were believed still to use HEU, compared to the sixty reactors that the program had enabled to use LEU fuel.[15] The explanation for this mixed record, and the lessons for future nonproliferation efforts, are explored below.

COOPERATION AND ITS LIMITS

The significant amount of cooperation ultimately achieved by the RERTR program is an interesting puzzle because initially, and to some extent persistently, operators of reactors and medical-isotope production facilities opposed converting from HEU to LEU. They expected conversion to provide no benefits but many costs, financial and otherwise: diminished performance due to reduced flux of thermal neutrons; higher prices for LEU fuel because of more complex fabrication techniques; unplanned expenses to replace HEU fuel before it was exhausted; relicensing by national authorities, often under regulations that had become stricter since the previous licensing; and possible shutdown due to public opposition during relicensing. The financial costs of each reactor conversion—for the new fuel and safety analysis—typically ranged from one to two million dollars.[16] As a U.S. official explained in 1987, "On the part of the other countries, there's really no incentive to convert. . . . If they have a machine that's working nicely and they have to convert, the operators are only asking for additional problems."[17]

By contrast, the expected benefit from eliminating the use of HEU was to international society as a whole. Operators typically dismissed this benefit on grounds that the theft or diversion of HEU from their facilities was implausible. They did not expect savings on security costs from switching to LEU because at the time the security measures required for HEU were no more stringent than those mandated to defend facilities against sabotage.[18]

Despite the resulting foreign opposition to conversion, the RERTR program made steady progress. As this book's theoretical framework suggests, U.S. leadership obviously was essential for launching the initiative. But that begs the harder question: what accounts for the extent and limitations of international cooperation under the RERTR program? Seven potential explanations are analyzed below, in descending order of importance.

Coercion

Coercion was the most important factor in the success of the RERTR program, especially in its early years. The United States had great leverage as virtually the sole supplier of HEU to the noncommunist world, and Washington communicated its intent to phase out exports of HEU to facilities that could convert to LEU. As reported in 1987, "To persuade operators of reactors in other countries to agree to abandon HEU, the United States sometimes threatens to cut off its exports of HEU to them." By contrast, merely appealing to a norm was insufficient to forge cooperation at the time; as a U.S. official explained, "It's not done just by talking."[19] Washington presented foreign reactor operators with a stark choice: convert to LEU or shut down. The operators could only hope to delay this choice by finding temporary alternative sources of HEU, either from leftover U.S.-origin stocks in Europe or—in two cases soon after the Cold War—from Russia.

Coercion, either implicit or explicit, was a persistent tool of the RERTR program, starting from its first annual international meeting in November 1978. At the time, foreign research reactor operators had no interest in converting to LEU fuel and were under no requirement to attend the meeting. Many did attend, however, because they had heard that the United States was planning to restrict HEU exports.[20] A number of these operators argued at the first meeting that they never would be able to convert their facilities. But the implicit threat of a fuel cutoff had brought them to the meeting to discuss the issue, which was an essential first step toward cooperation.

The United States subsequently utilized coercion when foreign operators applied to the U.S. NRC for additional HEU exports. In each case, the NRC asked Argonne to assess the feasibility of converting the facility to LEU, in order to provide guidance for the executive branch position on the proposed export. The foreign operators cooperated with Argonne on these studies but did so typically only to make the strongest case possible against the feasibility of converting to LEU, in hopes of avoiding a premature cutoff of HEU fuel.[21]

This coercive approach waned momentarily in the early 1990s, when the

The RERTR Program [53]

U.S. government slashed the RERTR program's budget for LEU fuel development and disregarded Argonne's stance against specific HEU exports, because of fading support for the conversion effort within the U.S. Energy and State Departments.[22] Partly in response, the U.S. Congress in 1992 passed the "Schumer Amendment"—named after its chief sponsor, Representative (now Senator) Charles E. Schumer (D-N.Y.)—which was signed into law as part of a larger energy bill.[23] The amendment prohibited HEU exports unless all of three conditions were met: the recipient could not currently use LEU, the recipient had pledged to convert to LEU as soon as possible, and the United States was actively developing an LEU fuel or target suitable for that recipient. This led to restoration of funding for LEU fuel development, prevented the exemption of any foreign facilities from the conversion requirement, and revived the RERTR program's watchdog role on HEU export license applications. Under the new statute, coercion to reduce HEU exports was transformed from an implicit policy to an explicit U.S. law. According to a State Department official, the NRC became much stricter about approving HEU exports.[24] An internal RERTR program document concurs that the Schumer "amendment quickly became a very effective tool to promote conversions abroad."[25]

Reliance on coercion also helps explain the originally limited scope of the RERTR program. Although more than two hundred HEU-fueled research reactors already existed worldwide in 1978, the program initially focused only on forty-two foreign reactors that required fresh HEU exports from the United States and thus were susceptible to coercion. In 1986, the scope expanded to include the conversion of medical-isotope production to LEU targets, based again on coercive leverage arising from the United States being the primary supplier of HEU for targets. This first paid dividends in 2002, when Argentina converted its medical isotope production from HEU to LEU targets after Washington made clear that it would no longer export HEU to that country.[26]

The original scope of the RERTR program omitted dozens of low- or zero-power reactors originally supplied by the United States, despite the fact that some of them contained large amounts of very lightly irradiated HEU that could be used to make multiple nuclear weapons. The main reason was that these facilities had "lifetime cores," which did not require fresh HEU exports, so the U.S. government lacked coercive leverage and thus saw little hope of persuading their operators to convert.[27] Moreover, converting reactors with lifetime cores would have imposed unexpected costs because the operators had never budgeted for purchasing fresh fuel.[28] By contrast, higher-power reactors routinely require refueling, so the costs of conversion are mainly the higher price of LEU fuel and relicensing.

Lack of coercive leverage also explains why the U.S.-based RERTR program excluded communist countries, which received their fuel from the Soviet Union.

The program's initial scope also excluded U.S. reactors—both nongovernmental research reactors and government reactors for research, naval propulsion, space missions, and nuclear weapons simulation—to avoid provoking domestic bureaucratic opposition, and in light of greater concern about foreign vulnerabilities.[29] Thus, the initial objective of the RERTR program was limited to reducing U.S. HEU exports, not minimizing worldwide civilian use of HEU.

Coercion's central role is further evidenced by the failure of the RERTR program in cases where the United States lacked leverage due to the availability of alternative supplies of HEU. Two European reactors, France's Orphee and Germany's FRM-II, successfully resisted conversion in the early 1990s—even though the 1992 Schumer Amendment barred export of fresh HEU to them—by managing to gain access to other HEU stocks in Europe that originally came from the United States and Russia. Another European reactor, the HFR-Petten in the Netherlands, temporarily suspended work on conversion in the 1990s, when it likewise gained access to several years' worth of U.S.-origin HEU in Europe. In France, the operator of the RHF-Grenoble reactor resisted committing to conversion and instead contracted in 1996 to obtain HEU from Russia. Only when Russia initially failed to supply the HEU for two years did the reactor operator in 1998 make a commitment to convert to LEU as soon as feasible, in order to qualify for U.S. HEU exports in the interim.[30] Germany's FRJ-2 delayed conversion for more than a decade after it had become feasible because the facility possessed adequate stocks of U.S.-origin HEU. After 1992, the Schumer Amendment, by barring HEU exports to facilities that refused to commit to convert as soon as possible, helped "dry up" the preexisting U.S.-origin stocks in Europe.[31] Over time, this decisively enhanced U.S. coercive leverage, especially because Russia refrained from further exporting HEU to Western Europe after the two shipments in the 1990s.

Inadequate coercive leverage also explains the RERTR program's decades-long failure to persuade the world's three biggest producers of medical isotopes—in the Netherlands, Belgium, and Canada—to convert their manufacturing processes from HEU to LEU targets. Until 2012, both the Dutch and Belgian companies obtained HEU mainly from existing stocks in Europe originally provided by the United States or Russia.[32] Accordingly, the companies could not be coerced by the Schumer Amendment that, from 1993 to 2005, prohibited U.S. export of HEU to medical isotope producers unless they cooperated on conversion.[33]

By contrast, the Canadian producer of medical isotopes, Nordion, was dependent on continued exports of HEU from the United States. This should have enabled U.S. coercion but did not for two reasons. First, the company successfully evaded and then succeeded at watering down U.S. law. Second, the United States was reciprocally dependent on importing medical isotopes from Canada. Nordion claimed to be working on converting to LEU targets, in order to qualify for U.S. HEU exports, but then refused to cooperate with Argonne on grounds that the company's technology was proprietary, thereby halting work on conversion.[34] The company also hired U.S. lobbyists, who drafted an amendment to create a loophole for Canada and warned Congress that any premature halt of HEU exports would endanger American patients' access to medical isotopes. This paid off when the United States enacted the Burr Amendment to the Energy Policy Act of 2005, exempting Canada and four other countries from some of the Schumer Amendment's restrictions on HEU exports.[35]

Perceived Costs Reduced

The second most important factor in persuading operators to convert to LEU was reducing their fear of negative impacts from the switch. At the first RERTR meeting in 1978, many operators declared that they never could convert to LEU because doing so would dramatically reduce the performance of their reactors.[36] Efforts to allay the operators' concerns were facilitated by interactions among scientists at the working level, which Knopf identifies as a common mechanism to forge cooperation on nonproliferation. Argonne feared that its own conversion studies would not be convincing, because some of the foreign operators disputed the calculations. To overcome this hurdle, the program and U.S. government officials devised a multilateral mechanism. In 1979, they initiated the drafting of an IAEA guidebook on conversion, which also would assess whether conversion degraded performance. At several IAEA meetings that year and the next, seven interested laboratories from around the world presented their own calculations. Most of the studies confirmed Argonne's findings, thereby compelling the few outliers to concede that their calculations fell outside the scientific consensus and probably were wrong.[37]

Rather than relying on coercion, in this instance cooperation was fostered by appealing to scientific integrity and consensus, enabled by an "epistemic community" of nuclear experts coordinated by an international institution, illustrating how various cooperative mechanisms can interact. As James Matos, an RERTR physicist, recalls, "IAEA involvement was crucial" and "resolved acrimony because [the operators] had thought that conversion to LEU fuel would significantly degrade the performance of their facilities."[38] Eventually, the IAEA effort was expanded to a seven-volume guidebook on conversion that shared best practices in areas such as safety and licensing, thereby reducing transaction costs to operators and national authorities, further facilitating cooperation.[39]

Scientists from foreign reactors also were brought to Argonne for extended periods so that they and the RERTR program jointly could prepare conversion feasibility studies for their facilities. Rather than Argonne simply telling reactor operators that conversion was feasible, which might have sparked skepticism and resistance, this practice enabled foreign scientists themselves to conclude that LEU fuel could provide roughly equivalent safety and performance at acceptable cost. It also facilitated foreign regulators issuing licenses for conversion to LEU, which averted potential diplomatic friction over U.S. restrictions on HEU exports. This is another example of Knopf's mechanism of cooperation being fostered by transnational relations at the working level.

The RERTR program further reduced the perceived costs of switching to LEU by converting two U.S. research reactors during the early years of the program, as demonstration projects, prior to any requirement for domestic conversion. In late 1981, the program substituted an entire core of LEU fuel in the University of Michigan's Ford reactor.[40] Then, over the course of 1985–86, the program gradually converted the core of the ORR reactor at Oak Ridge National Laboratory, substituting LEU when spent HEU fuel elements were removed. These initiatives proved to foreign operators that there were two methods to convert their reactors, neither of which significantly degraded performance.[41] The LEU fuel did cost approximately 15 to 30 percent more to fabricate, but it lasted as long as the HEU fuel, averting fears of additional costs from a shortened fuel cycle.[42] Another potential cost of conversion—new problems for waste disposal—was reduced in 1986, when the U.S. government announced that it would accept the return from foreign reactors of spent, high-density "silicide" LEU fuel that had been developed by the RERTR program but which Europe's main nuclear waste management company said it could not process.[43]

The role of costs is also illustrated by a temporary failure of cooperation. In Mexico, the operator of a TRIGA research reactor could not afford to pay for conversion to LEU fuel, so the facility continued to use some HEU fuel for many years longer than necessary. Eventually, the United States and Canada agreed to subsidize the conversion to LEU, which then proceeded expeditiously.[44]

The Soviet Union's parallel program to reduce the enrichment of fuel in Soviet-supplied reactors was also facilitated by the RERTR program's success at mitigating the perceived costs of conversion. Although the Soviet Union was not formally invited to participate in RERTR events during the Cold War, one leading Soviet nuclear official, Nikolai Archangelskiy, attended the 1981 annual RERTR meeting, where he discussed with Argonne officials the program's goals and methods. It was later learned that the Soviet Union had been observing the RERTR program from its beginning. The Soviet Union mimicked the program by reducing the enrichment of its research reactor fuel exports, although initially only to 36 percent rather than below 20 percent due to technical limitations on its fuel technology.[45] As program manager Armando Travelli says he discovered only when he visited Moscow in 1993, the Soviets had "a parallel universe that we didn't know about."[46] After 1989, Moscow halted exports of uranium enriched over 36 percent to Soviet-origin reactors.

The Soviet effort was facilitated by learning from the RERTR program that lowering fuel enrichment did not impose significant performance costs, and by Moscow's inherent security interest in reducing exports of bomb-grade uranium. Norm diffusion cannot explain this mimicking because the Soviet Union and later Russia refused for decades to convert their own research reactors, well after the United States had started converting its domestic reactors. Indeed, as late as February 2005, Russian president Vladimir Putin rejected entreaties from U.S. president George W. Bush to convert facilities in Russia and instead committed to convert reactors only "in third countries." Russia refused even to study the feasibility of converting its own reactors until a bilateral agreement in late 2010.[47]

China copycatted the RERTR program even more closely. In 1986, two Argonne scientists visited China on an IAEA mission, during which they viewed samples of LEU silicide fuel of the type designed by the RERTR program.[48] By 1991, China had fabricated such LEU silicide fuel to supply Pakistan's PARR reactor, which the United States was barred from doing by sanctions.[49] China may have been driven partially by norms, because it did later convert some of its own reactors. But most experts attribute these conversions to China's shortage of HEU rather than to its internalization of U.S.-promoted norms. Indeed, China has persistently refused to establish any formal cooperative relationship with the RERTR program, apparently to avoid even the perception of subordinating itself to U.S. normative leadership. Thus, China's "cooperation" is best attributed to de facto technology transfer that reduced the perceived costs of conversion.[50] The Russia and China examples also illustrate how direct contacts among scientists can assist cooperation, although typically only within parameters established by government officials on the basis of national interest.

Norms

Although not as important as coercion or reducing the perceived costs of converting to LEU, the emerging norm against civilian HEU commerce played several roles in fostering international cooperation with the RERTR program. First, the norm deserves primary credit for the conversion of at least one facility: Germany's FRG-1 reactor, which was switched to LEU fuel in 1991 despite having a stock of fresh HEU, because the facility's operator wanted to observe the norm.[51] In addition, the norm fostered cooperation less directly. In 2003, for example, Germany's coalition government of Social Democrats and Greens, which strongly supported the norm, declined a contractual option to import a second batch of HEU from Russia for the FRM-II, instead compelling the reactor's operator to agree to eventual conversion to lower-enriched uranium fuel.[52] The German coalition had embraced the norm as early as 1998, declaring that the use of HEU in the reactor was "problematic and dubious in terms of foreign policy."[53]

The norm's role is also illustrated by complaints from Europe during the 1980s and 1990s that U.S. government reactors were not subject to conversion. This apparent double standard violated a pledge made by a State Department official at the first RERTR meeting in 1978 that the United States would observe the norm: "The use of HEU in U.S. research and test reactors is being evaluated under essentially the same technical and economic criteria as are used to assess [HEU] export requests... to avoid giving a commercial advantage to any U.S." facility.[54] When the United States backtracked on that pledge, European officials declared that they would only convert their facilities if the norm were applied universally. Armando Travelli communicated such complaints to the DOE starting in the 1980s, and he urged that at least some U.S. government reactors be converted so that we "don't look hypocritical."[55] This image problem was exacerbated when the U.S. government, in the early 1990s, slashed funding for the development of ultra-high-density LEU fuel that was necessary to convert U.S. government and other high-performance reactors (see figure 3.4). Travelli says the budget cut "had a chilling effect on every meeting we had" at the time with foreign operators, some of whom responded by trying to evade the conversion requirement, claiming that their facilities too required the higher-density LEU fuel that no longer was under development.[56] This evidence that Washington's temporary flouting of the norm inhibited conversion efforts by foreign operators underscores the norm's role in fostering cooperation.

The most egregious example of the United States violating the norm also inflicted the greatest damage to international cooperation under the RERTR program. In the late 1980s, the DOE announced plans to build a new HEU-fueled reactor, the Advanced Neutron Source, despite preaching that other countries should use LEU fuel in new facilities.[57] This led to a near revolt at the 1987 annual RERTR meeting, as reported at the time: "DOE's decision to go ahead with a new reactor fueled with HEU, in apparent disregard for the RERTR program, led to open conflict during a conference in Grenoble, France.... The Europeans were not amused. French officials told DOE representatives flatly that they would insist on using HEU in their best research reactors if the United States builds the new facility."[58] The U.S. double standard also encouraged the operator of Germany's FRM-II, under development at the time, to embrace an HEU-fuel design on grounds that Washington had created an exception for state-of-the-art reactors.[59] As the German operator explained to a reporter in 1987, "To some extent, it's a matter of competition... I also think that it is a matter of fairness."[60]

Eight years later, in 1995, the U.S. government canceled its proposed HEU-fueled reactor and told Germany that it would not supply HEU for the FRM-II.[61] The German operator replied that too much design work and partial licensing

FIGURE 3.4   RERTR's Small and Fluctuating Budget (FY1978–2003)

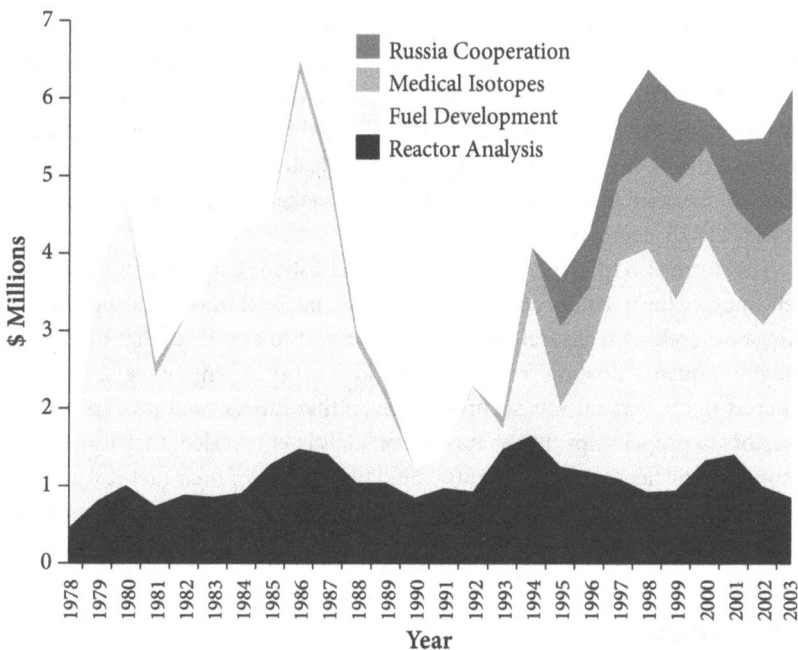

Source: Armando Travelli, personal communication, February 16, 2014. Current dollars.

already had been completed, so it proceeded to construct a core requiring HEU fuel, which eventually was obtained from preexisting U.S. stocks in Europe and an import from Russia. In this way, Washington's temporary flouting of the norm led adversely to construction of the world's first HEU-fueled reactor in more than a dozen years (excluding miniature facilities), further illustrating the norm's impact on cooperation.[62]

After undermining the norm for a decade, the United States reversed course in the mid-1990s, first by restoring funding for LEU fuel development and later by committing to convert its own government reactors. The impact on foreign operators was palpable at annual RERTR meetings, where cooperation grew to be almost universal, according to the program's top officials. James Matos reports that conversion to LEU "became the international norm," so that "resistance declined."[63] Armando Travelli likewise recalls that "at RERTR meetings, there were fewer dissenters saying 'why don't you like HEU?' . . . There is something funny about human nature, when someone hears something over and over again [that reactors are converting to LEU], they become more likely to do it."[64]

The norm's mechanisms for promoting cooperation are also illustrated in a song composed for the 1996 annual RERTR meeting, where it was sung by many of the participants from printed lyric sheets. The chorus stresses the mission: "We are, we are, we are, we are the RERTR / We can convert reactors, be they near, or be they far." A subsequent verse evokes the normative dynamic: "Give us your firm commitment and you will be walking tall / So come and join our company, you're sure to have a ball."[65] This lyric emphasizes that participants, by observing the norm, can feel pride and avoid being ostracized. Attendees fondly remember singing the song, which indicates that by 1996 they viewed themselves as subjects of a joint endeavor to make the world safer, not mere objects of U.S. coercion.

The norm also influenced the actions of at least one country that did not itself embrace the norm. Around 2000, a Russian national laboratory approached Argonne, seeking technical assistance to convert to LEU its design for a new, barge-mounted, "floating" reactor to provide energy in remote regions.[66] This interest in conversion was surprising, given that Russia used HEU in similar reactors to propel ships. But as Russian officials later revealed, they feared that exporting the floating power plants would be hindered if their fuel violated the emerging norm against HEU.[67] Thus, the Russians were constrained to observe the norm not because they had internalized it, but because others had done so.

Side Payments

The United States generally avoided offering inducements for conversion, because Washington sought to avoid precedents that could encourage further demands, and because any substantial financial incentives would have exceeded the RERTR program's modest budget. However, at least three inducements were utilized and may have been effective. First, in the early 1990s, the United States told foreign operators that it would accept the return of spent research reactor fuel and target material only from facilities that cooperated with the RERTR program to convert to LEU or shut down, a policy subsequently codified in 1996.[68] Considering that U.S. refusal to accept the return of spent nuclear material could impose significant costs on foreign operators or even force them to close their facilities, depending on their operating license requirements, this takeback conditionality provided a substantial incentive for operators to convert. Second, Washington provided subsidies for less developed countries to return their spent fuel to the United States, without which they might not have been able to afford the return and thus would have had less incentive to convert. These first two inducements clearly encouraged cooperation, but it is unknown whether either provision was decisive in persuading any operator to convert.

There was also one explicit financial incentive paid—to Russia in the 1990s for cooperation on LEU fuel development including test irradiations.[69] It is unclear whether that inducement was essential because Russia had its own interest in further reducing the enrichment of the fuel it exported. Russian officials claimed at the time, however, that they could not afford to conduct the required tests without partial U.S. funding.[70] Russia may have engaged in mild extortion, but the U.S. financial incentive may also have been necessary to achieve this cooperation.

Diplomacy

There is little evidence that U.S. diplomatic activity played a significant part in fostering cooperation with the RERTR program. Indeed, there is more evidence of reverse diplomatic pressure applied by other countries to curtail the RERTR program. The most common role of U.S. diplomacy was to assuage negative reactions abroad to U.S. refusals to provide HEU. In Travelli's words, this was "diplomacy that made it feel less like coercion."[71] For example, if the U.S. NRC decided that it was unlikely to approve a specific HEU export application, based on Argonne's classified assessment that the applicant could convert to LEU or was not cooperating toward conversion, U.S. diplomats conveyed this to their counterpart foreign ministry, which then explained the situation to the operator. In many cases, the operator then withdrew or modified the application, to avoid the embarrassment of being rejected.

But diplomacy also worked in the opposite direction. When faced with U.S. restrictions on HEU exports, foreign operators sometimes complained to their own government officials on two grounds: their facilities were not proliferation risks, and equivalent U.S. government facilities were not required to convert.[72] Foreign diplomats then conveyed those complaints to the U.S. State Department, which sometimes responded by advocating within the U.S. government in favor of the HEU exports—over Argonne's concerns. Travelli recalls a State Department official who told him to "calm down, don't take your job too seriously, we have other fish to fry" with these countries. In the 1980s, the State Department even reportedly tried to eliminate Argonne from the decision-making loop on HEU export applications.[73]

The State Department, by admission of its own officials from the time, did not view the RERTR program as a high priority. Even U.S. diplomats who were responsible for nuclear nonproliferation say that they focused on other aspects of this challenge—such as Pakistan, North Korea, nuclear cooperation agreements, and IAEA safeguards.[74] Bilateral meetings on reactor conversions typically were conducted at the technical, not diplomatic, level.[75] The head of the State Department's nonproliferation office during the 1990s concedes that most credit for the cooperation obtained from foreign operators during that era belongs to the RERTR program, not his department.[76]

U.S. diplomats did take some steps to promote the RERTR program, but seldom did this achieve cooperation. In the early 2000s, for example, the State Department complained to Canada's Ministry of Foreign Affairs that the medical isotope producer Nordion had halted work on conversion. However, this elicited merely a written reply from the Canadian government, rather than any renewed conversion effort by the company. The State Department also complained to Argentina about its reported diversion of HEU fuel to make targets for isotope production. But that country's eventual conversion of isotope production to LEU was driven not by diplomatic pressure but rather by a coercive cutoff of U.S. HEU exports.[77] In another example, when reports surfaced that Germany was planning to sell an HEU-fueled reactor to Indonesia, the State Department prevailed on the U.S. Export-Import Bank to clarify that it would not help finance the project.[78] However, that deal was a long shot in any case because Germany lacked HEU to fuel the reactor.

In 1993, to its credit, the State Department helped draft the Clinton administration declaration that the United States would "seek to minimize use of highly-enriched uranium in civilian nuclear programs,"[79] and explained to Germany that the policy applied to its forthcoming FRM-II reactor. However, this rare example of diplomatic boldness was remarkably short-lived. German Embassy officials soon visited the State Department to lodge a complaint, prompting the U.S. deputy assistant secretary of state for political-military affairs to tell his nonproliferation office to "back off."[80] After that, U.S. diplomats made no further effort to deter the use of HEU in the new German reactor, even though they had leverage arising from U.S. acceptance of spent fuel imports from other German reactors.

The two most significant contributions of diplomacy to the RERTR program were supplementary to other sources of cooperation. First, in the late 1980s, when foreign operators complained about the expiration of the U.S. policy of accepting the return of spent fuel from their reactors, the State Department urged the U.S. DOE to renew it.[81] DOE eventually did renew the take-back, but only for operators who cooperated with the RERTR program, thereby promoting conversion. Second, in the late 1990s, the State Department negotiated commitments from European countries to convert their high-performance research reactors to LEU fuel as soon as possible. These agreements were enabled mainly by the 1992 Schumer Amendment, which prohibited HEU exports in the absence of such commitments.[82] Yet, U.S. diplomats deserve credit for forging the agreements,[83] without which the foreign operators might have sought HEU from Russia.

On the other hand, the State Department made little or no effort to prevent a series of foreign actions that undermined the RERTR program. In the 1990s, a Dutch reactor operator halted cooperation on conversion and instead obtained U.S.-origin HEU that had been exported to Europe for other purposes.[84] In the mid-1990s, Russia agreed to export HEU to Europe for reactors in France and Germany, undercutting Washington's leverage with European operators who had refused to commit to conversion and thus were ineligible for U.S. exports. In addition, Russia refused to convert its own reactors, and Europe's two main producers of medical isotopes continued to use HEU targets. In none of these cases did the U.S. State Department attempt to avert the offending actions beforehand or even lodge a protest afterward.[85] It thus appears that diplomacy played only a marginal role in fostering cooperation under the RERTR program during its first quarter century.

Inherent Benefit

In only two instances did conversion to LEU improve a reactor's performance, and in neither case does it appear that the expectation of such benefit drove the decision to convert. At the University of Rhode Island reactor, in the United States, the operator opposed converting and did so only because it was mandated by the NRC in 1986. Afterward he conceded that conversion had enhanced his facility, as the more compact LEU core produced higher neutron flux. Germany's FRG-1 similarly benefited from improved neutron flux following conversion to a more compact LEU core, but the operator says he converted due to the emerging norm against HEU. That explanation is convincing because conversion entailed many costs and risks, including the possibility of permanent shutdown during relicensing, which made it otherwise unattractive.

Although operators of reactors and producers of medical isotopes typically expected conversion to impose net costs on their facilities, other interest groups anticipated benefits from the RERTR program. Fuel developers were paid to design and test high-density LEU fuels, and fuel fabricators typically could charge more and make higher profit for producing such exotic fuels. Even in 1978 at the first RERTR meeting, where reactor operators were highly resistant to the initiative, fuel developers and fabricators by contrast embraced it.[86] Inherent benefits of the RERTR program thus can help explain the successful development and commercialization of the higher-density LEU fuels and targets, but not the decision of reactor operators or isotope producers to convert to LEU.

Other Factors

Two additional dynamics fostered cooperation. First was the mimicking of RERTR by two countries. The Soviet Union ran a parallel program for more than a decade, without U.S. knowledge, prior to Russia initiating cooperation with Argonne after the Cold War. China likewise copied the LEU conversion effort, but still has not established a formal relationship with the RERTR program. This demonstrates that learning and emulation may expand cooperation even beyond its envisioned scope.

A second cooperative mechanism was the forging of unofficial, bilateral cooperative agreements, usually at the laboratory-to-laboratory level. These were essential for expediting elements of cooperation, such as rules for information sharing and intellectual property, especially when formal government negotiations bogged down. The informal agreements had no binding enforcement mechanisms, so compliance could be encouraged only by threatening to publicize violations. Travelli reports that he resorted to such pacts several times during his tenure. For example, around 2000, French officials began speaking of a "French fuel" and reducing their information sharing due to proprietary concerns. To restore transparency, Travelli says he negotiated an informal agreement between Argonne, the French fuel fabricator CERCA, and the French Atomic Energy Commission during a dinner near the U.S. laboratory. He conceded to his French counterparts that the deal was not legally binding but reminded them that "it is my word and your word, and if you break it, your name will be mud."[87]

Travelli says he used similar tactics in the late 1990s with Russian scientists in the face of slow-moving governmental negotiations on a bilateral cooperative agreement. To sidestep the red tape, he sent an email to the director of Russia's Bochvar laboratory, pledging his "gentleman's word" to cooperate. The Russian director reciprocated with a similar email, and work proceeded. Such cooperation was fostered by several factors: the potential for mutual gain, the desire of each side to preserve its reputation when facing the "shadow of the future," and the personal rapport between fellow scientists. Although subordinate to government-level decisions about whether to participate in nonproliferation initiatives, these examples illustrate how informal interaction among scientists can facilitate cooperation.

CONCLUSION

U.S. leadership brought RERTR into existence, but simply setting up the program did not guarantee that others would cooperate with it. Explanations for such cooperation during the program's first quarter century varied among countries and over time. Coercion was the most important factor, especially during the early years of the program. In light of the virtual U.S. monopoly on supply of HEU to noncommunist countries during the Cold War, the threat to restrict HEU exports was a necessary and sufficient condition for cooperation by many foreign operators. Other factors, however, were complementary and in some instances also sufficient for cooperation. For example, reducing the perceived costs of conversion—through consensus building by an epistemic community of nuclear experts coordinated by the IAEA—persuaded many foreign operators to acquiesce to conversion rather than demand that their governments pressure the United States to provide HEU. The emerging norm against civilian use of HEU played a growing role over time, especially as the United States complied with it. At two German reactors, the FRG-1 and FRM-II, the norm was directly or indirectly responsible for the eventual commitment to reduce fuel enrichment rather than utilize alternative supplies of HEU. A monetary inducement was employed only once, in the 1990s, for Russia—which was not subject to coercion because it possessed its own HEU stocks—and this incentive may have been necessary for the cooperation achieved. Other inducements in the form of accepting the return of spent fuel from operators who agreed to convert to LEU fuel, and subsidizing the take-back of such fuel from developing countries, further encouraged cooperation. Diplomacy played only a supplementary role, in part because the RERTR program was not a high priority at the U.S. State Department even among officials who focused on nuclear nonproliferation. Inherent benefit helps explain cooperation by fuel developers and fabricators but cannot explain conversion decisions because operators overwhelmingly expected that switching to LEU fuel would impose costs and reduce performance. Informal agreements between scientists facilitated cooperation, and emulation by Russia and China expanded the scope of cooperation.

Many of the above mechanisms required U.S. government support of the RERTR program, thereby subjecting international cooperation to the vagaries of domestic politics. Bureaucratic infighting in the United States endangered the program several times. Starting in 1981, some DOE officials sought to kill the program—apparently to avert possible future demands to convert U.S. government reactors—and the State Department sometimes reduced its support in response to foreign complaints.[88] The U.S. Congress intervened several times to restore funding for the RERTR program, and in 1992 to codify restrictions on HEU exports.[89] At times when neither the executive nor legislative branch supported the program, advocacy organizations such as the Nuclear Control Institute employed media tactics in hopes of restoring at least partial government support—with some success.[90] These advocacy efforts, however, frequently were opposed by nuclear industry lobbyists and trade associations.[91]

As Knopf has written, the success of a nonproliferation initiative can be measured by at least three different metrics: extent of cooperation, attainment of goals, and reduction in proliferation risk.[92] The RERTR program, during its first quarter century, elicited substantial cooperation from the vast majority of countries and individual operators that were asked to pursue conversion. By the year 2004, this had enabled four main achievements: thirty-nine reactors had been converted from HEU to LEU fuel, or were in the process of doing so; twenty-one new reactors had been designed to use LEU fuel; technology to produce medical isotopes without HEU had been successfully developed, and in one case adopted; and a norm of HEU minimization had emerged.

But for at least two reasons the RERTR program did not, during its first quarter century, fully achieve its stated goal of minimizing HEU commerce. First, progress was slow. As of 2004, some sixty-seven reactors within the program's scope still had not initiated conversion, and ultra-high-density LEU fuel had not yet been qualified to enable conversion of high-performance reactors. This was due partly to the inadequacy of the program's funding, which was provided almost exclusively by the United States. A few other countries did engage separately in fuel development—including France, Japan, Russia, and Germany—and additional countries provided in-kind support.[93] However, no efforts were made to solicit funding for the RERTR program from outside the United States, which in retrospect can be viewed as a failure of cooperation.

The second obstacle to HEU minimization was that the RERTR program's focus was artificially narrow. As of 2004, Argonne acknowledged that the scope of the program excluded fifty-six HEU-fueled nuclear facilities around the world—including critical assemblies, pulsed reactors, and Russian research reactors. This exclusion was somewhat understandable, in light of the expected opposition to conversion from the operators of such facilities, but it meant that the RERTR program failed to address the majority of worldwide use of HEU for nonmilitary purposes.[94]

Despite these shortcomings, the RERTR program did make a significant contribution to reducing risks of nuclear proliferation and nuclear terrorism from 1978 to 2004. Most important, it reduced annual HEU use at lightly guarded civilian facilities by hundreds of kilograms—sufficient for more than a dozen nuclear weapons per year—and thereby inhibited the spread of such weapons to states or substate organizations. The program's first quarter century also laid the technical and normative groundwork for further reductions in HEU commerce after 2004, when the GTRI had greater resources for that objective.

The history of the RERTR program offers several important insights for future efforts to promote international cooperation on nuclear nonproliferation, including but not limited to further reduction of HEU commerce. First, although the word "cooperation" connotes consensual action, it sometimes requires coercion. As with any collective action, promoting nuclear nonproliferation may require one or a few strong states to employ leverage to compel other states to do things that benefit everyone. On the other hand, exclusively relying on coercion would be inefficient and counterproductive. The RERTR experience demonstrates that three additional steps can greatly facilitate cooperation: technical investment to reduce the costs of compliance, building consensus via epistemic communities of international experts, and establishing norms based on shared sacrifice. HEU commerce was reduced not merely by U.S. export restrictions, but also by essential complementary actions: researchers developed higher-density LEU fuel and targets; the IAEA forged consensus that converting to LEU would not significantly degrade performance or increase costs at nuclear facilities; and the United States converted its own reactors. The history of the RERTR program also illustrates that cooperation may be expedited in certain instances by inducements, or by informal agreements between scientists. Compared to some of the other cases examined in this volume, transnational relationships among lower-level officials may not have been as crucial to the success of the RERTR program, but they helped.

Finally, diplomacy can and ideally should play a bigger role in promoting nuclear nonproliferation than was true for the RERTR program during its first quarter century. Foreign countries sometimes obstructed HEU minimization—such as when Germany built its HEU-fueled FRM-II reactor, or when Russia exported HEU to Europe—while the U.S. State Department failed to use its diplomatic leverage to try to dissuade them. By incorporating these lessons, and dedicating sufficient resources, future nonproliferation initiatives could exceed even the substantial progress that the RERTR program remarkably achieved with its limited funding and political support from 1978 to 2004.

Notes

Field research was supported by a grant from the Policy Research Institute, LBJ School of Public Affairs, University of Texas at Austin.

1. James Matos, former RERTR senior physicist, personal communication, July 8, 2013. The program also was supported by U.S. government personnel at the Nuclear Regulatory Commission, State Department, Arms Control and Disarmament Agency, and Department of Energy, including those working on take-back of spent fuel from foreign research reactors.

2. Anya Loukianova and Cristina Hansell, "Leveraging U.S. Policy for a Global Commitment to HEU Elimination," *Nonproliferation Review* 15, no. 2 (July 2008): 161.

3. Armando Travelli, then RERTR program manager, "The U.S. RERTR Program," in *Proceedings of the 1978 International Meeting on Reduced Enrichment for Research and Test Reactors* (Argonne, Ill., November 9–10, 1978), 3, 7.

4. Ibid., 4.

5. Loukianova and Hansell, "Leveraging U.S. Policy," 167; Oleg Bukharin, "Making Fuel Less Tempting," *Bulletin of the Atomic Scientists* 58, no. 4 (July–August 2002): 47.

6. U.S. Energy Secretary Spencer Abraham, presentation at the International Atomic Energy Agency, Vienna, May 26, 2004.

7. "RERTR Program Project Execution Plan (PEP)" (internal RERTR program document, February 24, 2004, in author's possession), 1.10.

8. These were in Argentina, Austria, Brazil, Canada (two reactors), Colombia, Denmark, France, Germany (two reactors), Iran, Japan (two reactors), Pakistan, the Philippines, Slovenia, Sweden (two reactors), Switzerland, and Taiwan. Armando Travelli, "Status and Progress of the RERTR Program in the Year 2004" (paper, International Meeting on Reduced Enrichment for Research and Test Reactors, Vienna, November 7–12, 2004), 6.

9. These were in Austria, Canada, Chile, Greece, the Netherlands, Romania, and Turkey. Travelli, "Status and Progress," 6.

10. Ann MacLachlan, "A Quarter-Century Later, RERTR Beset with Technical, Political Woes," *Nuclear Fuel*, November 22, 2004. Fourteen of these reactors had been completed by 2004. See "RERTR Program PEP," 1.10.

11. The one new HEU reactor is Germany's FRM-II, which commenced operation in 1996. See Alan J. Kuperman, "Civilian Highly Enriched Uranium and the Fissile Material Convention," in *Nuclear Power & the Spread of Nuclear Weapons*, ed. Paul L. Leventhal (Dulles, Va.: Brassey's, 2002), 249–60.

12. "RERTR Program PEP," 1.9–1.10.

13. These were in Bulgaria, Kazakhstan, Libya, Ukraine (two reactors), Uzbekistan, and Vietnam. Travelli, "Status and Progress," 6.

14. "RERTR Program PEP," 1.12, A-11, A-12.

15. For updated information on HEU use and minimization efforts, see Alan J. Kuperman, "Global HEU Phase-Out: Prospects & Challenges," in *Nuclear Terrorism and Global Security: The Challenge of Phasing out Highly Enriched Uranium*, ed. Alan J. Kuperman (New York: Routledge, 2013), 3–26.

16. "Some Typical Questions about Conversions" (2004), unpublished document in author's possession.

17. Daniel Charles, "DOE Undermines Own Nonproliferation Effort," *Science* 238, no. 4831 (November 27, 1987): 1224.

18. M. Kuechle, quoted in *Proceedings of the 1978 International Meeting*, 211. Since then, requirements for protecting HEU have become much stricter.

19. Charles, "DOE Undermines Own Nonproliferation Effort."

20. James Matos, interview, February 20, 2012.

21. Armando Travelli, interview, February 19, 2012.

22. Travelli, "Status and Progress," 2.

23. At the time, I was Representative Schumer's legislative director, responsible for drafting and promoting passage of the amendment.

24. Ellie Busick, former deputy director, Office of Nonproliferation and Export Policy, U.S. State Department, phone interview, June 8, 2012.

25. "RERTR Program PEP," 1.5.

26. Jared Berenter, "Argentina: Medical Isotope Production," in Kuperman, *Nuclear Terrorism and Global Security*, 29–41.

27. Such facilities also posed lower risks from the shipment of fresh and spent fuel, required only once each per reactor.

28. Matos, interview.

29. For further details, see Kuperman, "Global HEU Phase-Out." See also Rebecca Ward, "USA and France: Naval Propulsion," in Kuperman, *Nuclear Terrorism and Global Security*, 177–95.

30. Alison Abbott, "European Reactor Accepts U.S. Demands on Fuel Shift," *Nature* 396 (November 19, 1998): 203; Ann MacLachlan and Mark Hibbs, "French-Russian HEU Accord Signed; EC Agreed to Russian Prior Consent," *Nuclear Fuel* 21, no. 13 (June 17, 1996): 1; Mark Hibbs, "Euratom, Again, Accepts Russian Consent for HEU Transfer to FRM-2," *Nuclear Fuel* 23, no. 5 (March 9, 1998): 1. "Russian HEU Delivered to France for Use in Research Reactors," *WISE News Communiqué*, February 5, 1999. James Matos, personal communication, June 1, 2012.

31. Matos, interview. The FRJ-2 never converted and was shut down in 2006.

32. Alan J. Kuperman, "Quadripartite Agreement," in Kuperman, *Nuclear Terrorism and Global Security*, 92–94.
33. Matos, interview.
34. Matos, interview. "RERTR Program PEP," p. 1.10.
35. By this time, a Nordion executive had confessed to U.S. officials in a private meeting that the company would not convert to LEU even if the alleged technical hurdles could be overcome. Travelli, interview.
36. Matos, interview.
37. Ibid.; Travelli, interview.
38. Matos, interview.
39. The first volume: *Research Reactor Core Conversion from the Use of Highly Enriched Uranium to the Use of Low Enriched Uranium Fuels Guidebook* (Vienna: IAEA, 1980). The entire set: *Research Reactor Core Conversion Guidebook, Volumes 1–7* (Vienna: IAEA, 1992).
40. "RERTR Program PEP," 1.4.
41. The full-core replacement was particularly suited to reactors with lifetime cores, while gradual conversion was applicable to higher-power reactors.
42. Tests also certified the fuel fabrication processes of three large international companies: Babcock & Wilcox, NUKEM, and CERCA. Armando Travelli, personal communication, February 16, 2014.
43. Matos, interview.
44. J. Flores Callejas, "ININ TRIGA Mark III Reactor Plan Conversion to Use LEU Fuel Instead of HEU/LEU Standard Fuel" (RERTR 2011, Santiago, Chile, October 23–27, 2011); Pavel Podvig, "All HEU Is Removed from Mexico" (March 21, 2012), http://fissilematerials.org/blog/2012/03/all_heu_is_removed_from_m.html.
45. Matos, interview; James Matos, personal communication, March 28, 2012; Armando Travelli, "Using LEU in Research Reactors: The RERTR Program" (paper, Conference on Peaceful Uses of Nuclear Energy and Nonproliferation, San Carlos de Bariloche, Argentina, April 19–21, 1994), 8.
46. Travelli, interview. See also Sam Roe, "Nuclear Menace Made in U.S.: Cold War's Deadly Legacy; Atoms for Peace Debacle Triggers Global Quest to Regain Bomb Fuel," *Chicago Tribune*, January 28, 2007.
47. Putin's statement was made in Bratislava, Slovakia. See Braden Civins, "Russia: Research Reactors," in Kuperman, *Nuclear Terrorism and Global Security*, 146–61. Travelli, interview.
48. They were James Matos and James Snelgrove.
49. Matos, interview.
50. Shing-yao (Sandra) Feng, "China: Reactors and Nuclear Propulsion," in Kuperman, *Nuclear Terrorism and Global Security*, 100–118.
51. The operator was Wilfried Krull.
52. "Germany 'Canceled' Its Deal with Russia to Supply HEU to the FRM-2," *Nuclear News Flashes*, June 23, 2003.
53. Abbott, "European Reactor Accepts U.S. Demands."
54. Richard A. Lewis, "U.S. Non-proliferation Policy and Program Regarding Use of HEU in Research Reactors," in *Proceedings of the 1978 International Meeting*, 109.
55. Travelli, interview.
56. Ibid.
57. The reactor had been under development since 1983. Loukianova and Hansell, "Leveraging U.S. Policy," 164.

58. Charles, "DOE Undermines Own Nonproliferation Effort."
59. Roe, "Nuclear Menace."
60. Charles, "DOE Undermines Own Nonproliferation Effort," quoting Klaus Boening, Technical University Munich, West Germany.
61. At the time, the administration of President Bill Clinton stated that this decision was made at least partly because the HEU fuel presented "a non-proliferation policy concern." See, "DOE Facts: A New Neutron Source for the Nation" (U.S. Department of Energy, February 1995), 1.
62. See Kenneth Dayman, "Germany: The FRM-II Reactor," in Kuperman, *Nuclear Terrorism and Global Security*, 121–35.
63. Matos, interview.
64. Travelli, interview.
65. D and P, "The RERTR Song" (1996), in author's possession.
66. Matos, interview.
67. Christine Egnatuk, "Russia: Icebreaker Ships and Floating Reactors," in Kuperman, *Nuclear Terrorism and Global Security*, 66–82.
68. U.S. Department of Energy, "Record of Decision on a Nuclear Weapons Nonproliferation Policy Concerning Foreign Research Reactor Spent Nuclear Fuel" (DOE/EIS-0218F, May 13, 1996), 25099, www.gpo.gov/fdsys/pkg/FR-1996-05-17/pdf/96-12420.pdf, accessed March 27, 2012.
69. This was funded by $1.5 million from the U.S. State Department's Nonproliferation and Disarmament Fund. "RERTR Program PEP," 1.6.
70. Matos, interview.
71. Travelli, interview.
72. Busick, interview.
73. Travelli, interview.
74. Fred McGoldrick, former director (1991–98), Office of Nonproliferation and Export Policy, U.S. State Department, phone interview, June 11, 2012.
75. Allan Krass, former physical science officer, U.S. State Department, phone interview, June 8, 2012.
76. McGoldrick, interview, says "you have to give a lot of credit to Armando [Travelli] and Jim Matos."
77. Krass, interview.
78. Busick, interview.
79. White House, Office of the Press Secretary, "Fact Sheet: Nonproliferation and Export Control Policy" (September 27, 1993).
80. McGoldrick, interview.
81. Ibid.; Busick, interview.
82. Krass, interview.
83. Busick, interview.
84. Ibid.
85. McGoldrick, interview; Krass, interview; Busick, interview.
86. Matos, interview. Fuel fabricators included CERCA in France, NUKEM in Germany, and Atomics International, Babcock & Wilcox, and Texas Instruments in the United States. Travelli, personal communication.
87. Travelli, interview.
88. Roe, "Nuclear Menace"; Busick, interview. DOE itself often was divided between its nonproliferation officials, who supported the RERTR program, and its research-reactor officials who opposed it.

89. Loukianova and Hansell, "Leveraging U.S. Policy," 164.

90. In interviews, the Nuclear Control Institute was mentioned specifically by three former officials associated with the RERTR program: Travelli, interview; Matos, interview; and Krass, interview. See, for example, Alan J. Kuperman, "The A-Bomb Material in Civilian Reactors" (op-ed), *Washington Post*, September 23, 1987, cited on the same day at a U.S. Senate committee markup that restored half of the program's budget, which had been slated for elimination.

91. This is documented in Alan J. Kuperman, "Bomb-Grade Bazaar," *Bulletin of the Atomic Scientists* 62, no. 2 (March-April 2006): 44-50.

92. Jeffrey W. Knopf, "Multilateral Cooperation on Nonproliferation: Seeking Lessons" (paper, Multilateral Cooperation on Nonproliferation: Lessons Learned workshop, Naval Postgraduate School, Monterey, Calif., March 30, 2012), 19.

93. See, for example, Gerd H. Thamm, "Status of the German AF-Programme: Considerations with Respect to INFCE Recommendations and Criteria" (paper, 5th Annual International Meeting on Reduced Enrichment for Research and Test Reactors, RERTR, November 1982).

94. For details, see Kuperman, "Global HEU Phase-Out."

CHAPTER FOUR
Implementing Nonproliferation Programs
The Cooperative Threat Reduction Process in the Former Soviet Union

TOGZHAN KASSENOVA

DURING THE MONTHS PRIOR to the collapse of the Soviet Union, various nuclear nightmare scenarios occupied the minds of U.S. policy makers: a terrorist group might acquire enough Soviet nuclear material to make a bomb, Soviet scientists might go to work for a suspected proliferator such as North Korea, or a new and inexperienced government in one of the post-Soviet states might try to seize control over Soviet nuclear weapons stationed on its territory. Concerns about these risks led to the creation of the Nunn-Lugar Cooperative Threat Reduction (CTR) program. Managed initially by the U.S. Department of Defense (DOD), CTR evolved into several different programs administered not just by DOD but also by the Department of Energy (DOE), the Department of Commerce, the State Department, and other U.S. government agencies.

CTR programs have achieved remarkable success in minimizing proliferation risks in the former Soviet Union. The programs assisted with the denuclearization of three post-Soviet republics—Belarus, Kazakhstan, and Ukraine. CTR efforts helped Russia meet its START obligations by providing equipment for dismantlement of submarines, bombers, and missiles. Other elements of CTR have secured thousands of tons of vulnerable nuclear material, strengthened physical security at scores of nuclear facilities, and enhanced detection capabilities at borders to prevent nuclear material smuggling. CTR programs have also assisted in the mitigation of bio-threats, destruction of chemical weapons, and redirection of thousands of former weapons scientists into civilian projects aimed at preventing these scientists from seeking work with states or non-state actors who might be looking to develop nuclear weapons.

This chapter provides a historical overview of key CTR programs, with the primary focus on key nuclear-related CTR programs in Russia. While acknowledging CTR achievements, this chapter also examines the program's limitations, including problems in implementing cooperative nonproliferation projects, in order to draw lessons for future international nonproliferation endeavors. Consistent with a general theme of this volume, the chapter finds that good working-level relationships helped facilitate successful implementation of CTR programs. The CTR case also highlights some factors that affect cooperation that are not emphasized in chapter 1 by Knopf. These include a geopolitical context that encouraged lingering mistrust, the challenges of interagency coordination within the bureaucracies on both sides, a variety of technical challenges, and certain cultural differences.

In June 2013, the umbrella agreement that had governed U.S.-Russian CTR activities came to an end. The two countries agreed to a replacement effort that focused on a narrower set of activities and increased Russia's responsibilities. This scaled-down cooperation was supposed to continue until 2018, but in December 2014, partly as a result of deteriorated relations between the two countries over Ukraine, Russia told U.S. officials it will no longer proceed with cooperation on nuclear security.[1] The U.S. government continues to implement cooperative and global threat reduction programs in a variety of other countries, including some outside the former Soviet Union. This chapter derives lessons from the U.S.-Russian experience prior to the end of the original umbrella agreement.

ORIGINS OF THE COOPERATIVE THREAT REDUCTION PROGRAM

In the summer of 1991, top military and civilian officials conspired to overthrow the Soviet government. For three days, Soviet president Mikhail Gorbachev was under house arrest in his vacation residence away from Moscow, where he was cut off from the so-called nuclear football, a device to enable top Soviet decision makers to authorize a launch of nuclear weapons.[2] When U.S. senator Sam Nunn had a personal communication with Mikhail Gorbachev soon after, Gorbachev admitted that command and control of the Soviet nuclear arsenal during the coup had been unclear. Senator Nunn reflected, "I concluded that the Soviet Union was in great peril. In particular, I believed that we needed to do everything we could to help the Soviet authorities gain control and keep control over their own nuclear weapons."[3]

Although the attempt to overthrow the Soviet government did not succeed, the country was entering a profound crisis that would result in its dissolution by year's end. A group of scholars at Harvard University worked to analyze the unprecedented nuclear risks presented by the prospect of a Soviet collapse. Their report, *Soviet Nuclear Fission: Control of the Nuclear Arsenal in a Disintegrating Soviet Union*, laid an analytical foundation for the concept of cooperative threat reduction.[4] *Soviet Nuclear Fission* noted that the breakup of the Soviet Union would result in the appearance of four nuclear states instead of one. In addition to Russia, Soviet nuclear weapons were located in the territories of Belarus, Kazakhstan, and Ukraine. This raised the question of whether new governments in these young countries would try to retain possession of the arsenals stationed on their soil. In addition, the Harvard study reached the disturbing assessment that storage sites for weapons-grade nuclear material throughout the Soviet Union had inadequate systems for control and accounting, which made that material vulnerable to theft or diversion.

As the Soviet Union moved closer to the brink of collapse, Senators Sam Nunn and Richard Lugar argued that the United States had to take immediate measures to assist the disintegrating Soviet Union with minimizing the proliferation risks that might ensue. After an unsuccessful initial attempt to secure congressional funding for assistance to the Soviet Union, Senators Nunn and Lugar had a small group of outside experts including authors of *Soviet Nuclear Fission* brief key senators about the nuclear dangers posed by imminent Soviet disintegration.[5] Then, on November 25, 1991, the senators introduced the Soviet Nuclear Threat Reduction Act of 1991. It passed the Senate and the House, and on December 12, 1991, two weeks after the Soviet Union officially ceased to exist, President George H. W. Bush signed the Nunn-Lugar proposal into law.[6] Initial funding for the program came from the U.S. defense budget.

The initiative had a rough start for a number of reasons. Some members of Congress and executive branch officials strongly opposed the idea of spending U.S. defense money to address problems in the nuclear complex in another country. More fundamentally, they had no trust in Russia given that most Russian officials had until recently been part of the government of America's Cold War adversary, the Soviet Union. CTR skeptics were concerned that, by providing nonproliferation assistance, the United States would be freeing up Russia's own funds for weapons modernization.[7]

Similarly, in Russia, the CTR idea was met with substantial skepticism. Russian lawmakers, just like their U.S. colleagues, had little trust in the other party's motives. CTR critics raised concerns about the possible interest of the United States in "disarming Russia" and in learning Russia's nuclear secrets.[8] Despite these reservations on both sides, the passage of the 1991 legislation and the signing in June 1992 of a U.S.-Russian "umbrella agreement" meant that the U.S. Defense Department could begin implementing cooperative threat reduction activities.

THE EVOLUTION OF CTR

The objective of the initial Nunn-Lugar CTR program was to provide equipment, services, and technical support to the former Soviet Union to assist with transporting, dismantling, and securing weapons of mass destruction (WMD) and WMD materials and production facilities. Russia, Belarus, Kazakhstan, and Ukraine have been the main recipients of CTR assistance, with the bulk of CTR projects focusing on Russia.

There were fundamental differences in the environment for CTR in Russia compared to other post-Soviet states. As soon as the governments of Belarus, Kazakhstan, and Ukraine made a decision to surrender Soviet nuclear weapons, they viewed the purpose and goals of CTR as straightforward. CTR programs were to contribute to the dismantlement and removal of nuclear weapons, "redirection" into new employment of scientists with weapons expertise, and strengthening of nuclear material security. None of the three countries planned to keep a nuclear weapons capability. As a result, cooperation under the CTR framework was less sensitive.

In Russia's case, the situation was completely different. Russia was not planning to relinquish its nuclear arsenal.[9] More important, the main purpose of its nuclear arsenal was (and is) to counterbalance the nuclear might of the United States. In that context, any cooperation on nuclear matters was bound to touch upon issues extremely sensitive for Russia's national security.

Another important difference between Russia and the republics of Belarus, Kazakhstan, and Ukraine was in how they perceived the United States and the baggage (or lack thereof) that each country carried from the Cold War. The newly independent republics were more open to accepting nonproliferation assistance from the United States. They were far less affected by the Soviet "loss" in the Cold War and were keen on being integrated into the international community after the Soviet breakup, and it was clear that a good relationship with the United States would be critical in achieving that goal. For Russia, on the other hand, transitioning from being the only other superpower besides the United States to a fragmented empire in crisis was a hard pill to swallow. Accepting nonproliferation assistance and agreeing to cooperate on sensitive matters with a former archenemy on conditions imposed by it were psychologically difficult for Russia.

The original CTR program laid the foundation for several nuclear nonproliferation programs in the former Soviet Union. Efforts to improve material protection, control, and accounting (MPC&A) first started in 1992 in the form of government-to-government cooperation under the CTR program administered by the Defense Department. In 1994, the U.S. DOE launched a laboratory-to-laboratory program to work on MPC&A issues, and in 1996 DOE received responsibility for all MPC&A activities.[10]

In 1993, Russia and the United States signed the Highly Enriched Uranium (HEU) Purchase Agreement under which the United States would buy Russian uranium from dismantled weapons and eventually use it for electricity generation in the United States. Reflecting the idea that nuclear material from warheads would be converted into fuel for nuclear energy, the deal was popularly dubbed the "megatons to megawatts program." DOE administered the HEU Agreement until 1994, when the U.S. Enrichment Corporation (USEC) became the executive agent on the U.S. side. In 1994, the U.S. State Department established the International Science and Technology Center (ISTC) in Moscow to provide opportunities for former WMD scientists to engage in nonmilitary research. Between 1994 and 2000, DOE also launched a U.S.-Russian Plutonium Disposition program and two programs to redirect scientists to new projects— the Nuclear Cities Initiative and the Initiatives for Proliferation Prevention.

The "balkanization" of the Nunn-Lugar CTR program flowed to a large extent from a natural process of program development and expansion in the types of cooperation it involved.[11] Bringing in different agencies with their specific expertise was critical for effective implementation of the projects. The expansion of CTR programs and bringing on board new agencies also, however, created fresh challenges. The very first interagency meeting devoted to nonproliferation assistance work demonstrated that different agencies had different views and interests regarding how cooperation with Russia should proceed.[12] A multitude of players also resulted in some duplication of efforts due to a lack of interagency coordination.

Despite the challenges, the CTR process continued throughout two decades. In 2013 the CTR umbrella agreement signed in 1992 expired, and Russia made it clear that, given an improved economy and desire to play a greater role in the international system, it was not prepared to extend cooperation on the terms it had agreed to in the early 1990s. Russian nonproliferation specialists Vladimir Orlov and Alexander Cheban reflected prevailing sentiment in Russia when they argued that future efforts should be based on "equality" and "there should be no senior or junior partners, and no designation of countries as donors or recipients."[13] In the end, the two sides agreed on a new format for cooperation and signed an agreement to conduct joint efforts on nuclear security under the 2003 Framework Agreement on a Multilateral Nuclear Environmental Program in the Russian Federation and a related protocol. The new arrangement no longer included the Russian Ministry of Defense as a participant and did not cover two major areas of cooperation previously carried out under CTR: ballistic missile elimination and chemical weapons destruction.[14] As of the start of 2015, Russia had ceased participation in even this scaled-back agreement. Even if

Russia's involvement in CTR has come to an end, there are important lessons to be learned from the two decades when Russia did participate in the program.

THE CTR PROGRAM IN RUSSIA

The CTR process did not focus on reaching signed agreements, but instead emphasized implementation of practical activities at a variety of sites. This makes it important to study implementation. The remainder of this chapter does so by focusing on the nuclear aspects of CTR in Russia. Implementation of the CTR program in Russia has suffered from an array of problems. The challenges have included a lack of trust, residual Cold War attitudes among key participants, bureaucratic hurdles, and conditions attached to cooperation by the U.S. Congress.

Inside both countries, turf battles and lack of coordination between agencies played a negative role. Procedural issues—such as lengthy waits for personnel to receive authorization from their respective governments to travel, or to be granted visas by the other side—often delayed project implementation. On the Russian side, an agency tasked with regulatory oversight of nuclear facilities—Gosatomnadzor—had a tense relationship with the Ministry of Atomic Energy and the Ministry of Defense. Powerful ministries even defied government orders to allow Gosatomnadzor access to their sites. A former senior military official, General Evgenii Maslin, noted frequent bureaucratic struggles among implementing agencies. In a Russian study devoted to CTR, he lamented, "Funds are received not by the agency most critically in need, but by those who can better than others elbow their way in."[15] Intragovernmental issues in the United States had an impact on CTR implementation as well, including tensions that developed between the State Department and DOE.[16]

Concessions made to maintain support in Congress also created problems in implementation. A "Buy American" condition attached to the program had a particularly negative impact in the early years of cooperation. The original legislation stipulated that all equipment and services for CTR implementation had to be of U.S. origin. While this mandate helped gain congressional support for the program, it was resented in Russia.

The "Buy American" clause often caused problems. Russian specialists lamented that when equipment broke down, they had to wait months for spare parts to be shipped from the United States. They also complained that U.S.-supplied equipment could be used only for strictly specified purposes. That meant that certain equipment would often sit unused for long periods. Compared to procuring local Russian equipment, spending CTR funds on more expensive U.S.-made equipment constituted an inefficient use of program money. Russian specialists also pointed out that Russian-made equipment was more suitable for Russian conditions. Critics warned that the "Buy American" requirement was bound to impact the sustainability of any security and safety upgrades.[17]

An unequal donor-recipient relationship also limited the basis for sustained cooperation. When the idea for the CTR program was first introduced, the disintegrating Soviet Union was in a deep economic and political crisis. Having the United States directly provide nonproliferation assistance was the only viable way to carry out the program. The unfortunate downside of this initial framework was that Russia did not feel like an equal partner. Exclusion of Russians from the program's management positions and failure to be sensitive to Russian priorities for use of CTR funding decreased support for the programs in Russia. In the words of a Russian diplomat, Russia had "a very limited influence on the processes [of fund allocation and choice of subcontractors]," and that was "wrong."[18] Some Russian participants lamented that they received assistance (equipment or expertise) that was readily available in the United States, and that it did not necessarily match Russia's real needs.[19]

The question of access to Russia's nuclear sites became one of the key impediments to smooth implementation of CTR projects. A prolonged waiting period for U.S. personnel to gain access (not guaranteed to be granted) to "closed" cities and nuclear sites often plagued time-sensitive work.[20] Experts from Moscow's Center for Policy Studies in Russia (PIR Center) noted that "the problem of access to the Russian weapons complex site [was] one of the most 'painful' and hard to be solved problems in U.S.-Russian relations."[21] As a matter of principle, the U.S. government insisted that it had every right to monitor the implementation of the projects for which it provided funding. Russia viewed U.S. insistence on having access to almost any site in Russia as an intrusion on sensitive national security affairs. An important factor for Russia was a lack of reciprocity, as Russian specialists could not visit sensitive U.S. sites.

Throughout the years, Russia and the United States took steps to alleviate these challenges. The two sides signed the first formal agreement on access in 2001. The agreement stipulated how many visits could take place and how U.S. experts could operate at Russian sites, and it committed Russia to accepting certain on-site visits.[22] Progress in overcoming problems of access was modest but steady; in the aftermath of 9/11, Russia granted DOD access to a limited number of warhead sites and, following the Bush-Putin summit in Bratislava in 2005, provided access to an even larger number of warhead sites.[23]

Cultural differences and dissimilarities in standard operating procedures also played a role. For example, regular rotation of program management personnel is a common practice for the U.S. government. However, Russian participants who rely on trust and personal relationships built over time, especially in the sensitive nuclear field, found this high turnover among their U.S. counterparts disruptive to the implementation process.[24]

CTR ACHIEVEMENTS

Despite all the challenges encountered, the CTR program succeeded in making a tangible contribution to international security. It played a critical role in the denuclearization of Belarus, Kazakhstan, and Ukraine in the early 1990s. While it was not the only or decisive factor in the decision of the three republics to give up nuclear weapons, CTR made that decision easier. The governments of Belarus, Kazakhstan, and Ukraine were greatly concerned about the financial and technical challenges of dismantling and transporting weapons from their territories. A promise of CTR assistance answered that concern. By the end of FY2013, CTR had paid for deactivation of 7,616 nuclear warheads and destruction of 2,531 missiles and 1,187 launchers and silos, among many other tangible accomplishments.[25]

Cooperation under CTR also enabled a plethora of ties between military personnel, scientists, nuclear engineers, government officials, and policy experts from the United States and the former Soviet Union. CTR's intangible result was building a working relationship in the sensitive area of nuclear security between unlikely partners. At the same time, CTR helped Russia meet its START obligations and enabled the United States to assist Russia with securing its nuclear weapons, materials, and scientific expertise, thereby reducing possible risks of nuclear proliferation to threshold states or non-state actors. Some CTR activities proceeded more smoothly than others, making it useful to examine and compare some of the individual programs.

INDIVIDUAL PROGRAMS TO PREVENT NUCLEAR PROLIFERATION: A CLOSER LOOK

The subsequent sections of this chapter analyze in greater detail programs that addressed two specific categories of threats: the security of nuclear materials (the MPC&A program, the Plutonium Management and Disposition Agreement, and the HEU Purchase Agreement) and the potential leakage of sensitive expertise (the Nuclear Cities Initiative, the Initiatives for Proliferation Prevention, and the ISTC).

The MPC&A Program

At the time of its collapse, the Soviet Union possessed an estimated 650 metric tons of weapons-usable fissile material (HEU and plutonium).[26] The security of these materials varied significantly depending on the custodian agency. It was generally believed that military stocks of fissile material in custody of the defense establishment had satisfactory nuclear safeguards. The majority of other sites with fissile material in the former Soviet Union, however, had major security shortcomings. The less protected sites included research installations, naval fuel cycle facilities, and nonstandard fuel cycles. Problems with security at these sites included holes in the fences around the facilities, the use of wooden buildings to store nuclear materials, faulty locks, and a shortage of guards or security equipment.[27]

The first effort to assist the former Soviet Union with strengthening MPC&A began in 1992 in the form of a government-to-government program administered by the U.S. Defense Department. The initial negotiations on MPC&A cooperation were fraught with difficulties. Russia and the United States reached a first agreement on the development of national systems for physical protection, control, and accounting in September 1993, but the cooperation was limited to low-enriched uranium (LEU) only.[28]

There were three main reasons for the slow start of the government-to-government program. First, the Russian government was suspicious of U.S. motives and reluctant to provide access to facilities with fissile materials due to the sensitivity of such sites. Second, the key agency in charge of fissile material, the Ministry of Atomic Energy, was reluctant to acknowledge the supervisory role of the nuclear regulatory agency, Gosatomnadzor. Finally, the "Buy American" clause attached to cooperation on MPC&A irritated the Russian side.[29]

Although the initial stage of the MPC&A program was laden with complexities, it laid the foundation for what became unprecedented cooperation on fissile material security. The turning point for cooperation on MPC&A came in 1994 when the U.S. DOE launched a parallel laboratory-to-laboratory program. The lab-to-lab initiative was designed to nurture cooperation on MPC&A projects among scientists in a way that would circumvent any challenges at the political level of government-to-government cooperation. The lab-to-lab initiative played a critical role in building confidence between the United States and Russia, and it succeeded in moving forward agreements on specific MPC&A projects. Russian authorities started granting access to some of the facilities with HEU and plutonium. In 1994 both parties signed their first contracts for rapid MPC&A upgrades.[30]

The lab-to-lab program succeeded in moving cooperation on MPC&A forward because it adopted a bottom-up approach, and there were no requirements to negotiate and sign state-level agreements. The laboratories and facilities on both sides had an opportunity to establish direct links and reach agreements not subject to congressional approval or restrictions. The American and Russian scientists engaged in lab-to-lab cooperation developed personal ties and established a high level of mutual trust. According to experts familiar with MPC&A implementation, scientists from both countries shared a common understanding on the priorities and methods as far as MPC&A work was concerned.[31]

Once the scientific communities on both sides established priorities, they were in a position to influence their respective governments. Especially in the case of the Russian bureaucracy, Russian scientists played a critical role in raising awareness of the importance of security upgrades at Russian sites and promoted cooperation with the United States on those matters. U.S. observers acknowledged that Russian scientists understood how to deal with Russian bureaucracy and could be effective in influencing their government.[32]

MPC&A cooperation proceeded at these two levels (DOD's government-to-government and DOE's lab-to-lab programs) until 1996. In its early years, the lab-to-lab program succeeded in escaping bureaucratic and political problems, while the cooperation process under the government-to-government program was more ponderous.[33] The differences in the experiences of the government-to-government and the lab-to-lab programs serve as an example of how working-level relationships and epistemic communities affect cooperation in the nonproliferation field. The lab-to-lab program benefited from the trust and common perspectives shared by the scientific communities in the two countries.

In 1996, DOE received funding responsibilities for all MPC&A activities, and in February 1997, the DOE consolidated the government-to-government and lab-to-lab programs into the MPC&A program. Consolidation of MPC&A activities under a single program received a mixed assessment from the experts. Some believed that it was necessary to consolidate management of MPC&A projects and that consolidation did not affect the work process,[34] while others blamed consolidation for a diminished role of the lab-to-lab process.[35]

The MPC&A program encountered similar challenges to other initiatives under the CTR umbrella. Most notably, a lingering Cold War mind-set and mutual suspicions hampered cooperation in the extremely sensitive field of fissile material security. A lack of reciprocal access to U.S. nuclear sites fed Russia's concerns about the motives behind U.S.-funded MPC&A assistance.

Bureaucracies on both sides regularly delayed implementation of MPC&A projects by imposing burdensome clearance procedures on U.S. program managers and experts. After a scandal concerning Chinese espionage on U.S. nuclear weapons technology, as detailed in the 1999 Cox Report,[36] the DOE imposed strict restrictions on contacts between DOE employees and citizens from "sensitive countries," a category that included Russia.[37]

Implementation was also affected by two major shortcomings in the management of MPC&A: a frequent turnover of program participants on the U.S. side and insufficient participation of Russian experts. Russian participants complained that "each site was constantly having to accommodate itself to new team leaders with new approaches."[38] Russian experts blamed a frequent change in U.S. personnel for access issues, as it hampered the establishment of trust between the partners.[39] Russian specialists practically lost any involvement in the management of the MPC&A program after the consolidation of the lab-to-lab and the government-to-government programs. This undermined the spirit of partnership and negatively affected their commitment to the program.

The lack of an MPC&A culture in the former Soviet Union added to the challenges. The Soviet economic system had created paradoxical methods of accounting. Due to an obsession with production rates, Soviet nuclear facilities would produce extra volumes of plutonium without it being registered in order to compensate for a possible fall in production in the years to follow.[40] The Soviet-style accounting of fissile material left a problematic legacy. First, in the case of political and social upheavals, when the risk of diversion was extremely high, nobody knew the exact amount of fissile material. Second, it created an environment in which the insiders with knowledge of the accounting peculiarities could gradually divert nuclear material without being detected.

Fundamentally, during the Soviet times, proper accounting of nuclear material was not a priority for the government. The nature of the political system made an insider theft unlikely in the eyes of the government. The Soviet Union was isolated from the rest of the world, and the state exercised tight control on its citizens, even more so on the nuclear custodians. The nuclear complex employees also had a sense of belonging to an elite and privileged part of society, which further minimized any incentive to attempt diversion.

The implementation of MPC&A upgrades required intrusion into very sensitive areas and in this way gradually pushed the boundaries of what was considered possible in cooperative threat reduction. In practice, though, the effectiveness of MPC&A implementation has varied. For example, cooperation between the United States and the Russian Navy was more productive than with other Russian agencies. By 2006, the program completed upgrades at all navy sites, two years ahead of schedule. A former Russian senior military official praised U.S. MPC&A efforts for being more attentive to the needs of the Russian Navy, which resulted in fewer controversies on the type of upgrades.[41]

The successfully implemented MPC&A projects with the navy contain lessons on how to effectively engage partners in nonproliferation cooperation. At the outset, the Russian Navy insisted that the U.S. team be composed of a small group of experts with no or little turnover because of the highly sensitive nature of the navy sites. As a result, the two sides developed an atmosphere of mutual trust and created conditions for an effective work environment. The Russian program participants were ready to promote U.S. assistance efforts with their government, and the United States proved to be flexible and treated Russian needs, interests, and concerns with sensitivity. To give an example of the latter, the two parties agreed that Russian scientists and engineers would design and implement new security and accounting systems that relied almost exclusively on Russian equipment.[42] As U.S. nuclear nonproliferation expert Matthew Bunn summarized, "The U.S. team for the nuclear navy projects worked in genuine partnership with its Russian counterpart, and the Russian Navy leadership was strongly committed to the effort and willing to bend rules to move it forward."[43]

After the 1992 CTR umbrella agreement expired in 2013, there was a temporary halt on nuclear security activities due to disagreement on the terms for a new framework for cooperation. The replacement agreement reached in June 2013 enabled nuclear security activities such as MPC&A to continue, but not for long. Russia's announcement in December 2014 that it would curb all nuclear security cooperation with the United States marked the end of bilateral efforts in this area.[44]

The Plutonium Management and Disposition Agreement

In 1998, Russia and the United States signed a Scientific and Technical Cooperation Agreement to carry out tests of proposed technologies for plutonium disposition. Then, in 2000, the two governments signed the Plutonium Management and Disposition Agreement (PMDA), which stipulated that each country would dispose of thirty-four metric tons of weapons-grade plutonium. The agreement required Russia and the United States to start operating industrial-scale disposition facilities no later than December 2007 and dispose of two metric tons of plutonium annually.[45] The two countries had to answer a number of fundamental questions on issues such as the method of disposition, liability, and funding before the agreement could be implemented. Answering these questions delayed progress for about a decade, and as of this writing the method the United States will use for disposition remains uncertain.

Two methods for plutonium disposition received consideration: conversion into mixed oxide (MOX) fuel for use in nuclear reactors (MOX method) and vitrification with waste (immobilization method). The United States initially planned to pursue both methods, while Russia opted for the MOX method from the start, arguing that plutonium was a valuable energy resource. Russia had concerns that if the United States immobilized part of its plutonium, it would have an opportunity to reconstitute weapons-grade material at a later date. Eventually, Washington made a decision to pursue only the MOX method.[46] In 2013, however, due to huge cost overruns at the MOX fuel fabrication plant being constructed in South Carolina, the Obama administration asked DOE to slow construction work and once again study possible alternatives.[47] In its budget proposal for FY2015, the administration called for suspending work on the plant altogether, leading the state of South Carolina to sue the administration in an effort to save the planned MOX plant.[48]

Another reason for the decade-long stalling of the process was a failure to agree on several key issues, including liability in the case of MOX-fuel accidents, safeguarding and monitoring of disposition, and financial assistance arrangements.[49] For instance, when the 1998 technical agreement on plutonium disposition expired in July 2003, it could not be renewed for three years due to disagreements over how to address liability provisions. The U.S. Department of State wanted language under which Russia would be liable for any damages, even those caused by the actions of U.S. personnel. Not surprisingly, the Russian government refused to accept these terms. In 2006, the United States abandoned its demands and, after this three-year delay, the two governments finally resolved the standoff by agreeing on wording that reflected the status quo of 2003.[50]

Russia and the United States also did not work out the mechanics of financial assistance to Russia for its plutonium disposition before signing the agreement in 2000. Russia insisted it was not its responsibility to bear the costs if the international community wanted Russia to dispose of plutonium sooner than Russia considered it to be economical.[51] In 1999–2000, the United States pledged four hundred million dollars in assistance, but a decade elapsed before the two sides confirmed the commitment in the Plutonium Disposition Protocol signed during the Nuclear Security Summit in 2010.[52]

Following Russian Duma ratification, the PMDA finally entered into force in July 2011. After a decade of delays, both countries agreed they would start disposition by 2018. However, the 2014 request by the Obama administration to stop construction work on the planned U.S. facility to blend weapons-grade plutonium into MOX has cast doubt on whether this fuel-fabrication facility will ever be completed. Russia already has some capacity to fabricate MOX fuel on a limited basis and is considered to be well advanced in the process of constructing and modifying facilities to meet the disposition requirements under the PMDA.[53]

Overall, the nonproliferation value of the PMDA is limited. Even if fully implemented, the agreement addresses only part of the excess plutonium stocks in both countries. And, as of this writing, it remains unclear if full implementation will be achieved.

The HEU Purchase Agreement (Megatons to Megawatts Program)

Under the HEU Purchase Agreement signed in 1993, Russia agreed to take five hundred metric tons of HEU from dismantled weapons, down-blend it to LEU that could be used to generate nuclear energy, and sell it to the United States over a period of twenty years.[54] This goal was ultimately achieved, but not without difficulties. In theory, the HEU deal should have quickly become a successful nonproliferation initiative. Because LEU down-blended from Russian HEU was a valuable market product, the deal created an economic incentive for Russia to follow its arms reduction obligations and dismantle warheads; the U.S. market would receive a valuable source of energy; and extracted fissile material would be moved out of Russia, thereby reducing the threat of nuclear material proliferation.

In practice, however, implementation of the HEU deal involved challenges. These arose from tension between the nonproliferation and commercial drivers of the deal. The DOE served as the initial U.S. administrator of the deal. However, in 1992, U.S. law established USEC to manage DOE's civilian enrichment facilities, and in 1998 USEC became a private company. USEC was committed to purchase Russian LEU at a fixed price, and when market prices for LEU declined, this made it difficult for the company to sell the LEU it received from Russia at a profit. USEC's commercial interests led it to want to renegotiate its contract with Russia, which was problematic since the company was tasked with implementing a deal whose primary goal was removing HEU from Russia on an agreed schedule. The collision of U.S. nonproliferation objectives and USEC's commercial interests significantly strained the implementation process. USEC and Russia's Tenex, a company in charge of implementing the deal on the Russian side, eventually reached an agreement in 2002 under which USEC would pay a price dependent on average market conditions in the preceding three years.[55]

Despite the difficulties, the HEU deal can be considered one of the more successful CTR efforts. By 2014, the two countries had cooperated to downblend the full five hundred metric tons of weapons-grade HEU stipulated by the agreement—thereby removing nuclear materials that could have been used to produce twenty thousand warheads. The program was completed on schedule and phased out following a final shipment of LEU from Russia to the United States in December 2013.[56]

The Nuclear Cities Initiative

Potential leakage of scientific and technical expertise from the former Soviet Union was a serious concern in the early 1990s. The economic turmoil that followed the Soviet collapse had a devastating effect on the nuclear complex. Many nuclear scientists and engineers lost their jobs, and those who still had jobs were not paid for months. Morale was at an all-time low.

There were two worrying scenarios about how the crisis could contribute to proliferation. First, scientists and engineers with critical knowledge could be tempted to sell their expertise to nuclear aspirants (third countries or non-state actors). Second, disgruntled nuclear custodians could shirk their responsibilities, jeopardizing the security of nuclear weapons and materials.

The U.S. DOE launched the Nuclear Cities Initiative (NCI) in 1998 to promote the development of private industry and create nonmilitary job and research opportunities for newly unemployed scientists, engineers, and technical experts from the weapons complex. NCI specifically focused on Russia's "closed" cities, where most sensitive weapons work took place. Ten "closed" cities in Russia had been central to the Soviet nuclear weapons program, and they continued to be the backbone of Russia's nuclear weapons program. During Soviet times, the population in these cities enjoyed special privileges leading to a better quality of life than in the rest of the country.[57] By the time of the Soviet collapse, the "closed" cities went from being privileged parts of the country to struggling for survival. A survey published in 2001 revealed that 60 percent of Russia's nuclear complex workers had to supplement their income with second jobs, around 90 percent reported deterioration of their income, and 80 percent said they were willing to work for military programs of foreign countries.[58]

In 1998, NCI launched pilot projects in three "closed" cities: Sarov, Snezhinsk, and Zheleznogorsk. From the start, however, the underdeveloped economic and financial system, as well as corruption in Russia, complicated NCI's operations. Severe economic problems made it hard to attract foreign investment to "closed" cities for creating nonmilitary jobs. Russian businesses equally did not show much interest in investing in "closed" cities.

A strict access regime for foreign nationals proved to be a major problem for NCI implementation. Most of the "closed" cities are located far from big cities and have several layers of physical protection. The United States complained about the long waiting period for permission to visit the cities and numerous cases of denied access.[59] All foreign citizens who were granted access to "closed" cities required an escort at all times, with a few exceptions in some cities where foreigners were allowed to move on their own within a limited area.[60] NCI managers and their Russian counterparts sought creative solutions to problems with access. For example, NCI funded the construction of research facilities that provided job opportunities just outside of the fence in Sarov. This allowed Sarov inhabitants to forego moving out of the city or commuting to a remote city for work.[61]

While NCI's official goal was to assist Russia with providing nonmilitary job opportunities for Russian weapons scientists, the program spent on average almost 70 percent of its funding on U.S. national labs, with only about 30 percent spent in Russia.[62] NCI was also not the only U.S.-funded program designed to prevent "brain drain" from the former Soviet Union. As such, it had to compete for funding with other programs such as the ISTC and the Initiatives for Proliferation Prevention (IPP), discussed in subsequent sections. NCI and other programs with similar goals occasionally duplicated their efforts due to a lack of coordination between the implementing agencies.

In 2001, the DOE issued a new guidance for the NCI program that contained more detailed information on the project selection and approval process. While the move was welcome from a government oversight perspective, it was controversial as far as the nonproliferation objective was concerned. Starting in 2001, NCI projects were required to involve partners from industry or demonstrate commercial viability. Stricter conditions meant fewer NCI projects would be approved.

Perhaps the most serious challenge that NCI faced was opposition within the U.S. Congress. Members of Congress had a difficult time accepting the idea of spending taxpayer money to improve the economic situation of foreign scientists. In addition, unlike the CTR program, which could use hard data metrics to demonstrate its effectiveness (e.g., number of weapons destroyed), it was impossible to quantify and therefore demonstrate NCI's effectiveness.

After years of battling for its existence, NCI ended operations in 2006. At that time, it and the Initiatives for Proliferation Prevention were folded together into the Global Initiatives for Proliferation Prevention program. By its end, despite the challenges it confronted, NCI had helped to reemploy more than sixteen hundred scientists.[63]

The Initiatives for Proliferation Prevention

In 1994, DOE established the Initiatives for Proliferation Prevention (IPP). Unlike NCI, from the start IPP aimed at establishing commercially viable projects jointly implemented by entities from the United States and the former Soviet Union. Also unlike NCI, it was not limited to "closed" cities.

IPP adopted a multistage project implementation procedure. Initially, a U.S. company would approach a national lab, DOE, or the U.S. Industry Coalition (USIC) with a proposal for a cooperative project with a partner institution in Russia, Belarus, Kazakhstan, or Ukraine. The Inter-Laboratory Board, which consists of the representatives of the national labs and the Kansas City Plant, would identify an appropriate institution in the former Soviet Union and evaluate that institution's capabilities. USIC would be responsible for evaluating the commercial viability of the proposed project. DOE would make the final decision on which projects to fund.

IPP encountered problems of implementation similar to other CTR programs. The U.S. Government Accountability Office (GAO) criticized the program for the inadequate share of funding received by Russia (30–40 percent), a lack of sufficient data on the amount of funding actually reaching Russian scientists, vague priorities on the selection of institutions (creating concerns that the program was not targeting critical institutions and personnel), and most important, a lack of success with moving projects toward becoming commercially self-sustaining without government assistance.[64]

At the same time, there were two major concerns specific to the nature of IPP. First, unlike NCI, which targeted weapons scientists as they were leaving the weapons complex, IPP engaged weapons specialists who were still employed. In that respect, IPP managers had to address criticism that the program subsidized nuclear weapons activities. The DOE defended its approach by noting that preventing scientists from selling their expertise to foreign countries required providing opportunities both for scientists who were leaving jobs and those who continued to work. Second, the GAO raised concerns about the possibility of inadvertent sharing of critical information with former Soviet scientists during the process of project implementation.[65]

Despite the concerns, IPP can point to measurable achievements. Between 1994 and 2008, Global Initiatives for Proliferation Prevention, a program that combined IPP and NCI, created or sustained over 2,400 civilian jobs and attracted more than $280 million in investments. The program sustained more than thirty businesses, employed former weapons specialists, and achieved a 20 percent commercialization rate.[66]

The International Science and Technology Center

The ISTC is a multilateral effort to prevent the proliferation of weapons expertise from the former Soviet Union. The agreement to create it was signed in 1992; ISTC started operation in 1994. In this project, the European Union, Russia, the United States, and Japan joined efforts to create opportunities for weapons scientists and engineers in the former Soviet Union to work on nonmilitary projects.[67] At a later stage, Norway, South Korea, and Canada joined the ISTC as funders, and Armenia, Belarus, Georgia, Kazakhstan, Kyrgyzstan, and Tajikistan joined as recipient states. In addition to the ISTC, initially headquartered in Moscow, a parallel agreement signed in 1993 created a Science and Technology Center in Ukraine, based in Kiev.

The ISTC created opportunities for scientists from former Soviet republics to engage in new cutting-edge projects and for U.S. and other partners to benefit from the advanced level of Soviet fundamental sciences. As of December 2013, ISTC had funded 2,794 proposals, totaling $879 million. More than seventy-five thousand scientists had received ISTC research grants.[68]

Despite these achievements, several factors have limited cooperation under the ISTC. First, throughout the years, ISTC has suffered from a lack of funding. The number of project proposals has far exceeded the number of projects that ISTC could fund.[69] Second, the multilateral nature of ISTC has caused delays. The Board of Governors, consisting of representatives from Canada, the European Union, Japan, Russia, and the United States, operates on the rule of consensus. Reaching consensus on every single decision, especially when the EU needs approval from all member states, has inevitably taken time.

A more serious blow came in 2011, when the Russian government took a decision to pull out of the ISTC by 2015.⁷⁰ As a result, the ISTC had to look for a new host country. Kazakhstan volunteered for the role. By June 2014, Kazakhstan had inaugurated the ISTC's new office in Astana.⁷¹

To sum up, this section has examined six specific CTR programs. All six achieved some success and encountered some obstacles, but to varying degrees, with implementation proceeding better in some cases than others. It is now time to consider what might explain this pattern of cooperation.

EXPLAINING COOPERATION

The CTR case has implications for all seven factors that might affect cooperation listed in chapter 1. The CTR case also indicates the importance of some other factors not highlighted by Knopf. Self-interest, the first factor on the list, played an important but complex role in CTR. There were competing interests involved, which help account for both cooperation and its limits. From the standpoint of the United States, potential nuclear proliferation from the former Soviet Union was one of the most serious threats to its national security, creating a strong interest in cooperative threat reduction. For Russia, economic crisis created an interest in receiving financial assistance for dealing with pressing nuclear security needs and meeting arms control obligations. Security upgrades to its nuclear complex also reduced the risk of unauthorized groups within Russia getting access to weapons and materials and threatening the internal security situation. CTR thus benefited both parties in different ways.

But self-interest considerations cut both directions. Some in the U.S. government were wary about potentially subsidizing the weapons complex in a country that could still prove to be an adversary. And Russia worried about giving access to sensitive nuclear sites to U.S. personnel. Thus, interest calculations both fostered and limited cooperation.

U.S. leadership also played an obvious role, given that CTR was a U.S. initiative, but the type of leadership that stands out in this case was not simply a reflection of America's hegemonic status. The U.S. government did not act as a unitary actor. Instead, key individuals, including individuals outside the executive branch, such as Senators Nunn and Lugar, had to play an entrepreneurial role to convince the government to initiate CTR.

Norms and identity were not as directly important, but the related factor of culture had an impact. Differences in bureaucratic culture impeded efforts of the two sides to work together and hence served as another limiting factor on cooperation. Domestic politics played a similar role in constraining cooperation. This is demonstrated by the "Buy American" provision included by Congress, even though this provision reduced the effectiveness of CTR as a nonproliferation tool.

Capabilities and inducements were among the more important factors in this case. CTR was designed in large part to provide inducements—and direct assistance—to former Soviet republics to help them improve their capabilities in key areas such as MPC&A and security at nuclear sites. CTR also provides strong evidence in support of the hypothesis that working-level relationships can be important. Two of the most successful CTR efforts—the lab-to-lab program and the MPC&A project with the Russian Navy—succeeded in large part because they developed the greatest levels of trust and smoothest working-level relationships between participants on the two sides.

The CTR case also suggests a need to pay attention to some factors not emphasized by Knopf. The broader strategic context greatly affected the cooperation process. Because the two countries had just recently been major Cold War rivals, officials in the United States and Russia continued to harbor grave suspicions about each other, and this mistrust slowed CTR implementation. This case also shows the importance of bureaucratic politics. Institutional interests and standard operating procedures, and difficulties establishing interagency cooperation, created additional impediments to CTR implementation.

CONCLUSION

The CTR path was not an easy one: the first challenge was to get the program off the ground. There were two main factors that complicated translation of the Nunn-Lugar vision into a programmatic activity. First, it was not clear how seriously to take the potential nuclear dangers associated with the disintegrating Soviet Union. There was no evidence of an imminent loss of control of nuclear weapons or materials. Since governments have difficulties with prioritizing resources to deal with threats that are unquantifiable, securing support for CTR was not an easy feat. Second, CTR was a novel concept and required close U.S.-Russian cooperation on sensitive national security issues. Neither side was psychologically ready to wholeheartedly accept such a partnership. CTR hence met fierce opposition in both countries.

Both at the inception of the CTR program and over the course of two decades, CTR programs struggled with bureaucratic, political, technical, and cultural problems. The most common bureaucratic problems were conflicting organizational interests, time-consuming procedures, and a lack of interagency cooperation. The organizational culture of various CTR participants had a direct impact on the success, or lack thereof, of cooperative projects. More conservative organizations, such as military establishments and national security agencies, had a more difficult time with CTR, while scientific communities were quicker to embrace CTR projects. In the case of the HEU Purchase Agreement, the introduction of private entity, USEC, driven by commercial interests complicated the implementation process.

Conditions attached to cooperation impacted the implementation of CTR projects. The requirement to buy only U.S. equipment and expertise had both practical and political consequences. More often than not, using U.S.-made equipment was impractical and resulted in delays and more program money spent. More important, an imposition of rules that effectively prioritized U.S. economic interests over efficiency of program implementation negatively affected Russian participants' perception of CTR.

Unresolved issues in political relations further intensified bureaucratic challenges. A lack of trust or an existing U.S.-Russian partnership exacerbated already cumbersome procedures related to access to facilities and issuance of visas. Practically all CTR programs required access to "closed" cities or sensitive nuclear facilities. Both governments contributed to project delays by introducing cumbersome and lengthy procedures for authorizing travel for CTR participants. A lack of reciprocity compounded these problems. Russia sometimes responded to U.S. demands for unprecedented access to Russian nuclear facilities by noting that Russians did not have similar access to U.S. nuclear sites.

Political and bureaucratic limitations of the CTR process were directly linked to the role both countries continued to assign to nuclear weapons. Notwithstanding the end of the Cold War, nuclear weapons have remained critical in the national security strategies of Russia and the United States, with the numbers of their nuclear weapons still set to balance against each other. In the absence of a radical restructuring of strategic postures and in an environment of incomplete transition from an adversarial relationship to a partnership, cooperation in the nuclear field remains extremely sensitive for both sides.

In addition to political, bureaucratic, and cultural obstacles, CTR faced technical challenges. These were especially noticeable in the case of the PMDA. The two disposition methods under consideration both had drawbacks, and the two countries differed in opinion on which method was preferable. Resolving these differences delayed program implementation, and uncertainty on the U.S. side means full implementation is still in doubt.

The initial obstacles and problems of implementation make CTR's subsequent achievements even more impressive. There were several conditions that allowed CTR programs to succeed. Although U.S. policy makers debated the urgency and scope of the threat, they recognized that the threat of proliferation from the former Soviet Union was real. There was also a fortunate combination of key individuals in the United States from academia, the executive branch, and Congress who promoted the vision behind CTR. On a larger scale, when CTR began, U.S.-Russian relations were in a honeymoon period; both sides had high hopes for the transformation that was under way.

CTR programs deserve credit for averting a nuclear proliferation nightmare in the former Soviet Union. CTR significantly reduced proliferation threats from Russia and other post-Soviet states. The most important contribution of CTR to enhancing international security is the non-nuclear status of three post-Soviet republics—Belarus, Kazakhstan, and Ukraine. CTR paid for the removal and dismantlement of nuclear weapons and all weapons-related infrastructure in these three states. CTR assisted Russia with meeting its obligations under START by providing equipment for weapons dismantlement. CTR programs secured thousands of tons of vulnerable nuclear material and strengthened the physical security of scores of nuclear facilities. As far as we can tell today, no significant diversion of nuclear material occurred from the facilities in the former Soviet Union. The engagement of thousands of former weapons scientists in civilian projects became possible due to CTR. While the effectiveness of scientist redirection programs is not quantifiable, such engagement contributed to preventing a potential leak of expertise to third parties. Overall, CTR has proven to be one the most innovative and important nonproliferation initiatives of the post–Cold War period.

The expiration of the CTR umbrella agreement in 2013 and subsequent narrowing down of and eventual halt in CTR activities in Russia coincided with the worsening of U.S.-Russian relations over Ukraine. Yet, the crisis in relations was not the primary reason for the transformation in bilateral cooperative threat reduction. Rather, Russia's revival from its low point in the 1990s and desire to become a more assertive player on the world scene led it to look for ways to reduce and eventually end its reliance on U.S. nonproliferation assistance.

Given its achievements, the international community may want to use the CTR process as a model for future nonproliferation initiatives. Simply imitating the original Nunn-Lugar programs, however, is not likely to produce optimal results. To make future cooperative threat reduction efforts effective, it is important to pay due attention to the lessons from the operationalization and implementation of CTR programs in the former Soviet Union.

Notes

This chapter is based on the author's doctoral dissertation research conducted during 2000–2004 at the University of Leeds and subsequently published in *From Antagonism to Partnership: The Uneasy Path of the U.S.-Russian Cooperative Threat Reduction* (Stuttgart: Ibidem-Verlag, 2007). The author gratefully acknowledges research assistance provided by Wyatt Hoffman.

1. "Russia Ends U.S. Nuclear Security Alliance: Accord Worked to Keep Stockpiles Secure," *Boston Globe*, January 19, 2015.

2. Bruce Blair, *The Logic of an Accidental Nuclear War* (Washington, D.C.: Brookings Institution Press, 1993), 72.

3. Senator Sam Nunn, "Foreword: Changing Threats in the Post-Cold War World," in *Dismantling the Cold War: U.S. and NIS Perspectives on the Nunn-Lugar Cooperative Threat Reduction Program*, ed. John M. Shields and William C. Potter (Cambridge, Mass.: MIT Press, 1997), xvi.

4. Kurt Campbell, Ashton Carter, Steven Miller, and Charles Zraket, *Soviet Nuclear Fission: Control of the Nuclear Arsenal in a Disintegrating Soviet Union* (Cambridge, Mass.: Harvard University, Center for Science and International Affairs, 1991).

5. John Felton, "The Nunn-Lugar Vision: 1992–2002" (Washington, D.C.: Nuclear Threat Initiative [NTI], 2002), 5.

6. Text of the Soviet Nuclear Threat Reduction Act of 1991 is available on the website of the Federation of American Scientists, www.fas.org/nuke/control/ctr/docs/hr3807.html.

7. This concern haunted CTR in later years as well. For example, during a congressional debate on CTR funding for FY1997, Representative Solomon declared, "If we are giving them this money, it is freeing up other money.... We are subsidizing the Russian government to dismantle old nuclear missiles while they are still in the process of modernizing and building up other nuclear missiles." Quoted in Amy F. Woolf, "Nunn-Lugar Cooperative Threat Reduction Programs: Issues for Congress" (Congressional Research Service Report 97–1027, Washington, D.C., March 23, 2001), 16.

8. On Russian domestic critics, see Vladimir A. Orlov, "Perspectives of Russian Decision-Makers and Problems of Implementation," in Shields and Potter, *Dismantling the Cold War*, 85–102.

9. CTR programs to address the Soviet legacy in chemical and biological weapons also encountered difficulties in Russia, but these programs operated in a different context. Russia has made treaty commitments to eliminate chemical and biological weapons, which removes some of the national security concerns that surround nuclear activities.

10. Jessica Stern, "U.S. Assistance Programs to Improve MPC&A in the Former Soviet Union," *Nonproliferation Review* 3, no. 2 (Winter 1996): 17–32.

11. "Balkanization" is a term used by Rose Gottemoeller in "Presidential Priorities in Nuclear Policy," in Shields and Potter, *Dismantling the Cold War*, 69.

12. Individuals with direct experience in various programs' establishment and implementation, interviews, Washington, D.C., 2003.

13. Vladimir Orlov and Alexander Cheban, "Sochi 2014: G8 Must Set a New Benchmark for Global Partnership" (Moscow: PIR Center, 2013), 15.

14. Daniel Horner and Tom Z. Collina, "Nunn-Lugar Program Scaled Back," *Arms Control Today* 43, no. 6 (July–August 2013).

15. Evgenii Maslin, "Programma sovmestnogo umen'sheniya ugrozy i interesy natsional'noi bezopasnosti Rossii" [Cooperative threat reduction program and Russian's national security interests], in *Programma sovmestnogo umen'sheniya ugrozy: otsenka effektivnosti i perspektivy razvitiya [Cooperative threat reduction program: Assessing efficiency and development prospects)*, ed. Ivan Safranchuk (PIR Study Paper No. 13, Moscow, 2000), 7, translated from Russian by the author.

16. U.S. nonproliferation experts, interviews, Washington, D.C., 2003.

17. Russian nonproliferation experts, interviews, Moscow, 2003.

18. Valerii Semin, "Programma sovmestnogo umen'sheniya ugrozy imeet potentsial dal'neishego razvitiya" [Cooperative threat reduction program has potential for further development], in Safranchuk, *Programma sovmestnogo umen'sheniya ugrozy*, 9, translated from Russian by the author.

19. Russian nonproliferation experts, interviews, Moscow, 2003.

20. U.S. Government Accountability Office (GAO), "Weapons of Mass Destruction: Additional Russian Cooperation Needed to Facilitate U.S. Efforts to Improve Security at Russian Sites" (GAO-03-482, March 24, 2003), "Highlights," www.gao.gov/products/GAO-03-482.

21. "Sotrudnichestvo vo imya global'noi bezopasnosti" [Cooperation for the global security], *Nauchnye Zapiski PIR-Centra* 19, no. 1 (2002): 198, translated from Russian by the author.

22. DOE official, interview, Washington, D.C., 2003.

23. Matthew Bunn, "Cooperation to Secure Nuclear Stockpiles: A Case of Constrained Innovation," *Innovations* 1, no. 1 (Winter 2006): 128–29.

24. Russian nonproliferation experts, interviews, Moscow, 2003.

25. U.S. Defense Threat Reduction Agency (DTRA), "Nunn-Lugar CTR Scorecard 2014," www.dtra.mil/docs/trac/ctr-program-scorecard.pdf?sfvrsn=0. The "missiles" category on this scorecard includes intercontinental ballistic missiles, submarine-launched ballistic missiles, and nuclear air-to-surface missiles.

26. Jon Brook Wolfsthal, Cristina-Astrid Chuen, and Emily Ewell Daughtry, "Nuclear Status Report: Nuclear Weapons, Fissile Material and Export Controls in the Former Soviet Union" (Number 6, Monterey Institute of International Studies and Carnegie Endowment for International Peace, June 2001), 75, http://carnegieendowment.org/files/NSRFullTextEnglish.pdf.

27. Graham Allison, Owen R. Coté, Jr., Richard Falkenrath, and Steven Miller, *Avoiding Nuclear Anarchy: Containing the Threat of Loose Russian Nuclear Weapons and Fissile Material* (Cambridge, Mass.: MIT Press, 1996), 42.

28. Oleg Bukharin, Matthew Bunn, and Kenneth Luongo, "Renewing the Partnership: Recommendations for Accelerated Action to Secure Nuclear Material in the Former Soviet Union" (Princeton: Russian American Nuclear Security Advisory Council, August 2000), 46.

29. "Foreign Programs Reducing Russia's WMD Threats: Appraisals and Outlook" (report, Center for Strategic and International Studies Project on Strengthening Cooperative Threat Reduction with Russia: A U.S.-European Initiative, Moscow, April 15, 2002), 41.

30. Bukharin, Bunn, and Luongo, "Renewing the Partnership," 46.

31. U.S. and Russian nonproliferation experts, interviews, Washington, D.C., and Moscow, 2003.

32. U.S. nonproliferation experts, interviews, Washington, D.C., 2003.

33. Senior U.S. national lab official, interview, Washington, D.C., 2003.

34. Ibid.

35. Bukharin, Bunn, and Luongo, "Renewing the Partnership," 46.

36. Select Committee, U.S. House of Representatives, "U.S. National Security and Military/Commercial Concerns With the People's Republic of China" (January 3, 1999), www.house.gov/coxreport/.

37. Bukharin, Bunn, and Luongo, "Renewing the Partnership," 46.

38. Matthew Bunn, Oleg Bukharin, and Kenneth Luongo, "Renewing the Partnership: One Year Later," in *Proceedings of the 42nd Annual Meeting of the Institute of Nuclear Materials Management* (Indian Wells, Calif., July 15–19, 2001), 5.

39. "Sotrudnichestvo vo imya global'noi bezopasnosti," 104.

40. Jessica Eve Stern, "Cooperative Activities to Improve Fissile Material Protection, Control, and Accounting," in Shields and Potter, *Dismantling the Cold War*, 314.
41. Former Russian senior military official, interview, Moscow, 2003.
42. Bunn, "Cooperation to Secure Nuclear Stockpiles," 127.
43. Ibid., 127.
44. Even if Russia had not halted its involvement in these programs, it is not clear that the U.S. Congress would have agreed to fund U.S. nuclear security cooperation with Russia given the dispute over Ukraine.
45. Wolfsthal, Chuen, and Daughtry, "Nuclear Status Report," 65–66.
46. Elena Sokova, "Plutonium Disposition," NTI Analysis, September 16, 2010, www.nti.org/analysis/articles/plutonium-disposition-14/.
47. Tom Clements, Edwin Lyman, and Frank von Hippel, "The Future of Plutonium Disposition," *Arms Control Today* 43, no. 6 (July–August 2013).
48. Meg Kinnard, "Feds: Plans to Mothball Savannah River Site MOX Plant on Hold," Associated Press, April 29, 2014.
49. Douglas Brubaker and Leonard Spector, "Liability and Western Nonproliferation Assistance to Russia: Time for a Fresh Look?," *Nonproliferation Review* 10, no. 1 (Spring 2003): 1–39; Henry L. Stimson Center, "Liability Issues in WMD Threat Reduction and Nonproliferation Programs in Russia" (last updated June 1, 2007), www.stimson.org/liability-issues-in-cooperative-nonproliferation-programs-in-russia-/.
50. Matthew Bunn, "Troubled Disposition: Next Steps in Dealing with Excess Plutonium," *Arms Control Today* 37, no. 3 (April 2007).
51. Ibid.
52. U.S. State Department, "2000 Plutonium Management and Disposition Agreement" (Fact sheet, April 13, 2010), www.state.gov/r/pa/prs/ps/2010/04/140097.htm.
53. Ibid.; U.S. Defense Treaty Inspection Readiness Program, "Plutonium Management and Disposition Agreement (PMDA)," http://dtirp.dtra.mil/tic/synopses/pmda.aspx; Mark Holt and Mary Beth D. Nikitin, "Mixed-Oxide Fuel Fabrication Plant and Plutonium Disposition: Management and Policy Issues" (Congressional Research Service Report R43125, Washington, D.C., March 28, 2014).
54. USEC, "Megatons to Megawatts," www.usec.com/russian-contracts/megatons-megawatts.
55. J. Peter Scoblic, "United States, Russia Approve New 'HEU Deal' Contract," *Arms Control Today* 32, no. 6 (July–August 2002).
56. USEC, "Megatons to Megawatts."
57. Michael Dobbs, "Collapse of Soviet Union Proved Boom to Iranian Missile Program," *Washington Post*, January 13, 2002.
58. Valentin Tikhonov, *Russia's Nuclear and Missile Complex: The Human Factor in Proliferation* (Washington, D.C.: Carnegie Endowment for International Peace, 2001), 9–10.
59. GAO, "Nuclear Nonproliferation: DOE's Efforts to Assist Weapons Scientists in Russia's Nuclear Cities Face Challenge" (GAO-01-429, May 2001), 45.
60. Oleg Bukharin, "Appendix 3: What Are Russia's Closed Nuclear Cities?," in *Conversion and Job Creation in Russia's Closed Nuclear Cities: An Update, Based on a Workshop Held in Obninsk, Russia, June 27–29, 2000*, ed. Oleg Bukharin, Frank von Hippel, and Sharon K. Weiner (Program on Nuclear Policy Alternatives, Center for International Studies and Center for Energy and Environmental Studies, Princeton University, November 2000), 74.
61. NNSA, "Nuclear Cities Initiative," document accessed May 28, 2007 from NNSA website, no longer available online.

62. GAO, "Nuclear Nonproliferation: DOE's Efforts," 9.

63. Raphael Della Ratta, "Scientist Redirection, Bioproliferation Prevention, and Effective Measurements of Progress" (presentation, Biosecurity Group Roundtable, Washington, D.C., September 22, 2006).

64. GAO, "Nuclear Nonproliferation: Concerns with DOE's Efforts to Reduce the Risks Posed by Russia's Unemployed Weapons Scientists" (GAO/RCED-99-54, February 1999), 44.

65. Ibid.

66. U.S. Industry Coalition, "GIPP Program," http://old.usic.net/gipp-program/, website no longer available.

67. ISTC, "Agreement Establishing an International Science and Technology Center" (November 27, 1992), www.istc.ru/istc/istc.nsf/va_WebPages/StatutoryDocumentsAgreeEstabEngPrint.

68. ISTC, "ISTC Fact Sheet," http://istc.ru/istc/istc.nsf/va_WebPages/ISTCFactSheetEng.

69. John Crowley, U.S. State Department, interview, Washington, D.C., 2003.

70. Douglas Birch, "Russia Abandons $1B Western Aid to Weapons Program," Associated Press, April 20, 2011.

71. ISTC, "The New Office of ISTC Was Officially Opened at Nazarbayev University in Astana, Kazakhstan on 5 June, 2014," http://istc.ru/istc/istc.nsf/va_WebPages/New_office_NUEng.

CHAPTER FIVE
The G8 Global Partnership
A Glass Half Full

WYN Q. BOWEN AND ALAN HEYES

DRIVEN BY INCREASED CONCERNS following the terrorist attacks of September 11, 2001, that terrorists might harness and use chemical, biological, radiological, and nuclear (CBRN) materials, American officials began working with Canadian colleagues to establish a new multilateral initiative to address vulnerable CBRN materials. They used the Group of Eight (G8) meeting of leading industrialized nations to develop an initiative built along the lines of the U.S. Cooperative Threat Reduction (CTR) program. The result was the Global Partnership (GP) Against the Spread of Weapons and Materials of Mass Destruction, which was launched at the G8 Summit of June 2002 in Kananaskis, Canada. The GP was established as a mechanism to "support specific cooperation projects, initially in Russia, to address nonproliferation, disarmament, counterterrorism and nuclear safety issues." The initial priorities identified in 2002 included destroying chemical weapons, dismantling decommissioned nuclear submarines, disposing of fissile materials, and redirecting former weapons scientists into civilian employment (sometimes called "scientist redirection").[1] The GP was envisaged as a twenty-billion-dollar decade-long initiative with ten billion provided by the United States and the remaining ten billion to come from its G8 partners ("10+10 over 10").

This chapter examines the establishment and implementation of the GP from its formal announcement in June 2002 up until the Deauville G8 Summit in France of May 2011, with a brief discussion of developments since then.[2] At the Deauville Summit, the initiative was extended beyond its original ten-year mandate, which had been due to expire in 2012.[3] The chapter unfolds in five parts. The first examines the establishment and expansion of the GP. Consideration is given to the primary objectives of the GP and the motivations of the Bush administration as its principal originator. Attention is also given to how the GP was established as a functioning arrangement and how and why the initiative was extended beyond the original G8 members to encompass, as of 2011, a total of twenty-two states and the European Union (EU).

The second and third sections assess the accomplishments and failings of the GP, respectively, in the period up to 2012. Both sections examine the degree of cooperation achieved among the participating countries and the extent to which this resulted in a realization of the objectives and priorities laid out in 2002. Attention is also given to the degree to which the objectives and priorities contributed to successful proliferation prevention. The fourth section briefly considers developments in 2012 to 2014, especially the impact of the Ukrainian crisis and Russia's associated ejection from the G8. The final section relates the findings from the case study to the questions posed by Knopf in chapter 1. This section highlights four factors that help to explain cooperation in this case: (1) self-interest; (2) U.S. leadership; (3) norms and identity; and (4) ideas, learning, and transnational networks.

ESTABLISHING AND EXPANDING THE GP

The 9/11 attacks dramatically increased international concerns over the potential for terrorist groups like al-Qaeda to acquire and use CBRN weapons. In an October 2002 Senate hearing on the GP, for example, U.S. senator Richard Lugar noted, "Now we live in an era where catastrophic terrorism, using weapons of mass destruction, is our foremost security concern."[4] The perception of a growing CBRN terrorist threat prompted the Bush administration to secure the commitment of America's G8 partners to take more concerted action to address potential sources of CBRN materials and weapons, particularly in Russia and other former Soviet states. According to testimony at the Senate hearing by John Bolton, undersecretary of state for arms control and international security affairs in the Bush administration, "President Bush took the lead in working with G8 colleagues to come up with the 10+10 over 10 program" and in doing so secured "close to a doubling of the international resources" available for CBRN threat reduction work in the former Soviet Union (FSU). While the Bush administration provided the essential impetus for the negotiation and launch of the GP, Canadian officials also expended significant effort paving the way for the GP because of Canada's presidency of the G8 in 2002. Indeed, the role of the Canadian government was highlighted by Bolton, who noted that without Canada's work "we would not have come as far as we did" in setting up the GP.[5]

At the Kananaskis Summit, the G8 states signed up to a set of principles and guidelines designed to "prevent terrorists, or those that harbor them, from gaining access to weapons or materials of mass destruction." The G8 states agreed to put the initial focus on threat reduction projects in Russia in the areas of "the destruction of chemical weapons, the dismantlement of decommissioned nuclear submarines, the disposition of fissile materials and the employment of former weapons scientists."[6] The initial emphasis on these specific areas was driven by concerns that terrorists could potentially capitalize on the major holdings of poorly secured chemical and nuclear weapons and associated materials, or on the CBRN expertise of former weapons scientists and engineers, in Russia.

The G8 also agreed to "raise up to $20 billion" over ten years for projects to address vulnerabilities in these areas.[7] The United States would provide around ten billion, with the remainder coming from the other seven countries. This was an unprecedented pledge of resources for a multilateral initiative designed primarily to counter CBRN terrorism. The financial pledges also demonstrated the high level of political buy-in to a global threat reduction agenda. The long-term funding pledges made by the heads of state provided significant impetus to relevant government departments across the G8 states in terms of convincing their respective legislatures to support, and to approve the requisite resources for, national threat reduction programs. According to officials from some GP countries, their governments would probably not have been in a position to contribute to threat reduction work beyond their own countries in the absence of the GP.[8]

While the primary driver for the Bush administration to establish the GP was enhancing efforts to reduce the CBRN terrorist threat, a secondary driver was gaining a larger resource commitment from other G8 states for threat reduction projects. This partly reflected domestic politics, as the U.S. Congress had been pushing for American allies to carry a larger part of the burden. In October 2002, for example, Senator Joe Biden argued in relation to the GP that "at the very least, it may leverage increased funding on those important projects by our allies in Europe, Japan, and Canada."[9]

The G8 states also agreed in 2002 to "invite other countries that are prepared to adopt its common principles and guidelines to enter into discussions with us on participating in and contributing to this initiative." This was a clear statement of intent to expand the number of donors to the GP beyond the G8, as well as to enlarge the geographical recipient base. In the latter case, it was specifically stated that "the G8 would be willing to enter into negotiations with any other recipient countries, including those of the Former Soviet Union, prepared to adopt the guidelines, for inclusion in the Partnership."[10]

The GP subsequently expanded from the original membership to some twenty-two countries by 2011, all of which contributed funding to GP projects.[11] In addition, both the EU and the nongovernmental Nuclear Threat Initiative contributed funding to GP projects, while Kazakhstan and Ukraine later joined as additional recipient countries. Some of the motives for new participants to become involved reflected very specific national interests. For example, Finland, Norway, and Sweden participated in projects in northwest Russia for environmental reasons in order to address safety challenges associated with decaying

Russian nuclear submarines. Arguably, the submarines did not present a proliferation risk, although the spent fuel from them certainly presented safety and security challenges.

Finally, in terms of organizational structure, while no formalized bureaucracy was established to run the GP, a Working Group was set up consisting of senior diplomats from the G8 with a rotating chair drawn from the country hosting the G8 presidency. The group has reviewed the status of projects and has met up to five times annually. Importantly, those officials and contractors responsible for specific threat reduction projects and programs have met much more frequently to discuss progress and to share experiences. As shown later, it has been at this operational and more technical level where the GP has performed most effectively. Indeed, the role of the Working Group in providing effective strategic direction has been much less effective primarily because of its consensus approach to decision making.

In summary, the GP was established following the 9/11 terrorist attacks under the initiative of the Bush administration working in collaboration with the Canadian government because of its presidency of the G8 in 2002. It was designed to be an informal and flexible mechanism drawing on financial contributions and technical and project management expertise from the G8 states and, later on, from a widening group of GP participating governments. In this respect the GP helped to address congressional pressure for American allies to carry a larger part of the global threat reduction burden. While the Bush administration clearly acted in the U.S. national interest to establish the GP, its widening membership demonstrated that other countries also shared a sense of urgency over the CBRN legacy challenge in Russia and other former Soviet republics. While no legal framework was set up to oversee the implementation of the GP, a Working Group was established to provide guidance and to serve as a coordinating mechanism.

ACCOMPLISHMENTS

This section outlines the main accomplishments of the GP from June 2002 through May 2011. Some accomplishments were directly in line with the original priorities set out in 2002, some involved the development of operational mechanisms to deliver multilateral threat reduction programs and projects, while others are best described as spin-off benefits. Key accomplishments include submarine dismantlement, chemical weapons destruction, the establishment of implementation networks of technical and project management experts, the development of "piggybacking" options for financing and implementing projects, the provision of support to established international organizations, and spin-off benefits.

Submarines and Chemical Weapons

As a result of the GP, the majority of Russia's decommissioned nuclear submarines had been dismantled by mid-2011 (and dismantlement has since been fully completed); more than one hundred submarines had been awaiting dismantlement some nine years earlier in 2002. Importantly, these submarines did not really pose a proliferation risk, but the significant amount of spent fuel and other high-level waste, whether stored on board or ashore at poorly secured locations, presented security and safety challenges. Andreeva Bay and Gremiikha in northwest Russia were the two main onshore bases where such materials were stored; the former site was one of the world's largest repositories for military spent nuclear fuel.

G8 assistance enabled Russia to dismantle its decommissioned nuclear submarines when it lacked the financial and technical resources to do so in a reasonable timescale. A spin-off benefit of this dismantlement work was the role it played in improving the project management expertise of Russian agencies as a result of working with other GP countries that had long experience of running such large projects. Moreover, joint work in this and other areas contributed to the development of confidence and trust between GP donors and beneficiaries.

In 2002, some forty thousand metric tons of chemical weapons stocks remained to be destroyed as part of Russia's commitment under the Chemical Weapons Convention to do so by 2012.[12] Progress up until 2002 had not been rapid because Russia had not allocated sufficient resources to the destruction process. Securing the funding and technical assistance of the other GP countries to complete the task was therefore a significant achievement for Russia. Moscow subsequently announced in 2010 that it would probably take an additional three years to complete the destruction because of technical and funding challenges, although this timetable later proved too optimistic. However, around half of the stocks had been destroyed by mid-2011.[13] Without the $1.5 billion contributed by GP countries, along with technical and project management expertise, the quantity of chemical weapons still waiting to be destroyed would have been much greater.

Implementation Networks

Another major accomplishment of the GP has been its contribution to enhancing coordination and collaboration at the operational level in the areas of technical knowledge, risk assessment, and the sharing of lessons derived from the planning and implementation of actual threat reduction projects. One example of such a network is the Contact Expert Group,[14] which has enhanced cooperation between those donors operating in northwest Russia. Similarly, the

Shchuch'ye Co-ordinating Working Group was established as a means for Canada, Russia, the United Kingdom, and the United States to share information on their national efforts in the field of chemical weapons destruction in order to maximize the overall effect of the Shchuch'ye Chemical Weapons Destruction Project. In another example, the Border Monitoring Working Group was set up in 2005, and this has resulted in coordination among the EU, the IAEA, and the United States on detection equipment and training issues.

These networks have helped to implement many and varied GP-supported projects with a higher degree of confidence that they will be effectively and safely implemented. According to a senior GP-related official from an EU member state, "the sharing of information with others and the transparency the structure offered was of great value."[15] Another official from a GP country thought the GP set up "a fantastic mechanism to provide a picture of what others were doing on threat reduction, sharing lessons learned and avoiding duplication of effort."[16] Another European official highlighted the GP's contribution to ascertaining "best practice."[17]

One case helps to illustrate the benefits of the GP as a networking mechanism: efforts to move about thirty metric tons of highly radioactive spent fuel at Andreeva Bay. Nuclear experts and contractors from Russia, Italy, Norway, Sweden, the United Kingdom, and the European Bank for Reconstruction and Development (EBRD) worked together to develop a plan to safely remove the spent fuel following the construction of the requisite infrastructure. The GP facilitated a partnership approach to the work at Andreeva Bay, including the development of close working relations between technical experts from all of the involved parties. This work was characterized by a significant amount of interaction at the bilateral and multilateral levels. The result was raised confidence among the involved parties to a point where all developed mutual trust and respect for one another.[18] The shipping away of spent fuel is now scheduled to begin in 2016, in part on a ship built by Italy as a contribution to the GP; the task could take until 2030 to complete.[19]

Support to the IAEA's Nuclear Security Work

With the exception of the G8 states, Norway, and Sweden, the other GP participants have contributed their financial pledges to support projects run by either other GP countries through "piggybacking" arrangements or the IAEA or EBRD to be applied to threat reduction projects.[20] In these respects the GP has proved to be a highly flexible burden-sharing instrument. With the IAEA, for example, GP funds have been committed by several governments to its Nuclear Security Fund (NSF), which is used to support nuclear security activity in IAEA member states upon request.²¹ Committing funds in this way has meant that GP participants have been able to use the agency's legal framework to support projects in countries where they do not have their own projects in place.²² Funding of the agency's nuclear security work is almost completely derived from voluntary contributions, so the significance of GP funds being channeled into the NSF is clear. Examples of NSF contributions by GP participants include those pledged by Belgium, Norway, and the United Kingdom during the Nuclear Security Summit of April 2010. Moreover, involvement with the IAEA by funding the NSF has allowed some GP states to gain insights from, and to influence, much larger projects than they would have been able to run on their own.

Piggybacking

The administrative burdens associated with setting up the necessary legal agreements to work in Russia, as well as the project management infrastructure, have meant that many non-GP countries were not able to set up and run their own projects. In this respect the GP's "piggybacking" mechanism has proved to be an effective means for smaller donors to work with others in the delivery of large-scale threat reduction projects. In short, it has allowed smaller donors to provide funding to a lead country that has then run specific projects. One GP-related official noted that "piggybacking was a very effective mechanism to enable countries without the manpower or technical expertise to support and manage GP projects."²³ Indeed, numerous countries have provided important funding contributions via piggybacking. For example, Australia provided ten million dollars to Japan's submarine dismantlement projects in the Russian Far East; South Korea provided two hundred fifty thousand to submarine dismantlement projects run by Canada and Norway; ten countries and the EU provided funding to a set of United Kingdom–run chemical weapons destruction projects at Shchuch'ye; and six countries provided thirty million to the U.S.-run Elimination of Weapons-Grade Plutonium Production program.

Spin-off Benefits

The GP has also realized some accomplishments that were unforeseen in 2002. The contribution of scientist redirection work to opening up the scientific community in Russia has resulted in links being forged within the domestic community itself as well as between it and the wider scientific world. Redirection efforts have also provided donor states with a means to engage stakeholders in Russia and the wider FSU. In 2005, for example, then-Senator Barack Obama noted, "Part of the strength that I saw of the CTR program was it gives a means of us engaging with the Russians in a constructive way and at multiple levels, not just at the top levels, but you know, you have military officers, intelligence officers who are in a cooperative-joint venture several layers down." Obama added that such relationships give the United States insight into the thinking of a range of government officials and make it easier to promote "broader issues related to democratization and liberalization."[24] Luongo and Hoehn similarly observed in 2003 that these interactions had resulted in "an improved Russian appreciation of nonproliferation; heightened levels of trust between U.S. and Russian officials, military officers, and scientists; and new political linkages and relationships not thought possible during the Cold War."[25]

Summary

From 2002 through 2011, the GP realized significant accomplishments in two of the four areas prioritized at Kananaskis: submarine dismantlement and chemical weapons destruction. This progress was made possible largely by collaborative GP threat reduction programs and projects. However, both of these areas were prioritized by Russia, so it is unsurprising that such positive progress was made. This was not the case for the two other priorities identified at Kananaskis—fissile material disposition and scientist redirection—that posed a greater proliferation and CBRN security threat but were de-emphasized by the Russian government after 2002. Beyond this macro level, major accomplishments were made at the operational level including the support made available to the IAEA, the establishment of implementation networks, and the development of piggybacking mechanisms to enable funding from smaller donors to be applied to larger projects managed by other GP states.

FAILINGS

This section outlines the main failings of the GP through 2011. The consensus nature of GP decision making and the domination of Moscow's priorities put a brake on developing a more targeted, and truly global, approach to threat reduction. This situation was exacerbated by the Working Group, which proved largely incapable of providing strategic guidance, did not perform effective assessments of GP-related projects and programs, and did not facilitate meaningful discussions of priorities and implementation issues. As a result of all this, the GP paid insufficient attention to pressing challenges such as enhancing the security of nuclear, radiological, and biological materials and engaging scientists in Russia, other former Soviet republics, and beyond. A further significant failing was that some G8 countries did not meet their original financial pledges of 2002.

Limited Scope

Several issues interacted to reduce the scope of the GP's CBRN threat reduction work in line with the priorities laid out in 2002. To begin with, the consensus approach to decision making within the GP enabled the Russian government to adopt an intransigent position with regard to which of the priorities identified at Kananaskis it wished to promote: submarine dismantlement and chemical weapons destruction. This domination of one country's priorities determined the GP's principal focus from 2002 through 2011 at the expense of the initiative taking a more inclusive approach to threat reduction in both a thematic and geographical sense, an approach that arguably would have focused international efforts on issues of greater relevance to preventing CBRN terrorism. Moreover, despite the GP being established because of concerns over CBRN terrorism, Russia and several countries bordering or close to Russia (Finland, Japan, Norway, and Sweden) believed that environmental issues, notably those related to nuclear safety, were equally as important as the proliferation and security implications of the CBRN legacy.

According to a senior official from a European G8 member state, "it was not at all clear why all [the other] countries allowed Russia to dominate the priorities" in this way.[26] One problem, as a senior official from a different European G8 member noted, is that "the wording in the Kananaskis documents relating to 'initially in Russia' could have been better defined."[27] The result was the inability of the GP to pursue a flexible approach to geographical expansion given the absence of Russia's political support. Ultimately, this meant that at least 70 percent of GP donor funds were expended on projects in Russia.[28]

After 2002, Moscow decided to reduce the priority it gave to plutonium disposition within the GP framework and ceased seeking funding in this sector. This issue had been identified by the G8 at Kanaskis as a high priority because of its direct relevance to terrorists interested in building an improvised nuclear device. It took until April 2010 to see further movement on this issue when the Russian and U.S. governments inked a plutonium disposal protocol at the Nuclear Security Summit.[29] In addition to plutonium disposition, the focus on Russia's priorities of submarines and chemical weapons meant that other urgent issues were also relatively neglected. Important examples include scientist redirection, bio-security, securing nuclear and radiological material beyond Russia, enhanced border monitoring for the detection of nuclear and radiological materials, replacing highly enriched uranium (HEU) in research reactors with low-enriched uranium (LEU), and the provision of expertise and training to states seeking or needing to improve their threat reduction activities or to implement more effective export controls on dual-use technology and materials.[30]

Similar to plutonium disposition, the Russian government also de-emphasized scientist redirection in the years after the 2002 summit. The Russian government came to believe that it had become capable of securing the legacy workforces associated with past weapons programs so that they no longer posed a proliferation challenge. As a result, international agreements with Russia after Kananaskis did not encompass scientist redirection, and so no additional initiatives in this area were launched beyond the International Science and Technology Center (ISTC) in Moscow and the Science and Technology Center Ukraine (STCU) in Kiev. Indeed, although an emphasis was placed on human capital during the Italian presidency of the G8 in 2009,[31] very little new work on scientist engagement was set in motion in the immediately following years. Outside of the ISTC and STCU only four GP states—Canada, France, the United Kingdom, and the United States—have funded significant redirection activities. These include, for example, the State Department's WMD Personnel Engagement and Redirection Program in Iraq and Libya, Britain's biological nonproliferation and redirection of WMD expertise work in Georgia, Iraq, and Libya, and France's efforts to establish connections between Russian laboratories and French enterprises.[32] The French worked ended early in 2009 because of financial constraints on the country's GP program.[33]

Delivering on Pledges

Beyond Russia's de-emphasis of fissile material disposition and redirection, another shortcoming of the GP during the period 2002–11 was the failure of some of the GP states to deliver on their financial pledges (see table 5.1).

Table 5.1 provides data on the 2002 pledges made by the G8, their estimated spending and commitments up to 2010, as well as the estimated percentage of their pledges met by early 2010. The data show that, although U.S. government spending fell in real terms, in cash terms Washington maintained a significant funding level for threat reduction work in the FSU and further afield. Two countries—France and Italy—are conspicuous because they appeared to spend only 15 to 20 percent of their pledges. Other significant donors fell short of their pledges by 35 to 50 percent, including Canada, Germany, Japan, the United Kingdom, and the EU. A number of issues help to shed light on these shortfalls:

- Some GP states did not make much progress in setting up projects in Russia during the period 2002–5 because the process proved to be highly bureaucratic.
- Russia's decision to de-emphasize work on plutonium disposition meant that significant funds pledged by France and Japan for this work were not reallocated as domestic budgetary constraints in both countries seem to have prevented this from happening.[34]

Table 5.1   G8 Pledges and Spending, 2002–12

Donor	Pledge	Estimated Spending and Commitments to 2010*	Estimated Percentage of Pledge Met by Early 2010
United States	$10 billion	$10 billion	100
Canada	CA$1 billion	CA$650 million	65
EU	€1 billion	€600 million[†]	~60
France	€750 million	€135 million	18
Germany	Up to €1.5 billion	€925 million	62
Italy	€1 billion	€140 million	14
Japan	$200 million	$105 million	52
United Kingdom	Up to $750 million	$450 million[‡]	~60
Russia	$2 billion	$5.6 billion[§]	280
Total	~$20 billion	~$18 billion	

* Calculated from financial data published by the Global Partnership Working Group, "GPWG Annual Report 2010: Consolidated Report Data—ANNEX A" (June 2010), http://www.canadainternational.gc.ca /g8/assets/pdfs/FINAL%20-%20GPWG%20Report%202010%20-%20Annex%20A%20-%20June%20 17%20_2_.pdf, accessed 14 June 2011. Dollar figures are in U.S. dollars unless otherwise indicated.

[†] Only data on individual program budgets are presented in the GP annual report—totaling some €550 million. However, these budget figures include some expenditure incurred pre-2002 and also exclude contributions to the European Bank for Reconstruction and Development (EBRD) for Chernobyl and work in northwest Russia. The spending figure is therefore the authors' estimate of spending on GP-related work up to 2010.

[‡] Although the U.K. pledge was in U.S. dollars, its GP returns are in pounds. The exchange rate conversion for the purposes of this table is £1 = $1.45.

[§] Increased from $2 billion to $6 billion in 2006 at the 2006 St. Petersburg G8 Summit chaired by the Russian Federation.

- Russia's financial position improved substantially over the four years from 2002 and a perception quickly developed in other G8 countries that Moscow was now in a much better economic position to afford to pay for its own threat reduction work and that external financial help at the levels agreed in 2002 at Kananaskis was no longer necessary. The decision by Russia in 2006 to raise its GP pledge to six billion dollars from two billion in part mirrored the growing reluctance of its G8 partners to subsidize work in that country.
- Many of Moscow's G8 partners became increasingly concerned that as the GP progressed, the initiative was overly focused on Russia at the expense of more pressing CBRN challenges.

It is clear that, in the absence of the additional four billion dollars from Russia, the shortfalls in spending from other G8 states would have resulted in a much bigger overall shortfall from the target of twenty billion highlighted in 2002.

Working Group Failings

In addition to budget shortfalls and Russia's de-emphasis of fissile material disposition and scientist redirection, there were clear problems in the first decade of the GP with the operation of the GP Working Group. This was most notable with respect to the group's poor performance in providing strategic direction, conducting comprehensive assessments of work conducted, and monitoring progress. These problems were largely the result of its decision-making process and the lack of a standing body to ensure consistency of approach over multiple years.

In terms of strategic direction, a senior official from a G8 country noted that "the GP Working Group was not a particularly effective forum for driving forward new policy approaches largely due to the influence of the Russian Federation and the clear desire of all successive chairs of the Group to present a consensus way forward."[35] A different GP-related official stated that "because [the Working Group] spent some 60 to 70 percent of its time agreeing on the reporting statements for each presidency, it could only be a light touch on the political steering wheel and expecting it to undertake detailed strategic work was wishful thinking."[36] Moreover, there was a lack of coordination over priorities in terms of the projects to pursue, there was a lack of opportunity on the part of non-G8 GP countries to influence priorities despite the investment of significant financial and expertise resources by some of them,[37] and there was no significant role for the IAEA in GP discussions despite its central role in the context of nuclear and radiological security.[38]

More could have been done to promote the GP's successful projects as well as the implementation networks developed under the GP umbrella. This lack of effective promotion meant that the profile of the GP was not raised sufficiently with respect to attracting potential new participants, whether donors or recipients. Related to this failing has been the very limited nature of the official reviews of the GP that have been conducted. Reviews like the one conducted under the German G8 presidency in 2007 have not contained significant analysis and have been constrained by the importance attached to maintaining consensus.[39] According to a senior official from a European G8 member state, the group was "not an effective mechanism to undertake a detailed review and evaluation of the various GP programs."[40] While Russia's domination of the priorities made it difficult to conduct an in-depth assessment of the GP, the lack of comprehensive evaluations meant that accomplishments and failings were not effectively flagged and so did not prompt changes in priorities.

While the G8 stated their preparedness in 2002 to add new recipients to the GP, only Kazakhstan and Ukraine subsequently joined in this capacity.[41] In this respect the Working Group does not appear to have spent sufficient time recruiting new donors and potential recipients and lacked a strategy for doing so. This is despite the group's recognition of the importance of broadening the GP's geographical base.[42]

Summary

In terms of the main failings of the GP outlined above, a key factor was the apparent blocking role played by Russia in preventing both the geographical expansion of the GP as well as a more concerted focus on the two neglected Kananaskis priorities: fissile material disposition and scientist redirection. These other priorities are of much greater relevance to preventing proliferation and CBRN terrorism compared to submarine dismantlement and chemical weapons destruction, both of which were championed by Moscow. The Working Group also failed to provide strategic direction, to perform effective outreach, and to conduct thorough evaluations, all of which undermined the impact of the GP. The fact that several G8 countries also failed to live up to their 2002 funding pledges compounded these problems.

DEVELOPMENTS AFTER 2011

At the 2010 G8 Summit in Canada, participants outlined possible future directions for the GP. These included greater efforts in the areas of nuclear and radiological security, bio-security, scientist redirection, and support for UN Security Council Resolution (UNSCR) 1540, which calls on all states to implement a wide range of measures to criminalize and help prevent CBRN terrorism. The following year, the Deauville Summit decided to extend the GP indefinitely, but without securing new funding commitments. The Summit Declaration and a supporting study document called for completing existing projects in Russia while also broadening the scope of the GP. The 2011 summit endorsed the four areas of emphasis that were highlighted in 2010 and also called for efforts to add new members and to improve coordination with relevant international organizations.[43]

In 2012, the United States served as chair of the GP. In order to promote the priorities adopted in 2011, the GP under U.S. leadership established five sub-working groups, dealing with bio-security, membership expansion, promoting Centers of Excellence, nuclear and radiological security, and chemical security. The U.S. chair also began inviting relevant international organizations to attend GP meetings and sought to deepen the involvement of non-G8 GP members as well.[44]

The following year, the United Kingdom held the chair of the GP, and it sought to build on prior efforts to broaden the Partnership Program. In December 2013, the United Kingdom's report on its chairmanship highlighted just how far the program had developed. The GP priorities emphasized by the United Kingdom in 2013 included facilitating the implementation of UNSCR 1540 and expanding the membership of the GP, among other things. The United Kingdom also pioneered a new "match-making" approach to use the GP as a vehicle to more effectively, and on a timely basis, bring together expertise, funding, and specific CBRN security requirements, while emphasizing the centrality of "complementarity" to avoid duplication of effort with other nonproliferation-related groups and initiatives and support them instead.[45] One passage in the U.K. report of December 2013 was particularly prescient in terms of the events about to unfold in Ukraine:

> In its first decade since inception in 2002, the GP concentrated its threat reduction efforts on large scale projects in Russia and other FSU states. Many of these projects are now largely complete, and the GP decided to refocus towards projects in other regions of the world, in order to address broader WMD and terrorist threats. The GP has already broadened its identity by expanding beyond the core G8 and has moved away from a "donor and recipient" model towards one characterised by a genuine security partnership. Under the UK's presidency, steps were taken to expand this further and the Global Partnership now benefits from perspectives from previously underrepresented regions.[46]

Soon after this report, events in Ukraine raised questions about the future of the GP given Russia's ejection from the G8 in March 2014 following its annexation of Crimea. Russia had, rather ironically, been scheduled to host the next G8 Summit at Sochi on the Black Sea. Following its expulsion, the summit was moved to Brussels and reestablished under the G7 format of pre-1998. Despite these tumultuous developments, the GP continued to function in 2014. Indeed, the G7 Summit that June produced a declaration on nonproliferation in which the participants stated, "We affirm our commitment to the Global Partnership," describing this commitment as "unwavering." The statement also noted that since 2013 the GP had added the Philippines, Hungary, and Spain as new members.[47]

According to knowledgeable sources, both the remaining G7 states and non-G7 members of the GP had wanted to continue their work and feared losing momentum after the events in Ukraine. As a result, they scheduled a number of GP-related meetings in the months after the G7 Summit. Given the situation in Ukraine, the GP gave special focus to its projects in that country. Even before the events in Ukraine, work on GP projects in Russia had already slowed down, and the dispute over Ukraine means that GP work in Russia will continue to progress slowly if at all for the foreseeable future.[48]

It is important to note that if the events in Ukraine had occurred several years previously, then the GP would have confronted an entirely different and much more problematic situation, specifically because Russia had been so central to the evolution of the program over most of its first decade of existence. Indeed, the fact that the GP had evolved in recent years to become a much broader affair—in terms of membership, geographical scope, and functional focus—arguably made responding to Russia a much more straightforward exercise from a GP perspective than would have been the case just a few years earlier.

KEY FINDINGS

This section briefly summarizes findings with respect to the sources of cooperation with the GP and the program's effectiveness as a nonproliferation tool. Among the factors listed by Knopf in chapter 1 that can be helpful for explaining cooperation, four appear to be particularly relevant: (1) self-interest, (2) U.S. leadership, (3) norms and identity, and (4) ideas, learning, and transnational networks. Self-interest proved to be an important motivation for states participating in the GP. After 9/11, several of the G8 governments perceived a potential danger from CBRN terrorism, and many other participating states, while not likely targets of CBRN terrorism, also had good reason to be concerned about the potential risks because of their economic and political ties to important partner countries. Recipient countries also had a self-interest in the financial and technical assistance they would obtain.

The United States took the lead role in setting up the GP. Importantly, however, it did not and could not act alone. Canada also played a key role in launching the initiative. In addition, the explicitly multilateral nature of the program did much to facilitate participation by other states. U.S. leadership was effective in part because it was harnessed to a multilateral framework and capitalized on an altered strategic paradigm in the wake of 9/11.

Norms and identity also seem to have played a role, especially in the program's expansion. States that joined beyond the original G8 did not necessarily face a direct threat of CBRN terrorism. Instead, they more likely wanted to express solidarity with friends and allies at risk and to show they could be members of the club of states that take responsibility for addressing the threat of CBRN terror. The norm of multilateralism also contributed to the obligation states felt to support the initiative. The more recent emphasis placed by the GP on assisting states to fulfill their 1540 obligations further adds to the role of normative considerations, given that 1540 emerged from action by the UN Security Council.

Ideas and learning are also apparent in the way the GP built on the existing model of the Nunn-Lugar CTR program. The idea of threat reduction and the lesson learned from CTR that such a program could be largely successful paved the way for the GP. Indeed, some GP programs involved contributing funding to existing CTR efforts. Finally, transnational networks proved important in implementation. The technical and operational networks that developed at the working level proved relatively effective in ensuring implementation of projects, especially compared with the less effective cooperation witnessed at the strategic planning level.

Turning to effectiveness, the GP has had clear successes within an overall mixed record. The GP made good progress on two of its initial four priorities: submarine dismantlement and chemical weapons destruction. It made less progress on its other two priorities, however, even though these arguably were more directly related to preventing CBRN terrorism. The record of expansion is similarly mixed. Additional countries joined the GP, but threat reduction projects have not been implemented in as many countries as would be desirable.

It remains to be seen how effectively the GP will operate in the future with an expanded membership and a broader scope of activities, while simultaneously dealing with frictions with a key original participant, Russia. One pressing challenge going forward will be the financial aspect. While the original ten-year funding pledge seized headlines in 2002, specific funding commitments by GP members have dramatically diminished in number and scale since the GP was renewed at Deauville. In part this reflects the move away from large capital projects toward a portfolio of smaller, less costly projects.[49] But it also reflects the fact that GP states are still managing their economic recoveries from the great recession, and this continues to have an effect on government spending.

CONCLUSION

This chapter has examined the establishment and implementation of the GP, its accomplishments, and its failings. The initiative was established after 9/11 in response to a perceived heightening of the CBRN terrorist threat. The Bush administration played the guiding role as the instigator of the GP, but the widening of the GP beyond the original G8 states demonstrated that many other governments also perceived a significant risk to be posed by legacy CBRN materials and weapons in Russia and the wider former Soviet Union, although their reasons for concern were not always the same.

During the initial ten-year time frame set for the GP, significant progress on two of the four Kananaskis priorities—submarine dismantlement and chemical weapons destruction—was made possible because Russia supported these goals. Progress on the arguably more important priorities—fissile material disposition and scientist redirection—was stunted, however, because Moscow de-emphasized these after 2002, and the consensus approach to decision making made it difficult for the other G8 countries to rebalance the attention accorded to the four priorities in the period up to 2011. Russia also played a blocking role in terms of the geographical expansion of the GP for most of the period under study.

The informality and flexibility of the GP entailed both strengths and weaknesses. The strengths notably involved the operational level where accomplishments included the establishment of implementation networks, the development of piggybacking mechanisms to enable funding from smaller donors to be applied to larger projects managed by other GP states, and the support made available to the IAEA. The weaknesses were primarily at the strategic level and involved issues of strategic direction, prioritization, effective evaluation, and associated decision making. The fact the GP continued to function following the upheaval of Russia's expulsion from the G8 is a promising sign, but it will be up to participating states to take advantage of the opportunities created by maintaining the GP framework.

Notes

1. "Statement by G8 Leaders: The G8 Global Partnership Against the Spread of Weapons and Materials of Mass Destruction" (G8 Summit, Kananaskis, Canada, June 27, 2002), www.g8.utoronto.ca/summit/2002kananaskis/arms.html.

2. This chapter draws on and selectively updates a longer study by the authors. See Alan Heyes, Wyn Q. Bowen, and Hugh Chalmers, "The Global Partnership Against WMD: Success and Shortcomings of G8 Threat Reduction since 9/11" (Whitehall Paper 76, Royal United Services Institute [RUSI], 2011). That study, and this chapter, were informed by dozens of interviews with officials from numerous government departments, international organizations, project contractors, and nongovernmental organizations. These interviews were made possible by a grant from the MacArthur Foundation. All interviews were conducted on a not-for-attribution basis. The authors identify each interview subject in subsequent references by a unique letter and number code. Where other sources are not noted, information in this chapter comes from the research interviews and the larger RUSI report.

3. "G8 Global Partnership: Assessment and Options for Future Programming" (G8 Summit, Deauville, France, May 26–27, 2011), www.g20-g8.com/g8-g20/g8/english/the-2011-summit/declarations-and-reports/appendices/g8-global-partnership-assessment-and-options-for.1354.html; "Deauville G8 Declaration" (G8 Summit, Deauville, France, May 26–27, 2011), 21, www.whitehouse.gov/sites/default/files/uploads/deauville_declaration_final_-_eng_8h.pdf.

4. Statement by Senator Richard Lugar, in "A Progress Report on 10+10 over 10," Hearing before the Committee on Foreign Relations, United States Senate, 107th Congress, Second Session, 9 October 2002, S Hrg 107-799 (Washington, D.C.: Government Printing Office, 2003), 2.

5. Oral testimony of John Bolton, undersecretary of state for arms control and international security affairs, in ibid., 9–10.

6. "Statement by G8 Leaders."

7. Ibid.

8. Interview L, written communication, October 1, 2009; interview M2, May 28, 2009.

9. Opening statement by Senator Joe Biden, chairman, Senate Foreign Relations Committee, in "Progress Report on 10+10 over 10," 1.

10. "Statement by G8 Leaders."

11. The member states as of 2011 were Australia, Belgium, Canada, Czech Republic, Denmark, Finland, France, Germany, Ireland, Italy, Japan, the Netherlands, New Zealand, Norway, Poland, Republic of Korea, Russian Federation, Sweden, Switzerland, Ukraine, United Kingdom, and United States. The GP has continued to expand its membership since 2011, but Russia was expelled from the G8 following its annexation of Crimea in 2014.

12. Much of Russia's chemical weapons stockpile was weaponized, and around thirty thousand metric tons comprised nerve agents (sarin, soman, VX) contained in more than four million air-delivered, artillery, and rocket munitions, some of which were relatively portable and therefore at risk of theft.

13. Chris Schneidmiller, "Russia to Miss Chemical Weapons Disposal Deadline," *Global Security Newswire*, June 30, 2010, http://gsn.nti.org/gsn/nw_20100630_4072.php.

14. See International Atomic Energy Agency, "Contact Expert Group," www.iaea.org/OurWork/ST/NE/NEFW/CEG/index.html.

15. Interview E1, June 2, 2009.

16. Interview K3, June 1, 2009.

17. Interview B2, April 15, 2009.

18. For more details, see the brief case study in Heyes, Bowen, and Chalmers, "Global Partnership," annex C.

19. "Russian Waste Transport Ship Completes Test Mission," *World Nuclear News*, July 22, 2014, www.world-nuclear-news.org/WR-Russian-nuclear-waste-transport-ship-completes-test-mission-22071401.html.

20. The EBRD has received GP-labeled funding for the Northern Dimension Environmental Partnership's nuclear-related work in northwest Russia, which the bank manages. Interview C2, July 28, 2009.

21. Jack Boureston and Andrew K. Semmel, "The IAEA and Nuclear Security: Trends and Prospects" (Policy Analysis Brief, Stanley Foundation, December 2010), www.stanleyfoundation.org/publications/pab/Boureston_SemmelPAB1210.pdf.

22. The United Kingdom has, for example, contributed to NSF security upgrades at the radioactive waste repository near Fayzabad, Tajikistan, as well as security upgrades at the Armenian Nuclear Power Plant. See U.K. Department of Energy and Climate Change, Global Threat Reduction Programme, "Case Study: Nuclear Security Programme," www.gov.uk/government/case-studies/global-threat-reduction-programme-nuclear-security-programme.

23. Interview M1, May 28, 2009.

24. Richard G. Lugar and Barack Obama, "Challenges Ahead For Cooperative Threat Reduction" (Washington, D.C.: Council on Foreign Relations, November 1, 2005) (rush transcript, Federal News Service), www.cfr.org/publication/9138/.

25. Kenneth N. Luongo and William E. Hoehn III, "Reform and Expansion of Cooperative Threat Reduction," *Arms Control Today* 33, no. 5 (June 2003).

26. Interview D2, July 6, 2009.

27. Interview E1, June 2, 2009.

28. This figure is based on calculations derived from data in the "Global Partnership Working Group Annual Report, 2010," annex A, http://g8.gc.ca/about/past-summits/summit-documents-2004/global-partnership-report/. The financial labeling system in the report does not permit greater accuracy.

29. U.S. Department of State, "Signing of the Plutonium Disposal Protocol" (April 13, 2010), www.state.gov/secretary/rm/2010/04/140120.htm.

30. Comparatively few biological-related projects were launched under the GP in its first decade. The three countries to support projects in this field were Canada, the United King-

dom, and the U.S., which labeled them as "GP-related." As noted below, the GP is now giving greater attention to this area. Specific program details can be accessed from the Consolidated Report Data sections of the Global Partnership Annual Reports. Some of these are unfortunately no longer available online, but some have been collected and posted by the Partnership for Global Security at www.partnershipforglobalsecurity-archive.org/Official%20Documents/G-8%20Global%20Partnership/index.asp.

31. GP Working Group, "Recommendations for a Coordinated Approach in the Field of Global Weapons of Mass Destruction Knowledge Proliferation and Scientist Engagement" (G8 Summit, L'Aquila, Italy, 2009), www.g8italia2009.it/static/G8_Allegato/Annex_B,2.pdf.

32. "GPWG Annual Report 2009 Consolidated Report Data: Annex A" (G8 Summit, L'Aquila, Italy, July 8–10, 2009).

33. Interview D1, July 6, 2009.

34. Ibid.

35. Ibid.

36. Interview E1, 2 June 2009.

37. Interview L, written contribution, October 1, 2009; interview M1, May 28, 2009.

38. Interview H1, February 27, 2010; interview E1, June 2, 2009.

39. "Global Partnership Review" (G8 Summit, Heiligendamm, Germany, June 2007), www.g-8.de/Webs/G8/EN/G8Summit/SummitDocuments/summit-documents.html.

40. Interview K6, May 27, 2009.

41. The United States and United Kingdom gave funds and technical assistance to decommission Kazakhstan's B-350 reactor, which was used to produce weapons-grade plutonium, and for projects encompassing redirection of scientists to nonweapons work and the securing of radiological sources. The GP's work in Ukraine focused primarily on Chernobyl, although projects on redirection and enhancing the security of nuclear facilities were also pursued.

42. See, for example, "Global Partnership Review" (G8 2007 Heiligendamm Summit).

43. "G8 Global Partnership," and "Deauville G8 Declaration."

44. U.S. Department of State, Bureau of International Security and Nonproliferation, "2012 GP Report," www.state.gov/t/isn/gp2013/gpreport/index.htm.

45. U.K. Foreign & Commonwealth Office, "Global Partnership Against the Spread of Materials and Weapons of Mass Destruction: President's Report for 2013" (December 2013), 5, 9–10.

46. Ibid., 6.

47. Although not noted, Mexico also joined in late 2012. "G-7 Declaration on Non-Proliferation and Disarmament for 2014" (Brussels, Belgium, June 5, 2014), http://iipdigital.usembassy.gov/st/english/texttrans/2014/06/20140610301019.html#axzz387WP7uwU.

48. Personal communications by informed sources with Jeff Knopf, July 2014.

49. Alan Heyes, "The Global Partnership on WMD: A Work in Progress," *Arms Control Today* 43, no. 3 (April 2013): 8–13.

CHAPTER SIX

The Proliferation Security Initiative

The Achievements and Limits of an Informal Approach to Cooperation

EMMA BELCHER

THE PROLIFERATION SECURITY INITIATIVE (PSI) had controversial beginnings in the George W. Bush administration. Over time, however, it has become more widely accepted as one tool among others to prevent proliferation. The PSI is a nonbinding political pledge through which states voluntarily commit to efforts to interdict shipments of illicit materials related to weapons of mass destruction (WMD) to and from states and non-state actors.[1] President Bush announced the PSI in May 2003 along with a list of initial participants—Australia, France, Germany, Italy, Japan, the Netherlands, Poland, Portugal, Spain, the United Kingdom, and the United States. These initial participants released an agreed-upon Statement of Interdiction Principles in September 2003. Additional countries can join the PSI simply by endorsing its statement of principles. The founding members stressed that the PSI would be "an activity, not an organization."[2] This reflected a strong preference in the Bush administration, especially on the part of its undersecretary of state for arms control and international security, John Bolton, who played a leading role in establishing the PSI, to avoid creating a new, formal international bureaucracy.

At the outset, critics saw the PSI as an example of the Bush administration's "cowboy diplomacy" and charged it with undermining the nonproliferation regime and contravening international law.[3] Yet, the PSI quickly gathered momentum and perceived legitimacy, with membership growing from 11 states at its inception to 105 states by 2015.[4] To a degree, the PSI fits well with a larger theme of this volume concerning the growing prominence of operational activities and working-level relationships. Working-level relationships quickly became important in the rush to operationalize the vague high-level political commitment announced by President Bush in May 2003. Subsequent operational activities to implement the PSI have increased opportunities for transnational cooperation at the working level.

This chapter begins by tracing the origins and evolution of the PSI. It then explores explanations for cooperation, drawing on the seven factors Knopf derives from the literature. Next, it evaluates effectiveness of the PSI as a cooperative mechanism. The chapter concludes with a discussion of lessons of the PSI case. One key lesson is that an informal, nonbinding approach can be an effective way to launch international cooperation, but careful consideration must be given to which countries are excluded initially, because their resentment can lead to greater resistance to a new initiative than might otherwise occur.

ORIGINS AND EVOLUTION OF THE PSI

The PSI largely fits the four-stage cooperation process outlined by Knopf (proposal making, establishment, enlargement, and implementation), with a caveat: there were two distinct stages of implementation. One stage came after establishment, somewhat simultaneously with enlargement, and another implementation stage came after enlargement began, with the creation of the Operational Experts Group. President Bush's demand for swift creation of the PSI explains why implementation took place in these two stages: the first stage of implementation involved quickly turning a vague idea into something actual, while fleshing out the operational details took place in a later stage.

Proposal Making

The United States first proposed the idea of a cooperative mechanism to the United Kingdom and Australia following the interdiction of a Cambodian ship, the *So San*, in December 2002. U.S. officials had intelligence that the *So San* was transporting proliferation-related materials from the Democratic People's Republic of Korea (DPRK) to Yemen. U.S. officials asked Spanish authorities to interdict the ship.[5] The Spanish subsequently discovered twelve SCUD missiles concealed beneath thousands of bags of cement. Ultimately, at the request of the United States, the Spanish allowed the ship and its cargo to proceed. According to U.S. officials, the United States asked the Spanish to drop the case because the U.S. government valued Yemen as a partner against terrorism and did not want to alienate its government.[6] While the interdiction did not result in the seizure of proliferation-related materials, it did prompt serious thought within the U.S. government about how to deal with such situations in the future.[7]

The problem of illicit shipments of WMD-related materials was not new; it had been on the U.S. radar well before the *So San* incident. Nor was interdiction a new tool in combating illicit trafficking. U.S. and other navies had conducted interdictions for years to counter narcotics trafficking and other illicit activities, and had cooperated with each other on an ad hoc basis. Yet just prior to the *So San* interdiction, the United States had received intelligence that shipments of illicit material for WMD purposes were increasing in intensity. National Security Council (NSC) officials had established an Interdiction Sub-Policy Coordinating Committee just weeks before the *So San* episode to deal with the very problem.[8]

In the wake of the *So San* incident, President Bush, who reportedly took great personal interest in the issue,[9] directed his senior officials to investigate the issue of interdiction as a matter of priority. When government experts analyzed legal and operational issues of WMD-related interdiction, it became clear that the United States would need international support to maximize the chances of successful interdictions. As John Bolton notes, "Basically, we felt that better advance coordination among diplomatic, military, and intelligence components of like-minded governments would result in better planning and therefore better implementation of future interdiction efforts. Moreover, if interdiction had a higher political priority, there would surely be a significantly greater number of operations, and hence a significantly enhanced actual and deterrent effect against proliferation."[10] This shows that, even among administration officials reputed to have a strong preference for unilateral action, there was recognition that combating WMD proliferation would require a certain level of international cooperation. Thus, the United States sought to explicitly forge a commitment by states to cooperate on the particular issue of interdicting shipments that could aid WMD proliferation.

Although an in-depth examination of institutional design is beyond the scope of this chapter, it is important to understand the U.S. rationale for proposing cooperation in the form of a non–legally binding political pledge. Certainly, there were alternatives. One option was to pursue a change in international law to allow for interdiction absent flag-state permission in cases of WMD proliferation suspicion. To do this, the United States could have tried to build a new custom of interdiction over time by directly challenging current practice and interdicting on the high seas absent the proper legal authority. Undersecretary Bolton apparently supported this option.[11] Such a policy would have been fraught with political risk, however, as interdiction on this basis could have been viewed as an act of war.

Another option would have been to amend existing treaties, such as the United Nations Convention on the Law of the Sea (UNCLOS) or the Treaty on the Non-Proliferation of Nuclear Weapons (NPT), to permit interdiction on the basis of illicit WMD activities. However, this course of action would have been extremely difficult. The limited U.S. political capital due to its failure to ratify UNCLOS and the general difficulty of amending the NPT meant it was politically unrealistic to hold out any hope for amendment.

Yet another option was to attempt to negotiate a new treaty that would allow for interdiction based on suspicion of illicit WMD trafficking. Because of its legally binding nature, a treaty could have helped to grant legitimacy to interdiction and credibly signaled parties' intent to comply, thereby increasing the chances of deterring violations. However, the agreement would have applied only to those states that ratified it—which would likely not include all states of proliferation concern. Even if a critical mass of states did support a new treaty, it could have taken a long time to negotiate and enter into force, treaty terms might have been watered down to the lowest common denominator, and there would still be no guarantee of compliance. The United States wanted to deal with the matter urgently and sought a strong commitment from states whose reliability was not in question.

Recognizing that seeking a treaty was not optimal given their priorities, U.S. officials sought an alternative way to encourage states to cooperate. They decided to pursue a non–legally binding political pledge. Compared with a treaty, such a pledge might be easier to negotiate, contain stronger commitments, and be faster to implement. A political pledge was not without its risks, however. Without the gravity that legally binding commitments convey, states could more easily decide when to comply and, ultimately, could choose to abandon their commitment more easily. Nonetheless, U.S. officials decided a non–legally binding agreement was the best approach and made a proposal to other states accordingly.

Proposal making was itself a multistep process. The United States considered very carefully to which states it wanted to propose cooperation through the PSI and then approached potential partners sequentially. It wanted to secure commitments from like-minded states that viewed the threat of WMD proliferation in a similar light, would take action to prevent such proliferation, and were important from a proliferation standpoint. First, the United States approached the United Kingdom and Australia, close allies of the United States who shared intelligence with Washington and had been beside the United States in the Iraq war. Once the United Kingdom and Australia provided in-principle support, officials from the three countries conferred on which other countries to invite to join them. They used several criteria to consider potential candidates. States needed to be an important part of the global supply chain (with jurisdiction over brokers and traders who dealt in WMD-related materials), to be geostrategically significant, to have defense capabilities and a willingness to use them, and to hold a similar view of the threat. The three initial partners also considered which states were actively engaged on the North Korean proliferation issue. They gave special consideration to those that might have connections to and enough bilateral leverage over other important states that they could influence them and eventually bring them into the agreement. Japan, for example, was desirable given its geostrategic location in the north Pacific, its large port, and potential influence over South Korea.[12]

In determining which states to approach, one official reports the United States did not want to be seen to be acquiring only easy partners, or "low-hanging fruit."[13] According to this source, administration officials had learned lessons about coalition building from their experience in Iraq and felt they needed to be more inclusive of states with diverging views, and not just the war coalition. France and Germany were obvious candidates, and despite concerns among some U.S. officials that France and Germany might create roadblocks, President Bush made the decision that they should be included. Apparently, he felt it best to have France and Germany working with them on the inside, rather than potentially creating problems from the outside. Some U.S. officials also believed France and Germany saw this as an opportunity to reengage the United States following tensions over the Iraq war.[14]

Building the PSI was as much about who was excluded as who was included. The United States decided to exclude those they felt might make reaching agreement difficult. It viewed Russia and China as the main obstacles. According to Bolton, "One reason Russia and China were not in the Core Group to begin with was that we wanted to get something going that was not wishy-washy or watered down, and then bring others on board. . . . Gaining adherence to our statement was less important as a first step than [having] a strong statement."[15]

U.S. officials believed Russia needed to be involved at some point, not only for its WMD capabilities, but because of its status as one of the five permanent (P5) members of the UN Security Council. However, they excluded Russia at first because they feared including Russian officials in the initial negotiations would slow down agreement or even preclude reaching one altogether.[16] Furthermore, officials did not view Russia as one of the most problematic sources of illicit activities, such as training, acquisition, or selling of parts. This, in their view, made Russia less of an essential partner at the formation stage.[17]

U.S. officials had similar reservations about the prospect of reaching agreement with China. Chinese sensitivities in the South China Sea, U.S. sanctions on Chinese firms that had traded with the DPRK,[18] and a controversial interdiction in 1993, which had strained U.S.-China relations, meant China was likely to view the PSI with suspicion. The 1993 incident was sparked when Clinton administration officials believed a Chinese ship, the *Yinhe*, was transporting chemical weapons precursors to Iran and requested permission to board and search the ship. Chinese officials granted permission to a joint Saudi-U.S. team, which did not find any illicit material.[19] This experience seems to have made Chinese officials wary of cooperating with the United States on interdiction. Even if China had agreed to consider PSI participation at the initial stage, however, U.S. officials felt that Chinese wariness would have made reaching the type of agreement they wanted difficult.[20] They did keep Chinese and Russian officials informed as the PSI took shape, but did not seek their inclusion in developing the agreement.[21]

By limiting initial participation to states with a like-minded view of the WMD threat and a willingness to take action, the United States sought to quickly conclude an agreement on a strong statement of principles.[22] For this reason, it proposed cooperation through an informal mechanism. Ultimately, France, Germany, Italy, Japan, the Netherlands, Poland, Portugal, and Spain agreed to join the United States, the United Kingdom, and Australia.[23] These participants became known as the Core Group.

Establishment

The manner in which the United States established the PSI was novel. President Bush announced the PSI and its participants in a speech in Krakow, Poland, in May 2003, armed with only an in-principle agreement to cooperate on interdiction. The contours of the agreement were yet to be determined, and there was not even preliminary text for public release. Despite this, President Bush declared, "Today I announce a new effort to fight proliferation called the Proliferation Security Initiative. The United States and a number of our close allies, including Poland, have begun working on new agreements to search planes and ships carrying suspect cargo and to seize illegal weapons or missile technologies. Over time, we will extend this partnership as broadly as possible to keep the world's most destructive weapons away from our shores and out of the hands of our common enemies."[24] The U.S. rationale for announcing the PSI before it had a negotiated agreement was to creatively address a problem it saw as urgent and to enable PSI to have an immediate deterrent effect. States aimed to send a message to would-be proliferators that they were closely monitoring their movements and would not hesitate to take action against them. The ultimate goal was to change proliferators' risk-reward calculus and make interdiction unnecessary in the first instance. As one former official notes, making the announcement before there was a negotiated agreement meant the PSI was initially little more than a "bluff."[25]

Following the May 2003 announcement, working-level officials from participant states had the task of moving quickly to develop the PSI's text. As John Bolton recalls, "We needed to flesh out the two sentences in Bush's Krakow speech and make PSI as real as possible."[26] The principles and operating procedures would be hashed out in the first and second implementation stages, respectively.

Implementation—Stage 1

Officials of Core Group states met several times over the next few months to develop the PSI's principles. Negotiation was laborious,[27] even though the agreement was nonbinding. The negotiations involved several issues, including the PSI's relationship to existing international institutions and law and how specific the principles should be.

Early on, international partners insisted that the PSI adhere to existing international law, rather than endorse Bolton's vision of interdictions on the high seas absent flag state permission (in violation of international law).[28] This led to explicit language in the PSI's principles that it would be "consistent with national legal authorities and relevant international law and frameworks, including the UN Security Council."[29]

Participants considered explicitly defining WMD-related materials and actors of proliferation concern, but eventually decided against doing so. Regarding WMD-related material, participants decided not to reinvent the wheel and resolved to draw on lists developed by complementary regimes—including the Missile Technology Control Regime, the Nuclear Suppliers Group, and the Australia Group (dealing with chemical and biological weapons). This would avoid duplication of effort and allow participants to adapt as new technologies came on the market. Regarding actors of proliferation concern, PSI participants decided against naming specific states or non-state groups, so as not to exclude those that might emerge as threats in the future.[30]

By September 2003, the United States was eager to publish details as soon as possible, but it had not yet secured final agreement on a statement of principles. France, in particular, was unhappy with what it considered a lack of reference to international law, and requested additional time. To push the agreement through, a U.S. official reported that the United States gave participants the impression that the principles could be amended at a later stage, even though the United States knew it would be difficult to make changes down the road. Bolton also reminded the working-level officials that their heads of government had already publicly made an in-principle agreement with President Bush. Bolton informed the group he would announce the principles as they were and any state that did not agree with the text could withdraw from the PSI. This pressured the officials to agree to the principles, and no state withdrew.[31]

These tactics led to France's begrudging agreement, enabling the Core Group to release its Statement of Interdiction Principles after a PSI meeting on September 4, 2003.[32] These principles call on all states, whether or not they are part of the PSI, to interdict shipments of WMD-related materials to state and non-state actors of proliferation concern, to strengthen their own domestic frameworks to prevent illicit trade in such materials, to share relevant information about suspected proliferation activities, and to consider permitting their own vessels and aircraft to be inspected by others who have reasonable suspicions that they are being used to ship WMD materials. Through these principles, the vague commitment Bush announced in May was realized.

Enlargement

Initial PSI membership was restricted to an invitation-only basis. Once the United States had assembled its preferred partners, it opened the PSI to general membership. It is difficult to determine the rate of enlargement in the early months and years of the PSI because little information was publicly released about when states acceded. By the time the Interdiction Principles were released in September 2003, U.S. officials claimed that 50 states had expressed their support for the initiative, although they were not all publicly identified. By its ten-year anniversary there were 102 participant states. As of June 2015, there were 105 identified participants.

It is important to note that only the Core Group of participants (the original eleven states plus Singapore, which joined shortly after Bush announced the PSI in May 2013) had input into the crafting of the Interdiction Principles. Thus, enlargement was a carefully controlled process whereby the core states maintained control over the PSI's substantive direction while allowing for additional states to join on a take-it-or-leave-it basis.

Implementation—Stage 2 (or Operationalization)

After the Interdiction Principles were adopted, they needed to be operationalized so they could be implemented in practice. Technical experts held a series of meetings to determine the procedures for implementation. They created the Operational Experts Group (OEG), which consists of officials with legal, operational, and intelligence backgrounds from a subset of the most active PSI participants, including Argentina, Australia, Canada, Denmark, France, Germany, Greece, Italy, Japan, the Republic of Korea (ROK), the Netherlands, New Zealand, Norway, Poland, Portugal, Russia, Singapore, Spain, Turkey, the United Kingdom, and the United States.[33] Most of these states were Core Group members at the time the OEG formed.[34]

The OEG operationalized the Interdiction Principles by establishing points of contact and procedures for requesting interdictions, building relationships, organizing workshops and meetings for gaming potential scenarios, conducting joint interdiction exercises, and identifying interoperational difficulties participants might encounter during future interdictions. As of mid-2014, the PSI had held more than sixty activities, including interdiction exercises, workshops, and gaming scenarios.[35] Officials describe the PSI as a forum for developing best practices for conducting interdictions, rather than a mechanism for dealing with individual cases. States cooperate to conduct interdictions, but they prosecute WMD trafficking cases at the national level, and any request for additional assistance is made bilaterally outside the PSI.[36]

In addition to rehearsing potential interdiction scenarios and building transnational working relationships, the exercises are intended to have a deterrent effect. They are an attempt to indicate to would-be proliferators that the international community is actively taking steps to address the problem, and there is a possibility they will be caught. The first exercise, off the coast of Australia in September 2003, was highly publicized in order to send a message to this effect to the DPRK.[37]

Despite concerns it would violate international law, the PSI is designed to operate within existing boundaries of international and domestic legal frameworks. States seek flag-state permission to board a suspect vessel on the high seas, rather than interdict absent permission, because this would be a violation of customary law of the sea and UNCLOS. More often, however, states would interdict suspect vessels in ports where they have greater jurisdictional authority and conducting interdictions is operationally easier.[38]

Based on these attributes, the PSI can be classified as being somewhere at the midpoint of the cooperation spectrum — midway between minimal coordination and robust forms of collaboration. Participants coordinate by aligning their otherwise separate interdictions and sharing information (including points of contact so interdiction requests can be more quickly requested, considered, and acted upon), and they also collaborate by working jointly on problem solving, through both gaming exercises and actual interdictions.

KEY PARTICIPANTS AND NONPARTICIPANTS

PSI participation currently involves more than a hundred states. Some states are more relevant than others from a nonproliferation standpoint. The Netherlands is an important participant, given its naval capabilities. Singapore is important, given the size of its port, its role as a major cargo transit hub, and its location on the Strait of Malacca, through which much of the world's shipping flows. Russia is another key participant because of its nuclear weapon and missile possession, its nuclear exporter status, and its P5 membership. The ROK is important because of its location on the Korean Peninsula and close proximity to the DPRK. Saudi Arabia is likewise an important participant, for its location on the strategic trade route of the Red Sea.

Other participants are not as important from a strategic perspective, such as the Holy See and Lichtenstein. While their numbers help confer legitimacy to the effort, they do not bring significant resources.

Some key states are not PSI participants. China, in particular, would be an important participant for multiple reasons: its location in Northeast Asia, its relationship with and proximity to the DPRK, its major role in global trade, its nuclear weapon and missile possession, and its P5 membership. Similarly, India and Pakistan are key missing states. This is not only because they possess nuclear weapons and civilian industries with the potential for dual use, but also because they are located beside major Indian Ocean trade routes.

In Southeast Asia, Indonesia's absence weakens the PSI's coverage of the Strait of Malacca. Likewise, in the Middle East, Egypt's absence is problematic because of its strategic location on the Suez Canal. These states have jurisdiction over some of the world's critical trade choke points, through which proliferators would typically operate. Many of these nonparticipating states cite concerns about the legality of PSI activities as their reason for staying out, but as the next section discusses, this may not be the primary motivation for their objections.

EXPLANATION OF COOPERATION AND NONCOOPERATION

There are several plausible explanations for the cooperation, or lack thereof, of key players. *U.S. leadership* was clearly central to launching the PSI. The United States acted out of self-interest, in line with what it perceived as an urgent threat. While it is possible the U.S. power position as a hegemon could account for some latecomer states' decisions that cooperating with the United States was better than the alternative, it does not appear this was the strongest reason for many of the first movers.

To explain why other states have or have not joined PSI, among the factors Knopf identifies as potentially relevant in the theoretical framework for this volume, several stand out: self-interest, domestic political considerations (including political change), and norms and identity. Ideas, learning, and transnational networks, power, inducements, and capabilities appear to be more minor. In some cases, several factors were likely at play, but some explanations are more powerful than others.

Self-interest appears to have been a strong motivating factor for a number of PSI participants, particularly members of the original Core Group. The United Kingdom and Australia had reason to be concerned about WMD proliferation, as both a threat to international stability and a direct national security threat to their countries. They were particularly concerned about non-state actors acquiring and using WMD. Both had lost citizens in the 9/11 attacks (the United Kingdom more than sixty and Australia eleven), and more than eighty Australians had been recently killed in the October 2002 Bali bombing. U.K. and Australian citizens were clearly targets of terrorist groups, and a WMD attack could prove devastating. They hence had clear national security imperatives to be part of the new interdiction initiative.

Japan was also likely motivated by self-interest. It feared WMD acquisition by the DPRK, seeing it both as a regional threat to stability on the Korean Peninsula and as a direct threat to Japan. When U.S. officials approached Japan about the PSI, the DPRK had just announced its intention to withdraw from the NPT, which likely provided resonance to the U.S. request. On the non-state-actor front, Japan had experienced the sarin gas attacks in the Tokyo subway in 1995, in addition to losing over twenty citizens in the 9/11 attacks. Proliferation to both states and non-state actors would have been a clear security concern.

The above states joined at the beginning primarily for self-interest reasons. Yet, other states that might have had similar concerns (i.e., regional stability and terrorism) did not join, or joined only at a later date. What accounted for this?

Russia would have been an obvious candidate for PSI participation, given its interest in preventing proliferation to additional states and its concerns about terrorism. Yet, when the United States officially opened the PSI to additional participants, Russia refused to join, citing concerns about the PSI's legality. A U.S. official believes, however, that the real reason Russian officials objected was because Russia was excluded at inception, rather than because it had strong concerns about international law. When Russia did finally join the PSI in May 2004, it insisted on being classified as a Core Group member, lending credence to the argument that the real reason for its earlier opposition was its initial exclusion.[39] Ironically, U.S. officials disbanded the Core Group not long after Russia joined (but Russia did become part of the OEG).

The ROK is another interesting case. South Korea would have appeared to be a prime candidate to join for self-interest reasons. Like Japan, it feared WMD acquisition by the DPRK. On the non-state-actor front, the ROK lost twenty-eight citizens on 9/11. However, it appears the ROK did not initially join the PSI because of concerns about the DPRK's reaction.[40] Indeed, the DPRK did not react well to the PSI, claiming it was the PSI's main target and threatening that it would consider any PSI activity against it as an act of war. It warned the ROK not to become a participant.[41] The ROK refrained from joining until May 26, 2009, when, under new leadership, it joined in the wake of the North's second nuclear test. Thus, when the PSI first emerged, the ROK's fear of short-term retaliation by the DPRK created security interests that trumped other self-interest reasons for participation. Changes in both ROK leadership and the security environment altered this calculation in 2009.

Another key country that joined after initial hesitation is Saudi Arabia, which signed on in May 2008. Saudi Arabia's eventual cooperation was likely driven, at least in part, by its self-interest in preventing Iran from acquiring nuclear weapons. In sum, there are plausible self-interest explanations for many of the important participants.

Just as self-interest was a reason for cooperation by some states, it can equally be an explanation for noncooperation by others. Most states that have refused to participate cite international law concerns. But, it is probable there are more powerful explanations. China is a prime example. While Chinese officials proclaim several objections, the chief stated objection involves concern over international law. One official claims the PSI is only "weakly anchored" in international law because it is not a treaty and there is no UN Security Council (UNSC) resolution supporting it.[42] Yet, China played a critical role in preventing the United States from including any language in UNSC Resolution 1540 that endorsed the PSI. As James Holmes points out, such language could have alleviated China's legal concerns, and China's "effort to deny the initiative UN imprimatur suggests other motives were at work in Chinese diplomacy."[43]

There are a number of possible motives. China's special relationship with the DPRK might have led it to view PSI participation as contrary to its self-interest. China has a clear interest in preserving its relationship with and maintaining the DPRK's stability, even though proliferation to and from the DPRK is not in its strategic interests. An interdiction could foment instability on the Korean Peninsula, a deep fear for China. Another motive might have been China's economic interest in exporting nuclear materials and technology to other countries, particularly to Pakistan, and a fear that PSI participation might challenge these economic interests. The motive at the forefront of Chinese officials' minds, however, was most likely access to vital shipping lanes in Asia and the Pacific for resources and its claims to territory in the South China Sea.[44] Conferring legitimacy on a U.S.-led maritime initiative could make policy makers nervous about China's ability to operate in the maritime environment in the future. In this context, Chinese opposition to the PSI is understandable.

Yet, China is not opposed in principle to interdiction per se. It has reportedly cooperated behind the scenes with the United States in some interdiction activities, reflecting a shared concern about proliferation.[45] For the foreseeable future, however, China is much more likely to continue to cooperate behind the scenes, rather than risk exposing itself to unforeseen potential consequences in the future.

Like those of China, India's and Pakistan's objections to the PSI on legal grounds might be a smoke screen for more fundamental concerns. Both states might have self-interested reasons for not joining, given the nature of their nuclear weapons programs outside the NPT and the consequentially difficult means they have had to adopt to acquire parts and materials to sustain these programs. While both states have an interest in preventing further proliferation to each other as rivals, and in preventing non-state-actor WMD acquisition, both might view PSI participation as impeding their sovereign right to develop their own capabilities.

Moreover, for Pakistan, it is possible that the very concept of interdictions under PSI cuts too close to the bone. Pakistan built its nuclear weapons program in part through scientist A. Q. Khan's clandestine network, through which Khan procured nuclear-related parts and materials. Khan continued to operate this network beyond the Pakistan program's requirements for personal gain. The extensive network involved front companies and middlemen from multiple states including the United Arab Emirates, Germany, South Africa, and Malaysia. Ironically, a 2004 interdiction of the Libya-bound *BBC China* played a part in unraveling Khan's network.[46] Given the turbulent nature of U.S.-Pakistan relations over the past few years, it is difficult to imagine Pakistan joining a U.S.-led initiative.

Indonesia also appears to have taken a self-interest position when deciding not to participate in the PSI. It stood for a long time with Malaysia in questioning the PSI's legality.[47] Both countries also said they viewed the PSI as an attempt by Western states to impede their sovereign rights to develop their economies, claiming interdiction would slow down their ability to conduct trade at a pace their development required. Even though U.S. and Australian diplomats tried to reassure these countries that this was not the purpose of the PSI,[48] and that the impact on trade would be minimal at most, Indonesia and Malaysia both claimed to see the PSI in this light.[49] These perceived economic interests combined with other interests to preclude their participation.

Interestingly, Malaysia had a change of heart, acceding to the PSI in May 2014, more than ten years after its establishment. Malaysia's location on the Strait of Malacca and the involvement of some of its companies in the A. Q. Khan network had meant its long-standing absence was significant. Yet it appears Malaysia and the United States had already been cooperating in this realm to a certain extent. In announcing Malaysia's accession, Prime Minister Datuk Seri Najib Tun Razak said, "What we are doing today is to formalize it so that there will be a formal relationship. . . . This relationship will continue what we have done and also reflects strong will and desire on the Malaysian side, to not only cooperate with the U.S., but with the international community to stop proliferation of parts for nuclear weapons and WMD."[50] Indeed, Malaysia had been an observer at previous OEG exercises. Whether Malaysia ultimately decided to join after a period of learning about the PSI and its benefits, or whether the political dynamics had changed after the Bush administration left office, its accession was a coup for the Obama administration.

Self-interest is not the only relevant factor for PSI participation. The role of *domestic politics* also helps to explain state decisions. Nowhere is this more evident than for the ROK, whose decision to join in 2009 was undoubtedly catalyzed by the DPRK's second nuclear test. However, the change in government of February 2008, from Roh Moo-hyun's progressive party to the conservative party headed by Lee Myung-bak, had ushered in an improvement in relations with the United States, and a different, more confrontational approach to the DPRK. This was a necessary ingredient in the ROK's change in position toward the PSI, demonstrating the effect a change in domestic politics can have on a state's calculation of its national interest.

Domestic politics could be another reason that some key states have refused to participate in the PSI. In the cases of India and Indonesia, domestic political concerns over being perceived as too close to the United States likely precluded PSI participation. With respect to India, Holmes offers several reasons for its nonparticipation—many of which hinge on domestic political considerations. First, when the PSI was getting started, the prime minister from the Bharatiya Janata Party (BJP), Atal Behari Vajpayee, vocalized support for the initiative. This alienated some of the BJP's left-leaning adversaries, who might otherwise have supported the PSI. After coming to power in 2004, Manmohan Singh's Congress-led government, which relies on support from the left, avoided alignment with the PSI, particularly after reports became public that participation would be a condition of the U.S.-India nuclear deal. Second, Holmes argues, participation in the PSI could have been seen by many Indians as unpalatable given perceived maltreatment by the United States in the wake of India's 1998 nuclear tests, as well as a sign of acquiescence to an international nonproliferation regime many Indians regard as unjust. Third, for geostrategic reasons, India wants to maintain strong control over the Indian Ocean, and relegate the United States to a supporting role. If India joined the PSI, it might be perceived as entering into an arrangement in which the United States would play the role of policing India's own region, potentially inflaming domestic public opinion.[51] Moreover, India's participation without Pakistan's, and vice versa, could be politically fraught. While India has participated in PSI exercises as an observer, the above sensitivities have clearly outweighed any Indian interest in formal alignment with the PSI. Whether Narendra Modi's recent election and the apparent strengthening of the United States–India relationship affect India's calculus on PSI remains to be seen. If India did adhere, however, this could add weight to the domestic politics factor. Or, adherence could be related to U.S. support for India's entry into the Nuclear Suppliers Group, suggesting certain incentives at play.

Norms and identity are another relevant explanatory factor for cooperation. While a belief in the norm of nonproliferation likely added to some states' reasons for participating in the PSI—for example, Australia, the United Kingdom, and Japan—there are a number of states that do not appear to have any major self-interest reasons, based on rational cost-benefit calculations, for joining the PSI (beyond the recognition that WMD use in one part of the globe could significantly affect international peace and stability, as well as the global economy). Similarly, they have neither capabilities to contribute to PSI interdictions, nor industries that are part of the global supply chain. Yet, these states are members of the various WMD treaties, and several play active roles in promoting disarmament. Their cooperation might reflect a normative understanding of the importance of preventing WMD proliferation and cooperating in multilateral institutions. The Holy See, for example, could contribute few assets to an interdiction. Its participation indicates a belief in the norm of nonproliferation. A norms and identity explanation might also apply to former Eastern European communist countries, such as Poland, which have tended to show solidarity with the United States in appreciation for the U.S. role during the Cold War.

Power and the offer of explicit incentives as explanations of cooperation are not as strong as the other factors, but were likely present to some extent. A U.S. official reported that the United States did not seek to build the PSI coalition by offering any tangible incentives, positive or negative, in order to secure states' participation. He claims rather that some states proactively came to the United States, seeking to join the PSI without waiting to be invited.[52] Perhaps they hoped there might be future payoffs on other bilateral issues, but this does not appear to have been promised to any state explicitly.

In reality, the PSI has provided some benefits to participants, even if positive inducements were not explicitly offered. The training and interoperability exercises through the OEG have revealed important information to states about their own weaknesses, and enhanced information sharing among officials and their foreign counterparts. This benefit might not have been evident at the outset, before the OEG was set up, however. Thus, states that joined after the OEG began functioning might have perceived additional incentives for participation that early joiners did not.

Finally, states' *capabilities* to conduct interdictions do not appear to have been a decisive factor. PSI membership is not restricted to those that have the capabilities to participate in interdictions. While it was initially desirable to have states capable and willing to contribute resources, once a critical mass was established, there was no harm in having additional participants join. Officials interviewed about such expansion felt it only beneficial to have a greater number of states sign up.[53] By doing so, these added states were supporting the norm of interdiction on suspicion of illicit WMD activities. A lack of capabilities is likewise not a strong explanation for a lack of participation by some states.

The multistage process of the PSI's development had an impact on participation. Because the United States invited only a handful of states to join initially, and then opened the initiative to any state, it alienated certain states that might have joined had they not been initially excluded. Indonesia might fall into this category, although domestic political considerations were perhaps enough to preclude participation regardless. Other states that had plausible self-interest reasons for joining probably took longer to join than they would have had they been invited from the beginning. Russia likely falls into this category given its insistence on inclusion in the Core Group once it joined.

ASSESSING THE PSI'S EFFECTIVENESS

The PSI's primary objective was to help prevent WMD proliferation to states and non-state actors by intercepting shipments of related parts and materials. A linked objective was to dissuade would-be proliferators, by demonstrating a willingness to pursue illicit trade. Given the classified nature of its activities, it is difficult to assess how effective the PSI has been in reaching these objectives, but the limited information available suggests it has been partially but not wholly effective.

The U.S. government has released some information about interdictions it considers successful. In 2005, Condoleezza Rice credited the PSI with around a dozen interdictions in the previous nine months that had prevented states, including Iran, from receiving shipments of WMD-related technology.[54] In June 2008, the U.S. State Department released details of five interdictions that took place between February 2005 and July 2007.[55] The 2003 interdiction of the *BBC China* is the highest profile case to date. This German-owned ship was interdicted transporting centrifuge parts procured through the A. Q. Khan network to Libya. U.S. officials cite this as one factor in Muammar Gaddafi's decision to renounce Libya's WMD programs.[56] They contend that the interdiction of the *BBC China* would have taken much longer, potentially missing a crucial window of opportunity, had Germany and Italy not recently made the decision to participate in the PSI, and had points of contact not already been established.[57]

One case hints at effectiveness in the PSI's second objective—dissuasion. In 2011, the United States suspected a ship traveling from the DPRK and flying the Belize flag was transporting illicit parts to Myanmar. Belize, a PSI participant, gave the United States permission to interdict its ship. Political considerations ultimately precluded the United States from forcibly boarding the ship, but despite this the ship aborted its journey to Myanmar and returned to the DPRK.[58]

Other situations suggest limits to the PSI's effectiveness. The most pertinent example is the PSI's failure to thwart the DPRK's trade in proliferation-related materials with Syria. In September 2007, Israeli air strikes destroyed the nearly operational al Kibar facility in Syria. The U.S. intelligence community believes that the DPRK and Syria had engaged in an "intense level" of nuclear cooperation for over a decade by then and that officials from North Korea were involved in a cargo transfer from the DPRK to Syria in 2006.[59] This happened at a time when PSI participants would have been focused on precisely this type of activity. Given the DPRK's limited means to transship material, this example casts doubts on the PSI's effectiveness.

The absence of certain key states—such as China, India, Indonesia, and Egypt—also limits the effectiveness of the PSI. Without these states, which exert control over major trading choke points and are influential in their regions, the PSI is undoubtedly less effective than it could be. Nonetheless, reported ad hoc behind-the-scenes participation by China is at least encouraging.

The PSI has demonstrated particular effectiveness in building capacity, promoting learning, publicizing the issue, and strengthening the nonproliferation regime. Through the PSI, states have improved their practice of interdiction and developed operational working relationships. Exercises and actual interdictions have provided feedback loops for officials to learn from their experiences, communicate about best practices, and identify potential problems that require further collaboration. The relevant officials have established trust, which has strengthened their relationships and, accordingly, the WMD proliferation epistemic community.[60] One U.S. official even reported that he felt he had more in common with his international counterparts, than he did with his colleagues in the U.S. government.[61] To date, states have held around one hundred events, including more than twenty-five OEG meetings and sixty PSI activities (exercises, workshops, and gaming).[62] The rate of PSI activities has recently increased, after a lull at the beginning of the Obama administration. Participants from around the globe have shared hosting duties and provided equipment and personnel for exercises, an often costly endeavor lending credence to the claim the PSI is not solely a U.S. interest.

In May 2013, more than seventy participants attended the tenth anniversary meeting in Poland, where they affirmed four joint statements intended to strengthen elements of the PSI.[63] The statements contain explicit commitments, such as enhancing states' abilities through a Critical Capabilities and Practices effort. One statement encourages participants to consider acceding to relevant international instruments, such as the 2005 Protocol to the Convention for the Suppression of Unlawful Acts Against the Safety of Maritime Navigation (the SUA Protocol) and the 2010 Convention on the Suppression of Unlawful Acts Relating to International Civil Aviation (the Beijing Convention), and fully implementing the relevant UN resolutions, including Resolution 1540. The outcome of this meeting demonstrates the PSI's continued development and is further evidence of the value states accord to it.

At the implementation stage, the PSI has been a paradigmatic example of a broader hypothesis broached by Knopf in chapter 1: international cooperation on nonproliferation is incorporating more operational activities, and this in turn is creating a more important role for working-level relationships. The PSI has also been successful in directing high-level attention toward the issue of WMD proliferation and interdiction as a tool for combating it. It has helped move many states, though not all, toward consensus that interdiction is an important part of preventing proliferation, and it has aided legal developments in other areas of the WMD nonproliferation regime. In these ways, the PSI has bolstered the preexisting nonproliferation regime by helping address gaps in its ability to deal with shipments of WMD-related items.

As noted earlier, some observers have viewed the PSI as being contradictory to other elements of the global nonproliferation regime, but it is better interpreted as resting upon and being complementary to the regime. It clearly derived some of its legitimacy from the NPT. Even though amending the NPT was not politically viable, the norm against proliferation that the treaty codifies provides a basis for PSI activities. The PSI emerged in response to a gap in the NPT's ability to address the realities of trafficking in WMD-related materials through states and private-sector networks. It does not undermine the NPT's basic principles, as some have claimed it would.[64]

Although the PSI has remained an informal arrangement, it has helped facilitate some legally binding arrangements. In the years following its establishment, the United States has concluded legally binding bilateral ship-boarding agreements, while not formally part of the PSI, with open registry states. These agreements are similar in concept to the PSI's principles, but provide specific operational detail, such as expedited interdiction under specific conditions, as well as information-sharing and dispute-resolution mechanisms.[65] This helps avoid delay and the potential destruction of evidence.[66] According to an official who was closely involved, the PSI principles facilitated these legally binding agreements.[67] The United States sought them with open registry states, known for their relaxed maritime laws, history of illicit activity, and financial incentives to turn the other cheek (they earn significant revenue from their maritime commerce, and proliferators are most likely to attempt to traffic their goods under one of these states' flags). They cover more than 70 percent of the world's shipping tonnage and thus complement the PSI's activities to create a more robust interdiction regime.

The PSI has clear parallels with United Nations Security Council Resolution 1540, which was passed in April 2004 and requires states to criminalize WMD terrorism activities taking place within their jurisdictions. The United States pursued the resolution as a formal means of addressing the trafficking of WMD and related materials for illicit purposes, concurrent with its informal approach through the PSI. Some of the resolution's language is highly similar to the PSI's principles, although, at Chinese insistence, it does not explicitly mention the PSI. Officials report that the prior development and acceptance of the PSI's principles aided the passage of Resolution 1540.[68]

In addition, the epistemic community the PSI fostered helped bring about two international legal instruments. The International Maritime Organization's SUA Protocol of 2005 makes it an international offense to unlawfully and knowingly transport material for illicit WMD purposes by sea and provides for interdiction on the high seas.[69] Officials credit the WMD proliferation community with enabling the negotiation of the protocol, after trust had been built through the PSI.[70]

The second legal instrument whose development the PSI influenced is the Convention on the Suppression of Unlawful Acts Relating to International Civil Aviation. Concluded in Beijing in September 2010, the convention criminalizes the unlawful transport of WMD and related material by air and makes such smuggling punishable under the convention. Although not yet in force, it requires states to adopt domestic legislation criminalizing this conduct, and it promotes a norm against transport for illicit purposes. The Beijing Convention was not concluded through PSI channels, but officials report that the PSI's interdiction principles and the working-level relationships it had fostered facilitated the negotiation.[71]

Finally, the PSI has also served as an example of how an informal approach can be used in nonproliferation. U.S. officials have adopted the PSI's nonbinding approach to address other nuclear security objectives—namely the Global Initiative to Combat Nuclear Terrorism (GICNT) and the Nuclear Security Summit process, both subjects of study elsewhere in this volume.

LESSONS LEARNED

The PSI provides some distinct lessons. First, nonbinding agreements can help build consensus and develop norms around issues for which urgent attention is needed. Even if the agreements are met with resistance and skepticism at first, legitimacy can be built over time. Such agreements can usefully plug gaps in existing regimes and lead to a more robust governance structure. Second, nonbinding agreements need not become legally binding—in fact, pressure to transform their status could lead to disintegration.[72] Yet, they can influence norm development that leads to new and potentially legally binding agreements in other areas that make the overall governance framework more robust. The PSI's role in facilitating international maritime and aviation agreements concerning illicit WMD trafficking illustrates this point.

Third, states can take steps to ensure nonbinding agreements are successful despite their informal status. The PSI case suggests it is important to conclude the agreement at the head-of-government level. This communicates seriousness of intent, gives momentum to negotiations, and provides leverage should working-level officials get stuck. Developing the agreement in a sequential manner and carefully choosing partners allow the initiator and its allies to build a regime that suits their interests, without getting bogged down in protracted negotiations with potential spoilers. However, those launching an initiative should carefully consider the implications of excluding states important to the eventual success of the agreement, should they take offense at their initial exclusion and decide not to join.

Fourth, and finally, the PSI illustrates the potential value of transnational relationships in the implementation stage. Once states joined the PSI, officials at the working level—with technical, policy, and legal backgrounds—collaborated on the implementation process. As officials have shared information and identified potential problems that required further consideration and cooperation, they have established trust, which has strengthened their relationships and, accordingly, the WMD proliferation epistemic community. By collaborating in this way, officials from multiple states have reinforced the PSI and provided it additional momentum.

CONCLUSION

In May 2013, representatives from seventy-two member states met in Warsaw, commemorating the tenth anniversary of the PSI.[73] An initiative whose future seemed uncertain when it was announced appears to have become a relatively established part of global nonproliferation efforts. Although it has taken on some modest structure since its inception, such as the role of the OEG, the PSI remains primarily focused on facilitating operational activities, including both practice exercises and actual interdictions. It is noteworthy that the Obama administration has not moved to "institutionalize" the PSI, as it indicated it would prior to the president's 2009 inauguration.[74] Instead, the 2010 National Security Strategy indicates that the United States will seek to turn the PSI and GICNT into "durable international efforts."[75] The 2013 joint statements support this.

U.S. leadership got the PSI off the ground. Self-interest, domestic calculations, and normative concerns account for other states' participation in the PSI. Calculations of power, while possible factors in state cost-benefit considerations, do not appear to be prominent reasons for participation. One aspect of the PSI, the promise of belonging to its emerging epistemic community, might have provided additional impetus for others to join.

The PSI experience of proposal making, establishment, implementation, enlargement, and additional implementation has led to strengthening of the WMD proliferation epistemic community and facilitated relevant international legal developments. These have all served to foster the growing norm of interdiction of illicit WMD trade, and to strengthen the overall nonproliferation regime. Despite initial resistance, the model itself has been adopted to promote new nonproliferation initiatives, in recognition that its informality provides a valuable complement to formal mechanisms.

Notes

1. Interdiction is the stopping and searching of vessels, including aircraft, and potentially, but not necessarily, the seizing of materials and arresting of persons aboard. Douglas Guilfoyle, "Maritime Interdiction of Weapons of Mass Destruction," *Journal of Conflict and Security Law* 12, no. 1 (2007): 1.

2. "Proliferation Security Initiative: Chairman's Conclusions at Fourth Meeting" (London, October 10, 2003), www.state.gov/t/isn/115305.htm, accessed July 30, 2013.

3. Some critics objected to the PSI's "coalition-of-the-willing" nature and claimed it was a rejection of formal multilateralism and the United Nations. Other critics feared it would "dilute" other nonproliferation efforts. See Siew Gay Ong, "The PSI: A View from Asia," in *Global Non-proliferation and Counter-terrorism*, ed. Olivia Bosch and Peter van Ham (Washington, D.C.: Brookings Institution Press, 2007), 153–67; Mark Valencia, *The Proliferation Security Initiative: Making Waves in Asia*, Adelphi Paper (London: International Institute for Strategic Studies, 2005), 8.

4. As of June 2015, the U.S. Department of State listed 105 participants. For the complete list, see U.S. Department of State, Bureau of International Security and Nonproliferation, "Proliferation Security Initiative Participants" (Washington, D.C., June 9, 2015), www.state.gov/t/isn/c27732.htm, accessed July 2, 2015.

5. One reason the United States asked Spain to interdict was to avoid the perception that this was a predominantly U.S. concern. Former U.S. official B, interview, Washington, D.C., June 2008. (Note: As part of her dissertation research on the PSI, the author interviewed former and current government officials from the United States and Australia on condition of anonymity. To clarify when the same official is cited as a source in different notes, certain officials are referred to by a letter, as in official A, official B, etc.)

6. John Bolton, *Surrender Is Not an Option: Defending America at the United Nations and Abroad* (New York: Threshold Editions, 2007), 120–21, and former U.S. official A, interview, Washington, D.C., March 2008.

7. Bolton, *Surrender Is Not an Option*, 119–21.

8. Former U.S. official B, interview, June 2008.

9. Ibid.

10. Bolton, *Surrender Is Not an Option*, 122.

11. John Bolton, comment at Tufts University Fletcher School conference on preemptive use of force, September 30, 2004; author interviews.

12. Former U.S. official B, interview, June 2008.

13. Ibid.

14. Ibid.

15. Bolton, *Surrender Is Not an Option*, 126.

16. Former U.S. official C, interview, February 25, 2009.

17. Former U.S. official B, phone interview from Cambridge, Mass., October 20, 2009.
18. Former U.S. official B, interview, June 2008.
19. Patrick E. Tyler, "No Chemicals Aboard China Ship," *New York Times*, September 6, 1993.
20. Former U.S. official B, interview, June 2008; and Bolton, *Surrender Is Not an Option*, 126.
21. Bolton, *Surrender Is Not an Option*, 124–25.
22. Ibid., 126.
23. It is unknown whether any states were invited and declined in the beginning, or whether the eleven original participants represent the total number of states invited.
24. "Remarks by the President to the People of Poland" (Krakow, Poland, May 31, 2003), http://georgewbush-whitehouse.archives.gov/news/releases/2003/05/20030531-3.html, accessed May 16, 2010.
25. Former U.S. official D, interview, Washington, D.C., January 11, 2010.
26. Bolton, *Surrender Is Not an Option*, 122.
27. Former U.S. official B, interview, February 29, 2008.
28. Ibid.
29. U.S. State Department, Bureau of International Security and Nonproliferation, "Interdiction Principles for the Proliferation Security Initiative" (September 4, 2003), www.state.gov/t/isn/c27726.htm.
30. Former U.S. official B, interview, February 29, 2008.
31. Ibid.
32. See "Interdiction Principles for the Proliferation Security Initiative."
33. Government Accountability Office, "Nonproliferation: U.S. Agencies Have Taken Some Steps, but More Effort Is Needed to Strengthen and Expand the Proliferation Security Initiative" (GAO-09-34, Washington, D.C., November 3, 2008), 3n4, www.gao.gov/new.items/d0943.pdf. Since 2003, there have been more than twenty OEG-type meetings. See PSI Calendar of Events, available at www.state.gov/t/isn/c27700.htm, accessed July 12, 2014.
34. A U.S. official claims the United States did not dictate which states would be part of the OEG, but that the OEG formed from those states that were part of the Core Group at the time. Former U.S. official B, interview.
35. "Calendar of Events" (Washington, D.C., June 11, 2014), www.state.gov/t/isn/c27700.htm, accessed February 7, 2015. While not every PSI participant is an OEG member, all are allowed to take part in joint interdiction exercises.
36. Discussion with Australian government officials from the Department of Foreign Affairs and Trade, Canberra, June 12, 2009.
37. Former U.S. official D, interview, January 11, 2010.
38. Ibid.
39. Former U.S. official B, interview.
40. Discussions with government officials.
41. See DPRK Korean Central News Agency, "DPRK Regards S. Korea's Full Participation in PSI as Declaration of War against DPRK" (May 27, 2009), www.kcna.co.jp/item/2009/200905/news27/20090527-17ee.html, accessed June 8, 2009.
42. Ye Ru'an and Zhao Qinghai, "The PSI: Chinese Thinking and Concern," *Monitor: International Perspectives on Nonproliferation* 10, no. 1 (2004): 22–24.
43. James R. Holmes, "Sea Power with Asian Characteristics: China, India, and the Proliferation Security Initiative," *Southeast Review of Asian Studies* 29 (2007): 107.
44. See ibid. for a more thorough discussion of these objectives.

45. Interviews by author.

46. Mark Landler, "Trafficking in Nuclear Arms Called Widespread," *International Herald Tribune*, January 24, 2004. For a comprehensive analysis, see Mark Fitzpatrick, ed., *Nuclear Black Markets: Pakistan, A.Q. Khan and the Rise of Proliferation Networks* (London: International Institute for Strategic Studies, May 2007).

47. See "Indonesia Rejects U.S. Request to Join Proliferation Security Initiative," *BBC Monitoring Asia Pacific—Political*, March 18, 2006; "Paper Urges Indonesian to Join U.S.-led Proliferation Security Initiative," *BBC Monitoring Asia Pacific—Political*, September 14, 2009; Michael Richardson, "Testing the Water," *South China Morning Post*, October 5, 2007, 23.

48. Assurances along these lines were evident at an Indonesian government seminar open to the public and attended by the author, Jakarta, Indonesia, December 2007.

49. Discussions with Australian government officials.

50. See "Malaysia Endorses Initiative against WMD," *AsiaOne Malaysia*, April 28, 2014, http://news.asiaone.com/news/malaysia/malaysia-endorses-initiative-against-wmd, accessed July 18, 2014.

51. Holmes, "Sea Power with Asian Characteristics," 111–13.

52. Former U.S. official B, interview.

53. Government officials, interviews.

54. Condoleezza Rice, "Remarks on the Second Anniversary of the Proliferation Security Initiative" (Washington, D.C., May 31, 2005), http://2001-2009.state.gov/secretary/rm/2005/46951.htm, accessed August 5, 2009.

55. Wade Boese, "Interdiction Activities Assessed," *Arms Control Today* 38, no. 6 (July–August 2008).

56. U.S. Department of State, "Proliferation Security Initiative Frequently Asked Questions" (Washington, D.C., May 26, 2005), http://2001-2009.state.gov/t/isn/rls/fs/46839.htm, accessed August 5, 2010.

57. Former U.S. official A, interview, March 2008; former U.S. official B, interview, June 2008.

58. David E. Sanger, "U.S. Said to Turn Back North Korea Missile Shipment," *New York Times*, June 13, 2011, A4.

59. "Background Briefing with Senior U.S. Officials on Syria's Covert Nuclear Reactor with North Korea's Involvement" (Washington, D.C.: Office of the Director of National Intelligence, April 24, 2008), www.dni.gov/interviews/20080424_interview.pdf, accessed June 15, 2010.

60. Former U.S. official D, interview, January 11, 2010; discussion with Australian government officials, June 12, 2009.

61. Former U.S. official D, interview.

62. PSI Calendar of Events, www.state.gov/t/isn/c27700.htm, accessed July 12, 2014.

63. The statements address enhancing critical interdiction capabilities and practices, ensuring a robust initiative, expanding strategic communications, and strengthening authorities for action. See "Joint Statements with List of Affirming Countries," www.state.gov/t/isn/jtstmts/index.htm, accessed July 18, 2014.

64. Valencia, *Proliferation Security Initiative*.

65. The United States maintains these agreements with Antigua and Barbuda, the Bahamas, Belize, Croatia, Cyprus, Liberia, Malta, the Marshall Islands, Mongolia, Panama, and Saint Vincent and the Grenadines. See "Ship Boarding Agreements" (U.S. Department of State), www.state.gov/t/isn/c27733.htm, accessed August 7, 2013.

66. Ashley J. Roach, "Proliferation Security Initiative (PSI): Countering Proliferation by Sea" (paper, Law of the Sea Issues in the East and South China Seas conference, Xiamen, China, March 11, 2005),www.state.gov/s/l/2005/87344.htm, accessed August 5, 2010.

67. Former U.S. official B, interview.

68. Especially ibid.

69. Protocol of 2005 to the Convention for the Suppression of Unlawful Acts against the Safety of Maritime Navigation (SUA PROT 2005) (IMO DOC LEG/CONF.15/21, November 1, 2005), www.imo.org/inforesource/mainframe.asp?topic_id=835#04b.

70. Interviews by author.

71. Discussions with government officials.

72. According to officials interviewed by the author, some states would probably withdraw from the PSI if it were formalized into a legally binding treaty.

73. U.S. Department of State, "Proliferation Security Initiative 10th Anniversary High-Level Political Meeting," www.state.gov/t/isn/c10390.htm, accessed July 20, 2014.

74. Language to this effect was posted on the administration transition website in January 2009 and then on the whitehouse.gov website following inauguration but is no longer available. In his April 2009 Prague speech, Obama called on the international community to come together to turn efforts such as the PSI into "durable international institutions." See "Remarks by President Barack Obama" (Prague, Czech Republic, April 5, 2009), www.whitehouse.gov/the_press_office/Remarks-By-President-Barack-Obama-In-Prague-As-Delivered/, accessed May 16, 2010.

75. President of the United States, "National Security Strategy" (May 24, 2010), www.whitehouse.gov/sites/default/files/rss_viewer/national_security_strategy.pdf, accessed May 27, 2010.

CHAPTER SEVEN

UN Security Council Resolution 1540

Origins, Status, and Future Prospects

TANYA OGILVIE-WHITE

THIS CHAPTER EXPLORES the origins, goals, and effectiveness of UN Security Council Resolution 1540, which obligates states to take certain actions to help prevent terrorists from obtaining weapons of mass destruction (WMD). After a bumpy start, Resolution 1540 is emerging as a cornerstone of the nonproliferation and counterterrorism regimes, around which a complex framework of international security cooperation is being built. But while the vast majority of states now express support for the goals and objectives of the resolution, which is a major achievement in itself, implementation of the resolution still faces an uphill struggle. Technological and economic challenges are significant obstacles, but over the longer term, these can be surmounted through effective provision and coordination of international assistance by donor states, the 1540 Committee that was established by the resolution, and relevant international organizations. Thornier obstacles to implementation arise on the political side, stemming from the divided priorities of developed and developing states, different perceptions of threat and vulnerability, and competing concepts of sovereignty. Thanks to the flexibility and learning capacity of key actors—including proactive individuals—these political obstacles are gradually being worn down, but unless they are handled carefully they have the potential to reemerge. Of special significance is the style and character of U.S. nonproliferation and disarmament leadership, which has the potential to increase or undermine support for the initiative.

ORIGINS OF RESOLUTION 1540

The Security Council adopted Resolution 1540 in April 2004 with the aim of closing loopholes in the nonproliferation regime, especially those related to the potential for non-state actors to gain access to WMD materials. The resolution was adopted under Chapter VII of the UN Charter. This makes it legally binding, meaning that compliance is mandatory for all UN member states, regardless of their size, resources, or capabilities. Resolution 1540 is the first international legal instrument to cover all three major categories of WMD (i.e., nuclear, biological, and chemical weapons), their means of delivery, and related materials in a comprehensive and integrated manner.

The origins of the resolution lie in U.S. and U.K. efforts to set new international standards to criminalize WMD proliferation following the 9/11 terrorist attacks. In a speech to the UN General Assembly on September 23, 2003, U.S. president George W. Bush called for a new antiproliferation resolution, which would make it mandatory for all states to "enact strict export controls consistent with international standards, and to secure any and all sensitive materials within their own borders."[1] Two days later, U.K. foreign secretary Jack Straw reinforced Bush's proposal in his own speech to the General Assembly, urging the Security Council to take action to prevent WMD proliferation.[2]

In the following weeks, a U.S. and U.K. draft text of what eventually became Resolution 1540 began circulating among the P5 (the five permanent members of the Security Council). The original text underwent numerous revisions, most notably leading to the replacement of the phrase "interdict illicit [WMD] trafficking" with "take cooperative action to prevent illicit [WMD] trafficking."[3] The change was made at the insistence of China, which was determined to ensure that Resolution 1540 did not provide a basis in international law for the Proliferation Security Initiative (PSI). China has consistently argued that the PSI, a 2003 U.S. initiative to enlist states to interdict WMD-related international shipments, flouts international maritime law. This amendment was significant because the United States had indeed intended that 1540 would inject UN legitimacy into the PSI—and in informal diplomatic forums since 2004 U.S. scholars and officials have often made the claim that 1540 does so, despite the objections of their Chinese counterparts.[4]

The resolution's mandate initially ran for two years, but this was extended for another two-year period by Resolution 1673 (2006) and a further three-year period by Resolution 1810 (2008). In April 2011, the Security Council unanimously adopted Resolution 1977, which extended the mandate again, this time by a period of ten years.[5] This reflected a general recognition that the objectives set out in the resolution represent a long-term undertaking, requiring a huge collaborative effort, which will need to go beyond formal governmental initiatives to include civil society groups, academia, and relevant business interests.[6]

Resolution 1540 requires states to criminalize the proliferation of WMD to non-state actors and to implement and enforce measures to prevent WMD terrorism. The main requirements of the resolution are set out in operative paragraphs 2, 3 (a) and (b), and 3 (c) and (d), respectively:[7]

- Operative paragraph 2 obliges states to "adopt and enforce appropriate effective laws which prohibit any non-State actor to manufacture, acquire, possess, develop, transport, transfer or use nuclear, chemical or biological weapons and their means of delivery, in particular for terrorist purposes, as well as attempts to engage in any of the foregoing activities, participate in them as an accomplice, assist or finance them."
- Operative paragraphs 3 (a) and (b) require states to "develop and maintain appropriate effective measures to account for and secure [WMD] items in production, use, storage or transport" and to "develop and maintain appropriate effective physical protection measures."
- Operative paragraphs 3 (c) and (d) oblige states to "develop and maintain appropriate effective border controls and law enforcement efforts to detect, deter, prevent and combat, including through international cooperation when necessary, the illicit trafficking and brokering in [WMD]" and "establish, develop, review and maintain appropriate effective national export and trans-shipment controls over [WMD] items."

Under the resolution, member states were supposed to report to the Security Council no later than six months after the resolution's adoption on the steps they have taken, or plan to take, to implement its provisions. Fifty states met the original deadline of October 2004, but many states complained that the six-month deadline did not give them enough time to introduce appropriate laws or establish effective WMD measures and controls.[8]

The resolution made provision for the establishment of a Security Council committee to oversee its implementation. This is composed of the five permanent members of the Security Council and the ten nonpermanent members and is assisted by a small group of independent experts.[9] In addition to evaluating national reports and assessing progress in implementation, this body plays a role in raising awareness of Resolution 1540 through outreach and dialogue with member states, including (when specifically invited to do so) undertaking work in-country. It also plays a coordination role among the international organizations involved in implementing the resolution: the 1540 Committee engages the International Atomic Energy Agency (IAEA), the Organization for the Prohibition of Chemical Weapons (OPCW), and the Implementation Support Unit of the Biological Weapons Convention, as well as regional and subregional organizations.

One of the most useful roles that the 1540 Committee undertakes, with the support of its experts group, is the coordination and facilitation of technical assistance to member states, with the aim of national capacity-building. It matches offers of and requests for assistance through assistance templates, voluntary action plans, and country visits. Although the committee has limited capacity of its own, it has been able to play this role by leveraging the expertise and resources of member states and international governmental and nongovernmental organizations, including major assistance providers such as the European Union (EU) and the Group of Eight (G8, now back to the G7 after other states expelled Russia following its annexation of Crimea). Activities related to 1540 also receive financial support from the United Nations Trust Fund for Global and Regional Disarmament Activities, which is funded through voluntary contributions from member states. Contributions to the fund can be earmarked for specific UN-related initiatives, such as the effective implementation of Resolution 1540.[10]

The 1540 Committee and experts meet regularly to discuss work programs that set out short-term implementation goals. In 2009, the committee established four working groups to focus on specific areas of work: monitoring and national implementation; assistance; cooperation with international organizations, including the 1267 and 1373 Committees; and transparency and media outreach.[11]

STATUS OF RESOLUTION 1540 IMPLEMENTATION

The 1540 Committee reports provide the most comprehensive and up-to-date information on the current status of 1540 implementation. These are based on information supplied to the committee in national reports or acquired through its consultations with experts, member states, and international organizations. The 1540 Committee puts the data obtained by these means into a series of state-by-state matrices, which are used to create tables and charts that provide periodically updated assessments of implementation.

The most recent report (as of this writing), published on the 1540 Committee website in September 2011, reveals that since the adoption of the resolution in 2004, 168 states have submitted national reports on the steps they have taken or intend to take to implement 1540.[12] Of these, 105 states have submitted additional information at the request of the 1540 Committee, and at least 140 states have adopted legislative measures to prohibit proliferation of nuclear, chemical, and biological weapons (as compared to 65 states in 2006). But the report reveals significant gaps. For example, more states have measures in place prohibiting chemical weapons than nuclear or biological weapons, with higher numbers addressing chemical weapons in every mandated category except transport. In addition, more states have adopted legislation than have put in place enforcement measures. Furthermore, as of September 2011, 24 states had yet to submit their first national report to the 1540 Committee, most of them in Africa (Congo, Lesotho, Liberia, Malawi, and South Sudan have since submitted).[13] The report also identified a number of other critical areas in which implementation has been weak, including measures covering non-state-actor access to biological materials, means of delivery, and related materials; the creation of national control lists; and measures to prevent financing of illicit proliferation activities.

A cross-comparison of information provided in the September 2011 and July 2008 reports provides further insight into the scale and pace of national implementation of the resolution's key obligations, and especially the gaps in enforcement. This is illustrated in tables 7.1, 7.2, and 7.3.[14] In each table, the first number in each box relates to the number of states with legislative frameworks covering the specific provision, and the second is the number of states that have enforcement measures in place to punish violators. In the vast majority of cases, enforcement provisions lag far behind the drafting of legal frameworks.

Table 7.1 compares the number of states with a national legal framework in place to prohibit non-state WMD activities and enforcement provisions in place to penalize non-state-actor WMD activities. The figures show that one of the most rapid increases in implementation involved the introduction of national legal frameworks to prohibit the manufacture and production of WMD and the development of relevant penal measures regarding manufacture and production. The slowest increases (with the numbers almost unchanged) related to criminalizing the means of delivery.

Table 7.2 compares the number of states with a legal framework in place to

Table 7.1   Status of Implementation of Operative Paragraph 2

Obligation	Nuclear Weapons		Chemical Weapons		Biological Weapons	
	2011	2008	2011	2008	2011	2008
Manufacture/produce	115/92	97/76	135/123	105/96	112/95	86/83
Acquire	112/88	93/77	138/121	99/90	112/95	84/80
Possess	80/95	68/82	101/116	74/88	72/87	61/74
Stockpile/store	52/57	42/55	134/103	101/81	103/70	81/69
Develop	45/47	41/49	129/95	96/71	98/65	76/61
Transport	60/84	47/68	50/76	36/61	52/69	38/58
Transfer	75/83	76/71	140/122	101/91	104/89	86/73
Use	105/112	66/85	150/140	108/104	115/121	65/91
Means of delivery	39/37	30/35	54/48	46/45	90/43	77/45
Accomplice	98/102	58/72	116/119	69/84	106/110	64/78
Assist	103/102	67/74	140/125	97/88	115/110	75/79
Financing	125/120	66/78	128/122	71/87	121/114	64/75

Table 7.2   Status of Implementation of Operative Paragraph 3 (a) and (b)

Obligation	Nuclear Weapons		Chemical Weapons		Biological Weapons	
	2011	2008	2011	2008	2011	2008
Accounting						
Production	164/73	154/50	97/89	68/53	61/62	39/36
Use	165/73	155/53	96/86	67/52	62/63	39/38
Storage	165/71	154/49	97/92	64/53	61/61	38/38
Transport	78/72	58/44	78/73	49/38	60/57	39/35
Securing						
Production	81/72	62/56	74/69	60/45	60/62	53/44
Use	90/81	72/64	73/72	62/49	64/67	55/43
Storage	89/90	73/65	81/78	69/56	68/72	60/50
Transport	101/100	91/82	80/81	69/65	73/78	68/69
Physical protection						
Protect	74/61	61/48	53/45	37/27	46/35	39/25

account for, store, and physically protect materials related to nuclear, chemical, and biological weapons, and those that have introduced provisions to penalize those who fail to comply. The table shows that, again, more states have adopted measures in the legislative framework than in the enforcement area. Implementation has also been weak in the area of biological weapons—although more states have introduced provisions for criminal or administrative penalties to enforce measures related to the accounting and securing of biological materials, those that have done so still represent a minority of states, exposing a serious gap in the regime. This is most noticeable when the numbers are compared with those relating to the accounting of nuclear weapons materials, which are relatively well covered in legislative terms (although the same is not true regarding the physical protection of nuclear materials, which remains relatively weak).

Table 7.3 compares the number of states with a legal framework in place to control borders, trade, and transshipment and those that have enforcement measures in place to punish those who fail to comply with those measures. The numbers highlight an area of particular concern to the 1540 Committee: measures to prevent the financing of illicit transactions related to nuclear, chemical, and biological weapons, their means of delivery, and related materials. Although these measures have increased since 2008, as states have used their counter-terrorism legislation to cover financing of WMD activities, implementation remains low, with fewer than forty states reporting measures in place in 2011.[15]

Table 7.3 Status of Implementation of Operative Paragraph 3 (c) and (d)

Obligation	Nuclear Weapons		Chemical Weapons		Biological Weapons	
	2011	2008	2011	2008	2011	2008
Border control	163/148	114/99	166/151	118/111	163/148	114/99
Technical support of border control	87/121	88/*	84/117	87/*	87/120	88/*
Control of brokering	74/68	59/50	78/73	61/48	74/68	59/50
Enforcement agencies	111/142	74/101	116/146	78/111	111/142	74/101
Export control legislation	116/108	99/90	125/116	107/94	116/108	99/90
Licensing provisions	90/70	76/60	91/76	77/57	90/70	76/60
Exceptions from licensing	51/51	49/47	53/51	53/47	51/51	49/47
Licensing of deemed export/visa	43/24	22/12	41/22	19/11	43/24	22/12
National licensing authority	98	85	104	94	98	85
Interagency review for licenses	55	54	60	56	55	54
Control lists	79/47	68/69	85/54	80/81	79/47	69/69
Updating of lists	57	53	59	58	57	53
Inclusion of technologies	70/52	64/22	69/51	62/23	70/52	64/22
End-user controls	67	61	72	64	67	61
Catchall clause	59/44	56/20	57/42	54/20	59/44	56/20
Intangible transfers	59/50	47/25	61/53	46/26	59/50	47/25
Transit control	100/80	81/52	104/91	80/56	100/80	81/52
Transshipment control	77/65	62/35	84/72	66/43	77/65	62/35
Re-export control	80/65	72/45	85/71	73/46	80/65	72/45
Control of providing funds	35/35	30/25	39/39	30/26	35/35	30/25
Control of providing transport services	31/26	27/19	33/29	25/19	31/26	27/19
Control of importation	133/118	104/75	136/123	110/86	133/118	104/75
Extraterritorial applicability	34/36	31/31	39/42	32/35	34/37	31/31

* Data not provided in 2008 report for those categories in which a cell has only one number.

The same is true of the number of states that have measures against providing transport services for illicit WMD transactions—implementation is occurring, but only slowly.

THE EFFECTIVENESS OF RESOLUTION 1540

Evaluating the effectiveness of Resolution 1540 is difficult because the resolution covers every state and virtually every single mechanism of the long-established nonproliferation regime, along with various new initiatives that specifically relate to the prevention of WMD terrorism. Even a regional or subregional assessment would be a major undertaking. On one level, evaluation may appear to be aided by the fact that the 1540 Committee gathers and publishes information, including via regularly updated country-specific matrices and comprehensive reports. But there are potential sources of doubt about the reliability of these data, meaning caution is needed in interpreting the information contained in the tables.

First, some of the information provided in the national reports is distorted by member states' desire to be seen to be complying with their 1540 obligations, even when their level of implementation is low or patchy. And because there is little in-country monitoring except by invitation, it is difficult to gauge the accuracy of national implementation claims. This problem is accentuated by the gap between the largely supportive rhetoric of country missions in New York and Vienna, and the more wary reception that 1540 has received in some capitals, especially in the Global South.

Second, the 1540 Committee itself has a tendency to put a positive spin on implementation statistics, partly to emphasize the effectiveness of its own work, and possibly also to create forward momentum through upbeat claims of progress and consensus (thereby generating a positive self-fulfilling prophecy). Third, the figures in the committee's summary reports do not distinguish between long-standing domestic legislation that a state claims covers WMD prohibitions, some of it dating back decades, and domestic legislation that has been specifically drafted with the goal of prohibiting and punishing the illicit WMD activities of non-state actors. While individual country matrices go into more detail on these matters,[16] the information contained in them is difficult to verify, and there is little indication of whether measures are being enforced to the extent that prosecutions are taking place. Reliable information on prosecutions (which are critical to the effectiveness of any measure to criminalize proliferation) is hard to obtain.[17]

Even taking into account the distorted and patchy information that is available via the 1540 Committee apparatus, progress in some areas of 1540 implementation is clearly occurring. The most significant development is that Resolution 1540 is increasingly regarded as a legitimate and essential part of the nonproliferation regime, thanks to the careful, consultative coordination role that has been played by the 1540 Committee, its group of experts, and the direct and indirect assistance of many states and international organizations.[18] There have been many concrete, verifiable achievements, such as more states signing up to relevant nonproliferation and counterterrorism conventions, the emergence of new forms of nonproliferation cooperation including at the regional and subregional levels, a willingness among many developed states and organizations to provide relevant capacity-building assistance, and a parallel willingness among recipient states to take advantage of the help on offer. The resolution, primarily through the activities of the 1540 Committee and a myriad of international organizations, has been successful in raising awareness of WMD threats and in establishing new norms obliging states to minimize vulnerabilities.[19] This has led some scholars to regard the growing security apparatus associated with Resolution 1540 as a nascent form of future governance that will ensure global cooperation to address state and non-state threats efficiently and effectively.[20]

Although progress has been occurring, the steps needed to close off to non-state actors all avenues of access to WMD and related materials remain immense. As a result, there is frustration in some quarters—particularly among states that prioritize counterterrorism—that statements of strong support for the resolution in international, regional, and subregional forums are not being matched by a much faster pace of implementation on the ground.[21] In the early years, the slow pace was partly the result of confusion among states over their legal obligations—some believed that their membership in the main WMD treaties and conventions, which deal with state-to-state proliferation, satisfied their 1540 requirements, and as a result they were slow to take action.[22] But the 1540 Committee has worked with the UN Office of Disarmament Affairs and a number of international organizations to raise awareness that the requirements of 1540 focus on non-state actors and typically need specific additional legislation, especially provisions for penalizing the involvement of non-state actors in prohibited WMD activities, whether or not terrorist intent can be proved.[23] The IAEA, OPCW, and the UN Office on Drugs and Crime have been particularly active in this area of raising awareness and building capacity, helping provide tailor-made legislative assistance to member states that request their help.

Nevertheless, huge gaps in implementation remain, despite the best efforts of the majority of states and relevant international organizations. Inevitably, there has been a great deal of haphazard "muddling through" as the 1540 Committee and expert group have tried to carve out the new regime, and a corresponding trial and error approach by member states and international organizations, leading to duplication of tasks, wasted opportunities, and inefficient use of resources. There have also been charges of secrecy and claims that the 1540 Committee and group of experts have been overstepping their mandate given the reservations of some member states.[24]

These problems were highlighted in 2009, when the committee held a comprehensive review of the status of 1540 implementation, which included an open meeting to which all member states and relevant organizations were invited. The review addressed three areas: the evolution of risks and threats, critical gaps in the regime, and new approaches to implementation to improve effective cooperation. As a result of the review, participants agreed on suggestions for the 1540 Committee to increase its capacity to gather information on the status of implementation, improve its role in matching requests for assistance with offers, develop formal and informal cooperative arrangements with relevant institutions at all levels, and do far more to share information on lessons learned and best practices.[25] To this end, a decision was taken to hold regular open meetings, to help raise the level of dialogue between the committee and member states, and to generate consensus over the need to extend the resolution for a longer term, with a clearer mandate to address critical gaps.[26] This approach succeeded, leading to the unanimous adoption of Security Council Resolution 1977 in April 2011, which extended the mandate for ten years and boosted the 1540 Committee's authority in the areas of assistance coordination and implementation oversight.[27]

To sum up, implementation of Resolution 1540 has been slow and patchy, despite the efforts of the 1540 Committee, group of experts, donor states, and a host of international organizations and individuals, and despite the growing support for the resolution of the majority of states. Although some of the slow rate of progress can be ascribed to the challenges associated with regime-building efforts by the Security Council, the most serious obstacles to effectiveness can be found at the national level. Key gaps in many states include failures to implement controls on WMD delivery systems, enforce WMD legislation, prevent the financing of illicit WMD-related transactions, and control many areas of biological research and development.

However, these shortcomings do not mean the effectiveness of 1540 should be judged negatively. It would be unrealistic to expect an initiative of the scope of 1540 to develop without experiencing major growing pains. As with the other major counterterrorism resolutions, 1267 and 1373, implementation of Resolution 1540 was always going to be a long-term undertaking, fraught with practical and political difficulties. Several areas show gradually improving effectiveness. The most important are that (1) most states now accept the need for 1540; (2) at a minimum, the resolution has raised awareness among states of the need to prevent illicit access to WMD materials; (3) though slow, national implementation of the resolution is growing each year; and (4) the international infrastructure needed to support the initiative is expanding, taking into account lessons learned.

EXPLAINING CHANGING ATTITUDES TO RESOLUTION 1540

The reasons most states have supported the goals and objectives of Resolution 1540 are straightforward and unsurprising. The resolution was partly a reaction to the horrific attacks of September 11, 2001, which dramatically increased fears of WMD terrorism and a sense of shared vulnerability to it. With this came the awareness that no single state has the capacity to prevent WMD terrorism acting alone or even in concert with others; it requires collective action on a scale never seen before—a global campaign in which all states and multiple international and regional organizations need to be committed. Most state and non-state organizations that support the resolution are driven by this goal: support is based on the close alignment of self-interest and common interest, which is the essential foundation of any successful international regime. Others comply because they want to uphold and reinforce international law (New Zealand is the perfect example here), or because they want to attract development assistance and/or consolidate alliances by being seen to be good international citizens (Pacific Island countries and numerous other small and microstates fit into this category).[28]

Explaining the early resistance to the resolution among many developing states—and the gradual reduction in this resistance over a number of years—is more challenging. Why were some states wary of Resolution 1540 in the first few years after it was passed? Why has "buy-in" among many of these states increased, and how has this been achieved? The following analysis highlights three factors: capacity issues, conflicting norms, and the different ways states view U.S. hegemonic leadership.

Capacity Challenges and the Availability of Assistance

Explanations for the early resistance to Resolution 1540 and for ongoing implementation challenges have to begin with an understanding of the immense practical obstacles that have slowed progress. Even states that have always fully supported the objectives of Resolution 1540 consider its obligations to be burdensome and have difficulty implementing many of its provisions.[29] This is especially true of developing states, most of which are stretched by the resolution's reporting requirements alone. Complying with Resolution 1540 strains the economic, technological, and governmental capacities of even the most advanced states, so it is hardly surprising that, from the moment the resolution was passed, many states in the Global South felt overwhelmed by what they feared would be unachievable new nonproliferation standards.[30]

Official statements made in the open meetings of the Security Council, and in other international and regional forums, provide copious evidence that capacity problems are the primary obstacle to compliance and the main cause of the huge variance in the extent to which states have implemented the key provisions set out in operative paragraphs 2 and 3. A quantitative study published in 2011 likewise found that poor capacity is the key factor behind variance in implementation of export controls under operative paragraph 3 (d)—an area of low implementation that is most often attributed to self-interested economic factors, such as concerns that export controls undermine trade. The authors evaluated thirty proliferation-salient states that had the potential to serve as WMD transshipment points and concluded that capacity levels are the strongest determinant of noncompliance.[31]

The capacity challenges posed by Resolution 1540 were predicted from the start, but the lack of an institutional framework dedicated to capacity-building compounded these challenges, especially in the early years. The drafters of the resolution were aware that implementation would be beyond the capabilities of many states, so they inserted operative paragraph 5, which "recognizes that some States may require assistance in implementing the provisions of this Resolution within their territories and invites States in a position to do so to offer assistance as appropriate in response to specific requests to the States lacking the legal and regulatory infrastructure, implementation experience and/or resources for fulfilling the above provisions." However, at the outset, the 1540 Committee was primarily tasked with overseeing the reporting obligation, and it had neither the mandate nor the resources to connect the many requests for assistance with the offers being made by donors. This lack of assistance coordination led to frustration, exacerbating perceptions that the resolution placed an unfair burden on developing states.[32]

It is probably in this area of assistance that the 1540 Committee, international organizations, and member states have had the most to learn, the most important lesson being that multilateral assistance coordination is a huge task that needs to be mandated and systematized at the international level from the outset. Haphazard, uncoordinated assistance provision has proven to be inefficient in practical terms, but it has also resulted in wasted opportunities that are less obvious. For example, the past failure of the committee to oversee the implementation of operative paragraph 5 has meant that an accurate, publicly available Security Council record of which states have provided what kinds of assistance does not exist. In addition to making progress more difficult to assess, this has led to a missed opportunity to promote the work of the states and organizations that have been most active in capacity-building.

Despite the criticisms of a minority of states, which claim that developed states are not fulfilling their obligations under paragraph 5 to provide assistance,[33] international capacity-building initiatives have been multiplying, are paying dividends, and are partly responsible for generating wider support for Resolution 1540 over time. The European Union, United States, and G8/G7 have been leading the way, along with international organizations such as the IAEA, OPCW, INTERPOL, and International Maritime Organization and issue-specific NGOs such as VERTIC. Those involved in these outreach and assistance efforts have had to address traditional concerns among developing states that the measures required by 1540 will impose an economic burden and that the export control elements will limit their access to trade.[34] In response, assistance providers have stressed that cooperative efforts to help states comply with the obligations set out in Resolution 1540 should be welcomed on the basis that security and development are linked. Progress in implementing domestic WMD controls can assist states in their wider efforts to stem other forms of criminal activity, such as money laundering, human trafficking, and drug smuggling, all of which can undermine economic development and hamper licit trade.[35]

To help counter perceptions that domestic measures to curb proliferation are an unwelcome burden and a drain on scarce resources, assistance providers have been working to increase awareness of the wider, capacity-building benefits that WMD controls can have on economies and societies. This strategy of using development-focused assistance and outreach activities to induce compliance has been very effective in some areas, especially where resources are stretched thin and competing development priorities meant that Resolution 1540 was initially regarded as an obligation too far. For example, New Zealand has been providing important technical assistance to states in the South Pacific (in the areas of aviation, port, and shipping security, customs and immigration processes, and legislative drafting) through its Pacific Security Fund. These capacity-building projects have proved helpful in a region where many leaders are most concerned with what they refer to as basic "fish and rice issues" and are more willing to implement WMD controls if they can be shown to have a clear link to development priorities.[36]

Competing Norms

While capacity challenges explain much of the early resistance to 1540 and the variance in 1540 implementation, they do not tell the whole story. A large part of the early unpopularity of the resolution stems from the different attitudes among UN member states over the appropriate role of the Security Council, especially given its limited membership relative to the General Assembly. Some take a maximalist view and are happy to see the Security Council expanding its authority, especially in the area of counterterrorism cooperation; others are firmly within the minimalist camp, preferring to protect their national sovereignty and limit the Security Council's role to within a strict interpretation of the UN Charter.

It is useful to think of the tensions that arise from these different attitudes in terms of competing norms: the norm of noninterference versus that of common security.[37] Some states objected to Resolution 1540 because it appeared to undermine the first norm and elevate the second by adding to the lawmaking authority of the Security Council. This exacerbated concerns that had already been raised by the passage of Resolution 1373 in 2001, which mandated states to prevent and suppress the financing of terrorist acts, criminalize certain acts related to terrorism, and freeze the funds or financial assets of certain individuals. Both resolutions introduced a vertical, uniform, global lawmaking process that disturbed perceptions of the balance of power between UN member states and the Security Council, appearing to significantly increase the power of the latter.[38]

To understand the significance of this shift and the reasons it sparked so much unease, it helps to understand a key principle of international law known as "conferral," which has traditionally protected national sovereignty and the norm of noninterference. Conferral refers to the voluntary agreement of states to transfer certain powers to an international organization. When states join international organizations they do so on condition that such power is carefully delineated: they transfer specific competences to the organization in order to achieve common objectives, but they protect themselves against any subsequent power grabbing by that international organization by limiting its authority via treaty provisions and by making action dependent on consent. When the UN Security Council passed resolutions 1373 and 1540 under Chapter VII of the UN Charter, some states believed it had undermined the principle of conferral by making it mandatory for all states to introduce domestic legislation to counter specific terrorist activities even though states had not explicitly conferred to the Security Council the power to act in this way. They regarded this as a dramatic and unwarranted expansion of the Security Council's power, pitting its authority against their own.[39]

This helps explain why Resolution 1540 had a particularly poor reception in Southeast Asia, where attitudes are colored by a general suspicion of global instruments that are highly formalized, legalistic, and intrusive in nature. ASEAN members are highly protective of the norm of noninterference and the principle of conferral in the UN context. Even at the regional level, they are much more comfortable with the locally bred, informal political culture that underpins their own institutional frameworks, favoring the principle of quiet consultation, known as *musyawarah*, as the basis for dealing with neighbors.[40] Largely reflecting this informal, consultative approach, all instruments of ASEAN and the ASEAN Regional Forum work on a voluntary basis; there are no institutionalized enforcement structures, verification mechanisms, or official sanctions for uncooperative behavior. Given this political culture, it was not surprising to find some resistance to Security Council Resolution 1540, which imposed formal, legislative obligations on all states, whether or not they regard WMD terrorism as a serious threat.[41] Similar concerns have been expressed by states in Africa and in the South Pacific.[42]

The 1540 Committee, with the help of states, international organizations, and NGOs, has worked hard to overcome the perception that Resolution 1540 represents a form of quiet, unsanctioned power grabbing by the Security Council at the expense of weaker states in the international system. In doing so, it has benefitted from the efforts of committed individuals, such as the former U.S. 1540 coordinator, Tom Wuchte, and numerous members of the 1540 group of experts, who were quick to identify these concerns and ensure that they are addressed. Rather than stressing the Chapter VII origins of the resolution and using the language of compliance and enforcement, these individuals have sought to coax wary states into accepting the need for a global rollout of uniform domestic counterterrorism measures to prevent the proliferation of WMD to non-state actors. The nature of the committee's dialogue with states is consultative in character and informal where possible, emphasizing the common good and the need for a new level of partnership between the Security Council and UN member states.[43] Crucially, this effort also draws on opportunities to operate according to the principle of subsidiarity, whereby authority is not concentrated at the international level but where possible is exercised at regional, subregional, and national levels.[44] The appointment of regional 1540 coordinators—an initiative that was proposed and championed by Wuchte—has helped in this regard, with the coordinators serving as focal points for specific geographic regions and alleviating concerns that states are being dictated to from the global level.

This approach is gradually paying off, as more states accept that the Security Council needed to intervene in an area that lacked a global and uniform regulatory framework, and recognize that it is doing so by means that are as nonintrusive as possible, empowering states to decide how to translate their new obligations into domestic law as they see fit.[45] The result is that even states that were initially wary or even hostile toward the resolution are willing to engage in dialogue on implementation and best practices with the 1540 Committee and experts as well as states and international organizations.[46] Most are also now willing to accept capacity-building assistance and are forging new working relationships across government bureaucracies and across regions in order to address WMD terrorism risks.

U.S. Hegemonic Leadership and Domestic Political Factors

In addition to the complex UN dynamics outlined above, Resolution 1540 is caught up in North-South political divisions—especially resentments over U.S. hegemony. These resentments were significantly heightened during the first term of the Bush administration, when many states believed the United States abused its leadership position by trying to force an unpopular security agenda on the rest of the world. States especially objected to the policy of preemption and a strategy of abandoning multilateralism in favor of coalitions of the willing. Opposition to U.S. hegemonic leadership peaked during the Iraq war and its immediate aftermath, causing deep schisms that seriously undermined UN-mandated multilateral cooperation. Initial reactions to Resolution 1540 need to be understood in this context, as many states viewed it as an extension of U.S. grand strategy, despite the fact the text was also drafted by France, Russia, and the United Kingdom (China was not involved in the drafting process until the very end).[47]

Due to this perception, reactions to Resolution 1540 also became embedded in domestic political dynamics: states whose populations were hostile to the Bush administration's security agenda and especially to the "war on terror" were openly critical of the resolution, arguing that it lacked legitimacy because it had been pushed through the Security Council without their consent.[48] They argued that, in promoting Resolution 1540, the United States was using the UN system to pursue a selfish agenda via "a la carte multilateralism," and they said they would not be bullied into accepting new and burdensome nonproliferation and counterterrorism obligations that served U.S. interests above their own. From 2004 to 2009, some of the more strident members of the Non-Aligned Movement expressed these views quite frankly during informal meetings held under the Chatham House Rule (i.e., nonattribution).[49]

The rocky reception that Resolution 1540 received in 2004, the early resistance to it among some states, and the gradual growth in its acceptance can all be partially explained by the leadership characteristics of the Bush and Obama administrations. While both emphasized nonproliferation from the start, the Bush administration was largely unperturbed by the legitimacy deficit associated with its own approach, whereas the Obama administration made the pursuit of broad-based international support a greater priority. The dismissive response of key figures in the Bush administration to international criticism of its counterproliferation initiatives led its efforts to show leadership on Resolution 1540 to backfire. John Bolton, for example, made no secret of his belief that perceptions of the lack of legitimacy of U.S. nonproliferation leadership were irrelevant when he stated, "Our actions . . . require no separate, external validation to make them legitimate. Whether it is removing a rogue Iraqi regime and replacing it, [or] preventing WMD proliferation . . . the United States will utilize its institutions of representative government, adhere to its constitutional strictures, and follow its values when measuring the legitimacy of its actions."[50] This attitude undermined U.S. leadership on 1540, especially during 2005–6, when Bolton served as U.S. permanent representative to the United Nations during a sensitive period shortly after Resolution 1540 was passed.[51]

In contrast, the Obama administration placed a premium on restoring U.S. legitimacy as a world leader, reflected in the early conciliatory speeches that Obama delivered in Prague, Istanbul, and Cairo.[52] At the UN, U.S. representative Susan Rice made a point of demonstrating U.S. sensitivity to North-South tensions, especially over competing security and development priorities.[53] The result was a gradual rebuilding of the legitimacy that was lost during the Bush administration, which can help explain the growth in support for 1540, both on a rhetorical level in UN forums and in increased national implementation of 1540 obligations.[54]

The Obama administration's early efforts to redress imbalances in the nuclear nonproliferation regime were a crucial part of its legitimacy-building strategy. Much of the early criticism of Resolution 1540 reflected a broader concern that the United States had an unbalanced view of state obligations under the Nuclear Non-Proliferation Treaty (NPT). A traditional interpretation holds that the NPT has three pillars: nonproliferation, good-faith efforts at nuclear disarmament, and access to the peaceful uses of the atom. Non-nuclear-weapon states contend that most of the nuclear weapon states, and especially the United States, place too much emphasis on nonproliferation at the expense of progress on nuclear disarmament and to the detriment of international cooperation on the peaceful uses of nuclear energy.

Early debates in the UN over Resolution 1540 exposed this as a major bone of contention, as critics complained that the resolution text focused exclusively on nonproliferation, reinforcing the deeply unpopular nuclear status quo.[55] Many states considered this to be unjust, given that only a handful of countries possess the most dangerous weapons in the world, and yet all UN member states, however large or small and whatever their capabilities, are bound by the obligations set out in Resolution 1540. As many representatives stressed at the time (and continue to stress), the best way to keep nuclear weapons out of the hands of non-state actors is to pursue universal nuclear disarmament, a point that the Bush administration seemed to dismiss. This undermined support for Resolution 1540, reinforcing perceptions that the United States and its allies were imposing increasingly burdensome nonproliferation obligations on the international community while shirking their own disarmament commitments. The Obama administration's reassertion of proactive U.S. disarmament leadership reduced some of this resentment, and may be partly responsible for accelerated progress in 1540 implementation during Obama's first term.[56]

Summarizing the Explanation

In chapter 1, Knopf identifies seven factors that could be associated with cooperation on international nonproliferation initiatives. As the foregoing makes clear, all seven have played some role in the course of Resolution 1540, with capabilities being the most central to the progress that has been made so far. U.S. leadership, in conjunction with other permanent members of the Security Council (other than China), was decisive early on in erecting this new framework for keeping WMD out of the hands of terrorists. Self-interest, in the broad sense that many states share the perception of a global threat from WMD terrorism, accounts for much of the support for 1540. Norms also played a role, but this case shows that conflicting norms can be involved. Concerns about sovereignty worked in a contrary direction to antiterrorism norms, as some states were reluctant to grant the Security Council the authority to mandate domestic legislation for UN member states. Domestic politics also functioned as a constraint in some developing nations, because popular disapproval of U.S. policy made some governments reluctant to sign on to what some saw as just another expression of U.S. hegemony.

Turning from rhetorical support to implementation brings the remaining three factors into play. For many states, capacity shortfalls have been the key factor limiting their ability to meet the extensive obligations associated with Resolution 1540. In this situation, inducements and persuasion have been important tools in helping states address some of these capacity issues. The 1540 Committee, donor states, international organizations, and NGOs have all offered important sources of assistance to states that need it. They have also figured out how to persuade some reluctant recipients to accept assistance, by arguing that activities to implement 1540 will actually benefit rather than hamper economic development. Finally, learning and working relationships in transnational networks have also been critical. The 1540 framework did not initially contain appropriate arrangements to coordinate the provision of assistance, but through a learning process there has been improvement in this area. Certain lower-level officials, such as Tom Wuchte, have also been instrumental in helping build the connections that are leading to greater progress in implementing the obligations of Resolution 1540.

CONCLUSION

Since the UN Security Council adopted it in 2004, Resolution 1540 has become a core part of the nonproliferation and counterterrorism regimes. Its legitimacy has grown, its mechanisms are becoming more coordinated, and although compliance with its obligations is uneven and patchy, implementation is growing thanks to a combination of capacity-building assistance, norm consolidation, and more effective leadership at the national, regional, and international levels. Many of the huge challenges associated with preventing WMD terrorism remain, but the actors involved have been engaged in a learning process that has resulted in an increasingly successful nonproliferation partnership among the UN Security Council, member states, and international organizations. While it would be unrealistic to expect Resolution 1540, alone, to prevent WMD terrorism, it plays an important part in increasing awareness of the relevant threats and vulnerabilities and helping states to increase their capacity to reduce them.

This analysis offers some clear lessons. The first is that to have any chance of success, any nonproliferation initiative on the scale of Resolution 1540 requires a well-coordinated assistance mechanism, and the sooner this can start to operate, the better. Allowing assistance to occur on an ad hoc basis, with little oversight, results in inefficiency and missed opportunities, and can provide another reason for inaction among states that are critical of or resistant to global nonproliferation efforts.

The second lesson is that norm emergence and consolidation can take time, and can involve a bumpy period of norm recalibration, as existing norms compete with new norms. In the case of 1540, some states feared that the new obligations set out in the resolution had undermined the norm of noninterference and the principle of conferral, and it required sensitive handling on the part of key individuals, the 1540 Committee, and international organizations to encourage these states to adjust to the changing balance of power between themselves and the Security Council. Last, while the linkages between the nonproliferation, disarmament, and peaceful-use pillars of the NPT often seem counterproductive, they cannot be dismissed without serious penalty. All states need to be seen to take these linkages seriously in order to generate the trust and goodwill that are crucial to multilateral nonproliferation cooperation. The Bush administration ignored this to its detriment, as its efforts to show leadership on Resolution 1540 backfired. The Obama administration tried to address this problem by reasserting U.S. disarmament leadership, but this needs to be sustained if support for Resolution 1540 is to continue to grow.

Notes

1. Address by George W. Bush, UN General Assembly (58th General Session, 7th Plenary Meeting, A/58/PV.7, September 23, 2003), 11.

2. Jack Straw, speech to the 58th session of the UN General Assembly (September 25, 2003), www.un.org/webcast/ga/58/statements/ukeng030925.htm. In early 2003, the U.K. government had circulated a non-paper within the EU proposing the creation of a UN counterproliferation committee. See Masahiko Asada, "WMD Terrorism and Security Council Resolution

1540: Conditions for Legitimacy in International Legislation" (International Law and Justice Working Papers, New York University School of Law, September 2007), 10.

3. Merav Datan, "Security Council Resolution 1540: WMD and Non-state Trafficking," *Disarmament Diplomacy*, no. 79 (May 28, 2004), www.acronym.org.uk/dd/dd79/79md.htm.

4. Author discussions with U.S. and Chinese representatives at several study group meetings on "Countering the Proliferation of Weapons of Mass Destruction in the Asia-Pacific" (Council on Security Cooperation in the Asia-Pacific [CSCAP], 2006–12).

5. UN Security Council Resolution 1977, April 20, 2011, S/RES/1977 (2011).

6. Author discussions with representatives of UN missions, Stanley Foundation 42nd Annual UN Issues Conference, "UN Security Council Resolution 1540: Identity, Extension, and Implementation" (Tarrytown, N.Y., February 25–27, 2011).

7. S/RES/1540 (2004).

8. Report of the Committee Established Pursuant to Security Council Resolution 1540 (2004) (S/2011/579, September 14, 2011), available at www.un.org/en/sc/1540/reports-and-briefings/committee-reports.shtml.

9. See Richard T. Cupitt, "Nearly at the Brink: The Tasks and Capacity of the 1540 Committee," *Arms Control Today* 42, no. 7 (September 2012). Current and past members are listed at www.un.org/en/sc/1540/committee/expert-group.shtml.

10. For example, in March 2011, the United States made a voluntary contribution to this UN Trust Fund to support the assistance efforts of the 1540 Committee. Note Verbale of the EU Delegation and U.S. Mission to the United Nations (New York, October 31, 2011).

11. Security Council Resolution 1267 in 1999 placed sanctions on al-Qaeda and associated entities and individuals, and the 1267 Committee monitors implementation. Resolution 1373, adopted under Chapter VII shortly after 9/11, mandates various measures to combat terrorism and established the Counter-Terrorism (1373) Committee to monitor progress.

12. 1540 Committee Report, S/2011/579.

13. As of January 2015, the nonreporting states are Cape Verde, Central African Republic, Chad, Comoros, Democratic People's Republic of North Korea, Equatorial Guinea, Gambia, Guinea, Guinea-Bissau, Haiti, Mali, Mauritania, Mozambique, Sao Tome and Principe, Solomon Islands, Somalia, Swaziland, Timor-Leste, Zambia, and Zimbabwe. The chair of the committee, as well as members states, the EU, African Union, and G8 (now G7), have been working with some of the nonreporting states to help them submit their first report, and it is clear from these meetings that the main reason for nonreporting is capacity challenges.

14. These tables have been compiled using the data provided in the 2011 and 2008 reports of the 1540 Committee. Reports S/2011/579, September 14, 2011; and S/2008/493, July 30, 2008. As of January 2015, no further reports have been published since September 2011, but a third report of the 1540 Committee is expected before the end of 2016.

15. The intergovernmental Financial Action Task Force (FATF) keeps a list of states that are falling behind with their obligation to squeeze the financing of terrorism, and has started to focus its attention on the financing of non-state WMD activities. In February 2014, there were nineteen countries on the FATF blacklist, including Albania, Angola, Argentina, Cuba, Iraq, Kenya, Kuwait, Kyrgyzstan, Lao PDR, Mongolia, Namibia, Nepal, Nicaragua, Papua New Guinea, Sudan, Tajikistan, Tanzania, Uganda, and Zimbabwe. In addition, Afghanistan and Cambodia were singled out as making the least progress. For further information, see www.fatf-gafi.org/documents/news/fatf-compliance-feb-2014.html.

16. See, for example, Thailand's 1540 Matrix, as approved by the 1540 Committee on December 30, 2010, available at www.un.org/en/sc/1540/docs/matrices/Thailand%20revised%20matrix.pdf.

17. Some limited information on prosecutions is available via the Nuclear Threat Initiative's website. See, for example, "South Asia 1540 Reporting," *NTI Analysis*, January 9, 2014, www.nti.org/analysis/reports/south-asia-1540-reporting/.

18. The Stanley Foundation, "UNSCR 1540: Identity, Extension, and Implementation," *Policy Dialogue Brief* (summary report, 42nd UN Issues Conference, Tarrytown, N.Y., February 25-27, 2011).

19. This rising level of awareness of WMD terrorism threats and gradual process of norm acceptance is on display during debates in the UN First Committee, UN counterterrorism committees, regional forums, and track 2 (informal) diplomatic workshops and seminars worldwide.

20. M. Patrick Cottrell, "Hope or Hype? Legitimacy and U.S. Leadership in a Global Age," *Foreign Policy Analysis* 7, no. 3 (July 2011): 337-58; William B. Messmer and Carlos L. Yordan, "A Partnership to Counter International Terrorism: The UN Security Council and the UN Member States," *Studies in Conflict and Terrorism* 34, no. 11 (October 2011): 843-61; Heinz Gartner, "Towards a Theory of Arms Export Control," *International Politics* 47, no. 1 (January 2010): 125-43.

21. Author discussions with state representatives at the Stanley Foundation's 42nd Annual UN Issues Conference, February 2011.

22. 1540 Committee Report, S/2011/579; Annette Ahrnens, "A Quest for Legitimacy: Debating UN Security Council Rules on Terrorism and Nonproliferation" (Lund Political Studies 148, Lund University, Sweden, 2007), 165-69.

23. 1540 Committee Report, S/2011/579.

24. Summary Records of the 25th-30th 1540 Committee Open Meetings, UN Security Council (September 30-October 2, 2009), www.un.org/en/sc/1540/comprehensive-review/summaryrecords.shtml.

25. "Final Document on the 2009 Comprehensive Review of the Status of Implementation of Resolution 1540 (2004): Key Findings and Recommendations" (S/2010/52, February 1, 2010), www.un.org/ga/search/view_doc.asp?symbol=S/2010/52.

26. Ibid.

27. UN Security Council Resolution 1977, S/RES/1977 (2011).

28. Tanya Ogilvie-White, "Facilitating Implementation of UN Security Council Resolution 1540 in Southeast Asia and the Pacific," in *Facilitating Implementation of Resolution 1540: The Role of Regional Organizations*, ed. Lawrence Scheinman (Geneva: UNIDIR, 2008), 43-79.

29. Summary Records of the 25th-30th 1540 Committee Open Meetings.

30. The Stanley Foundation, "Perceptions, Resources Challenge Implementation of UN Security Council Resolution 1540 Ahead of April Renewal" (Policy memo, March 1, 2011).

31. Douglas M. Stinnett, Bryan R. Early, Cale Horne, and Johannes Karreth, "Complying by Denying: Explaining Why States Develop Nonproliferation Export Controls," *International Studies Perspectives* 12, no. 3 (August 2011): 308-26.

32. Tanya Ogilvie-White, report for CSCAP New Zealand following the 15th Meeting of the CSCAP Study Group on Countering the Proliferation of Weapons of Mass Destruction in the Asia Pacific (Sydney, Australia, March 5-7, 2012).

33. These criticisms were on display following the May 2011 Security Council briefings by the antiterrorism committee chairs. Representatives from Bosnia and Herzegovina and Gabon made it clear that they were not satisfied with the level of assistance on offer. UN Security Council, SC/10252, May 16, 2011.

34. Traditionally, the economic interests of developing states and the belief that export controls hamper trade and development have obstructed cooperation on strategic trade con-

trols. For an analysis of tactical noncooperation in this area, see Gartner, "Towards a Theory of Arms Export Control."

35. Brian Finlay, Johan Bergenas, and Veronica Tessler, "Beyond Boundaries in Eastern Africa: Bridging the Security/Development Divide with International Security Assistance" (Henry L. Stimson Center and Stanley Foundation report, March 2011), www.stanleyfoundation.org/publications/report/EArpt311.pdf.

36. Ogilvie-White, "Facilitating Implementation," 55.

37. The tensions between these competing norms are observable in most areas of UN debate, and are especially pronounced in disputes over the "responsibility to protect" principle and peace support operations.

38. For a detailed discussion of this issue, see Ahrnens, "Quest for Legitimacy."

39. Nicholas Tsagourias, "Security Council Legislation, Article 2(7) of the UN Charter and the Principle of Subsidiarity" (Adam Smith Research Foundation Working Papers, August 2011), 4.

40. Regional diplomatic culture involves seeking agreement, harmony, and consensus rather than confrontation; accepting the need for sensitivity, politeness, and agreeability in dealings with others; and engaging in private elitist diplomacy over frank, open discussion of disagreements. See Tanya Ogilvie-White, "Nonproliferation and Counterterrorism Cooperation in Southeast Asia," *Contemporary Southeast Asia* 28, no. 1 (April 2006): 1–26.

41. Peter van Ham and Olivia Bosch, eds., *Global Non-proliferation and Counter-terrorism: The Role of Resolution 1540 and Its Implications* (Washington, D.C.: Brookings Institution Press, 2007), 8.

42. Dominique Dye, "African Perspectives on Countering Weapons of Mass Destruction" (Institute for Security Studies Paper 167, Pretoria, South Africa, September 2008), 5; Ogilvie-White, "Facilitating Implementation."

43. This partnership approach is explained in Messmer and Yordan, "Partnership to Counter International Terrorism."

44. Tsagourias, "Security Council Legislation," 7–8.

45. Stanley Foundation, "Perceptions, Resources Challenge Implementation," 1.

46. Malaysia provides the most striking example of a state that has changed its attitude to Resolution 1540. The Malaysian government was originally one of the resolution's most outspoken critics. Yet in 2010, it introduced the Strategic Trade Act, which aims to curb the export and transshipment of WMD-related materials. The law was developed with the assistance of the United States, EU, and Japan.

47. Dye, "African Perspectives on Countering Weapons of Mass Destruction," 3; Ogilvie-White, "Nonproliferation and Counterterrorism Cooperation," 6.

48. Members of the Non-Aligned Movement (NAM) pushed hard to have some input into the drafting process, but their input was carefully controlled and had limited impact. Lars Olberg, "Implementing Resolution 1540: What the National Reports Indicate," *Disarmament Diplomacy*, no. 82 (Spring 2006), www.acronym.org.uk/dd/dd82/82lo.htm.

49. For example, see the chairman's reports from the CSCAP Study Group on Countering the Proliferation of Weapons of Mass Destruction, especially for 2006–7.

50. John R. Bolton, "'Legitimacy' in International Affairs: The American Perspective in Theory and Operation" (remarks, Federalist Society, Washington, D.C., November 13, 2003).

51. Representatives from the UN permanent missions of India, Indonesia, Iran, Malaysia, and Pakistan, interviews, New York, September–October 2006.

52. Cottrell, "Hope or Hype?," 338.

53. Insight into the Obama administration's approach to North-South issues can be found in Susan M. Rice, "A New Course in the World: A New Approach at the UN" (remarks, New York University Center for Global Affairs and Center on International Cooperation, New York, August 12, 2009), http://paei.state.gov/usun.state.gov/usun/briefing/statements/2009/august/127953.htm.

54. This growth in support can be observed in the national statements following the open Security Council briefings by the chairs of the antiterrorism committees, including the 1540 Committee.

55. Datan, "Security Council Resolution 1540."

56. Tanya Ogilvie-White and David Santoro, "Conclusion," in *Slaying the Nuclear Dragon: Disarmament Dynamics in the Twenty-First Century*, ed. Ogilvie-White and Santoro (Athens: University of Georgia Press, 2012), 304–23. A perceived backtracking on disarmament by the United States and other nuclear weapon states during the 2015 NPT Review Conference could have an adverse effect on future implementation of Resolution 1540.

CHAPTER EIGHT

Formal and Informal Mechanisms for Countering Nuclear Terrorism
The ICSANT and the GICNT

GAVIN CAMERON

THE ISSUE OF NUCLEAR TERRORISM falls at the intersection of concerns about proliferation and concerns about terrorism. As such, it has been addressed through both nonproliferation and antiterrorism measures. In addition to general efforts in these areas, there are a handful of initiatives that deal specifically with the danger of nuclear terrorism. The Convention on the Physical Protection of Nuclear Material (CPPNM), which opened for signature in 1980 and entered into force in 1987, represents an early but limited attempt at international cooperation in this area. It focuses on ensuring the security of international shipments of nuclear materials intended for peaceful purposes and also promotes interstate cooperation in the event materials are stolen. An amendment approved in 2005, which has not yet entered into force, adds legally binding commitments to protect nuclear facilities and materials during domestic use, storage, or transport. Shortly after the terrorist attacks on September 11, 2001, the UN Security Council (UNSC) approved Resolution 1373. Adopted under Chapter VII of the UN Charter, which makes it legally binding, this resolution mandates a range of antiterrorist actions, focused on terrorism in general rather than nuclear terrorism. Following this precedent, the UNSC later adopted Resolution 1540 (the subject of a separate chapter in this volume), which creates a set of legally binding obligations on states intended to make it harder for non-state actors to acquire not just nuclear but also biological or chemical weapons. This chapter analyzes two other international efforts to reduce the risk of nuclear terrorism. These make for an interesting comparison because they reflect two different approaches to promoting international cooperation.

The United Nations International Convention for the Suppression of Acts of Nuclear Terrorism (ICSANT) came into force in 2007, two years after it was opened for signature. The Global Initiative to Combat Nuclear Terrorism

(GICNT) was established in 2006 to facilitate cooperation against the threat of nuclear terrorism, through the sharing of information and knowledge. The ICSANT and GICNT represent, respectively, formal and informal mechanisms to respond to the threat of nuclear terrorism. Although such efforts are not solely a product of the post–September 11 world, the events of that day and the subsequent international responses provided a major impetus to discussions that, in the case of ICSANT, had been stalled for several years. However, the two mechanisms differ substantially and the GICNT, an initially bilateral arrangement that has developed into a coalition of the willing, has enjoyed earlier and more willing participation than the more traditionally multilateral ICSANT.

The following analysis finds that several factors identified in chapter 1, including self-interest, norms, and U.S. leadership (or its absence), have played a role in explaining cooperation on these two initiatives. The analysis also supports the suggestion that informal, working-level approaches are becoming more prominent, but this does not mean that they are fully effective. International cooperation to counter nuclear terrorism has remained incomplete, with states in the Global South generally being the least interested in participating.

THE INTERNATIONAL CONVENTION FOR THE SUPPRESSION OF ACTS OF NUCLEAR TERRORISM

Background

In 1996, UN General Assembly Resolution 50/53 required that the UN secretary-general prepare a report on the current legal frameworks pertaining to international terrorism. The resulting report concluded that significant gaps existed within the then existing instruments. In response, the General Assembly, in Resolution 51/210, established an Ad Hoc Committee with instructions that it develop, among other measures, an International Convention for the Suppression of Acts of Nuclear Terrorism. This need was pressing due to continuing concerns over nuclear smuggling within the former Soviet Union and because, as Russia argued, the only on-point convention, the CPPNM, dealt solely with nuclear material used for peaceful purposes. New measures were required that would deal also with military nuclear material.[1] Russia proposed a draft convention, emphasizing in particular the importance of preventing an act of nuclear terrorism and of mitigating its consequences.

The convention was unanimously approved by the General Assembly on April 13, 2005. It opened for signature on September 14, 2005, and entered into force on July 7, 2007, with the ratification of Bangladesh, the twenty-second state to ratify the convention.[2]

The ICSANT reflected one of the major concerns of policy makers: the potential for an act of terrorism that utilized nuclear means. Although present earlier, such fears increased in the early 1990s with alarm at the prospect of "loose nukes" in the former Soviet Union and then in the wake of Aum Shinrikyo's use of a chemical weapon in Tokyo in 1995. The attacks of September 11, 2001, reinforced beliefs that mass casualty terrorism with unconventional weapons was more likely than in the past. In the United States, both President George W. Bush and President Barack Obama supported a variety of initiatives, including the GICNT and the ICSANT, to counter the threat. However, even following the attacks of September 11, 2001, the international community has never agreed on a single uniform definition of terrorism, and many states lack the ability materially or institutionally to fulfill their obligations under UNSC Resolution 1373.[3] This has limited the extent of international cooperation against terrorism, and some of the challenges to promoting cooperation against terrorism in general have also affected the ICSANT.

What ICSANT Does

Although the convention does not offer an official definition of the term "nuclear terrorism," Article 2 lists a set of offenses that amount to a de facto definition. Most of the article encompasses a broad but relatively mainstream understanding of the phenomenon: nuclear terrorism is the intentional and unlawful damage to either people or property through the use of radioactive materials or devices or through damage to a nuclear facility that causes the release of radioactive material. It includes also the threat or attempt to do any of these actions or the participation as an accomplice, conspirator, or planner in any such actions. However, Article 2.2b extends the definition, so that nuclear terrorism includes not only the use or attempted use of a device, but also the acquisition or attempted acquisition of "radioactive material, a device or a nuclear facility by [making a] threat, under circumstances which indicate the credibility of the threat, or by use of force."[4]

The convention defines its scope broadly, so that it covers a greater range of materials and facilities than does the CPPNM. The ICSANT applies to both nuclear material and other radioactive material and also to any facility or vehicle "used for the production, storage, processing or transport of radioactive material," including those such as submarines where such materials are used in reactors as a means of propulsion. The convention also concerns itself with injury, property damage, and environmental harm caused by the malicious use of nuclear or radiological materials (i.e., both nuclear devices and radiological or "dirty" weapons).[5] The ICSANT, while covering both military and peaceful applications, deals exclusively with individuals' actions, so it does not consider either the activities of military forces during a conflict or exercise, or the issue of nuclear nonproliferation or nuclear threats, as these pertain to either states or intergovernmental organizations. The convention requires states to use national legislation to criminalize and appropriately punish acts of nuclear terrorism.[6] In addition, Article 7 of the convention obligates states parties to cooperate by "taking all practicable measures . . . to prevent and counter preparations" to commit an act of nuclear terrorism and to exchange "accurate and verified information . . . to detect, prevent, suppress and investigate the offences set forth in article 2 and also in order to institute criminal proceedings against persons alleged to have committed those crimes."[7] The ICSANT also calls on states to "make every effort to adopt appropriate measures to ensure the physical protection of radioactive materials."[8]

States' Reservations

As of mid-2015, ninety-nine states have become parties to the ICSANT, but a number of important states have not joined, including some surprising holdouts. Among the countries that have signed but not ratified the convention are Argentina, Egypt, Israel, Italy, New Zealand, Syria, and the United States. Several of these, including the currently unstable Syria, have weapons-usable nuclear materials.[9] States that have neither signed nor ratified the convention include several of proliferation and/or terrorism concern, such as Iran, Pakistan, and North Korea.[10] Such a list reflects a mixture of motivations and concerns about the convention. It includes official NPT nuclear weapon states, states that have long criticized what they see as the unequal obligations imposed by the NPT, and even states that have traditionally been strongly supportive of multilateral approaches to international security problems, generally, and the nuclear nonproliferation regime specifically. It also includes states for which nuclear terrorism is a critical concern.

Some of the challenges to obtaining participation in an international convention dealing with nuclear terrorism were already visible in the negotiation process. The process between initial proposal and eventual General Assembly approval of the convention took nine years (1996–2005), reflecting several key problems. First, drafts of the ICSANT contained no definition of terrorism per se, while addressing and defining a series of related issues. The absence of such a definition permits potential ambiguity about the actors and actions that are covered by the convention. For this reason, in hopes it would produce an agreed definition, some states preferred to focus first on a draft International Convention on International Terrorism, another product of the Ad Hoc Committee created by UN General Assembly Resolution 51/210 in 1996. As yet, negotiations remain ongoing toward such a comprehensive convention, with the key challenge remaining one of defining terrorism.

Second, the scope of the convention was a source of dispute. Some states, notably those from the Non-Aligned Movement, sought to include language on the illegality of nuclear weapons use or threatened use by the armed forces of the nuclear weapon states, and rejected any language that appeared to legitimize such use.[11] Other states argued that since the convention dealt with individuals perpetrating acts of nuclear terrorism and since conduct of states' armed forces was already regulated by international law, such inclusive language was unnecessary. Ultimately, this dispute was resolved by the inclusion of balancing language within the Preamble and Article 4 that excluded states' armed forces from the scope of the convention while not condoning or legitimizing such forces.[12]

Convention language about arbitration has also been a source of reservations. Some states, such as Argentina (which has still to ratify the convention) and India (which has done so), objected to Article 23.1, which opened the possibility that disagreements over interpretation of the convention might ultimately be referred to the International Court of Justice, the jurisdiction of which some such states disputed.[13]

Despite the various disputes that attended the drafting of the convention, many states have joined it. For obvious reasons, all states signing and/or ratifying the convention emphasize the importance of nuclear security and the dangers of nuclear terrorism. However, some countries had multiple motives for joining the ICSANT. For example, India's eagerness reflected not only significant concerns about nuclear terrorism, but also an attempt to strengthen its strategic relationship with one of the key proponents of the convention, Russia.[14] Because India cannot join the NPT as an official nuclear weapon state, it is interested in joining other international arrangements as a way to be acknowledged as a responsible nuclear power and to gain international prestige for acting as a good global citizen.[15]

Since the ICSANT came into force in 2007, the most significant holdout state has been the United States. Other states are waiting for U.S. ratification of the ICSANT before beginning their own ratification processes.[16] The U.S. failure to ratify the convention does not reflect any deep objections to the treaty, but instead has to do with the challenges of passing domestic legislation required by the convention. In September 2007, the Bush administration submitted the ICSANT to the U.S. Senate, which approved resolutions of advice and consent to ratification for these agreements in September 2008. In order to complete the ratification process, however, the United States needs to pass criminal legislation dealing with a range of offenses covered within the ICSANT and the 2005 amendment to the CPPNM. The House of Representatives passed the legislation on June 28, 2012, and again in May 2013. Senate approval, however, was delayed by disputes within the Senate Judiciary Committee over whether certain crimes under the legislation should be capital offences.[17] In addition to the death penalty issue, previous versions of the bill became bogged down over the information-sharing provisions within the ICSANT, the potential legal ramifications of possible military actions against foreign nuclear facilities, concerns at the overlap and potential lack of consistency between provisions within the new legislation and current U.S. counterterrorism laws, and concerns about wiretap provisions in the legislation.[18] A major additional issue is that the legislation that would permit U.S. ratification of the ICSANT simply has not been a priority for Congress.[19] Finally, in June 2015, Congress passed the implementing legislation that will enable Senate ratification.

The low priority given to passing necessary legislation to permit ratification of the ICSANT also accounts for the slow progress toward full membership of the convention by two close U.S. allies, both of which are often at the forefront of nonproliferation efforts: New Zealand and Canada. New Zealand officials have been working on legislation since 2005 and have blamed a crowded legislative agenda for slow progress.[20] In its progress report for the 2014 Nuclear Security Summit, New Zealand promised that its parliament is "soon to consider the domestic legislation necessary to complete implementation."[21] Canada introduced changes to the Criminal Code via legislation that came into effect on November 1, 2013.[22] However, the Canadian government waited until March 2012 to introduce such changes, suggesting that ratification of the ICSANT was not a legislative priority.

The issue for Canada has not been doubts about the threat of nuclear terrorism, but rather a preference for pursuing efforts to combat that threat through means other than the ICSANT. When Canada finally moved to ratify the ICSANT, norms and identity provided much of the motivation. Testimony and debate in the Canadian parliament suggest that the decision to amend the Canadian Criminal Code to permit ratification of the ICSANT reflected recognition that nuclear terrorism was a problem as well as a belief that ratification was an international obligation and was necessary to maintain Canadian leadership on nonproliferation.[23]

In summary, the ICSANT suffered from a long and contentious negotiation process. This resulted in compromises that both reduced its attractiveness to some potential members, including several key states within the international system, and limited its potential efficacy as an instrument by which nuclear terrorism might be countered. The criminal legislative requirements for states to ratify the convention ensure that there is a domestic political burden to participating in the regime, while the rewards for doing so are limited by the lack of domestic pressure or desire for such action in several key states. This last tendency both reflects and contributes to the limited prominence of the ICSANT. These factors should not be exaggerated: the number of states signing and ratifying the convention is steadily increasing, and states are choosing to do so for a variety of reasons. However, the difficulties of the ICSANT do encourage the many states concerned by the threat of nuclear terrorism to seek less burdensome and potentially more effective mechanisms, such as the GICNT, to alleviate that threat.

THE GLOBAL INITIATIVE TO COMBAT NUCLEAR TERRORISM

Background

The GICNT was announced on July 15, 2006, by U.S. president Bush and President Vladimir Putin of Russia, who called on other states to join in a project to further develop existing efforts to prevent nuclear terrorism.[24] The initiative met with an early positive response, and thirteen states—Australia, Canada, China, France, Germany, Italy, Japan, Kazakhstan, Morocco, Russia, Turkey, the United Kingdom, and the United States—attended the initial meeting in October 2006, which produced a Statement of Principles. According to the U.S. Department of State, "The eight principles within the [GICNT Statement of Principles] aim to develop partnership capacity to combat nuclear terrorism on a determined and systematic basis, consistent with national legal authorities and obligations as well as relevant international legal frameworks such as the Convention for the Suppression of Acts of Nuclear Terrorism, the Convention on the Physical Protection of Nuclear Material, and United Nations Security Council Resolutions 1373 and 1540."[25] This cooperation and international capacity-building is to be achieved "by conducting multilateral activities that strengthen the plans, policies, procedures, and interoperability of partner nations."[26]

What the GICNT Does

The GICNT offers a means by which partner states can share information and best practices and enhance the efficacy of individual and collective efforts to counter nuclear terrorism through meetings, seminars, workshops, and exercises. Partners participate in the GICNT by taking part in such collective activities, either as hosts or organizers or simply as attendees. Senior-level officials from GICNT partners also meet periodically. Such meetings initially took place about once per year, but are now scheduled once every two years; since 2008 these meetings have been called the GICNT Plenary. Coordination and prioritization of efforts within the GICNT is undertaken by the Implementation and Assessment Group (IAG), which serves as a mechanism to establish working groups and focus efforts upon activities that have been identified by the Plenary. The IAG was established at the 2010 Plenary session in Abu Dhabi and is open to all partners of the GICNT. Spain was elected as the Group Coordinator until

2013, followed by South Korea. States wishing to host an activity relevant to the GICNT approach the IAG Coordinator to do so. Such events may also receive financial assistance or other forms of logistical help from one of the co-chairs (Russia and the United States until 2019).[27]

So far, partners within the GICNT have participated in nine senior-level meetings (the first in Rabat, Morocco, in 2006, the most recent in Finland in 2015).[28] The practical work promoted by GICNT, however, takes place in other meetings, conferences, and exercises that have focused on more specific elements of the GICNT's objectives. These objectives include improving material protection, control, and accounting (MPC&A) of nuclear and radiological materials, combating nuclear trafficking, reinforcing national legal measures to combat terrorism including the financing of terrorism, and enhancing consequence-mitigation efforts in the event of a nuclear terrorism incident. One example of such an event is the Global Initiative Law Enforcement Conference, held in the United States in June 2007, at which there was discussion of the role of law enforcement and the potential challenges that such organizations faced across the nuclear fuel cycle.[29]

The 2010 and 2011 Plenary meetings identified three priorities by which "enhanced implementation" could be pursued with a view to promoting the GICNT as a durable international institution: nuclear detection, nuclear forensics, and response and mitigation. Working groups in these three areas were led by the Netherlands, Australia, and Morocco, respectively. At the 2013 Plenary meeting in Mexico, the three working groups reported on their activities in the preceding two years and their plans for future activities. The 2013 Plenary also endorsed three documents which, as a result, became official products of the GICNT. These dealt with fundamentals of nuclear forensics, best practices for training and exercises, and guidelines for planning and organization of nuclear detection efforts.[30]

Participants

States that wish to join the GICNT write to one of the initiative co-chairs, endorsing the eight principles. Upon the agreement of the co-chairs, the state joins the initiative as a partner. The process for admitting an observer organization is similar, but such observer status is limited to intergovernmental organizations. Membership of the GICNT is voluntary and as of 2015 the initiative has eighty-six partner states and five observer organizations: the International Atomic Energy Agency (IAEA), the UN Office on Drugs and Crime, the UN Interregional Crime and Justice Research Institute, INTERPOL, and the European Union. Of these, the IAEA is the most significant, given what IAEA efforts, knowledge, and resources could contribute to the GICNT.[31]

As with the ICSANT, states' participation in the GICNT reflects multiple motives and objectives. Successive U.S. administrations have been genuinely committed to preventing nuclear terrorism. Likewise, Russia's long-standing concern on the issue is obvious from its leadership of different multilateral initiatives, including relevant UN conventions. Part of the GICNT's purpose was to fill perceived gaps in the nuclear material security regime while avoiding a replication of the protracted international negotiations and substantive compromises that accompanied the ICSANT and CPPNM Amendment.[32] Despite the sluggishness of U.S. ratification of the ICSANT, the U.S. executive branch has seen the GICNT as a supplement rather than an alternative to the convention: a key U.S. official described it as a "necessary platform for implementing the provisions of the Nuclear Terrorism Convention" and a measure that builds upon and complements other efforts being taken both internationally and within the United States. He added that the initiative also offers a means for the United States to push other states into doing more toward combating nuclear terrorism: "Our goal is to galvanize our partners to invest greater resources in their own capabilities to protect nuclear material on their territory.... [T]he Global Initiative will ensure that our strategies for combating nuclear terrorism are tailored to the conditions prevailing with our partner nations."[33]

The announcement of the GICNT corresponded with Russia's presidency of the G8 and hosting of the G8 Summit in St. Petersburg. The initiative reflected two of the three themes that Russia emphasized during its presidency: counterterrorism and nuclear nonproliferation. As such, the announcement offered Moscow a means to help set the international agenda and give impetus to an issue of major concern to Russia. The GICNT also strengthened U.S.-Russian relations and provided international prestige for Russia. This fit into Russia's concerns with being a peer of the United States and maintaining its power and influence, while also helping it "appear to be a responsible member of the international community."[34]

Other states also emphasized the importance of preventing nuclear terrorism in the decision to participate in the GICNT. India's foreign secretary, Nirupama Rao, said, "We believe that the challenges of nuclear terrorism and nuclear security have to be addressed. We have been affected by clandestine nuclear proliferation in our neighborhood. We are naturally concerned about the possibility of nuclear terrorism given the security situation in our neighborhood."[35] The GICNT emphasizes states' domestic efforts to counter nuclear terrorism. This enabled the participation of countries, such as China, that have resisted joining in other international efforts that they perceive as interventions in states' internal affairs, such as the Proliferation Security Initiative (PSI). For the same reason, China welcomed both the exclusive focus on terrorism rather than state-level nuclear activities and the opportunity to be a founding member of the GICNT and thereby shape its future development to reflect China's ongoing concerns over the appropriate parameters of such an agreement.[36]

EFFICACY OF THE ICSANT AND GICNT

Both the ICSANT and the GICNT have lent some momentum to efforts to reduce the risks of nuclear terrorism, though in comparative terms the GICNT has generated more visible activity than has the convention. Yet both measures also have limitations. While the ICSANT expanded the global nuclear materials control regime beyond the original version of the CPPNM to include military material, state participation in the convention has been relatively slow to develop. Instead, many states have chosen to pursue nuclear material control through less formal and more practically oriented schemes, such as the G8 (now G7) Global Partnership, PSI, or GICNT. This distinction can be seen in the final communiqué from the 2014 Nuclear Security Summit, which gave credit to the achievements of the GICNT while suggesting more needs to be done with respect to the ICSANT:

> We underline the importance of the International Convention for the Suppression of Acts of Nuclear Terrorism and stress the need for all contracting Parties to comply fully with all its provisions. We welcome the new ratifications and accessions since the Seoul Summit and encourage all States to become party to this Convention.... We recognize the contribution made by the Global Initiative to Combat Nuclear Terrorism (GICNT) and the Global Partnership Against the Spread of Weapons and Materials of Mass Destruction since the 2010 and 2012 Nuclear Security Summits.... Both have expanded in membership and have become valuable platforms for coordination and cooperation on nuclear security.[37]

Arguably, the language of the convention reduces its effectiveness. Calling on states to "*make every effort* to adopt appropriate measures to ensure the protection of radioactive material, taking into account the relevant recommendations and functions of the International Atomic Energy Agency,"[38] fails to provide a clear set of standards or obligations for member states and precludes effective enforcement of the convention's provisions. Seemingly, states will have met their responsibilities so long as they try to implement security measures (rather than necessarily succeeding in doing so) and they take into account (rather than necessarily operationalizing) the appropriate IAEA recommendations. This permits significant variance in practice that appears at odds with a robust regime for safeguarding radiological material.[39]

Christopher Joyner disagrees with such an assessment, citing the use of the strong diplomatic language, "all practicable means," in Article 7. He argues that the ICSANT increases the international legal basis for responding to nuclear terrorism by increasing the scope for cooperation and information sharing, and by obligating member states to pass domestic legislation that criminalizes a range of core activities connected to nuclear terrorism. Joyner acknowledges, however, that legal mechanisms are necessary, rather than sufficient, conditions for countering nuclear terrorism. Although the ICSANT creates new norms and rules by defining and proscribing nuclear terrorism, and imposes duties on states to operationalize such rules, the implementation of the convention is contingent on countries' actions, which may be predicated on such nonlegal factors as political will and state capacity.[40]

The GICNT initially enjoyed more rapid membership growth than the ICSANT. However, it would be a mistake to assume that either participation or effectiveness is synonymous with such membership. Although participation in the GICNT has grown steadily, it remains a "coalition of the willing" and has relatively few partners from the Global South, relative to the total numbers of such states. The rate at which additional states are joining the initiative appears to be actually slowing, an especially disappointing development as this comes at a time when the Obama administration was giving high-profile priority to nuclear security through the National Security Summit process and other initiatives.[41]

The GICNT does assist states to fulfill their existing commitments to combat nuclear terrorism. UN Security Council Resolution 1540, although calling on states to make "meaningful" and "effective" measures to fulfill their obligations, left the meaning of such phrases vague, and offered little material support to facilitate such compliance.[42] The GICNT, by offering practical if limited material support, helps to alleviate this problem. The U.S. State Department identifies several key contributions made by the GICNT working groups. These include fostering cooperation among governments to reduce vulnerabilities, identifying capabilities in which investments should be considered, and developing a guide to enable resource-limited states to have a capacity to cope with nuclear terrorism.[43]

There have been more than seventy events, under the GICNT's auspices, that have enhanced states' capabilities for "preventing, detecting, deterring and responding to nuclear terrorist incidents."[44] For example, in September 2012, Russia hosted an exercise involving representatives of over fifty states and international organizations that sought to share best practices on counteracting nuclear and radioactive materials trafficking.[45] Crucially, the GICNT encourages and facilitates efforts involving both the state and the private sector, although only states may be initiative partners.[46] The advantage of the GICNT approach is not only that it encourages efforts fitted to individual states' needs and abilities, rather than a one-size-fits-all approach, but also that it encourages states other than the major powers to take a leadership role in promoting such capacity-building. In December 2006, for example, Australia, a close ally of the United States and early supporter of the Global Initiative, pledged to conduct outreach in Southeast Asia in support of the GICNT.[47] More recently, Spain and Morocco conducted a joint exercise in 2013 to showcase the role of international cooperation in response to a radiological attack.[48]

Despite these examples, however, arguably the GICNT represents the agenda of just a few of the major powers, rather than of the entire international community. Governments in countries or regions without nuclear weapons or extensive civil nuclear energy programs are less likely to be convinced that nuclear terrorism represents a substantial threat for their state.[49] Bonnie Jenkins, cooperative threat reduction coordinator at the Department of State, has noted that "one of the reasons cited by some African states for nonparticipation is that they do not perceive nuclear terrorism as a direct threat to their interests." She argues that there is a need to persuade such states that the issue should be of concern to them.[50]

Moreover, many of the partners within the GICNT have been passive participants, seeing it as a largely cost-free means of maintaining good relations with key countries, mostly notably the United States, for as long as these countries continue to emphasize efforts against terrorism generally and against nuclear terrorism in particular. Both aspects of the initiative reflect the way in which it has been pursued from the outset. In the initial joint statement, "The United States and Russia call[ed] upon *like-minded nations* to expand and accelerate efforts that develop partnership capacity to combat nuclear terrorism on a determined and systematic basis.... *We will be prepared to work with all those who share our views* to strengthen mechanisms for multilateral and bilateral cooperation to suppress acts of nuclear terrorism."[51] Obviously, such language is likely to be a disincentive to participation by states that do not share same view of nuclear terrorism as that held by the initiative's founders. For example, the GICNT ignores military nuclear technology and facilities, so nuclear terrorism is framed as an exclusively substate rather than state-level challenge.[52]

Limited participation, both in numbers and in scale of activities, is in some respects an asset for the GICNT. The U.S. State Department suggests that "the voluntary nature of the GICNT partnership allows for a large degree of flexibility and the ability to achieve a maximalist impact. Because the GICNT is not constrained by consensus decision-making, partner nations bring with them and contribute the maximum that their resources and capabilities allow for.... The GICNT also expands the network of resources available to partners and helps partner nations identify and build the core competencies required to effectively combat nuclear terrorism."[53] The effort to "expand the network of resources available to partners," even if the resources discussed are ideational, technical, or practical, rather than financial, does require some monetary support. The initiative is not intended primarily as a means for channeling funds to close gaps in states' nuclear security measures (unlike the G8 Global Partnership, for example). However, the level of funding for the GICNT is low even for an effort to promote meetings and exercises that could help boost states' own capacities.[54]

Furthermore, Turpen and others see the lack of benchmark standards as a key weakness, arguing that the GICNT's principles set goals and activities to be pursued, but do not set a level of achievement to be attained either collectively or by individual states. Turpen also criticizes the informal and voluntary nature of the initiative, suggesting that it ensures that the GICNT lacks legitimacy and a robust institutional or legal framework that would increase pressure on states to participate in the initiative.[55] Reflecting this concern, in his 2009 Prague speech, President Obama called for turning both the GICNT and the PSI into "durable institutional institutions."[56] So far, however, despite such statements by President Obama and others, little has been done to give the initiative the character of a permanent institution.[57]

WHAT THE ICSANT AND THE GICNT TELL US ABOUT INTERNATIONAL COOPERATION

Both the ICSANT and the GICNT fit several of the themes identified in chapter 1. However, it is the GICNT that conforms to the basic hypothesis of the volume, which suggests that recent nonproliferation activity features informal and practical working-level cooperation rather than the more traditional and formal model represented by the NPT, for example. The ICSANT, in contrast, represents a recent example of this more traditional variety of institution.

Among the factors identified by Knopf as potentially relevant to explaining cooperation, self-interest has been key, but its correlation with cooperation is not perfect. States that perceive nuclear terrorism as a major threat are more likely than others to participate in the ICSANT and the GICNT, but there are exceptions, especially with regard to some states that have not yet ratified the convention. Norms have also played a role, for example in the case of Canada, which ratified the ICSANT more out of obligation than a sense of the convention's intrinsic value.

U.S. leadership also correlates well with the outcomes. While Russia was at the forefront of both the ICSANT and GICNT processes, the United States gave more weight to the initiative than to the formal convention. This contrast in U.S. leadership priorities played a role in the early struggles and successes, respectively, of the convention and initiative, which reinforces arguments for the importance of a hegemonic actor in multilateral cooperation.

The two arrangements were not just products of interests and norms, but are also helping to shape them. The ICSANT resulted from long-standing and broad concerns over both nuclear security and the international response to terrorism. The GICNT was the product of U.S.-Russian partnership, intended to facilitate states' ability to fulfill their existing commitments to countering nuclear terrorism. The ICSANT reinforces the international campaign against nuclear terrorism by obligating states to cooperate with one another to this end. It also reinforces a norm of nuclear security and places key international organizations, the UN and the IAEA, as essential instruments in developing this norm.[58] The GICNT has also made an important contribution, emphasizing as it does the importance of developing a transnational network to enhance learning. As a U.S. State Department official put it, "While there may not be a single, universal solution to preventing nuclear terrorism, the notion of 'best practices' teaches us that a successful approach in one country can be applied to others who may be facing similar threats. This is a central theme of the Global Initiative."[59] However, only relatively low commitment levels are currently required for participants. This has meant that although the GICNT conforms to the concept outlined earlier in this volume that multilateral cooperation on nonproliferation needs to be seen as a dynamic rather than static entity, as practical action rather than signatures on a formal treaty, all too often this has been more true in theory than in reality.

In chapter 1, Knopf noted that even when they broadly favor nonproliferation, states may not participate in specific efforts or may do so only reluctantly or halfheartedly. Certainly, this applies to many states' responses to the ICSANT, where even states that have been traditional supporters of multilateral nonproliferation have been slow to pursue the requisite steps to enable ratification of the convention. In some cases, domestic politics may play a role: both the Conservative government of Canada, which came to power in 2006, and the National government of New Zealand, which came to power in 2008, were substantially less committed to such approaches than were their predecessors. However, such an account can be only a partial explanation. In the United States, concerns over the ICSANT and support for the GICNT have not broken down cleanly across partisan lines. Miles Pomper suggests that part of the reason that legislation was bogged down in the U.S. House of Representatives is that the ICSANT is "sort of obscure to your average congressman, and they're not going to win or lose an election on it."[60] Similar criticism can be levied at the current regime to prevent nuclear terrorism, as a whole. An editorial in one of South Korea's major newspapers, written during the Seoul Nuclear Security Summit, noted that "[the] Summit . . . can hardly grab the attention of the ordinary public with all the technical acronyms [including both the ICSANT and GICNT] . . . and a theme too broad and opaque for common understanding."[61] In that sense, difficulties over cooperation are not the result of opposition by domestic constituencies, so much as of indifference. In some countries, legislators have reflected that and prioritized other legislation, as in the United States and New Zealand, or pursed legislation only as a matter of international commitment, as in Canada.

CONCLUSION

Both the GICNT and the ICSANT too often have been reflections of the interests and concerns of the major world powers, rather than of the international community as a whole, which has reduced each measure's legitimacy. This critique suggests that a shared ideational basis may be significant in the successful pursuit of nonproliferation cooperation. The absence of such a widespread ideational base has been a key limitation on the broadening of the ICSANT and the deepening of the GICNT. The number of activities under the auspices of the initiative may have increased the quantity and ultimately depth of nonproliferation collaboration among like-minded states, but has had limited effect beyond this group.

The initiative's flexibility has considerable potential as a means to enhance and complement compliance with the more formal efforts to counter nuclear terrorism, such as the ICSANT and UNSCRs 1373 and 1540, but the depth and breadth of collaboration have been limited because of the focus on what some see as a narrow agenda and an inability to fully address some states' lack of capacity. Although establishing the basis for a capacity against nuclear terrorism even in resource-poor states is one of the major objectives of the GICNT, the initiative has struggled to overcome the gap in priorities and capacity that would move cooperation from a core of developed states to the international community as a whole. In the terminology of chapter 1, the GICNT has struggled to move beyond the establishment of cooperation to the enlargement stage. The fourth stage of cooperation identified in chapter 1, implementation, is hampered in both cases by a governance gap and unclear standards or benchmarks.

Finally, disagreement over the best way to deal with nuclear terrorism has further limited the scope of multilateral collaboration. Although the pursuit of multiple initiatives has involved efforts that are mostly complementary, it has also ensured that the political attentions of key driver states, such as the United States, have been spread more thinly than desired. Skepticism over the value of the convention or preferences for alternative measures, including a desire for prior completion of a comprehensive international convention on terrorism that contains a consensus definition of terrorism, have limited full participation in the ICSANT. States' preferences for some of the overlapping measures over others have also often reflected idiosyncratic reasons. Just as Russia's leadership of the GICNT reflected in part its G8 role in 2006, Canada's emphasis of the Global Partnership can be partially attributed to the program's formation at the Canada-led 2002 Kananaskis Summit and a desire to burnish its international prestige as a result. India's support for the ICSANT and GICNT reflected not only concern about nuclear terrorism, but also a desire to enhance its strategic relationship with a key backer of both, Russia, and a wish to augment its nonproliferation credentials given its inability to join the NPT. China's enthusiasm for the GICNT is partly a reflection of its concerns about more intrusive measures such as the PSI. Clearly, based on these examples, extraneous factors are an important aspect of the shape cooperation takes. The cooperation literature certainly includes such considerations, but the point appears especially acute here, where states have a choice over the nonproliferation instrument they choose to prioritize.

Notes

1. Rohan Perera, "International Convention for the Suppression of Acts of Nuclear Terrorism, New York, 13 April 2005" UN Audiovisual Library of International Law, http://legal.un.org/avl/ha/icsant/icsant.html, accessed February 3, 2015.

2. James Martin Center for Nonproliferation Studies (CNS), "International Convention for the Suppression of Acts of Nuclear Terrorism," http://cns.miis.edu/inventory/pdfs/nucterr.pdf, accessed January 10, 2012. The convention currently has 115 signatories and 99 states parties. For a list, see UN, "Status: International Convention for the Suppression of Acts of Nuclear Terrorism," United Nations Treaty Collection, chap. 18, item 15, https://treaties.un.org/Pages/ViewDetailsIII.aspx?&src=UNTSONLINE&mtdsg_no=XVIII~15&chapter=18&Temp=mtdsg3&lang=en#Participants, accessed June 12, 2014.

3. W. Andy Knight and Tom Keating, *Global Politics: Emerging Networks, Trends & Challenges* (New York: Oxford University Press, 2010), 323.

4. United Nations, International Convention for the Suppression of Acts of Nuclear Terrorism, www.un-documents.net/icsant.htm, accessed January 10, 2012.

5. Ibid.

6. Perera, "International Convention."

7. United Nations, International Convention for the Suppression of Acts of Nuclear Terrorism, Article 7.1.

8. Ibid.; Matthew Bunn, Eben Harrell, and Martin B. Malin, *Progress on Securing Nuclear Weapons and Materials: The Four-Year Effort and Beyond* (Managing the Atom Project, Belfer Center for Science & International Affairs, Harvard Kennedy School, March 2012), 17.

9. Bunn, Harrell, and Malin, *Progress on Securing Nuclear Weapons and Materials*, 18.

10. United Nations, "Status: International Convention."

11. CNS, "International Convention for the Suppression of Acts of Nuclear Terrorism"; Perera, "International Convention."

12. United Nations, International Convention for the Suppression of Acts of Nuclear Terrorism.

13. United Nations, "Status: International Convention."

14. Vladimir Radyuhin, "India, Russia for Greater Effort against Terrorism," *Hindu*, September 18, 2003, http://global.factiva.com.ezproxy.lib.ucalgary.ca/ha/default.aspx, accessed May 22, 2012.

15. "Terrorism: Nod for Signing Convention," *Hindu*, June 17, 2006, http://global.factiva.com.ezproxy.lib.ucalgary.ca/ha/default.aspx, accessed May 22, 2012.

16. Fissile Materials Working Group, "Two Treaties. One Congress. No Time to Wait," *Bulletin of the Atomic Scientists*, September 15, 2011, www.thebulletin.org/web-edition/columnists/fissile-materials-working-group/two-treaties-one-congress-no-time-to-wait, accessed January 10, 2012.

17. Diane Barnes, "House Panel Clears Bill to Adopt Nuclear Security Pacts," *Global Security Newswire*, June 6 2012, www.nti.org/gsn/article/us-house-panel-clears-bill-adopt-nuclear-security-pacts/, accessed June 13, 2012; Library of Congress, "Bill Summary & Status, 112th Congress (2011–2012), H.R.5889, Major Congressional Actions," http://thomas.loc.gov/cgi-bin/bdquery/z?d112:HR05889:@@@R, accessed July 9, 2012; Miles Pomper and Kingston Reif, "U.S. Delay on Anti-nuclear Terror Measures Hinders Global Efforts," *World Politics Review*, May 17, 2013, www.worldpoliticsreview.com/articles/12958/u-s-delay-on-anti-nuclear-terror-measures-hinders-global-efforts, accessed June 10, 2013.

18. Barnes, "House Panel Clears Bill"; Jack Bourseton and Tanya Ogilvie-White, "Seeking Nuclear Security through Greater International Cooperation" (working paper, International Institutions and Global Governance Program, Council on Foreign Relations, March 2010), 4, www.cfr.org/international-law/seeking-nuclear-security-through-greater-international-coordination/p21709.

19. Diane Barnes, "Legislative Quagmire Grips Nuclear Security Pacts in the U.S." *National Journal*, March 12, 2012, www.nationaljournal.com/congress/legislative-quagmire-grips-nuclear-security-pacts-in-u-s—20120312, accessed on May 22, 2012.

20. Andrea Vance, "Summit Aims to Stop Nuclear Terrorism," *Dominion Post*, March 26, 2012, http://global.factiva.com.ezproxy.lib.ucalgary.ca/ha/default.aspx, accessed May 22, 2012.

21. "Nuclear Security Summit 2014 National Progress Report New Zealand," www.nss2014.com/sites/default/files/documents/new_zealand.pdf, accessed April 3, 2014.

22. Department of Justice, Canada, "Government Introduces Legislation to Combat Nuclear Terrorism" (March 27, 2012), www.justice.gc.ca/eng/news-nouv/nr-cp/2012/doc_32717.html, accessed May 25, 2012; Parliament of Canada, "Senate Government Bill, 41st Parliament, 1st Session, s-9—An Act to Amend the Criminal Code, Short Title, Nuclear Terrorism Act," www.parl.gc.ca/LegisInfo/BillDetails.aspx?Language=E&Mode=1&Bill=S9&Parl=41&Ses=1, accessed November 13, 2013.

23. Parliament of Canada, "Senate Committees: Transcripts & Minutes," www.parl.gc.ca/SenCommitteeBusiness/CommitteeTranscripts.aspx?parl=41&ses=1&Language=E&comm_id=612, accessed July 9, 2012; Parliament of Canada, "41st Parliament, 1st Session, Edited Hansard, Number 161, Monday, October 15, 2012, Government Orders, Nuclear Terrorism Act," www.parl.gc.ca/HousePublications/Publication.aspx?Pub=Hansard&Doc=161&Parl=41&Ses=1&Language=E&Mode=1#int-7712722, accessed June 10, 2013.

24. U.S. Department of State, "Announcing the Global Initiative to Combat Nuclear Terrorism," http://2001-2009.state.gov/p/eur/rls/or/69021.htm, accessed April 28, 2014.

25. U.S. Department of State, "The Global Initiative to Combat Nuclear Terrorism: Frequently Asked Questions," www.state.gov/t/isn/c37072.htm, accessed March 1, 2012.

26. U.S. Department of State, "Global Initiative to Combat Nuclear Terrorism: Factsheet," www.gicnt.org/download/sop/GICNT_Fact_Sheet_-_December_2013.pdf, accessed April 28, 2014.

27. U.S. Department of State, "Global Initiative to Combat Nuclear Terrorism: Frequently Asked Questions"; U.S. Department of State, "2013 Global Initiative to Combat Nuclear Ter-

rorism Plenary Meeting Joint Co-chair Statement," May 24, 2013, www.state.gov/t/isn/rls/prsrl/2013/210575.htm, accessed July 2, 2013.

28. Ibid.

29. U.S. Department of State, "Global Initiative to Combat Nuclear Terrorism: Key Multilateral Workshops and Exercises," www.state.gov/documents/organization/172982.pdf, accessed March 1, 2012.

30. Michelle Cann, Kelsey Davenport, and Margaret Balza, *The Nuclear Security Summit: Assessment of National Commitments* (Arms Control Association and Partnership for Global Security, March 20, 2012), www.armscontrol.org/files/ACA_NSS_Report_2012.pdf, 12; U.S. Department of State, "2013 Global Initiative to Combat Nuclear Terrorism Plenary Meeting Joint Co-chair Statement."

31. U.S. Department of State, "Global Initiative to Combat Nuclear Terrorism: Statement of Principles," www.state.gov/t/isn/rls/other/126995.htm, accessed March 1, 2012. For a list of the eighty-six partner states, see Global Initiative to Combat Nuclear Terrorism, "GICNT Partner Nations and Official Observer Organizations," www.gicnt.org/partners.htm, accessed June 12, 2015.

32. Wyn Q. Bowen, Matthew Cottee, and Christopher Hobbs, "Multilateral Cooperation and the Prevention of Nuclear Terrorism: Pragmatism over Idealism," *International Affairs* 88, no. 2 (March 2012): 362–63.

33. U.S. Department of State, "Robert G. Joseph's Remarks on the Global Initiative to Combat Nuclear Terrorism as Prepared for Delivery at the Capitol Hill Club" (July 18, 2006), http://search.proquest.com.ezproxy.lib.ucalgary.ca/docview/467181022, accessed May 23, 2012.

34. Pamela A. Jordan, "International and Domestic Dimensions of Russia's G8 Presidency in 2006," *Canadian Slavonic Papers* 50, nos. 3–4 (September–December 2008): 411, 417.

35. "India Concerned over Possibility of 'Nuclear Terrorism' in Region," *BBC Monitoring International Reports*, September 21, 2010, Academic OneFile, http://ezproxy.lib.ucalgary.ca/login?url=http://search.proquest.com.ezproxy.lib.ucalgary.ca/docview/751864078?accountid=9838, accessed February 3, 2015.

36. Michael Richardson, "Testing the Water Crossroads," *South China Morning Post*, October 5, 2007, www.scmp.com, accessed May 22, 2012.

37. Hague Nuclear Security Summit Communiqué, March 2014, https://www.nss2014.com/sites/default/files/documents/the_hague_nuclear_security_summit_communique_final.pdf, accessed June 13, 2014.

38. United Nations, International Convention for the Suppression of Acts of Nuclear Terrorism, Article 8, emphasis added.

39. "The Incentive Gap: Reassessing U.S. Policies to Secure Nuclear Arsenals Worldwide," *Harvard Law Review* 121, no. 7 (May 2008): 1875–77.

40. Christopher C. Joyner, "Countering Nuclear Terrorism: A Conventional Response," *European Journal of International Law* 18, no. 2 (2007): 236, 250–51.

41. Bunn, Harrell, and Malin, *Progress on Securing Nuclear Weapons and Materials*, 19.

42. See, for example, Johan Bergenäs, "Beyond UNSCR 1540: The Forging of a WMD Terrorism Treaty" (James Martin Center for Nonproliferation Studies, 2008), cns.miis.edu/stories/081022_beyond_1540.htm, accessed January 10, 2012.

43. U.S. Department of State, "Joint Statement on the Contributions of the Global Initiative to Combat Nuclear Terrorism (GICNT) to Enhance Nuclear Security" (March 21, 2012), www.state.gov/r/pa/prs/ps/2012/03/186611.htm, accessed June 11, 2013.

44. U.S. Department of State, "Global Initiative to Combat Nuclear Terrorism: Frequently Asked Questions."

45. Vladimir Orlov, "The Global Initiative to Combat Nuclear Terrorism, PSI, and Global Partnership Against Proliferation: Progress and Future Challenges" (paper, Korea-United Nations Joint Conference on Disarmament and Non-proliferation Issues, Jeju, ROK, November 14–15, 2013).

46. Bourseton and Ogilvie-White, "Seeking Nuclear Security," 8.

47. "Australia and the United States Ministerial Consultations Joint Communiqué" (December 12, 2006), reprinted in *DISAM Journal* 27, no. 2 (April 2007): 112, www.disam.dsca.mil/Pubs/Indexes/Vol%2029_2/Media%20Note.pdf, accessed May 21, 2012.

48. U.S. Department of State, "2013 Global Initiative to Combat Nuclear Terrorism Plenary Meeting Joint Co-chair Statement."

49. Bowen, Cottee, and Hobbs, "Multilateral Cooperation," 355.

50. Bonnie Jenkins, "Adapting to the Times: The Evolution of U.S. Threat Reduction Programs," *Arms Control Today* 41, no. 1 (January–February 2011).

51. U.S. Department of State, "Announcing the Global Initiative," emphasis added.

52. Henry L. Stimson Center, "The Global Initiative to Combat Nuclear Terrorism" (May 30, 2007), www.stimson.org/the-global-initiative-to-combat-nuclear-terrorism-/, accessed June 11, 2013.

53. U.S. Department of State, " Global Initiative to Combat Nuclear Terrorism: Frequently Asked Questions."

54. For example, the U.S. State Department requested just six million dollars for the GICNT in FY 2012 and five million in FY 2013 (Miles Pomper and Meghan Warren, "Progress since the 2010 Washington Nuclear Security Summit: Successes, Shortcomings, and Options for the Future" [James Martin Center for Nonproliferation Studies], http://cns.miis.edu/stories/pdfs/120316_nuclear_security_summit_pomper_warren.pdf, accessed March 4, 2012). The request for FY 2014 was also five million (U.S. Department of State, *Congressional Budget Justification Fiscal Year 2014—Volume 2: Foreign Operations*, 161, www.state.gov/documents/organization/208290.pdf, accessed July 5, 2013).

55. Elizabeth Turpen, "Nuclear Security: Key Instruments and Initiatives" (working paper, Stanley Foundation, December 2, 2009), 8–9, www.fissilematerialsworkinggroup.org/SiteFiles/Turpen_Nuclear_Security_Tools_Dec09.pdf, accessed March 10, 2012; Henry L. Stimson Center, " Global Initiative to Combat Nuclear Terrorism."

56. "Remarks by President Obama, Prague, Czech Republic" (April 9, 2009), www.whitehouse.gov/the_press_office/Remarks-By-President-Barack-Obama-In-Prague-As-Delivered.

57. Bunn, Harrell, and Malin, *Progress on Securing Nuclear Weapons and Materials*, 19.

58. Bourseton and Ogilvie-White, "Seeking Nuclear Security," 3.

59. C. S. Eliot Kang, "Remarks at the 2009 Plenary Meeting of the Global Initiative to Combat Nuclear Terrorism, The Hague, Netherlands" (U.S. Department of State, June 16, 2009), www.state.gov/t/isn/rls/rm/125349.htm, accessed March 20, 2012.

60. Quoted in Barnes, "Legislative Quagmire Grips Nuclear Security Pacts."

61. "South Korean Article Says Better to Ignore North's Rocket Launch," *BBC Monitoring International Reports*, March 30, 2012, http://go.galegroup.com.ezproxy.lib.ucalgary.ca/ps/i.do?id=GALE%7CA284741292&v=2.1&u=ucalgary&it=r&p=AONE&sw=w, accessed May 22, 2012.

CHAPTER NINE

The Nuclear Security Summit Experiment

Has It Been a Catalyst for Action?

ELIZABETH TURPEN

IN PRESIDENT OBAMA'S historic Prague speech on April 5, 2009, he outlined a long-range vision of a world free of nuclear weapons. Obama also declared a more immediate goal of securing vulnerable fissile materials to address U.S. and international concerns regarding nuclear terrorism. To lend momentum to this latter goal, the president announced a commitment to host a nuclear security summit within the year with the objective to eliminate, within four years, the risk that inadequately secured fissile materials could fall into terrorist hands.[1]

Obama's Prague commitment led to an unprecedented summit in Washington, D.C., on April 13, 2010, attended by thirty-eight heads of state, several high-level delegations from other states, and representation by three international organizations—the United Nations, International Atomic Energy Agency (IAEA), and European Union (EU).[2] The forty-seven states that participated in the 2010 Nuclear Security Summit (NSS) included both nuclear weapon states and non-nuclear-weapon states, with the distinctive feature that the nuclear-armed participants included both Nuclear Non-Proliferation Treaty (NPT) signatories and non-NPT states (India, Pakistan, and Israel); summit participants also ranged from major nuclear energy users to states still aspiring to use nuclear power to address rising energy demands. A second NSS took place in Seoul, South Korea, in March 2012, and a third followed in 2014 hosted by the Netherlands. What is expected to be a final summit is scheduled to take place again in the United States in 2016.

According to the U.S. State Department, the NSS's primary objective was to "energize, enhance, empower and elevate the many existing multilateral, cooperative institutions and structures aimed at securing nuclear materials and preventing nuclear smuggling. The summit process is not intended to replace or compete with established processes, nor is it intended to be permanent."[3] In practice, much of the focus of the summit process has been on securing or eliminating vulnerable fissile materials—a goal sometimes referred to as a "Global Lockdown."

The 2010 summit resulted in a communiqué that embraced President Obama's goal of addressing vulnerable fissile materials and delineated the key multilateral instruments to mitigate the threat of nuclear terrorism. In addition, the summit produced an extensive work plan that detailed various initiatives and activities to address the immediate challenges and provided a notional foundation for a potential long-term nuclear security regime. Although later summits added action items to the list agreed upon in 2010, one of the important purposes of the follow-on summits has been to monitor and facilitate progress on items in the work plan from the initial Washington Summit.

The communiqué and work plan were nonbinding, and their action items mostly put forward general goals rather than detailed plans. Hence, rather than a checklist of specific objectives met, the real measure of the NSS experiment's success will be whether the high-level attention achieved through summitry can transform the previously existing nuclear security standards and the long-standing donor-recipient model of nonproliferation cooperation into a collective security response. Such a transition will require each state to recognize its sovereign responsibilities and take the corresponding cooperative actions to address the transnational threat of nuclear terrorism. If this transition is achieved, then the broadly framed, nonbinding summit aspirations could become sufficiently organized, operationalized, and sustained to achieve the ambitious goals announced in Obama's Prague speech.

This chapter begins by describing the origins of the 2010 NSS and explaining the reasons why many countries responded positively. Next, the chapter summarizes the main elements of the communiqué and work plan and how they relate to existing international commitments. The chapter then identifies and discusses several challenges that have confronted this far-reaching endeavor. A brief review of the 2012 and 2014 summits follows. The final sections of the chapter evaluate the success of the NSS experiment so far in order to derive preliminary lessons from what might be considered the "sprint phase" of a long-term effort to address the perils of inadequate fissile material and nuclear facility security.

In relation to the broader themes of this volume, the NSS experience shows that cooperation still sometimes takes place at the head-of-state level rather than primarily at working levels of government, but it also reveals that a summit process can prompt new requirements for cooperation at the working level. In this case, U.S. leadership and states' self-interest emerge as the most obvious drivers of cooperation. The case study also shows, however, how summit meetings can serve as a context to enable persuasion, learning, and the gradual recognition of norms concerning sovereign responsibilities and the international cooperation necessary to address nuclear security. Although states have not fully embraced nuclear security as a priority goal of the nonproliferation regime, they have become more comfortable with the discourse of nuclear security as a result of the summit process. This makes it possible that the summit process could set in motion the creation of a well-defined organizational mechanism to supplement what have largely been ad hoc efforts to address nuclear security.

ORIGINS AND OVERVIEW OF THE 2010 SUMMIT

The NSS's focus on a "Global Lockdown" of nuclear materials emerged several years before Barack Obama became a presidential candidate. Its academic genesis, which used the phrase "Global Cleanout," can be found in a March 2003 publication of the Belfer Center at Harvard University.[4] Following that report, the 2004 Democratic presidential candidate John Kerry endorsed the global cleanout goal, and President Bush's second term saw a bilateral U.S.-Russian agreement to accelerate cooperation on security at fissile material sites.[5] By the time of the 2008 presidential campaign the stage was set for Senator Obama to embrace global cleanout as a key component of his national security platform.

Fortunately, candidate Obama was no newcomer to the legacies of the Cold War and the potential threat of nuclear terrorism. Prior to arriving in the Senate, Barack Obama had written papers in graduate school about negotiating nuclear arms reductions with the Soviets and the goal of nuclear disarmament.[6] Perhaps more significant, his first official trip as a newly minted senator from Illinois was a tour of Cooperative Threat Reduction (CTR) projects with Senator Richard Lugar, the coauthor of the CTR legislation. Senator Obama's public remarks following that trip offer an early glimpse of his thinking on the global cleanout challenge. Obama commented that "sources that can be used to construct improvised nuclear weapons and radiological devices [must be] brought under control. . . . This should become an increasing priority for the Nunn-Lugar program, the Congress and the Russians."[7] President Obama's long-standing interest in nuclear issues, combined with Senator Lugar's influence, resulted in nuclear nonproliferation becoming a focal point among his immediate foreign policy priorities. Moreover, many of his senior advisors and political appointees were adherents of the global cleanout agenda.

The Prague address established the overarching script for the Obama administration's approach to nuclear threats. The administration's first eighteen months in office already involved the multidimensional challenge of performing a congressionally mandated Nuclear Posture Review, negotiating a new treaty with Russia prior to expiration of the Strategic Arms Reduction Treaty in December 2009, and preparing for an NPT Review Conference in May 2010. The Prague NSS commitment added an additional deadline and dimension to this list—tackling the threat of nuclear terrorism head-on. As one example of the priority placed on nuclear terrorism, the Executive Summary of the 2010 Nuclear Posture Review states, "Today's most immediate and extreme danger is nuclear terrorism.... The vulnerability to theft or seizure of vast stocks of ... nuclear materials around the world, and the availability of sensitive equipment and technologies in the nuclear black market, create a serious risk that terrorists may acquire what they need to build a nuclear weapon."[8]

The prominence of global lockdown on President Obama's agenda represented the result of approximately twenty years of increasing concern. Since the collapse of the Soviet Union, the United States has used its sole superpower status, immense technical skills, and once-brimming coffers to initiate and support measures to address the threat of nuclear terrorism. However, despite these years of effort, there is still no existing international mechanism or regime focused explicitly on nuclear security that could serve as a basis to organize cooperation or enforce compliance around nuclear security standards. Instead, the United States has struggled both internally and with international partners in establishing priorities and orchestrating a comprehensive approach.

The reordering of U.S. national security priorities, in conjunction with lessons from twenty years of U.S. leadership in providing nonproliferation assistance, pointed to a summit as the logical solution.[9] The decision to use a summit process to drive this agenda appears to have been an intuitive one, arising from the urgency of the threat, the need to cajole consensus, and the high-level attention needed to cut through bureaucratic malaise and catalyze the cooperation requisite for faster progress.[10] The lessons of prior experience also suggested that only purely voluntary commitments would have merit in light of variations in how individual states perceive the threat, the scope of domestic nuclear materials or facilities they have at risk, and the priority they assign to addressing the threat.

As the launching point for global lockdown, the 2010 summit itself was a remarkable success. This unprecedented gathering of heads of state and relevant international organizations put nuclear terrorism at the forefront of the global agenda and produced a communiqué and work plan setting forth objectives and actions to achieve sustainable global lockdown. Two essential and interrelated factors led to the summit's success: President Obama's "rock star status" and the positive momentum created by the Prague speech.[11] President Obama—and by extension U.S. leadership—was riding a global tide of goodwill in the immediate aftermath of the Bush administration's departure and the positive attention garnered by the Prague speech. U.S. leadership, given the particular characteristics and vision of the new president and the stalwart efforts of his national security staff, served to ensure the success of the 2010 Washington Summit. As a secondary factor that points to the role of norms, many states desired to participate in a signature step toward creating "a nuclear weapons free world"—the focus of the Prague speech. The subtle irony and still prevalent fissure with respect to this motivation is that, for reasons described below, the summits were actually designed to break out of the existing disarmament debate.

Although the foregoing explains participation in the summit process itself, it does not touch on all the key factors playing into states' decisions with respect to making commitments at the Washington Summit. Many states announced new policy commitments, referred to as "house gifts," immediately before or during the summit. When states were invited to the 2010 summit, the U.S. administration made quite clear to them what commitments it sought. In several cases, the priority was to accelerate long-standing cooperative efforts to address a specific stockpile or site. By and large, states contributed house gifts due to a combination of persuasion plus the inducements of maintaining good relations with the Obama administration and garnering positive international attention by making significant commitments as summit participants.[12]

Beyond individual state commitments through house gifts, the 2010 summit also produced an agreed-upon communiqué and work plan. These laid out a lengthy agenda for future cooperative efforts to improve nuclear security.

The Communiqué

The 2010 Washington Summit Communiqué set forth the broad objectives regarding nuclear security sought by the summit. At the outset, the communiqué stated the shared goals of nuclear disarmament, nuclear nonproliferation, and peaceful uses of nuclear energy. These goals mirror the three "pillars" embodied in the NPT. In the same line, however, the participating states also asserted their shared objective of "nuclear security," thereby adding this dimension to the nuclear agenda among a geographically diverse and highly relevant group of states.[13] The communiqué also promoted the following:

- efforts to improve the security and accounting of nuclear materials and strengthen regulations on plutonium and highly enriched uranium (HEU)
- consolidation of HEU and plutonium stocks and a reduction in the use of HEU
- quick ratification of key treaties on nuclear security and nuclear terrorism
- the importance of the Global Initiative to Combat Nuclear Terrorism (GICNT) in capacity-building among law enforcement, industry, and technical personnel
- additional resources for the IAEA to develop and facilitate implementation of nuclear security guidelines
- nuclear industry sharing of best practices

The summit also endorsed a set of actions that would help achieve the broad objectives described in the communiqué. These were contained in a separate work plan document.

The Nuclear Security Summit Experiment [187]

The Work Plan

The 2010 Summit Work Plan contained eleven broad goals, and under each it enumerated a set of steps that would advance that goal.[14] Some elements of the work plan described specific steps with respect to fissile material security and nuclear controls intended to help participants achieve and sustain the communiqué's overarching objectives. The Summit Work Plan also set forth nonspecific commitments intended to promote progress on other existing efforts while connoting shared responsibility. It stipulated that all participating states will work to ratify, implement, and ensure compliance with the numerous existing international mechanisms pertinent to nuclear security. In this regard, the work plan specifically identified the Convention on the Physical Protection of Nuclear Materials (CPPNM), the International Convention for the Suppression of Acts of Nuclear Terrorism (ICSANT), UN Security Council Resolution 1540 (Operative Paragraph 3), the G8 Global Partnership, and the Global Initiative to Combat Nuclear Terrorism (GICNT) as relevant instruments. (Several of these efforts are discussed in greater detail in other chapters in this volume.) The shared responsibility for compliance came in the form of an ill-defined commitment soliciting requests for and offers of assistance among the states in attendance. This formulation mirrored that of Resolution 1540 and explicitly acknowledged the cooperation requisite to address the legal, technical, and financial burdens that the work plan commitments would entail.

In addition, the Summit Work Plan contained strong support for the role of the IAEA in providing technical assistance to states and promulgating best practices, including a call for quick completion of the fifth revision of the IAEA's Information Circular 225 on "The Physical Protection of Nuclear Material and Nuclear Facilities" (INFCIRC/225/rev.5). The work plan further urged the consolidation of materials, attention to security during transport, and reduction in HEU use. It also specified separated plutonium and other radioactive substances as objects of concern, but without calling for reduced use of these materials. The final items in the document underscored the need at the domestic level in each state for a robust, independent regulatory infrastructure; the critical role of the nuclear industry; the importance of the "human dimension," including personnel training and security culture; and efforts to detect and prevent illicit trafficking.

When viewed in tandem, the Summit Communiqué and Work Plan could be seen as establishing an embryonic and evolving framework for an international nuclear security regime based largely on existing treaties and multilateral instruments. As was noted prior to the 2010 summit by high-level U.S. officials, there was no appetite in the international community for creating a "new regime" specifically to address nuclear material security.[15] For this reason, the NSS experiment's success must be assessed in terms of its ability to catalyze commitments and enhance collaboration primarily in the context of existing international frameworks. Forward movement has required managing several tricky dilemmas that have the potential to derail progress in this particularly sensitive and highly secretive international terrain.

DILEMMAS AND CHALLENGES FOR THE NUCLEAR SECURITY SUMMIT EXPERIMENT

Efforts to address nuclear security have had to navigate several challenges and dilemmas, starting with a trade-off between maximizing international legitimacy and expediting progress. The instruments selected for inclusion in the NSS documents run the gamut—from treaty-based efforts (the CPPNM and ICSANT) to UN Security Council–legislated obligations (Resolution 1540) and a multilateral initiative void of an institutional framework (the GICNT). As treaties, the CPPNM and ICSANT represent the most traditional and legitimate means of establishing an international nuclear security regime. However, treaty regimes entail lengthy multilateral negotiations and a prolonged process of ratification. Although treaties enhance legitimacy, such an approach is anything but expeditious. In the "race between cooperation and catastrophe," as former Senator Sam Nunn has couched it, this traditional approach has been supplanted by a more informal and cooperative approach that protagonists hope will offer a quicker means to address a burgeoning and swiftly evolving challenge.[16] For this reason, U.S. policy makers have increasingly relied on UN Security Council mandates or "coalition of the willing" approaches, such as the GICNT or the Proliferation Security Initiative, to address WMD proliferation challenges.

The legitimacy vice expediency conundrum is only one dimension of import that affects the summit process. Another dimension involves the role of the existing nonproliferation regime. Some non-nuclear-weapon states perceive the nuclear security agenda as an attempt to revise the existing nonproliferation "grand bargain" in a way that will impose additional obligations and restrictions on them while deflecting attention from their efforts to get the nuclear weapon states to do more on nuclear disarmament or circumscribing their access to civilian nuclear technology.[17] Reflecting efforts to assuage this concern, the Summit Communiqué echoes the three "pillars" of the NPT, and the summit documents repeatedly underscore the right to peaceful uses of nuclear energy. In addition, attention to and resources for the IAEA enjoy a prominent place in the summit documents and in unilateral commitments made by many states. At the same time, U.S. officials wanted to steer clear of the ideological debates surrounding the NPT, debates that have led some nonaligned states to resist further efforts to strengthen nonproliferation until they see greater progress toward nuclear disarmament. The summit process, in other words, was an attempt to "reset" traditional talking points mired in a nuclear haves versus have-nots, North-South dynamic, and shift to a cooperative dialogue framed around collective security that demanded only voluntary contributions—the so-called house gifts approach—and sought to spur actions focused exclusively on preventing nuclear terrorism.[18]

Beyond the need to focus global leadership and limit the dialogue to nuclear security vice disarmament, efforts to achieve the summit's objectives would confront additional impediments to implementation. These impediments can be viewed in two groupings of interrelated and mutually reinforcing concerns: issues surrounding standards, sovereignty, and legitimacy, and impediments to operationalization that reside at the nexus of domestic priorities and indigenous capacity. An additional question that arises with respect to capacity is how or whether the donor-recipient dynamic assumed as part of the cooperation necessary for implementation will foster or hinder efforts to persuade states to view global lockdown as a collective responsibility. These will be discussed briefly in turn, prior to assessing the NSS experiment's impact.

Standards, Sovereignty, and Legitimacy

One potential obstacle to progress on nuclear security is the difficulty in defining clear standards for what such security entails. Standards have been difficult to establish because provisions for nuclear security are usually shrouded in secrecy and viewed as a closely held issue of national sovereignty. For this reason, perceptions regarding the legitimacy of the instruments and the exercise itself can either catalyze or confound progress. No approach has fully squared the circle, and as a result each type of initiative has confronted problems in establishing clear standards. Even the relevant treaties do not contain agreed-upon standards. Decisions about how to handle the potential diversion or theft of nuclear materials, the physical security of materials or facilities, and anything associated with nuclear security beyond existing IAEA safeguards commitments, including enforcement, have largely remained the prerogative of either the facilities themselves or the sovereign domain of individual governments. As treaties, the ICSANT and the CPPNM represent the most legitimate approach, but these took eleven and seventeen years, respectively, to negotiate and bring into force. With agreement on the 2005 CPPNM amendment, more than eighty states to date have consented to new standards for protection of nuclear materials, but the standards agreed to are largely discretionary.[19] In short, when concerns about sovereignty and legitimacy prevail, the attempt to define clear standards in the nuclear security domain can appear impossible.

States can try to get around this by avoiding formal treaty negotiations, but the "treaty by fiat" approach does not fully solve the problem. Resolution 1540, as only the second iteration of the Security Council legislating functional obligations under its Chapter VII authority, confronts a legitimacy deficit when compared to preexisting treaty obligations, including those relevant to nuclear weapons states encompassed in Article VI of the NPT.[20] Moreover, UNSCR 1540 only calls on states to implement "appropriate effective physical protection measures" to ensure the security of nuclear material and facilities. What this means remains undefined, and any standards reside only in the form of guidelines promulgated by the IAEA. Hence, the effort to bypass multilateral negotiations does not necessarily result in more expeditious execution of measures or clearly defined standards.

As a purely voluntary multilateral initiative, the GICNT confronts no legitimacy hurdles, and its Statement of Principles specifies the goals and depicts the potential types of activities to be undertaken. However, there are no specific details regarding the level of standards or degree of participation to be met. The GICNT continues to gain additional participants, and its relevance was certainly elevated through its inclusion in the NSS final document. Enthusiasm for the GICNT could still be constrained, however, by its "tiered membership," in which some states belong to the Implementation and Assessment Group and others remain outside it, given how this mirrors the debilitating haves versus have-nots cleavage of the nuclear nonproliferation regime itself. In addition, it lacks any institutional framework upon which to build a universal and obligatory basis for fulfillment of its principles. The GICNT manages to articulate some standards while respecting concerns about sovereignty and legitimacy, but at a price—participation is far from universal, obligations are not legally binding, and the standards are still left vaguely defined.

The success of the NSS process can be gauged by whether the dilemmas arising from the interplay of sovereignty, legitimacy, and standards are being overcome. Based on initial indicators, the record is decidedly mixed, but as is discussed below, there are some signs that progress is being made at least in raising awareness and implementation of voluntary standards.

Low Priority and Insufficient Capacity

Another challenge for the nuclear security agenda is that not all states perceive this as being an important national interest. Many states view the threat of nuclear terrorism as remote and the physical protection of materials or facilities as esoteric at best. The states that consider nuclear security a low priority also often have inadequate indigenous capacity to implement the actions being requested, a combination that creates a high potential for inaction on the nuclear terrorism agenda. Initiatives such as the GICNT list over eighty participating states and the NSS process has marshaled several new recruits, but many of those listed lack any real capacity to contribute to actual activities contained in its Statement of Principles.[21] Therefore, while the effort may attain near global "buy-in" regarding the principles, many states' wherewithal to contribute is circumscribed by the low priority assigned to nuclear terrorism and the allocation of resources that follows. In addition, the tiered membership system embedded in the effort may foster a free-rider problem, in which many participants look to the core group to do all the heavy lifting.

The Donor-Recipient Conundrum in Collective Security

Related to the free-rider problem is the reality that nuclear security is a highly technical and potentially cost-prohibitive arena for many states to address without significant international assistance. The summit documents assumed that some of the commitments states made would follow a donor-recipient model, in which wealthier and more capable states would help others with capacity-building. This presents an additional challenge because the donor-recipient model becomes a hard habit to break. Most states are happy to receive technical assistance and potentially the high-tech equipment that accompanies it, but without requisite buy-in regarding its value, they will be hard pressed to sustain the activities or maintain the hardware when donor funding ends. Unless the cooperation is based on mutually identified needs and requisite ownership of the outcomes is established, donor states cannot be assured of a long-term return on investment. The donor-recipient model compounds this problem because it also tends to align with the split between haves and have-nots in the larger nonproliferation regime, and by reinforcing this cleavage can remind developing countries of reasons why they are reluctant to embrace new commitments. The work plan's detailed litany of actions required to improve nuclear security can be addressed only by attaining widespread consensus regarding the threat, leading to states accepting it as their sovereign responsibility to address this global threat, and then all states willingly assigning priority and resources to a collective solution.

The NSS experiment certainly has raised awareness and achieved some degree of consensus at the highest levels regarding the threat. The question remains, however, as to whether this process sufficiently elevates nuclear security as a priority and engenders models of cooperation that not only attain more rapid progress on the agenda, but do not fall prey to questions of sustainment when the spotlight moves on or donor funding sunsets.

Assessment of the 2010 Nuclear Security Summit

The primary goal of the process engendered by the 2010 Washington Summit was to bolster existing multilateral, cooperative instruments for securing nuclear materials and preventing nuclear smuggling. The summit process was not intended to replace or compete with other mechanisms or to be permanent. At the same time, however, negotiators obviously recognized that providing security for today's fissile materials does not guarantee their security in perpetuity; the effectiveness of the summit process hinges on addressing the ongoing use and production of materials, for both civilian and military purposes. Although an obvious measure of the 2010 summit's success would be a tabulation of fissile materials that were safely secured or eliminated to date, this is only a partial metric for assessing the success or failure of the NSS experiment in addressing the more enduring facets of the nuclear security challenge. Nevertheless, reports that examined such short-term metrics reached encouraging conclusions. For example, the Obama administration's own tally of successes prior to the 2012 Seoul Summit included multiple new ratifications of the amended CPPNM and the ICSANT, extension of the UNSCR 1540 Committee's mandate, extension of the G8 Global Partnership, enhancement of the IAEA's role and more voluntary contributions to its mission, updates to domestic legislation by the United States and others, a "Principles of Conduct" agreed to by industry, twelve new Centers of Excellence (COEs) around the world to assist in training of relevant personnel, almost four hundred kilograms of HEU removed from ten countries for elimination, and conversion of several reactors from HEU to low-enriched uranium (LEU) fuel.[22]

All of these actions indicate summit success at one level, but the fullest measure of success will be whether these activities attain an enduring impact. With this in mind, the following sections provide a brief overview of the 2012 and 2014 summits with a focus on new innovations and major commitments they generated, a general assessment of the potency of the NSS process in strengthening the elements of a potential nuclear security regime, and, last, a discussion of lessons learned and indications of progress from the first four years of this experiment.

THE 2012 AND 2014 SUMMITS

The Washington Summit set in motion three follow-on summits, with current expectations being that the 2016 summit will be the last meeting held in a summit format. Prior to the close of the 2010 summit, the Republic of Korea volunteered to host the 2012 summit; similarly, the Netherlands was on-line for 2014 by the time the Seoul Summit commenced. Self-interest and status considerations were prime motivations for both countries' commitments to host summits. As noted by observers, South Korea was a strange choice in that it possesses neither nuclear weapons nor the materials to produce them.[23] However, when Russia turned down the opportunity, South Korean president Lee

Myung-bak embraced it as neatly folding into his "global Korea" strategy, an effort to promote South Korea on the world stage and enhance its "competence and status internationally."[24] In addition, the NSS also offered a rare opportunity for Seoul to showcase its nuclear industry. South Korea is now the world's fifth largest nuclear energy producer and has emerged as a new nuclear plant exporter. As such, performing the host role was clearly in South Korea's political and commercial interests.[25]

The Netherlands' reasons for hosting in 2014 were more diffuse, reflecting a mix of self-interest, status, and national identity considerations. Dutch officials noted that first and foremost, the Obama administration requested that they do so; moreover, the Netherlands historically has played a prominent role in multilateral disarmament and nonproliferation efforts. Other motivations included their awareness that A. Q. Khan had started setting up his clandestine network while working in the Netherlands, and, related to this, the role of Netherlands-based URENCO as a major producer of enriched uranium for civilian reactors. Last, the Dutch do perceive nuclear terrorism and illicit trafficking as a threat given their role as a major transshipment point within Europe.[26]

At the 2012 and 2014 summits, the participant list was expanded to fifty-three countries, an increase of six from the roster at the Washington Summit.[27] In addition to the three international organizations at the 2010 summit (the IAEA, EU, and UN), INTERPOL joined the process. Both the Seoul and Hague Summits produced a communiqué but no separate work plan. Instead, new action priorities agreed to at later summits were incorporated into their communiqués. This reflected the intent to signal continuity with and give priority to the work plan set forth at the Washington Summit.[28]

The Seoul Communiqué identified eleven key priorities and listed a number of actions that could be taken voluntarily to further these priorities. The list of priorities began by reaffirming the value of multilateral instruments in "the global nuclear security architecture" as well as "the role of the IAEA" and ended with calls to enhance "information security" while increasing "international cooperation." Recommended action items ranged widely from minimizing HEU use to several steps to reduce the danger of radiological terrorism to strengthening national nuclear security cultures.[29]

The Seoul Summit also exposed some significant shortfalls in a summit process as a forcing mechanism for addressing nuclear security. Although South Korea desired to see concrete progress on efforts to minimize the use of HEU via "HEU Management Guidelines," this effort ran into opposition from some developing countries. Several countries, such as South Africa, desired to see this discussed within the IAEA where they hold more sway. Several participants also refused to make commitments with respect to down-blending their existing HEU stockpiles or converting their HEU-fueled civilian research reactors.

Russia and Canada were also successful in impeding efforts to set a deadline of 2015 for conversion of medical isotope production facilities from HEU to LEU. Last, the Seoul Summit made no concrete progress on setting legal standards or establishing measures to ensure standards are being achieved,[30] although a Joint Declaration made at the Hague Summit might provide a context for breaking through this barrier.

Although the results were not as dramatic as those achieved in Washington, the 2012 summit still involved some important accomplishments. Noteworthy products of the Seoul Summit included ensuring that national commitments from the 2010 summit were achieved, garnering new commitments, a continued emphasis on and commitment to greater coordination among COEs, and the advent of so-called gift baskets—collective pledges made by various sets of states. With respect to the 2010 commitments, participating states reported that many of the national commitments they made as "house gifts" in 2010 had been met. Perhaps the most important among the state-specific efforts was the successful removal of 234 kilograms of HEU from Ukraine to Russia.[31] A March 2012 report by the Arms Control Association found that "approximately 80 percent of the national commitments" from the 2010 summit had been completed.[32]

New house gifts emanating from both the 2012 and 2014 summits have included more treaty ratifications, additional commitments to establishing COEs, and multiple states taking the leadership role in orchestrating gift baskets. One striking feature of the national declarations in Seoul is the number of states that made no commitments in 2010, particularly from the Non-Aligned Movement, that offered house gifts in Seoul. In addition, the move from individual-state "house gifts" to joint "gift baskets" represents perhaps the most significant innovation and catalyst for new forms of nuclear security cooperation from the summit process thus far.[33]

The potential value of gift baskets is illustrated by one of the major accomplishments from the 2014 Hague Summit, the Joint Declaration on Strengthening Nuclear Security Implementation signed by thirty-five states (although not Russia, China, India, or Pakistan). Signatories pledged to meet or exceed the nuclear security recommendations in relevant IAEA documents and to conduct self-assessments and host peer reviews to gauge how well they are doing. The 2014 summit also produced a significant state commitment when Japan announced it would ship out five hundred kilograms of HEU and plutonium to their countries of origin (the United States and United Kingdom). One innovation at The Hague was participation by state leaders in a scenario-based simulation involving a potential radiological incident. A final noteworthy accomplishment was greater emphasis on plutonium; past summits had called for minimizing HEU stocks, but the 2014 communiqué added a call to keep separated plutonium stockpiles "to the minimum level."[34]

After three summits, one can identify a number of positive accomplishments. However, academic and NGO experts also point to places where the summit process has fallen short. Most obviously, by the 2014 summit, it was clear the process would not achieve President Obama's 2010 objective of securing all vulnerable materials within four years. More problematically, the process has yet to identify a mechanism to address the 85 percent of weapons-usable materials that are devoted to military use, such as fuel for nuclear-powered aircraft carriers and submarines.[35] To evaluate the prospects for further progress moving forward, it is important to consider the reasons for the substantial cooperation achieved so far, and then to identify factors that will affect the chances of sustaining a long-term commitment that could close some of the remaining gaps in the global nuclear security architecture.

EXPLAINING COOPERATION

Fifty-three nations have participated in a process that will result in at least four multilateral summit meetings, which in turn have encouraged various other forms of international cooperation. In 2014, Russia announced that it would not attend the 2016 summit, but this does not diminish the record of cooperation achieved to date.[36] To account for this cooperation, several factors discussed by Knopf in chapter 1 are relevant. U.S. leadership stands out as the most obvious. The NSS experiment began as an initiative by Washington. It is not simply the fact of U.S. status as the world's leading power that matters, however. Also important were the identity of the U.S. leader and the timing of the initiative. President Obama succeeded an administration whose policies were unpopular in many world governments, and his Prague speech received a highly positive response. Many countries wanted to support the new U.S. president and his disarmament agenda, and this created favorable circumstances for the exercise of U.S. leadership.

For many participating states, self-interest has been an important motivation, although the interests involved can be complex. States that perceive nuclear and radiological terrorism as threats are the most likely to participate. Some states have also seen the summits and associated national commitments as a way to achieve international status, maintain good relations with the United States, and support shifts in U.S. policy that they wish to see continue. In this sense, the summit process is not merely a reflection of interest calculations; the summits are also a source of feedback that creates new national interests in being part of the process.

Because individual state commitments are voluntary, persuasion, learning, and the gradual development of norms regarding sovereign responsibilities and the collective actions these require have been relevant factors. Some states have had to be convinced that actions to strengthen nuclear security are in their own interests and will contribute to collective security globally. Capacity is also a consideration. States that lack capacity to act have been among the most likely to hold back, and offers of assistance have been required to bring them into the process. Yet, as discussed above, this donor-recipient approach can be problematic if states use it as a reason not to take ownership of the responsibility for nuclear security.

Finally, the NSS experience appears to run counter to the observation that much cooperation has been moving to the working levels of government. Summits, by definition, involve heads of state. Yet summits also require preparation and potentially follow-through. As the Washington Summit has evolved into a summit process, coordination at the working levels of national governments has become necessary. Participating countries have designated certain government officials to be their head delegates and deputy delegates to meetings to plan each succeeding summit. These delegates, officially called "Sherpas" and "sous-Sherpas," represent another manifestation of the role of working-level relationships and potentially an embryonic epistemic community in international cooperation on nuclear security challenges. It remains unclear whether or in what form this cooperation will continue should the summits end after 2016; however, experts appear to be converging around the notion that they will move to a departmental/ministerial level and heavily rely on working-level agreements and actions.

PRELIMINARY LESSONS FROM THE NSS EXPERIMENT

This section identifies and examines factors that are likely to be central to the long-term impact of the NSS process on the overall objective of sustainable global lockdown. Five considerations discussed here are the ability to sustain focus, the effort to strengthen standards, the challenges of coordination and low-capacity states, the long-run impact of new innovations such as gift baskets, and the role of the IAEA.

Maintaining Focus and High-Level Engagement

Sustaining the summit process will be difficult given how many other concerns compete for the attention of heads of state. If some form of the process is to continue, it will likely involve transferring responsibility elsewhere. Options include putting a set of officials below the head-of-state level in a core group of states in charge or else finding a home in an existing institution such as the IAEA.

From the beginning, maintaining focus at the head-of-state level on nuclear security, especially if the agenda would be limited to fissile materials, hit strong headwinds. Immediate difficulties prior to the 2010 summit surrounded the issue of radiological materials, a higher priority of some European states.[37] In 2012, the mere location of the Seoul Summit cast a spotlight on nuclear safety issues due to the one-year anniversary of the Fukushima disaster in Japan as well as on concerns about nuclear stability on the Korean Peninsula. In the run-up to the Seoul Summit, the agenda expanded to include greater emphasis on radiological materials and recognition of the safety-security nexus, thereby diluting the focus on fissile materials.[38] Media coverage has reinforced the challenges to maintaining focus. Rather than nuclear terrorism and materials security, media attention during the Seoul Summit focused on other issues including Fukushima, Pyongyang's signaling of an upcoming rocket launch, and President Obama's "hot mic" incident in which he promised his Russian counterpart greater flexibility on missile defense after the 2012 election. Simultaneously, due to the Euro crisis, several European leaders, including the prime minister and host for the 2014 summit from the Netherlands, opted not to attend the Seoul Summit and sent high-level delegations in their stead.

According to senior U.S. officials, one factor in deliberations about whether or in what form to extend the summit process was concern about "fatigue" for such biannual, high-level engagements.[39] Within weeks of these comments, however, the United States announced it would host the 2016 summit. Presumably, the fatigue factor did not outweigh the potential benefit of creating a stronger basis for nuclear security prior to transferring the process to other venues.[40]

Making Progress toward Tighter Standards

Despite the ability of U.S. leadership to spearhead the summit process and cajole consensus at the highest levels among a diverse array of countries, the constraining effect of sovereignty and legitimacy concerns on discussions of security standards remains a difficult barrier through which to break. Standards remain discretionary and a closely held sovereign domain. At the same time, there is evidence that the NSS process has set activities in motion that may eventually break through this barrier. The prime examples are the progress made on INFCIRC/225/Revision 5 and The Hague Joint Declaration on Implementation.

As previously noted, the 2010 Summit Work Plan called for the completion of the fifth revision of the IAEA's Information Circular 225. Since 1975, INFCIRC/225, "The Physical Protection of Nuclear Material and Nuclear Facilities," has been the cornerstone of the international physical protection regime for nuclear materials and facilities. This nonbinding guidelines document is commonly leveraged as a binding legal commitment in bilateral agreements regarding security of materials.[41] Given that the last revision occurred in 1999, the United States had long pushed for INFCIRC/225 to be revised again to address the post–September 11, 2001, threat environment and to conform with and provide implementation guidance for the amended CPPNM and relevant UNSCR 1540 obligations. In light of its potential value in imparting guidelines relevant to these key instruments within the broader nuclear security framework, revision of INFCIRC/225 was a high priority. Closely following the 2010 summit, the IAEA completed Revision 5 and published the updated guidelines in January 2011.[42]

According to senior U.S. officials, the NSS helped prompt finalization of these revisions to this critical IAEA standard reference document. In the context of the sensitivities surrounding the elucidation of standards, the NSS process provided the political will, while the IAEA provided the crucible of legitimacy for significant gains that will follow from routine use of these newly issued guidelines. In addition, the NSS process helped raise awareness of the recent developments in this reference document, thereby prompting greater attention to its implementation.[43]

Although this example should be touted as a success for the NSS process, the standards remain discretionary and the IAEA's resources to promote them remain limited. For these reasons, consensus on and enforcement of standards remain critical to ensure adequate security of all materials and facilities. The Hague gift basket on Strengthening Nuclear Security Implementation signed by thirty-five states represents a significant move toward this objective.[44] As stated in the Hague Communiqué and underscored by this Joint Declaration, the IAEA will remain the crucible of legitimacy for such efforts. However, the IAEA's authorities and its financial and personnel capacity are too circumscribed to fully service this objective. Hence, in addition to top-down efforts such as holding summits or promulgating guidelines through IAEA publications, activities from the bottom-up such as the self-assessments and peer reviews called for in the Nuclear Security Implementation Initiative should improve implementation and adherence to IAEA guidelines and may offer new forums and mechanisms to achieve and enforce adequate standards over time.

Indigenous Capacity, Coordination, and the Donor-Recipient Conundrum

The NSS experiment has encountered challenges that reflect capacity-building needs in many states, inadequate multilateral coordination, and reliance on a donor-recipient model to address the capacity gap. The promotion across the three summits to date of COEs illustrates the challenges, but also suggests it may be possible to overcome them. The 2010 Summit Communiqué and Work Plan focused extensively on the goals of enhancing expertise and promoting a nuclear security culture, while also calling for international cooperation and assistance to help states build capacity. In support of these goals, several states at the 2010 summit announced plans to expand their efforts at existing training centers or to establish national or regional COEs to train specialists in best practices regarding nuclear security. Prior to 2010, several such entities already existed or were in planning, including in Brazil, South Korea, the United Kingdom, and the European Union. The 2010 Washington declarations added commitments to create COEs on the part of China, Japan, Italy, Kazakhstan, India, and France. In Seoul, several additional countries announced their intent to also establish such centers or in some cases, such as Algeria, reported that they had already done so.[45]

The lack of coordination among the various centers and with stakeholders gave rise to significant concerns regarding the credibility and sustainability of these centers. Before the 2012 summit, numerous questions were raised with respect to the role served by the COEs, the standards they were meant to uphold, and their viability over time. Analysts suggested that to ensure the quality of the training, especially of international audiences, these centers should undergo some sort of accreditation process. In addition, to date these COEs had been supported primarily by the United States, EU, and IAEA, so their sustainment would be subject to successful transfer of custody to the host governments. Last, early assessments included widespread recognition that coordination among these centers needed to be improved.[46]

These concerns have started to be addressed. Prior to the 2012 summit, the IAEA began organizing a network to improve coordination among the various centers, and this effort was formally endorsed at the 2012 summit.[47] At the 2014 summit, thirty-one states offered a gift basket in which they pledged to support greater cooperation through the IAEA's Nuclear Security Training and Support Centre network.[48]

Despite the coordination challenges involved, the commitment to create centers to support national or regional capacity-building needs does signal recognition by states of their sovereign responsibilities and presumably the intent to create and sustain the capacity necessary to address their own nuclear security requirements. In particular, the COEs' linkage to reference documents promulgated by the IAEA again suggests growing momentum for specific "standards," even if not yet—except potentially in the form of an accreditation process—enforcement of such. These activities, with the IAEA acting as coordinator, could set in motion the initial steps toward a peer review process for setting training standards, leading eventually to standards for implementation. Assuming adequate coordination, some form of accreditation process, and forthcoming commitments from host governments to support and sustain their COEs, the summit process may be viewed as having catalyzed a solution to the problem of ensuring states have the requisite technical capacity to meet nuclear security needs. Establishing an accredited curriculum at these centers could also be a way of facilitating adoption of defined standards for security.

From House Gifts to Gift Baskets

The summit process has also prompted new forms of cooperation among small groups of states on specific tasks, namely, the transition from unilateral house gifts to the gift basket approach. In fact, related to the COEs above, the U.S.-led gift basket at the Seoul Summit announced several states' intent to collaborate in the International Network for Nuclear Security Training and Support Centres, which will aim at building "a cadre of highly qualified and well trained personnel, provide specific technical support for effective use and maintenance of instruments . . . as well as provide scientific support for the detection of and response to nuclear security events in a country."[49] This was one of thirteen multinational joint statements made at the Seoul Summit;[50] at the Hague Summit, states offered eighteen joint declarations.[51]

The ultimate impact of the gift basket approach cannot yet be assessed, but its strong showing at The Hague, especially the thirty-five-state joint declaration focusing on implementation, offers an optimistic future. At a minimum, these efforts signal overt acknowledgment that sovereignty and secrecy do not outweigh the need for at least limited international cooperation to tackle the standards question and address the threat. In addition, these commitments will create additional forums for collaboration and are likely not to exclude the possibility of expanded participation as the efforts evolve. The gift baskets are a good example of the summit process working successfully to energize and enhance international cooperation, but in this case in ways that may go beyond the existing multilateral instruments.

International Institutions: The IAEA Role

To date, the biggest remaining deficit in the summit process is bolstering the budget and authorities of the IAEA. As the primary promulgator of guidance on security standards and the focal point for networking among the COEs and for the thirty-five-state implementation gift basket, the IAEA has a burgeoning agenda with respect to providing coherence, and, perhaps, institutionalizing the follow-on from the NSS experiment, at a minimum in parallel with Sherpa- or ministerial-level activities. The IAEA is the one international organization that can bridge the legitimacy gap and serve as an honest broker in advancing the standards requisite to ensure adequate nuclear security measures are in place worldwide.

However, as noted by a Government Accountability Office (GAO) report in

2013, three key issues limit the agency's ability to ensure that its nuclear security resources are used efficiently and effectively. First, the IAEA's nuclear security program relies almost exclusively on extrabudgetary contributions from donor countries; this makes planning difficult and could foreshadow significant shortfalls when the NSS spotlight is no longer present. Second, the IAEA does not conduct any needs-based assessment of the resources required beyond its two-year budget cycle; this is again a limiting factor in securing the resources necessary to address a broadening mandate. Third, the GAO faulted the IAEA for not systematically reporting on the results of measures used to assess the agency's performance in its nuclear security program.[52]

If the IAEA is to adequately address, on top of its myriad other functions, an added role in promulgating standards, servicing capacity-building needs, and providing coordination for the nuclear security agenda in perpetuity, the summit process must go beyond voluntary contributions and focus on new authorities for the long-term success of this international institution.

CONCLUSION

The National Security Summit experiment was intended to "energize, enhance, empower and elevate" the multilateral instruments and initiatives focused on nuclear security and preventing nuclear terrorism. Seeking a balanced course between the requirements of legitimacy and expediency, the Obama administration tried to weave together the pertinent instruments, garner consensus on a wide-ranging work plan, and focus high-level attention on the need for action on this multifaceted and technically complex agenda. Four years into the recently extended timeline for the experiment, when judged within the context of the challenges it faced, the NSS experiment has been remarkably successful.

Within the NSS context, there is concrete evidence of states recognizing their sovereign responsibility to address this transnational threat. The evidence includes new leadership emerging on a range of issues, the establishment of national or regional COEs, and greater domestic attention to ratification and implementation of relevant treaties. The gift baskets, especially the implementation basket signed by thirty-five countries at The Hague, extrapolate this recognition to new forms of international cooperation among coalitions of the willing focused on implementation.

Cooperation in the NSS experiment reflects U.S. leadership and states' self-interest calculations, but state perceptions of their interests—and their responsibilities—have also been changing as a result of persuasion, learning, and the deepening of norms during the summit process. Capacity remains a barrier for some states that the donor-recipient model of assistance cannot fully address because it does not necessarily lead states to take sovereign "ownership" of nuclear security needs; however the NSS process has shown significant innovation and may be moving toward efforts that will better establish domestic capacity and nuclear security cultures in the participating states. As a single summit became a summit process, and with hopes to sustain some form of nuclear security effort after 2016, an event organized at the head-of-state level has led to the development of new working-level relationships among "Sherpas" and "sous-Sherpas" as well.

It would be premature, however, to render judgment on the experiment overall. It remains clear that the summit experiment has catalyzed some impressive gains on fissile and radioactive materials security, even while it has fallen short in achievement of binding and enforceable standards for nuclear security. Even though more remains to be done, the summit process seems to have garnered sufficient global consensus to set in motion various mechanisms for making progress that would have been deemed infeasible in 2010. As one expert noted, due to the NSS process the "climate has shifted," and whereas few outside experts were calling for such things as binding standards or a peer review process to ensure compliance in 2010, this is now becoming commonplace in the dialogue surrounding the NSS process.[53] This shift has created an opportunity for suggesting that a roadmap for a true nuclear security regime is feasible in Washington in 2016.

Notes

1. By "nuclear security," the U.S. government, and increasingly the international community, means efforts to protect weapons-useable nuclear materials—primarily plutonium and highly enriched uranium (HEU)—so they do not fall into the hands of terrorists or other undesirable actors. This is distinguished from nuclear safety, which focuses on preventing accidents at nuclear reactors and other nuclear sites.

2. Josh Rogin, "White House Announces Nuclear Summit Attendees," *Foreign Policy*, April 10, 2010, http://thecable.foreignpolicy.com/posts/2010/04/10/white_house_announces_nuclear_summit_attendees.

3. U.S. Department of State, "Nuclear Security Summit 2012," www.state.gov/t/isn/nuclearsecuritysummit/2012/index.htm.

4. Matthew Bunn, Anthony Wier, and John P. Holdren, *Controlling Nuclear Warheads and Materials: A Report Card and Action Plan* (Cambridge, Mass.: Harvard University, March 2003), 115–37.

5. Matthew Bunn, interview, July 18, 2012. The agreement referred to is the 2005 Bratislava Agreement between Bush and Russian president Putin.

6. William J. Broad and David E. Sanger, "Obama's Youth Shaped His Nuclear-Free Vision," *New York Times*, July 4, 2009, www.nytimes.com/2009/07/05/world/05nuclear.html?_r=1&pagewanted=all. See also David Sanger, *Confront and Conceal: Obama's Secret Wars and Surprising Use of American Power* (New York: Random House, 2012), 235–37.

7. Transcript of a discussion with Senators Barack Obama and Richard Lugar, Council on Foreign Relations, November 1, 2005, www.cfr.org/international-peace-and-security

/challenges-ahead-cooperative-threat-reduction-rush-transcript-federal-news-service-inc/p9138, accessed August 14, 2012.

8. U.S. Department of Defense, *Nuclear Posture Review Report* (April 2010), iv.

9. William Tobey, "Planning for Success at the 2012 Seoul Nuclear Security Summit" (Policy Analysis Brief, Stanley Foundation, June 2011), 1.

10. National Security Council official, interview, July 10, 2012. See also Tobey, "Planning for Success."

11. "Rock star status" was a direct quote offered by several sources interviewed for this chapter. An official from the Netherlands indicated that the Prague speech created a "euphoria"— a real sense that "he's going to change the world." Officials at the embassy of the Royal Kingdom of the Netherlands, interview, July 25, 2012.

12. Senior National Security Council official, interview, July 10, 2012.

13. This chapter uses "nuclear security" for activities ranging from source security to detection, interdiction, and information sharing. This is consistent with the summit documents and assumes that measures targeting immediate lockdown of existing vulnerable materials must take into account the continued use and production of such materials for the foreseeable future. "Communiqué of the Washington Nuclear Security Summit" (April 13, 2010), http://whitehouse.blogs.foxnews.com/2010/04/13/nuclear-security-summit-communique-and-work-plan, accessed August 13, 2010.

14. "Work Plan of the Washington Nuclear Security Summit" (April 13, 2010), www.whitehouse.gov/the-press-office/work-plan-washington-nuclear-security-summit.

15. Senior National Security Council official in a briefing preceding the 2010 summit held on April 11, 2010.

16. Sam Nunn, "The Race between Cooperation and Catastrophe" (talk, American Academy in Berlin, June 12, 2008), www.nti.org/c_press/speech_Nunn_Germany61208.pdf, accessed August 13, 2012.

17. See, for example, Tobey, "Planning for Success," 2.

18. Obama administration official, interview, March 15, 2012.

19. George Bunn, "Enforcing International Standards: Protecting Nuclear Materials from Terrorists Post-9/11," *Arms Control Today* 37, no. 1 (January–February 2007).

20. Olivia Bosch and Peter van Ham, "Global Non-proliferation and Counter-terrorism: The Role of Resolution 1540 and Its Implications," in *Global Non-proliferation and Counter-terrorism: The Impact of UNSCR 1540*, ed. Bosch and van Ham (Washington, D.C.: Brookings Institution Press, 2007), 7.

21. The current tally includes eighty-five states and can be viewed at the Global Initiative to Combat Nuclear Terrorism "Partner Nations List," www.state.gov/t/isn/c37083.htm, accessed June 29, 2014.

22. Laura Holgate, "Progress since the 2010 Washington Nuclear Security Summit" (remarks, Washington, D.C., October 7, 2011), www.state.gov/t/isn/rls/rm/184951.htm.

23. Miles Pomper, "The Seoul Nuclear Summit: How Much a Success?" (Korea Economic Institute, May 23, 2012), 3.

24. Duyeon Kim, "2012 Nuclear Security Summit: The Korean Twist" (Korea Economic Institute, September 2011), 1. See also Bong-Geon Jun, "Road to the 2012 Seoul Nuclear Security Summit" (U.S.-Korea Institute at SAIS, February 2012), 7–8.

25. Pomper, " Seoul Nuclear Summit," 3.

26. Representatives at the embassy of the Royal Kingdom of the Netherlands, interview, July 25, 2012.

27. The new countries are Azerbaijan, Denmark, Gabon, Hungary, Lithuania, and Romania.

28. Duyeon Kim, "Fact Sheet: 2012 Seoul Nuclear Security Summit Results" (Center for Arms Control and Non-Proliferation, August 2012), http://armscontrolcenter.org/issues/nuclearterrorism/articles/fact_sheet_2012_seoul_nuclear_security_summit_results/.

29. U.S. Department of State, "Key Facts on the 2012 Seoul Nuclear Security Summit" (March 28, 2012), www.state.gov/t/isn/rls/fs/187208.htm.

30. Pomper, " Seoul Nuclear Summit," 4.

31. Although cooperation was already under way for removal of these materials, such expeditious completion of this removal would not have happened without the high-level commitment and attention that were brought to bear following the Washington Summit and prior to Seoul. Senior National Security Council official, interview, July 10, 2012.

32. Michelle Cann, Kelsey Davenport, and Margaret Balza, *The Nuclear Security Summit: Assessment of National Commitments* (Arms Control Association, March 2012), 3.

33. Michelle Cann, Kelsey Davenport, and Sarah Williams, *The Nuclear Security Summit: Progress Report*, appendix I (Arms Control Association, July 2013).

34. For reviews of the 2014 summit, see Sebastian Sprenger, "Nearly Three Dozen Nations Sign Hague Statement on Nuclear Security Framework," *Global Security Newswire*, March 25, 2014; Sharon Squassoni, "Outcomes from the 2014 Nuclear Security Summit" (Center for Strategic and International Studies, March 25, 2014), csis.org/publications/outcomes-2014-nuclear-security-summit; Arms Control Association, "Nuclear Security Summitry at a Glance" (updated April 2014), https://www.armscontrol.org/factsheets/NuclearSecurity Summit.

35. Squassoni, "Outcomes from the 2014 Nuclear Security Summit"; Nuclear Threat Initiative, "NSS 2014: Significant Progress but More to Do" (April 2, 2014), www.nti.org/analysis/opinions/nss-2014-significant-progress-more-do/.

36. The number of attendees in 2016 and the impact of Russia's withdrawal from the NSS process remain to be determined. In the midst of the Ukraine crisis, Russia announced in November 2014 that it would not participate in the 2016 summit. Officials stated that Russia did not see any "added value" coming out of the meetings and that they would prefer to support organizations, such as the IAEA, which were "created by all of us to deal with these issues." See Karen de Young, "Russia to Skip Nuclear Security Summit Scheduled for 2016 in Washington," *Washington Post*, November 5, 2014, www.washingtonpost.com/world/national-security/russia-to-skip-nuclear-security-summit-scheduled-for-2016-in-washington/2014/11/05/1daa5bca-6535-11e4-bb14-4cfea1e742d5_story.html, accessed January 26, 2015.

37. Administration official, interview, March 12, 2012.

38. Kim, "2012 Nuclear Security Summit."

39. Diane Barnes, "Stay Tuned for Future Word on Summits, U.S. Coordinator Says," *Global Security Newswire*, June 7, 2013, www.nti.rsvp1.com/gsn/article/q-stay-tuned-word-future-nuclear-security-summits-lead-us-organizer-says/?mgh=http%3A%2F%2Fwww.nti.org&mgf=1.

40. Daniel Horner, "Samore Suggests 2016 Summit," *Arms Control Today* 43, no. 2 (March 2013).

41. For example, INFCIRC/225's recommendations are the criteria by which the adequacy of physical protection of nuclear material and facilities is judged by the United States during bilateral assessment visits to countries holding U.S.-obligated nuclear material; it also provides the foundation for the IAEA's International Physical Protection Advisory Service (IPPAS) missions. See Craig Everton, Stephan Bayer, and John Carlson, "Developments in the IAEA's Nuclear Security Series and Physical Protection Guidance Document INFCIRC225/5," in *Institute of Nuclear Materials Management Proceedings* (Baltimore, July 11–15, 2010), 5–6.

42. INFCIRC/225/Rev. 5 is available at www-pub.iaea.org/MTCD/Publications/PDF/Pub1481_web.pdf.

43. Obama administration official, interview, March 7, 2012.

44. For a detailed analysis, see Jonathan Herbach, "The Nuclear Security Implementation Initiative: A Catalyst for Needed Action," *Arms Control Today* 44, no. 5 (June 2014): 8–12.

45. Alan Heyes, "An Assessment of the Nuclear Security Centers of Excellence" (Policy Analysis Brief, Stanley Foundation, May 2012).

46. Ibid.

47. Sharon Squassoni, "Building a Nuclear Security Framework from the Ground Up: Encouraging Coordination among Centers of Excellence in Northeast Asia" (Policy Analysis Brief, Stanley Foundation, March 2013), 3.

48. Bonnie D. Jenkins, "National Security Centers of Excellence," *Nuclear Security Matters*, Belfer Center, Harvard University, April 21, 2014, http://nuclearsecuritymatters.belfercenter.org/blog/nuclear-security-center-excellence.

49. This gift basket was offered on behalf of Algeria, Australia, Canada, Chile, Czech Republic, Germany, Hungary, Indonesia, Italy, Japan, Jordan, Kazakhstan, Republic of Korea, Lithuania, Malaysia, Mexico, Morocco, Netherlands, Pakistan, Philippines, Ukraine, United Arab Emirates, the United Kingdom, and the United States.

50. Cann, Davenport, and Williams, *Nuclear Security Summit*, 5.

51. Nuclear Security Matters, Belfer Center, Harvard University, http://nuclearsecuritymatters.belfercenter.org/files/nuclearmatters/files/2014_nss_joint_statements_-_by_statement.pdf. In contrast, the official site of the Netherlands summit lists only fourteen items under "gift baskets"—see https://www.nss2014.com/en/nss-2014/reference-documents.

52. U.S. Government Accountability Office, "Nuclear Nonproliferation: IAEA Has Made Progress in Implementing Critical Programs but Continues to Face Challenges" (GAO-13-139, May 2013), 29.

53. Ken Luongo, "Nuclear Security Governance for the 21st Century: An Action Plan for Progress" (paper, Nuclear Security Governance Experts Group Workshop on Improving Nuclear Security Regime Cohesion, Seoul, South Korea, July 18–19, 2012), 1.

CHAPTER TEN

Cooperating Regionally, Denuclearizing Globally

Multilateral Nuclear-Weapon-Free-Zone Initiatives

MICHAEL HAMEL-GREEN

THERE ARE MANY STRINGS to the nuclear nonproliferation bow. The central ones include the Non-Proliferation Treaty (NPT), International Atomic Energy Agency (IAEA) safeguards, and the Comprehensive Test Ban Treaty (CTBT). Supplementing these are supply-side measures, such as the Nuclear Suppliers Group and the Proliferation Security Initiative. Then there are other strings in the form of regional measures, particularly nuclear-weapon-free zones (NWFZs). NWFZs involve groups of countries cooperating regionally through multilateral agreements to forgo acquisition or stationing of nuclear weapons within their territories. Such zones are envisaged under the NPT's Article 7, which affirms "the right of any group of States to conclude regional treaties in order to assure the total absence of nuclear weapons in their respective territories."[1]

Even before the NPT was signed in 1968, regional NWFZ initiatives had already been successfully implemented in the form of the 1959 Antarctic Treaty and the 1967 Tlatelolco Latin American NWFZ (LANWFZ) Treaty. Four more followed: the 1985 Rarotonga South Pacific Nuclear Free Zone (SPNFZ) Treaty, the 1995 Bangkok Southeast Asian NWFZ (SEANFWZ) Treaty, the 1996 Pelindaba African NWFZ (AFNWFZ) Treaty, and the 2006 Semipalatinsk Central Asian NWFZ (CANWFZ) Treaty. As of 2012, 138 out of 193 UN member states were party to at least one of the existing NWFZ treaties. In the case of the five zones in populated regions, by June 2014, 96 UN member states had signed and ratified NWFZ treaties applying to their regions, and a further 15 states had signed but not yet ratified (all of the latter within Africa). In the case of the Antarctic Treaty, 50 states have as of this writing become parties, including the United States, the United Kingdom, and Russia.[2] This chapter analyses the six multilateral treaties that designate a land-based region as nuclear-free.[3]

All of the existing six treaties involved intensive multilateral negotiations at the regional level, and between the regional states and the five NPT-recognized nuclear weapon states (NWS): the United States, the United Kingdom, France, Russia, and China. The success of these multilateral negotiations, involving some two thirds of all UN member states, suggests that there are practical policy lessons to be learned from how regional dynamics and processes contribute to nonproliferation. The spread of NWFZs also raises theoretical questions about how best to explain such extensive multilateral regional cooperation.

Dan Deudney notes that "the diffusion of nuclear weapons has been much less than anticipated, and is greatly less than is possible." Like many analysts, Deudney ascribes this unexpected phenomenon to the role of a hegemonic state, the United States, through its provision of extended deterrence (the "nuclear umbrella") to a range of friends and allies in Europe and East Asia.[4] Certainly, U.S. security guarantees have played a key role in dissuading parties such as Taiwan and South Korea from acquiring nuclear weapons, but, unfortunately for this hypothesis, almost all of the ninety-six countries that have signed and ratified NWFZ treaties in populated regions are states that do not rely on U.S. extended deterrence as part of their security arrangements. Conversely, all but a few of the countries with which the United States does have explicit or implicit extended deterrence arrangements have so far declined to participate in NWFZs in their regions (the exceptions include Australia and the Philippines). Other explanations need to be found for the surprisingly large number of nations that have decided to eschew the assumed "benefits" of being nuclear armed—enhanced national power, prestige, and deterrence—that seem to count so heavily in the thinking of the nine nuclear-armed states.

The following analysis examines how and why, at a regional level, so many states have made legally binding nonproliferation commitments in the form of regional denuclearization treaties. After describing the genesis and evolution of the NWFZ concept, it identifies the key participants and nonparticipants (including holdouts) in each of the existing NWFZ treaty initiatives and traces the role of the most salient factors for explaining the successful regional negotiation outcomes. These factors include regional and national perceptions of nuclear crises or threats affecting or potentially affecting the region; the role of leadership including "advocate leaders" in key states; domestic political factors, including democratic compared to nondemocratic polities and the role of civil society groups and movements; the role of nonproliferation norms and normative frameworks; and the role of the nuclear weapon states. The analysis then evaluates the relative effectiveness of the six established NWFZs and suggests some lessons for further such multilateral nonproliferation negotiations, including implications for NWFZ initiatives in the Middle East, Northeast Asia, and South Asia.

ORIGINS AND EVOLUTION OF NWFZS

The concept of an NWFZ first emerged in the form of the 1957 Rapacki Plan advanced by the Polish foreign minister Adam Rapacki.[5] While there were earlier proposals for buffer zones between East and West in Central Europe, Rapacki's proposal was the first to focus specifically on a zone that would ban all nuclear weapons within the territories of East and West Germany, Poland, and Czechoslovakia. The United States and NATO rejected the Rapacki Plan on the grounds that nuclear weapons were needed in Europe to counter what were perceived to be numerically superior Warsaw Pact conventional forces. Even though it was unsuccessful, the Rapacki Plan represented the first initiative to define the essential features of all subsequent regional NWFZ treaties: nuclear weapon absence within the zone, multilateral inspection and verification systems, a binding commitment by nuclear weapon states not to use nuclear weapons against zone territories, and enactment through a treaty and related legally binding protocols. In subsequent years, the United Nations would codify the concept, beginning with its 1975 study of NWFZs and culminating with a 1999 report by the UN Disarmament Commission (UNDC) that set out NWFZ guidelines.[6]

Despite U.S. opposition to the Rapacki Plan, it was to be the United States that played the leadership role in establishing the very first NWFZ. The 1959 Antarctic Treaty, negotiated in Washington, D.C., affirmed that Antarctica "shall be used for peaceful purposes only," and created an NWFZ through its ban on nuclear explosions (Article 5).[7] Inspired by international Antarctic scientific cooperation in the 1957–58 International Geophysical Year, the treaty was signed by twelve countries with territorial claims or interests in Antarctica. It served to address strategic concerns of both the United States and Soviet Union to deny each other military toeholds in Antarctica, and to manage the problem of competing territorial claims (which the treaty froze rather than extinguished).

Eight years later Latin American countries established the first NWFZ in a populated region. This followed regional concerns over the 1962 Cuban Missile Crisis and global concerns over fallout from atmospheric nuclear weapons tests. The Tlatelolco Treaty was negotiated between 1964 and 1967 through the Preparatory Commission for the Denuclearization of Latin America.[8] The treaty included the main Rapacki elements: bans on nuclear weapon acquisition and stationing, verification and compliance systems (including a regional oversight body, OPANAL), and a legally binding protocol obligating nuclear weapon states not to use or threaten to use nuclear weapons against zone states (a provision known as a "negative security assurance"). In addition to creating a legal barrier to horizontal proliferation within the region, the treaty's prohibitions on nuclear stationing also helped prevent vertical proliferation in the form of nuclear weapons deployment by external nuclear powers (as attempted by the Soviet Union in Cuba).

In the decades that followed, further evolution of the nuclear-weapon-free-zone approach took place through the negotiation of four more zones, starting with the South Pacific.[9] The 1985 Rarotonga Treaty, including Australia, New Zealand, Fiji, Papua New Guinea, and other independent Pacific island states, was negotiated by a South Pacific Forum Working Party chaired by Australia in close consultation with the United States.[10] It included the same core prohibitions as the Tlatelolco Treaty but extended the concept to include a protocol prohibiting all nuclear weapons testing within the designated boundaries of the zone, including the high seas and Exclusive Economic Zones (EEZs).

Ten years later, following the end of the Cold War, the Association of Southeast Asian Nations (ASEAN) negotiated the 1995 Bangkok NWFZ Treaty.[11] The treaty was signed not only by the seven existing ASEAN members but also by Cambodia, Laos, and Myanmar, which were to become ASEAN members not long afterward. The ASEAN states had already in 1971 declared the region a Zone of Peace, Freedom, and Neutrality, reflecting concerns arising from the experience of major conflict in the region in the form of the Vietnam War and the presence of bases of major nuclear weapon powers (initially the United States and later Russia). It was only after Russia and the United States withdrew from their respective military bases in Vietnam and the Philippines that ASEAN was able to proceed with establishing a full-fledged NWFZ. The Bangkok Treaty included many of the provisions found in the preceding Tlatelolco and Rarotonga Treaties but also sought to extend the reach of the zone to its two-hundred-mile EEZ boundaries. This has led to continuing difficulties with securing the signature and ratification of the NWS on the protocol providing negative security assurances, with NWS expressing concerns about their rights of transit for nuclear-armed vessels.

The Pelindaba Treaty was negotiated between 1991 and 1996 by a regional grouping of experts established under the joint auspices of the regional body, the Organization of African Unity (now the African Union), and the United Nations.[12] South Africa's moves in 1990–94 to end the apartheid regime opened the way politically to pursuing the long-standing regional interest in establishing an NWFZ. The revelation that South Africa had built and then dismantled a small nuclear arsenal added to the momentum for creating the zone. The African NWFZ involved similar core provisions to the Tlatelolco and Rarotonga Treaties but also, given that proliferation had, due to the prior South African program, already occurred on the continent, the Pelindaba Treaty extended the NWFZ concept to include the dismantlement of existing nuclear-weapon-related facilities.

The most recent NWFZ to be established is the Central Asian zone. The Semipalatinsk Treaty was negotiated between 1997 and 2006 by Kazakhstan, Kyrgyzstan, Tajikistan, Turkmenistan, and Uzbekistan, all of which gained their independence in 1991 following the collapse of the former Soviet Union.[13] Together with comparable core denuclearization provisions to previous NWFZs, the Semipalatinsk Treaty extended the concept to require all zone members to accept the more intrusive and rigorous IAEA Additional Protocol safeguards.

Beyond the already established six multilateral NWFZs, there are proposals to create new such zones in various regions of the world, including the Middle East, South Asia, and Northeast Asia. As a way to gain Arab support for indefinite extension of the NPT, the 1995 Review Conference called for establishing a Middle East zone. To promote this goal, the 2010 NPT Review Conference unanimously called for convening a conference on a possible Middle East WMD-free zone (WMDFZ) by December 2012. The conference was postponed, however, largely due to U.S. requests in light of concerns expressed by Israel, and was not convened before the 2015 NPT Review. At the 2015 Review Conference, efforts by Egypt and other Middle East states to set a fixed date for the WMDFZ conference were opposed by the United States, Canada, and the United Kingdom. Reflecting this stalemate, the Review Conference failed to reach consensus on a final document. The failure to hold the Middle East WMDFZ conference and collapse of the 2015 NPT Review Conference could jeopardize Arab states' and Iran's commitment to the NPT and possibly even the treaty's future. This makes it all the more important to understand the lessons from successfully negotiated NWFZs.

KEY ACTORS IN ESTABLISHING ZONES AND REMAINING NON-PARTICIPANTS

For each region in which an NWFZ has been established, several types of actors have typically contributed to this development. At the core of the process, national government and diplomatic leaders have played key roles in proposing, negotiating, and implementing NWFZ treaties. In addition, regional organizations have sometimes provided forums for the negotiation of such treaties. Domestic or regional advocacy and support for such zones have also been provided by civil society actors, including political parties, nongovernmental organizations, epistemic communities, and wider nuclear disarmament advocacy groups and movements.

Beyond each region, there are further participants. The UN, in particular, has furnished international political support and guidelines for NWFZs, legitimized such zones in the General Assembly, encouraged linkages between NWFZs and the NPT and IAEA, and directly facilitated NWFZ negotiations. In the first NWFZ to be created in a populated region, the 1967 Latin American Tlatelolco Treaty, the UN secretary-general appointed a special advisor to the negotiations (William Epstein). The African Pelindaba NWFZ Treaty was negotiated under the joint auspices of the Organization of African Unity (OAU) and the UN, the latter providing not only diplomatic advisors but also experts in arms control law and legislation. The UN provided similar assistance in the case of the Central Asia Semipalatinsk NWFZ negotiations, offering particular support for the negotiations through its UN Regional Centre for Peace and Disarmament in Asia and the Pacific, whose director, Japan's Tsutomu Ishiguri, chaired the negotiations.

Also outside each region (but sometimes possessing administered territories within a particular zone), the five official nuclear weapon states also have key roles. These states are relevant participants because they are enjoined under UN Disarmament Commission NWFZ guidelines to sign negative security assurance protocols in which they guarantee not to use or threaten to use nuclear weapons against zonal states.

There is also the issue of regional states that decline to participate in an NWFZ arrangement for shorter or longer periods. All of the existing NWFZs have involved some states that have initially withheld participation for extended periods, although today only in Africa does one find states that have not ratified the relevant treaty. The reasons for initial or protracted nonparticipation vary. For many African states, the reasons are essentially technical, reflecting limited government capacity and the low salience of the issue. In other cases, such as the twenty-seven-year delay before Argentina and Brazil brought the Tlatelolco Treaty into force on their territories in 1994, nonparticipation was related to their interest in keeping open the nuclear weapons option.

FACTORS AFFECTING COOPERATION IN NWFZS

A number of factors have influenced how and why regional participants have decided to cooperate (or not to cooperate) in establishing regional NWFZs. This section discusses five especially salient factors: regional nuclear threats and crises, advocate leaders, domestic political factors, norms and normative frameworks, and the positions of the nuclear weapon states.

Regional Nuclear Threats and Crises

Consistent with the first factor identified by Knopf in chapter 1, self-interest, mainly in the form of a shared perception of threat, has helped promote regional cooperation. One precipitating factor that stands out clearly across most if not all of the six established NWFZ treaties is a common perception among regional states of a potential threat involving nuclear weapon activity as it affects the region. In each of the six zones, potential or actually experienced nuclear threats have been cited as key reasons for establishing an NWFZ.

In Antarctica, at the height of a nuclear arms race between the United States and the Soviet Union, there was a joint concern about potential future strategic use of Antarctica, particularly on the U.S. side concerning the Soviet Union. A 1958 U.S. National Security Council report proposed a multilateral treaty as a way to address concerns raised by "increased Soviet activity" in the region.[14]

In Latin America, the actual deployment of Soviet nuclear weapons in Cuba leading to the 1962 Cuban Missile Crisis sent shock waves through the region that created much of the impetus for creating an NWFZ. In addition, there were also concerns about a potential nuclear rivalry between Argentina and Brazil.

In the South Pacific, regional concerns focused on radioactive fallout and associated legacies from French nuclear testing in Polynesia, and earlier American and British nuclear testing in the Marshall Islands, Christmas Island, and Australia. Between 1946 and 1996, these nuclear powers carried out a total of 321 nuclear tests in the Pacific.[15]

In Southeast Asia, there was an acute awareness, during and after the Vietnam War, of the threat of nuclear weapon use in conflicts within the region, and the possibility that tactical nuclear weapons were deployed at U.S. and Soviet bases in the region. In Africa, concerns focused initially on French nuclear testing in the Sahara in the early 1960s, and later on the South African apartheid regime's nuclear weapon program, as well as suspicions about a potential nuclear-weapon-related program in Libya. Finally, in Central Asia, there was an extensive history of nuclear weapons testing and deployment by the Soviet Union prior to the Central Asian states gaining their independence. This, coupled with the region's central strategic location and the presence of both Russian and U.S. military bases that could potentially be used to store tactical nuclear weapons, served to prompt interest in a nuclear-free zone.

While a common facilitating factor in regional moves to set up NWFZs, the existence of perceived nuclear threats is not, in and of itself, sufficient for multilateral cooperation to emerge. Equally possible, of course, is increased adversarial competition and arms racing to match or deter regional rivals or external powers perceived to be a threat. The evidence from the available case studies of NWFZs established in each region suggests that several other factors were important in successful NWFZ treaty negotiation and implementation.

Advocate Leaders

One crucial factor for translating interests into action has been the role of advocate leaders, especially in the larger or more influential states within, or having interests in, each region. Advocate leaders may be defined as leaders prepared to pursue and argue for the merits of a measure both privately within their governments and publicly before domestic, regional, and international audiences. Key national leaders have played an especially important role, as most of the existing zones have been initiated through declarations of support for such arrangements by presidents or other government leaders of regional states.

In the Antarctic, U.S. president Eisenhower's advocacy was particularly crucial in both affirming the principle of Antarctica being reserved for peaceful purposes, and in taking the step of convening a multilateral conference to achieve this.[16] The further development of the initiative during its negotiation and implementation stages benefitted greatly from the skills and advocacy of the chair of the negotiation conference, U.S. Ambassador Herman Phleger, along with Ambassador Paul Daniels (special adviser to the secretary of state on Antarctica).

For Latin America, the five presidents of Brazil, Bolivia, Chile, Ecuador, and Mexico provided the initial NWFZ advocacy role with a Joint Declaration on April 29, 1963, calling for denuclearization of the region.[17] The Mexican diplomat, Alfonso Garcia Robles, enlisted wider support for the concept and chaired the treaty negotiations. Robles (later to be awarded the Nobel Peace Prize for his work) is widely credited, together with the UN's William Epstein, for much of the drafting of the treaty. Its key features included an innovative, flexible entry into force mechanism in Article 28 that recognized the political reality that Brazil and Argentina (following their respective 1964 military coups) were not ready to bring the treaty into force at the time of the negotiations.[18]

In the South Pacific, advocacy for a regional NWFZ was broadly based across the region, with successive waves of advocacy occurring in the early 1960s, the early to mid-1970s, and the early 1980s. In this last period, the new Labor prime ministers in Australia (Robert Hawke) and New Zealand (David Lange) and the Australian foreign minister, Bill Hayden, became important advocates for the treaty and steered it through talks that led to the 1985 Rarotonga Treaty.[19]

In the case of Southeast Asia, Indonesian leaders, such as Indonesian foreign ministers Mochtar Kusuma-Atmadja and his successor Ali Alatas, were leading advocates for establishing a regional NWFZ treaty to implement the 1971 Zone of Peace, Freedom, and Neutrality. As the Cold War wound down, and the United States and Russia withdrew from their bases in the Philippines and Vietnam, respectively, Mochtar Kusuma-Adtmadja—identified by subsequent Indonesian foreign minister Marty Natalegawa as the chief architect of the SEANWFZ proposal—argued in 1988 that the aim of the NWFZ proposal was to "reduce the risk of renewed rivalry and strategic competition in Southeast Asia."[20]

The African NWFZ had the lengthiest period of gestation of any of the NWFZs. Over three decades elapsed between 1964, when the Cairo Declaration of thirty-four OAU states called for the denuclearization of Africa, and 1996 when the declaration came to fruition in Cairo with the signing of the Pelindaba Treaty. Progress was made possible by two near-simultaneous developments: the end to the Cold War and South African president Frederick de Klerk's commitment to ending apartheid. These opened the path for reconsideration of the African NWFZ proposal. President de Klerk moved in 1991 to have South Africa accede to the NPT, and he announced in 1993 that South Africa had destroyed the six nuclear weapons it had previously built and dismantled its nuclear weapon facilities. This meant that the one country on the continent that had possessed a nuclear arsenal was now nuclear-free and thereby able to join the proposed zone. The key African figure in advocating and pursuing the African NWFZ negotiations was the chair of the OAU International Group of Experts, Nigerian Ambassador Oluyemi Adeniji, credited by Isaac Ayewah as "the driving force in the concretization and eventual negotiation of the Treaty that gave a legal basis for the zone."[21]

A regional NWFZ in Central Asia was first advocated in September 1992 at the UN General Assembly by Mongolia's first president, Punsalmaagin Ochirbatthe.[22] The president of Uzbekistan, Islam Karimov, was the first leader from the five former Soviet Central Asian states to specifically call, in 1993, for an NWFZ covering these five states. A key step involved denuclearizing Kazakhstan, which had nuclear weapons and ballistic missiles from the former Soviet Union on its soil. Return of these weapons to Russia was completed in 1995–96, and following this removal of nuclear arms from the region the five Central Asian presidents called for Central Asia to become an NWFZ.[23] The presidents invited Tsutomu Ishiguri, director of the UN Regional Centre for Peace and Disarmament in Asia and the Pacific, to chair a working group of diplomats and experts. Working together with UN undersecretary-general for disarmament affairs, Jayantha Dhanapala, Ishiguri showed extraordinary diplomatic acumen and persistence in facilitating the protracted decade-long negotiations that culminated in the 2006 signing of the CANWFZ Treaty.

For all six of the established NWFZ treaties, the crucial role of two kinds of leadership is evident. First, at least some of the regional leaders must step forward to both advocate and lobby within regional or multilateral forums for the establishment of each zone. Second, successful completion of an actual agreement takes highly skilled senior diplomats committed to pursuing the detailed and demanding work of negotiating zone treaties between multiple regional states, each with their own political agendas and exigencies. Consistent with what Knopf suggests, leadership is important. But in contrast to where he places the emphasis, with the exception of the Antarctic Treaty, the cases examined here did not depend on the leadership of a hegemonic global power. Instead, regional states and individual diplomats provided the key leadership roles.

Domestic Political Factors

None of the NWFZ advocate leaders acted in a political vacuum. Key political factors for the development and implementation of NWFZ arrangements have included changes in domestic political structures in a more democratic direction, the role of civil society groups and their engagement with political parties and governments, and the role of epistemic communities.

Democratic structures were important conditions for the Latin American NWFZ initiatives to be advanced in the first place, incorporated into regional agendas, and then negotiated. All five of the presidents (from Mexico, Brazil, Bolivia, Chile, and Ecuador) who joined together in the April 1963 declaration to create the zone were democratically elected at the time. The most significant holdout states in Latin America in terms of extended delays in bringing the NWFZ treaty into force for their own territories were the two states (Brazil and Argentina) that experienced military coups in the course of the treaty negotiations, and the Castro regime in Cuba. Studies by Redick and Serrano have demonstrated that different approaches by Argentina and Brazil on the one hand, and Mexico on the other, reflected military rule in the former and civilian government in the latter.[24]

The role of democratic systems was equally apparent in the South Pacific and Southeast Asian NWFZ initiatives. In Southeast Asia, the Philippines under President Marcos withheld support for a SEANWFZ but eventually reversed policy following the 1986 People's Revolution. In the South Pacific, the Tonga monarchy withheld ratification of the SPNFWZ until 2000, a decade and a half after the treaty was first signed.

In two of the zones, grassroots domestic political pressure also played a role in influencing political parties and national leaderships to pursue NWFZ arrangements. In the case of the South Pacific NFZ Treaty, the initiative occurred in a period of mounting regional concern over atmospheric nuclear testing in the region and the health effects of radioactive fallout. After earlier waves of public concern over nuclear testing during the 1960s and the early 1970s, a new wave of domestic political pressure occurred from 1976 to 1985. This involved civil society antinuclear groups, such as the Independent and Nuclear Free Pacific Movement. This group promoted the NWFZ idea, particularly at 1975, 1978, and 1980 regional conferences that brought together representatives from indigenous people's groups and Australian and New Zealand nongovernmental organizations.[25] Recently declassified Australian Cabinet documents have revealed that, in advancing the SPNFZ negotiations, the Australian government was responding directly to mounting contemporary civil society antinuclear and antitesting pressures while seeking to avoid provisions that might adversely affect Australia's ANZUS alliance with the United States.[26]

In the case of Southeast Asia, Indonesia and Malaysia took the lead in advocating for an NWFZ. This was based on their concerns about potential nuclear conflicts involving NWS bases in the region, including Soviet use of Vietnamese ports at Cam Ranh Bay and Da Nang and U.S. bases in the Philippines. Grassroots activity also played a role, however, when efforts in the Philippines helped remove the latter issue as a potential obstacle to a zone. Following the February 1986 People's Revolution that toppled Marcos and replaced his regime with a democratic government headed by Corazon Aquino, a civil society Nuclear-Free Philippines Coalition grassroots campaign focused on concerns about nuclear weapons at U.S. bases and the country potentially becoming a nuclear target. This helped convince the Philippines government to reconsider previous government reservations about how an NWFZ might affect U.S. bases in the country and adopt a nuclear-free provision in the country's 1987 Constitution. The Philippines then participated fully with fellow ASEAN states in negotiating the Bangkok Treaty.[27]

Epistemic Communities

At the civil society level, there is also the special role played by epistemic communities, that is, networks of experts or professionals in particular disciplines who share understandings of their field that lead them to support certain policy prescriptions. For example, nonproliferation advocacy by scientists in Argentina and Brazil played an important part in securing the two countries' adherence to the wider Latin American NWFZ Treaty. The Argentinean and Brazilian decisions to bring the Tlatelolco Treaty into force for their territories were announced through the same 1990 Argentina-Brazil Declaration that led to the creation of the Brazilian-Argentine Agency for Accounting and Control of Nuclear Materials (ABACC). As Wrobel and Redick note, the Brazilian Physics Society (Sociedade Brasileira de Fisica, SBF) was successful, under a democratic civilian administration, in having the 1988 Brazilian Constitution include a paragraph "which requires that nuclear activities in Brazil be pursued only for peaceful purposes," and, as early as 1983, Brazil's and Argentina's physics societies, the SBF and the Asociación Física Argentina, called for nuclear disarmament, avoidance of an arms race in the region, and establishment of mutual inspections of nuclear facilities.[28]

In two zones, the African and Central Asian, legal and academic experts made important contributions. Jozef Goldblat from the United Nations Institute for Disarmament Research acted as a UN consultant during both the African and Central Asian NWFZ negotiations. In the Central Asian case, William Potter, director of the Center for Nonproliferation Studies at the Monterey Institute of International Studies, played a key role in facilitating the treaty negotiations through consultative advice, meetings with leaders, and workshop presentations for the UN-facilitated Working Group on the Central Asian Nuclear-Weapon-Free Zone.[29]

Norms and Normative Frameworks

The international community has long sought, through both legal instruments and moral suasion, to achieve adherence to norms concerning weapons of mass destruction that could inflict indiscriminate death and injury, particularly to civilians. From the mid-1950s onward, a strong "taboo" developed against use of nuclear weapons.[30] The role of international norms in facilitating establishment of the six existing regional NWFZs is evident in their respective preambles and in the statements of negotiators at the time the zones were created.

The 1959 Antarctic Treaty referred to the need to "ensure the use of Antarctica for peaceful purposes" as a way of furthering the UN Charter; it also required parties to observe international agreements concerning "nuclear explosions and the disposal of radioactive waste material."[31] The Antarctic Treaty's denuclearization provisions were, in part, a response to the emerging taboo on nuclear weapon use, and the treaty also furthered this development by creating the first legally binding norm against nuclear weapon presence and use in a particular region.

The 1967 Latin American Treaty preamble affirmed that the "incalculable destructive power of nuclear weapons has made it imperative that the legal prohibition of war should be strictly observed."[32] Treaty architect Garcia Robles acted with awareness that the normative framework created by the Tlatelolco Treaty would provide "lessons for all States wishing to contribute to the broadening of the areas of the world from which those terrible instruments of mass destruction . . . would be forever proscribed."[33] Robles's hopes for the Tlatelolco Treaty as a normative and legal precedent for other regions were borne out in the ensuing four decades as the other regional NWFZs took inspiration from the Tlatelolco example and built upon its normative scaffolding. For instance, the most recent 2006 Central Asian NWFZ Treaty acknowledged Robles's vision with its preamble's reference to the goal of "striving to broaden such regimes throughout the planet for the good of all living things."[34]

Another normative role of NWFZ treaties involves the way in which, once established, they exert influence on holdout states, if not in the short term, then at least in the longer term. None of the existing treaties in populated regions were successful in gaining immediate ratification by all states within their region. Their failure to achieve complete ratification immediately after treaty signature could be interpreted as rendering the zones ineffective; yet, in the context of a longer time frame, such an interpretation would be premature. The regional normative frameworks established by NWFZ treaties have contributed to eventual adherence of all holdout states in four out of the five NWFZs in populated regions, and there has been a positive trend in the African NWFZ toward securing complete adherence.

The act of negotiating regional NWFZ treaties creates normative nonproliferation frameworks and confidence-building processes that can engage reluctant or holdout states at both diplomatic and civil society levels, and ultimately secure their adherence, particularly in the context of domestic political changes. The NWFZ role in developing regional nonproliferation norms has been analyzed most closely in the case of the Tlatelolco Treaty. Redick observes that "the Tlatelolco negotiating process... had a subtle but important impact on Argentine-Brazilian relations in the nuclear policy area. For the first time, two suspicious rivals discussed fully and frankly the most sensitive issues of nuclear policy and reached common positions.... The coordination of nuclear policy by Argentina and Brazil relative to the NPT and during the Tlatelolco negotiations was a first substantive step in a lengthy nuclear confidence-building process."[35] These confidence-building processes were to continue under both military and democratic governments, until the two countries ratified the LANWFZ in the 1990s. As Ambassador Thomas Graham, Jr. has noted with respect to Argentina and Brazil, "Even countries that are not Party to a nuclear-weapon-free zone treaty... cannot avoid the regional norm of nonproliferation established by that treaty."[36]

The Tlatelolco Treaty contained a key mechanism for enabling, and allowing time for, regional nonproliferation norms to take hold in initially resistant states: its flexible entry-into-force mechanism. The entry-into-force provision in the original Article 28 (29 in the amended treaty) allowed regional states to bring the treaty into force for their own territories ahead of the wider objective of having the treaty in force for the whole of Latin America. This was achieved by giving each state the right to waive the requirements that designate the treaty coming into force for the whole of Latin America and the Caribbean. In this way, each state brought the treaty into force for its territory by lodging an Article 28 waiver declaration. States such as Brazil, Argentina, and Cuba could sign and even ratify the treaty, but decline to bring it into force by not lodging their waiver. In practice, this mechanism allowed the treaty to come into force gradually across the region over a span of three decades.

Other NWFZs have not followed the Tlatelolco Article 28 precedent of including a waiver process. However, the South Pacific, Southeast Asia, and Africa zones achieved a similar effect by not requiring all regional states to ratify as a precondition to entry into force; they instead required a specified minimum number of ratifications, in each case involving more than half of the relevant states. In this way, these zones also created some flexibility, permitting initial holdout states to opt for joining at a later date. All of the existing NWFZs, other than the African NWFZ, have now secured universal adherence; yet, if universal adherence had been required as the price of entry into force, many would not have entered into force.

Nuclear Weapon States

While there is nothing to prevent regional groups of countries from exercising their sovereign right to negotiate and implement NWFZs within their own regions, NWS can and do play both positive and negative roles in regional cooperation on such zones. All five of the official NWS have agreed to the 1999 UNDC NWFZ guidelines, but they have tended to be selective in their support for such zones. In particular, the NWS have been slow in ratifying the protocols to NWFZ treaties that would create legally binding obligations, such as negative security assurances, for the five official NPT nuclear powers. As a result, only Protocol 2 of the Latin American zone has been ratified by all five.

As of this writing, Tlatelolco remains the only such treaty the United States has ratified, while the other four NWS have also ratified protocols to the Rarotonga and Pelindaba accords. The United States did provide some initial support for the 1985 South Pacific NWFZ and the 1996 African NWFZ treaties, signing the protocols for the SPNFZ treaty in 1996 (after France had ceased testing in the region) and the AFNWFZ Treaty in the same year. However, U.S. ratification of the two treaties has been long delayed. Only in May 2011 did the Obama administration present ratification documents to the Senate, which has so far not acted on them. The Obama administration has also taken an initial step forward on the Central Asian NWFZ, signing its protocols containing negative security assurances on May 6, 2014, together with the other four NWS.[37] The United States has been less forthcoming about the Southeast Asian NWFZ, declining so far to sign, let alone ratify, the relevant protocols. As noted above, the NWS have objections to provisions in the Bangkok Treaty that extend it to EEZs, which would preclude nuclear states from launching sea-based nuclear weapons from within the zone against states outside the zone.

Russia and China have shown similar patterns of selective support and delays in fully supporting NWFZs. Russia has signed and ratified the Antarctic, LANWFZ, SPNFZ, and AFNWFZ, but delayed its ratifications of the Tlatelolco Treaty for twelve years and the Pelindaba Treaty for fifteen years. China has similarly signed and ratified the same treaties, but delayed its ratification of the Tlatelolco Treaty for seven years. Like the United States, neither Russia nor China has so far been prepared to sign or ratify the SEANWFZ protocol.

THE EFFECTIVENESS OF EXISTING NWFZS

NWFZs have several key objectives. They seek to prevent horizontal and vertical proliferation, improve regional security against nuclear threats from outside the region, contribute to wider global efforts to promote nonproliferation and elimination of nuclear weapons, and, in the case of some treaties, address health and environmental effects of past or potential future nuclear activities. The existing NWFZs have largely been effective in achieving these objectives, though not completely so.

On the objective of preventing horizontal proliferation, there have been no major breaches by any of the member states of NWFZs. In four out of the five zones in populated regions, all states have become parties; only the African NWFZ has yet to achieve complete adherence of relevant states. In Africa, the NWFZ has involved the dismantling of previous nuclear weapon facilities in South Africa. In Latin America, the Tlatelolco Treaty has contributed to reversing previous military control of nuclear energy programs in Argentina and Brazil. While NWFZ treaties are not immune from potential treaty withdrawals, no ratifying NWFZ state has so far withdrawn; and the legally binding nature of the treaties means that any noncompliance would face national, regional, and conceivably UN Security Council scrutiny and potential sanctions. There have been few examples to date of NWFZ-ratifying states that have even come under suspicion of noncompliance with NWFZ obligations.

The related aim of strengthening international nonproliferation systems has certainly been achieved by all the existing NWFZs in populated regions as a result of mandatory requirements for member states to bring into force IAEA safeguards on all their nuclear activities. In the case of Latin America, this represented a reversal of policy for Argentina and Brazil, both of which had previously declined to accept IAEA safeguards.

In terms of preventing vertical proliferation activities, all of the NWFZs appear to have been successful to date in preventing stationing of nuclear weapons. This includes regions such as Central Asia and Latin America where such weapons were stationed in the past.

Some treaties also prohibit NWS from conducting nuclear tests within designated zone boundaries, including in some cases in international waters. Following relevant NWS protocol ratifications, there has been no further testing of such weapons in any of the zones, including the South Pacific, Africa, and Central Asia, all of which were sites for extensive nuclear testing by one or other of the nuclear weapon states. Prior to French ratification of the SPNFZ protocols, however, France continued nuclear testing in the South Pacific region for over a decade after the treaty came into force. France signed the treaty only after ceasing the tests in 1996 following an upsurge in regional civil society and government protests over the tests. This is also the year the CTBT was concluded, and that treaty has also contributed to the cessation of nuclear testing by the five NWS.

On the question of how effective the existing NWFZS are in reducing the risks of nuclear use or threat of use against NWFZ regions, there has been little evidence of such threats to date. There is, however, the issue of securing the required negative security assurances. The Latin American NWFZ treaty remains the only one for which all five of the NWS have ratified such guarantees. In the case of the South Pacific and African NWFZS, the relevant protocols have been ratified by all the NWS except the United States. Although the Obama administration submitted these protocols to the Senate for advice and consent in 2011, there has been little evidence since then of Senate movement to ratify them.

LESSONS FROM THE EXISTING NWFZS

A number of lessons may be drawn from the negotiation and contexts of the six established NWFZS. First, consistent with the first factor listed by Knopf in the theory chapter, self-interest plays a role in facilitating cooperation. The zones have all represented responses to past or potential nuclear threats specifically affecting each region. In the South Pacific, African, and Central Asian zones, concerns centered on nuclear testing and its radioactive legacy. In other zones, regional actors had concerns about becoming a target in a nuclear conflict between the nuclear weapon states as a consequence of the stationing or deployment of nuclear weapons within the region. This was particularly the case in Latin America and Southeast Asia. The NWFZS also reflected concerns about horizontal proliferation within the region, especially in Latin America and Africa. Such perceived threats are key factors in creating the political impetus for establishing a regional NWFZ.

Second, NWFZS have been greatly facilitated by regional organizations. Regional organizations have played major roles in providing the forums, negotiation mechanisms, and mutual trust and respect that helped establish NWFZS in those regions. However, it should not be concluded that the absence of permanent regional organizations precludes NWFZ establishment. The Latin American, Antarctic, and Central Asian NWFZ treaties were all successfully negotiated through specially created regional negotiation bodies. This observation is similar to the proposition from chapter 1 that transnational networks can be important. In this case, however, working-level relationships have not been as central as Knopf suggests. Regional organizations have mattered more for the reasons typically emphasized in the literature: they reduced transaction costs and promoted a shared regional identity.

Third, the success of each of the existing NWFZS has relied in no small part on advocate leaders in one or several of the regional states. Such leaders have pursued the NWFZ initiative not only in the context of their domestic political environments but also in regional and international forums. This confirms the importance of leadership, but also shows that it need not come from a global power such as the United States.

Fourth, in line with another factor proposed by Knopf, each NWFZ has depended on favorable domestic political contexts. In the South Pacific and Southeast Asian zones, active civil society campaigns over a number of years were an important factor in creating the political will to implement the zones. The existence, or coming to power, of democratic civilian governments has also been a key factor in some zones, particularly the Latin American NWFZ.

Fifth, NWFZS are not overnight panaceas for averting or reversing horizontal nuclear proliferation in a particular region. Many have taken extended periods, almost three decades in the case of the Latin American NWFZ, to secure complete adherence within a region. However, even in contexts where they have not secured relatively quick adherence from all regional states, they have functioned to provide and promote regional nonproliferation normative frameworks, incentives, and forums for dialogue and discussion that can lead to eventual adherence to regional and global nonproliferation arrangements. This supports the proposition in the theory chapter that norms can be important, while also showing that their impact can take time to develop.

Sixth, while NWFZS do not depend on prior assent by the nuclear weapon states, they cannot be assumed to be effective in terms of reducing risks of nuclear threat or use by the NWS until they have secured the requisite protocol negative security assurances from all NWS. The NWS have signed the protocols for all the zones but that in Southeast Asia. But only one NWFZ in a populated region has so far successfully achieved ratification from all five NWS, the LANWFZ.

Compared to what can be achieved through unilateral or bilateral policies, NWFZ multilateral initiatives are long-term projects that may take many years or even decades to yield their intended outcomes. As Peter Piot, former UN HIV/AIDS coordinator, reminds us, there is an old proverb, "If you want to go fast, go alone, but if you want to go far, don't."[38]

In line with the framework identified in chapter 1, the lessons from the six regional NWFZs confirm that the initial formal outcomes at the time of treaty negotiation and signature are only parts of the story. Just as important are the evolving processes of multilateral cooperation, regional confidence and trust building, and progressive adherence to regional and global nonproliferation norms that serve to prevent or even reverse proliferation in a specific region. There is also a learning process evident in successive treaty provisions, with negotiators of each new zone learning from the outcomes and experience of previous zones. Furthermore, NWFZ advocacy, negotiation, and implementation have tended to be multitrack in character, frequently involving not just cooperation at the government level, but also between governments, civil society, epistemic communities, and global organizations, particularly UN bodies. The influence of domestic political change was evident in a number of the NWFZs, at least at the stage where they were first proposed, while in all of the treaties the advocacy role of political leaders was critical. At the same time, many of the NWFZ treaties reflected a clear sense of national self-interest in protecting participants from becoming involved in a nuclear conflict either as a result of an adversary in their own region acquiring nuclear weapons or as part of a wider nuclear conflict.

IMPLICATIONS FOR NEW NWFZ INITIATIVES

There are three regions facing critical stages in nuclear proliferation in the coming years: the Middle East, Northeast Asia, and South Asia. In all three regions, proliferation has already occurred. In the absence of regional denuclearization measures, such proliferation is likely to extend further, and it could undermine the global NPT-based nonproliferation regime.

There are a number of lessons for the Middle East that may be drawn from previous NWFZ experience. The region lacks the kind of regional security forum that many other regions have. However, the proposed Middle East conference may, if successfully held, serve to create the necessary regional structures. The Tlatelolco Article 28 mechanism continues to be relevant in allowing reluctant states (most likely Israel and Iran) to give in-principle acceptance of a regional nonproliferation framework while not bringing such a framework into force until such states feel assured that adequate verification systems are in place and their respective security concerns can be assured.[39] A particular need, and rationale, for an NWFZ in the Middle East region is a greatly enhanced regional inspection and verification system. Again the Latin American experience offers precedents in the form of the OPANAL and ABACC monitoring bodies.

Northeast Asian governments, unlike some of the Middle Eastern states, have so far not pursued the concept of a region-wide NWFZ in either UN or NPT forums, nor collectively agreed on a region-wide zone. A more geographically circumscribed arrangement briefly appeared to be in reach when bilateral North-South negotiations culminated in the 1992 Joint Declaration on the Denuclearization of the Korean Peninsula, but this agreement was never fully implemented. The opportunity remains for Northeast Asian leaders to consider a phased introduction into force of a wider Northeast Asian NWFZ. North Korea could be encouraged to join a rigorously verified zone and dismantle its nuclear weapon program through a combination of NWFZ treaty incentives, such as negative security assurances from the United States and other nuclear powers, a final peace settlement, and economic and energy assistance. As in the Middle

East, there is potential for the progressive bringing into force of a regional NWFZ on the Tlatelolco Article 28 precedent since South Korea and Japan are already nuclear free and could jointly negotiate such a zone with North Korea.[40] The treaty could include initial acceptance in principle by North Korea and provide incentives for a subsequent North Korean decision to bring the treaty into force for its territory. If necessary, as Morton Halperin has proposed, a time window could be built into a Northeast Asia NWFZ treaty jointly negotiated by South Korea and Japan allowing withdrawal if North Korea had not joined within three to five years.[41]

In South Asia, like Northeast Asia, there are currently no initiatives at a governmental level to create a regional NWFZ. Historically Pakistan sought such a zone at the UN General Assembly from 1974 to 1997, but the idea was rejected by India on the grounds of needing to counter Chinese nuclear weapons. However, the South Asian NWFZ concept continued to be endorsed at the 2000 NPT Review Conference, and fellow regional states, such as Bangladesh, Nepal, and Sri Lanka, might play the same role as Mexico in developing an NWFZ framework that India and Pakistan could be encouraged to join at a later date.

CONCLUSION

This chapter differs from others in the volume in that it focuses on formal treaties rather than less formal arrangements. More than fifty years since the original Rapacki Plan, the process of creating NWFZs contains many lessons for international cooperation on nonproliferation, starting with the basic insight that treaty-based mechanisms can still make valuable contributions. Regional groupings of like-minded countries have demonstrably succeeded in creating a mosaic of denuclearized zones across the globe. NWFZs now embrace the whole Southern Hemisphere as well as north-of-equator parts of Latin America, Africa, and Southeast Asia plus Central Asia and Mongolia (a self-declared single-state NWFZ). Almost half of all UN member states have now ratified NWFZs.

The negotiation of each of these denuclearized zones was the outcome of a number of key factors. All have been motivated by concerns among regional decision makers and their constituencies about regional threats posed by nuclear weapons activities, whether in the forms of nuclear testing, nuclear weapons stationing or deployment, or potential involvement in nuclear conflicts between nuclear weapon states. In some zones, regional concerns were identified and pursued by civil society groups and movements that influenced domestic political parties and leaderships. In all cases, advocate leaders played a key role, both in persuading domestic constituencies and in diplomacy with fellow regional leaders.

Permanent regional organizations greatly assisted negotiation in the case of some NWFZs, as in the South Pacific, Southeast Asian, and African treaties; but ad hoc conferences, commissions, or working groups also proved sufficient in such regions as Antarctica, Latin America, and Central Asia. Regional negotiations, such as for the African and Central Asian NWFZs, were also assisted by UN and independent experts.

Yet it would be a mistake to assume that NWFZs are an instant solution for the proliferation problems and dilemmas of a particular region. While requiring much effort and leadership to bring into being, NWFZs do not necessarily secure immediate adherence by all the relevant parties, whether relevant regional states or external nuclear powers. Where NWFZs have not secured complete adherence from the beginning (the case in most of the zones), their role has been to create a normative nonproliferation framework, including mechanisms for regional dialogue, that serve to build confidence within a region, and between that region and the nuclear powers. This confidence- and norm-development role can, and usually does, take an extended period.

There are important lessons to be drawn from the six existing NWFZ treaties for successful negotiation of further such zones, and for other regional nonproliferation measures. The proposed conference on the Middle East WMDFZ highlights the continued relevance of the NWFZ concept to regions facing serious proliferation developments and risks. These lessons extend to how the nuclear powers respond to NWFZ initiatives. The potential threat of an unraveling of the whole nonproliferation regime warrants NWS recalculation of the nonproliferation benefits of supporting and giving security guarantees to NWFZs compared to hypothetical needs for forward deployment of nuclear weapons in NWFZ regions.

Multilateral negotiations are rarely easy, particularly in regions with many states and enduring rivalries. The successful negotiation of the six existing NWFZs demonstrates what is feasible in securing commitment to nonproliferation norms given the necessary conditions, advocacy, leadership, and political will within each region. The incalculable risks of death and destruction from inadvertent or deliberate use of nuclear weapons suggest that new multilateral NWFZ initiatives are more urgently needed than ever if the future risk of a nuclear holocaust is to be averted.

Notes

1. Treaty on the Non-Proliferation of Nuclear Weapons (NPT), United Nations Office for Disarmament Affairs (UNODA), Disarmament Treaties Database, http://disarmament.un.org/treaties/, accessed July 12, 2012.

2. Antarctic Treaty, Treaty of Tlatelolco, Treaty of Rarotonga, Bangkok Treaty, Pelindaba Treaty, and Treaty on a Nuclear-Weapon-Free Zone in Central Asia, UNODA, Disarmament

Treaties Database. In the South Pacific, two island microstates that are not UN members have also joined the treaty, and in Africa as of this writing newly independent South Sudan has yet to sign the Pelindaba Treaty.

3. There are also treaties prohibiting nuclear weapons in outer space and on the seabed, and the UN recognizes Mongolia as a single-state NWFZ, but these zones are not discussed here.

4. Daniel Deudney, "Unipolarity and Nuclear Weapons," in *International Relations Theory and the Consequences of Unipolarity*, ed. G. John Ikenberry, Michael Mastanduno, and William C. Wohlforth (New York: Cambridge University Press, 2011), 303–5.

5. James R. Ozinga, *The Rapacki Plan* (Jefferson, N.C.: McFarland, 1989).

6. Conference of the Committee on Disarmament, *Comprehensive Study of the Question of Nuclear-Weapon-Free Zones in All Its Aspects* (New York: United Nations General Assembly Official Records, 30th Session, Supplement No. 27A, A/10027/Add.1, October 8, 1975); United Nations, *UN Disarmament Yearbook 1978* (New York: United Nations, 1979), 50–51; United Nations, *Report of the Disarmament Commission* (New York: UN General Assembly Official Records, 54th Session, Supplement No. 42, A/54/42, annex 1, May 16, 1999), 7–10.

7. Antarctic Treaty.

8. Alfonso Garcia Robles, *The Denuclearization of Latin America* (Washington, D.C.: Carnegie Endowment for International Peace, 1967); Alfonso Garcia Robles, *The Latin American Nuclear-Weapon-Free Zone* (Muscatine, Iowa: Stanley Foundation, 1979); Davis R. Robinson, "The Treaty of Tlatelolco and the United States: A Latin American Nuclear Free Zone," *American Journal of International Law* 64, no. 2 (April 1970): 282–309; John R. Redick, "Regional Nuclear Arms Control in Latin America," *International Organization* 29, no. 2 (Spring 1975): 415–45; John R. Redick, "The Tlatelolco Regime and Nonproliferation in Latin America," *International Organization* 35, no. 1 (Winter 1981): 103–34; Monica Serrano, *Common Security in Latin America: The 1967 Treaty of Tlatelolco* (London: Institute of Latin American Studies, London University, 1992); Monica Serrano, "Latin America: The Treaty of Tlatelolco," in *Nuclear Weapons-Free Zones*, ed. Ramesh Thakur (London: Macmillan, 1998), 35–58; John R. Redick, "Precedents and Legacies: Tlatelolco's Contribution to the 21st Century," in *Nuclear-Weapon-Free Zones in the 21st Century*, ed. Pericles Gasparini Alves and Daiana B. Cipollone (Geneva: United Nations Institute for Disarmament Research [UNIDIR], 1997), 39–48.

9. For NWFZ overviews, see James Martin Center for Nonproliferation Studies, *Nuclear-Weapon-Free-Zone (NWFZ) Clearinghouse*, cns.miis.edu/nwfz_clearinghouse; Jozef Goldblat, *Arms Control: The New Guide to Negotiations and Agreements* (London: Sage, 2002), 196–219; Michael Hamel-Green, "Peeling the Orange: Regional Paths to a Nuclear-Weapon-Free World," *Disarmament Forum*, UNIDIR, no. 2 (2011): 3–14; Thakur, *Nuclear Weapons-Free Zones*; Alves and Cipollone, *Nuclear-Weapon-Free Zones*.

10. Michael Hamel-Green, *The South Pacific Nuclear Free Zone Treaty: A Critical Assessment* (Canberra: Peace Research Centre, Research School of Pacific Studies, Australian National University, 1990); Greg Fry, "Regional Arms Control in the South Pacific," in *Nuclear-Free Zones*, ed. David Pitt and Gordon Thompson (London: Croom Helm, 1987), 46–66.

11. R. M. Marty M. Natalegawa, "The Southeast Asian Nuclear Weapon Free Zone Proposal: Retrospect and Prospect" (Ph.D. thesis, Australian National University, 1993); J. S. Djiwandono, *Southeast Asia as a Nuclear-Weapons-Free Zone* (Kuala Lumpur: Institute of Strategic and International Studies, 1987); Carolina G. Hernandez, "Southeast Asia: The Treaty of Bangkok," in Thakur, *Nuclear Weapons-Free Zones*, 81–92; Bilveer Singh, *ASEAN, the Southeast Asia Nuclear-Weapon-Free Zone and the Challenge of Denuclearization in Southeast Asia* (Canberra Papers on Strategy and Defence No. 138, Strategic and Defence Studies Centre, Australian National University, Canberra, 2000).

12. Oluyemi Adeniji, *The Treaty of Pelindaba on the African Nuclear-Weapon-Free Zone* (Geneva: UNIDIR, 2002); Julius O. Ihonvbee, "Africa—The Treaty of Pelindaba," in Thakur, *Nuclear Weapons-Free Zones*, 93–120.

13. Marco Roscini, "Something Old, Something New: The 2006 Semipalatinsk Treaty on a Nuclear Weapon-Free Zone in Central Asia," *Chinese Journal of International Law* 7, no. 3 (2008): 593–624; Jozef Goldblat, "Denuclearization of Central Asia," *Disarmament Forum* UNIDIR, no. 4 (2007): 25–32.

14. U.S. Department of State, "National Security Council Report NSC 5804/1 8 March 1958: Statement of U.S. Policy on Antarctica" (Washington, D.C.: U.S. Office of the Historian), www.history.state.gov/historicaldocuments/frus1958-60v02/d269, 1 and 4, accessed March 23, 2012.

15. Michael Hamel-Green, "Nuclear Tests in the Pacific," in *The Oxford Encyclopaedia of Peace*, vol. 3, ed. Nigel J. Young (Oxford: Oxford University Press, 2010), 264–69; U.S. Department of Energy (DOE), *United States Nuclear Tests, July 1954 through September 1992* (Washington, D.C.: Department of Energy, NV-209, Rev.15, 2001); Bruno Barrillot, *Les Essais Nucléaires Français 1960–1996: Conséquences sur l'environnement et la santé* (Lyon: Centre de Documentation et de Recherche sur la Paix et les Conflits, 1996); Vitali Fedchenko and Ragnhild Ferm Hellgren, "Nuclear Explosions, 1945–2006," in *SIPRI Yearbook 2007* (Oxford: Oxford University Press, 2007), 555–57.

16. Paul A. Berkman, "President Eisenhower, the Antarctic Treaty and the Origin of International Spaces," in *Science Diplomacy*, ed. Paul A. Berkman, Michael A. Lang, David W. H. Walton and Oran R. Young (Washington, D.C.: Smithsonian Institution Scholarly Press, 2011), 23.

17. Presidents of the Republics of Bolivia, Brazil, Chile, Ecuador, and Mexico, *Joint Declaration of 29 April 1963 on the Denuclearization of Latin America* (New York: UN General Assembly Official Record, 18th Session, 1963, A/51415/rev.1 annex).

18. Robinson, "Treaty of Tlatelolco," 283–84; Redick, "Regional Nuclear Arms Control," 146.

19. Hamel-Green, *South Pacific Nuclear Free Zone Treaty*, 1–6 and 55–82.

20. Natalegawa, "Southeast Asian Nuclear Weapon Free Zone Proposal," 308–9.

21. Isaac E. Ayewah, "The Treaty on the Nuclear-Weapon-Free Zone in Africa," in Alves and Cipollone, *Nuclear-Weapon-Free Zones*, 56.

22. Scott Parrish, "Prospects for a Central Asian Nuclear-Weapon-Free Zone," *Nonproliferation Review* 8, no. 1 (Spring 2001): 142.

23. United Nations General Assembly, *Almaty Declaration, Letter Dated 14 March 1997 from the Representatives of Kazakhstan, Kyrgyzstan, Tajikistan, Turkmenistan and Uzbekistan to the United Nations Addressed to the Secretary-General* (New York: United Nations General Assembly, A/52/112, March 18, 1997).

24. Redick, "Regional Nuclear Arms Control"; Redick, "Tlatelolco Regime and Nonproliferation"; Redick, "Precedents and Legacies," 39–48; Serrano, *Common Security in Latin America*.

25. Hamel-Green, *South Pacific Nuclear Free Zone Treaty*, 1–6, 55–104.

26. Australian Government Cabinet, "South Pacific Nuclear Free Zone—Major Issues, Minister for Foreign Affairs Bill Hayden's Report to Cabinet on Progress Achieved by the South Pacific Forum's Working Group on a South Pacific Nuclear Free Zone (SPNFZ)" (Submission No. 2806, April 24, 1985; declassified 2013).

27. Natalegawa, "Southeast Asian Nuclear Weapon Free Zone Proposal," 300–383, esp. 359–77.

28. Paulo S. Wrobel and John R. Redick, "Nuclear Cooperation in South America: The Role of Scientists in the Argentine-Brazilian Rapprochement," *Annals of the New York Academy of Sciences* 866 (December 1998): 165–81.

29. Oumirserik Kasenov, "On the Creation of a Nuclear-Weapon-Free Zone in Central Asia," *Nonproliferation Review* 6, no. 1 (Fall 1998): 144–47; Parrish, "Prospects for a Central Asian Nuclear-Weapon-Free Zone," 141–48.

30. Nina Tannewald, *The Nuclear Taboo: The United States and the Non-use of Nuclear Weapons since 1945* (Cambridge: Cambridge University Press, 2007).

31. Antarctic Treaty.

32. Treaty of Tlatelolco.

33. Alfonso Garcia Robles, "The Treaty for the Prohibition of Nuclear Weapons in Latin America," in Pitt and Thompson, *Nuclear-Free Zones*, 21.

34. Central Asia Nuclear-Weapon-Free-Zone Treaty.

35. John R. Redick, "Nuclear Illusions: Argentina and Brazil" (Occasional Paper 25, Henry L. Stimson Center, Washington, D.C., December 1995), 19.

36. Thomas Graham, Jr., "The Treaty of Tlatelolco: Its Role in the International Regime of Non-Proliferation" (OPANAL, collection articles on the 30th Anniversary of the Tlatelolco Treaty, February 1997), www.opanal.org/Articles/Aniv-30/graham.htm, accessed May 11, 2012.

37. U.S. Department of State, "United States Signs Protocol to Central Asian Nuclear-Weapon-Free Zone Treaty," www.state.gov/r/pa/prs/ps/2014/05/225681.htm, accessed May 21, 2014. The United States, United Kingdom, and France had delayed signing the protocol due to concern about language in the Semipalatinsk Treaty that preserves prior agreements, fearing this might allow Russia to deploy nuclear weapons to regional parties under a Collective Security Treaty involving the Commonwealth of Independent States. These concerns were apparently sufficiently alleviated to enable the five NWS to make a demonstration of their commitment to negative security assurances by signing the protocols during a meeting of NPT parties. At the 2015 NPT Review Conference, the United States and Russia announced they had now submitted the protocols for ratification.

38. Peter Piot, "Chasing Down Deadly Viruses," interview with Debora MacKenzie, *New Scientist* 215, no. 2872 (July 7, 2012): 46.

39. See Redick, "Precedents and Legacies," 42.

40. Michael Hamel-Green and Peter Hayes, "The Path Not Taken, the Way Still Open: Denuclearizing the Korean Peninsula and Northeast Asia," *Asia-Pacific Journal* 50-1-09 (December 14, 2009), http://japanfocus.org/-Michael-Hamel_Green/3267.

41. Morton Halperin, "Promoting Security in Northeast Asia: A New Approach" (Nautilus Institute, NAPSNet Policy Forum, October 30, 2012), http://nautilus.org/napsnet/napsnet-policy-forum/promoting-security-in-northeast-asia-a-new-approach/, accessed January 2, 2013.

CHAPTER ELEVEN

Bilateral Cooperation on Nonproliferation
The Role of an Epistemic Community in Argentina and Brazil's Creation of a Joint Safeguards Arrangement

SARA Z. KUTCHESFAHANI

ONE OF THE MOST SUCCESSFUL, yet least studied, examples of bilateral cooperation on nuclear nonproliferation is the Brazilian-Argentine Agency for Accounting and Control of Nuclear Materials (ABACC). ABACC differs from the other cases in this volume. It emerged from a process that initially took place outside the existing multilateral nonproliferation arrangements and with no direct U.S. involvement. Yet ABACC contributed significantly to the nonproliferation outcomes in Argentina and Brazil. It created a binational system of mutual inspections of each state's hitherto non-safeguarded nuclear installations. This system enabled each side to verify the other's non-nuclear-weapon status to its satisfaction. This created confidence in both Argentina and Brazil that each could safely renounce nuclear weapons without having to fear its rival was still secretly pursing them.

Between the 1950s and the 1980s, Argentina and Brazil were widely suspected by the international community—as well as by each other—to be pursuing covert nuclear weapons programs. Several factors lay behind these suspicions. First, both countries had long competed for regional hegemony and were for much of this time ruled by military leaderships. Their military rivalry made nuclear weapons appear to be a logical next step. Second, in these decades both nations indigenously developed aspects of the nuclear fuel cycle, resulting in a situation in which both possessed nuclear facilities that were not subject to international safeguards. Third, both nations refused to participate in the international nuclear nonproliferation regime. They rejected the Nuclear Non-Proliferation Treaty (NPT), full-scope International Atomic Energy Agency (IAEA) safeguards, the Nuclear Suppliers Group (NSG), and the Tlatelolco Treaty to create a Latin American nuclear-weapon-free zone. These factors fueled widespread suspicion that the two countries were intent on acquiring a nuclear weapons capability.[1]

By the following decade, the two countries had reversed this situation and committed themselves to refraining from nuclear weapons development. Their agreement in July 1991 to establish ABACC represented a milestone in this process because it created a mechanism to verify the non-nuclear-weapon status of Argentina and Brazil. Using data collected primarily from interviews with Argentine and Brazilian decision makers (conducted face to face, over the phone, and via email from December 2008 to October 2009) as well as information accessed from open sources (including conference proceedings and the ABACC website), this chapter analyzes the process that led Argentine and Brazilian decision makers to create ABACC. The chapter focuses on the role of an Argentine-Brazilian epistemic community—a transnational group of like-minded technical experts—in ABACC's creation.

This focus is not meant to suggest that the epistemic community provides a monocausal explanation for the two states' decisions to commit to nuclear nonproliferation. In this chapter, the epistemic community is treated not as an alternative explanation, but rather as an intervening mechanism in a larger process. Many studies of why Argentina and Brazil renounced the nuclear weapons option agree that no single factor can alone explain this outcome.[2] This chapter recognizes that several other explanatory factors played a role, including transitions to democracy and the embracing of economic liberalism. However, the role of an epistemic community in creating ABACC has remained an unexplored aspect of the story in the nonproliferation literature. This chapter complements previous studies of the Argentina and Brazil cases by showing how a transnational network of technical and diplomatic specialists contributed to making cooperation on nonproliferation possible.

The first part of the chapter summarizes the epistemic community framework and applies it to the case of ABACC. The second part of the chapter considers how the cooperation between the two states relates to the possible factors outlined in Knopf's introduction. Finally, the chapter concludes with a discussion of "lessons learned," analyzing how successful and effective ABACC has been since it was created. This section points to the importance of dialogue, trust-building processes, and political leadership.

REASONS TO APPLY THE EPISTEMIC COMMUNITY FRAMEWORK TO THE ABACC CASE

The epistemic community framework was introduced to international relations scholars by Peter Haas as a way to study the role of ideas in international policy coordination.[3] Haas defined an epistemic community as a "network of professionals with recognized expertise and competence in a particular domain and an authoritative claim to policy-relevant knowledge within that domain or issue area."[4] In a special issue of *International Organization* edited by Haas, scholars suggested that the concept of an epistemic community should be treated as an alternative to prevailing approaches to the study of international cooperation.[5] The volume concluded that, under certain conditions, epistemic communities can influence state decisions.[6] When they are credited with possessing unique expertise in highly technical issue areas, enjoy a reasonable degree of consensus in their views, and have access to decision makers, members of an epistemic community influence policy when decision makers experience uncertainty about how to handle complex situations. In such circumstances, state decision makers often seek out relevant scientific or technical information and expertise. Epistemic communities are one possible provider of such information, and decision makers will defer to their advice when they perceive the epistemic community to be the main source of policy-relevant knowledge.

The epistemic community framework has been applied to studies of international environmental regimes, international economic policy, and U.S.-Soviet nuclear arms control, but it has not been given much attention in studies of nuclear nonproliferation. In order to supplement existing explanations and gain a more complete understanding of nonproliferation outcomes, studies of nuclear proliferation and restraint need to broaden explanations to include more actors (such as scientists and other experts), moving away from traditional state-centric approaches. The epistemic community approach does this by focusing on the potential role of transnational groups of experts working behind the scenes in policy formulation and subsequent implementation. Consequently, it provides a crucial insight into the link between actors and nonproliferation policy. The nonproliferation literature currently lacks a good understanding of the origins of the idea behind ABACC. As such, the epistemic community approach provides a useful framework through which to analyze the origins of this nuclear nonproliferation agreement.

Scholars have offered a number of reasons for why Argentina and Brazil did not become nuclear weapon states. These include both countries' transitions to democracy (Argentina in 1983, Brazil in 1985), the pursuit of economic liberalization in the mid- to late 1980s, trust building through confidence-building measures, a learning process over time, and the rise of less nationalistic new leaders.[7] These explanations are not incorrect, but they are incomplete. They do not account for all the domestic influences on policy or how the two sides came to embrace a binational inspection arrangement as the technical basis for cooperation that made possible a nonproliferation outcome. Although their efforts to develop a nuclear weapons option ceased only after they became democracies, it is important to note that negotiations on nuclear issues between the two states began in 1980, when both nations were ruled by military leaderships. These negotiations continued throughout the 1980s and early 1990s, prompting the creation of ABACC as part of the Guadalajara Agreement of July 1991. The creation of ABACC was a remarkable accomplishment given that the two nations had only a short time before been competing and generating mutual mistrust through their efforts in the sensitive area of nuclear technology development.

CASE OVERVIEW: THE PATH TO ESTABLISHING ABACC

The end of Argentina and Brazil's larger geopolitical rivalry took place in part through a gradual nuclear rapprochement process, which can be traced back to the late 1960s and early 1970s. Even though the two sides maintained an intense rivalry in this period (particularly in the nuclear sphere), they also developed a common position during the negotiations on the Tlatelolco Treaty in the mid-1960s and a shared opposition to the global nuclear nonproliferation regime that emerged with the NPT. These common policy positions facilitated the process of entering into nuclear cooperation.[8] The irony of this case is that cooperation that began out of common opposition to the nonproliferation regime ended up facilitating a nonproliferation outcome.

The two sides signed their first joint nuclear agreement, calling for cooperation on peaceful applications of nuclear technology, in May 1980. From then through December 1991, when they reached the Quadripartite Agreement to have ABACC work with the IAEA on full-scope safeguards, Argentina and Brazil signed a total of ten nuclear cooperation agreements. These progressively facilitated closer cooperation on technology and foreign policy between the two sides while also enabling them to build mutual confidence in each other's peaceful intentions.

The path to the creation of ABACC involved three distinct phases: (1) May 1980, (2) 1983–89, and (3) 1990–91.[9] Phase 1 saw initial steps taken by the military governments of President Jorge Rafael Videla of Argentina and President Joâo Baptista de Oliveira Figueiredo of Brazil. In May 1980, they signed the Cooperative Agreement for the Development and Application of the Peaceful Uses of Nuclear Energy. This accord called for cooperation on developing civil nuclear technology, but did not produce much progress before the end of military rule. Phase 2 saw these steps pursued and strengthened by the countries' first democratic governments when President Raúl Alfonsín of Argentina and President José Sarney of Brazil signed five nuclear cooperation agreements. During the second phase, the 1985 Foz de Iguaçu joint declaration established the Joint Working Group on Nuclear Affairs (JWG). This became institutionalized as the Permanent Committee on Nuclear Affairs (PCNA) as a result of the 1988 Iperó joint declaration on nuclear policy. The JWG and PCNA would provide a vital foundation for the work of the epistemic community in this case.

In addition, during the 1983–89 period, reciprocal presidential and technical visits to unsafeguarded and sensitive nuclear facilities began. In July 1987, President Alfonsín invited President Sarney to an exclusive tour of Argentina's unsafeguarded Pilcaniyeu pilot uranium enrichment facility. In response, in April 1988, Sarney invited Alfonsín to the navy-controlled Aramar uranium enrichment facility in the Iperó nuclear complex in São Paulo. Similar to the Pilcaniyeu pilot uranium enrichment facility in Argentina, the Aramar uranium enrichment facility had once been a secret nuclear installation.[10] Sarney made the final of the presidential visits to the Ezeiza nuclear facility, near Buenos Aires, in November 1988.

In phase three the initial May 1980 steps were brought to full conclusion by President Carlos Menem of Argentina (elected in 1989) and President Fernando Collor de Mello of Brazil (elected in 1990)—the successors of Alfonsín and Sarney, respectively. Presidents Menem and Collor signed a further four nuclear cooperation agreements. In the second Foz de Iguaçu joint declaration, issued in 1990, the two sides agreed to a Common System of Accounting and Control (SCCC), which outlined how they would implement bilateral full-scope safeguards. The subsequent Guadalajara Agreement of 18 July 1991 established ABACC as the agency to administer and verify the SCCC.

These steps were sufficient to convince Argentina and Brazil of each other's peaceful intentions in the nuclear sphere, but did not fully convince important outside parties, notably the United States. Hence, in December 1991, the two states and ABACC signed the Quadripartite Agreement with the IAEA to establish coordination between it and ABACC on full-scope safeguards. Their bilateral cooperation and subsequent agreement with the IAEA made it possible for Argentina and Brazil to reconsider their opposition to existing nonproliferation treaties. By the end of the decade, both countries had acceded to the Tlatelolco Treaty and the NPT and become members of the NSG.

THE EPISTEMIC COMMUNITY BEHIND ABACC

The epistemic community involved in the creation of ABACC emerged out of an incipient epistemic community that began to develop during the 1965–80 period. This incipient epistemic community reflected the common Argentine and Brazilian positions taken against the international nuclear nonproliferation regime. By the 1980–91 period, however, the epistemic community had realigned in ways that made a process of cooperation, and by extension, ABACC, possible.

In particular, in this period, Argentine and Brazilian scientists began calling for bilateral nuclear cooperation and mutual inspections. For example, in November 1983, the Brazilian Physics Society (SBF) and the Argentine Physics Association (AFA) issued their first joint declaration, which contained a paragraph asking both governments to exchange nuclear information and to establish mutual inspections of nuclear facilities. For the first time, both physics societies began to share the view that some (bi)national control over their respective nuclear programs was desirable, and that they should work together to establish this objective.[11] In November 1984, the two physics societies released a further joint declaration stating their opposition toward nuclear weapons and labeling as "morally unacceptable the participation of physicists in the development of nuclear weapons."[12] These declarations show that the scientists met the criteria that define an epistemic community: shared causal beliefs and normative views, leading to shared policy recommendations.

The epistemic community gained legitimacy and greater access to policy makers when the 1985 joint declaration of nuclear policy established the JWG; in 1988, this originally ad hoc group was institutionalized as the PCNA. The JWG/PCNA—the institutionalized epistemic community—comprised a mix of Argentine and Brazilian scientists (including representatives from CNEA and CNEN—the nuclear energy commissions in both states) and government officials (including representatives from the foreign ministries). These experts participated in periodic meetings where they engaged in a mutual exchange of information, consulted about scientific, technical, and military issues, and discussed the nature of a possible mutual safeguards system. Reflecting a period in which newly democratic governments were seeking to consolidate democracy and limit the military's role, the epistemic community operated independently from and had little interaction with the militaries in the two countries.[13] Through their technical work and regular interactions, members of the epistemic community helped change the Argentine-Brazilian nuclear relationship from one of rivalry to one of cooperation. Over the years, they stressed the importance of a bilateral mutual inspections regime, which would verify Argentina and Brazil's non-nuclear-weapon status. Their proposals were adopted and implemented by the presidents of both Argentina and Brazil (Menem and Collor, respectively), culminating in the establishment of ABACC in 1991.

EVIDENCE FOR THE EPISTEMIC COMMUNITY'S INFLUENCE

The Argentine and Brazilian representatives from the JWG/PCNA fit Haas's definition of an epistemic community. These experts included both prominent members of the scientific community (particularly representatives from national energy commissions) and state officials charged with making nuclear policy (especially representatives from the foreign ministries). Both groupings were equally important in the process that led to ABACC's establishment. On the one hand, the scientists were responsible for outlining the ways in which a mutual safeguards regime could be created, from a scientific and technical perspective. On the other hand, the state officials promoted the negotiations for bilateral nuclear inspections. While government officials endorsed the idea behind ABACC and ultimately implemented it as policy, it was primarily the scientists who came up with the concept and developed the framework for operationalizing it.

Support for this conclusion comes through consistently in interviews I conducted with eighteen individuals who either participated in or were familiar with the activities of JWG/PCNA.[14] These individuals generally agreed on the division of labor between scientists and government officials and on the areas where scientists had a major influence. Dr. Paulo Wrobel, a former advisor on science and technology at the Brazilian Embassy in London, summarized the consensus view that a "combination of political leadership and physicists" lay behind the thought process leading to ABACC. As various interviewees explained, "ABACC was the idea of scientists" and in particular "the scientists offered the structure behind ABACC." Yet interviewees usually described the decision to create ABACC as, ultimately, "a political decision" or "a government decision."

The scientists and government officials also functioned like a community, with good communication and productive working relationships. Argentine Ambassador Vicente Espeche Gil, a former director of nuclear affairs in the Argentine Foreign Service, remarked that "the communication between our delegations was both among diplomats, and mixed, with scientists from the two countries." Dr. Marco Marzo, a former Brazilian ABACC inspector, spoke for many when he observed that the epistemic community was "very influential and their role was fundamental" in the creation of ABACC.

The epistemic community was not limited solely to the delegates to the JWG/PCNA. The scientific community in both states, particularly nuclear physicists and engineers, also actively promoted Argentine-Brazilian nuclear cooperation. In both states, scientists and their professional societies (i.e., the Brazilian Physics Society; the Brazilian Society for the Advancement of Science, SBPC; and the Argentine Physics Association) promoted public discussions on the need for regional nuclear arms control.[15] In 1987, Naren Bali, president of the AFA, urged nuclear commission officials to open up facilities that were still off-limits.[16] These professional scientific societies were key lobbying elements before the Argentine and Brazilian congresses and presidents. The epistemic community built support for ABACC step by step. According to Marco Marzo, from 1987 onward, the "Argentinean and Brazilian nuclear delegations began to develop their joint inspection program between country and country, and amongst scientists and scientists," paving the way for the creation of ABACC.

HOW THE ABACC CASE FITS THE EPISTEMIC COMMUNITY FRAMEWORK

Having described who was behind the idea for ABACC, this chapter next examines how well the details of ABACC's creation correspond to theoretical framework of the epistemic community approach. According to Adler and Haas, epistemic communities gain influence when policy makers who are uncertain about what policies best serve the national interest believe the epistemic community has authoritative knowledge in that policy domain and when members of the community gain access to policy makers, often through appointments to the bureaucracy.[17] This section examines how—through having recognized knowledge and expertise and access to decision makers—the Argentine-Brazilian epistemic community outlined above facilitated official acceptance of the idea for ABACC and its subsequent implementation as policy.

The Role of Knowledge and Expertise

An important element in the epistemic community's influence was the acceptance of its knowledge and expertise in certain areas. Policy makers relied on the scientists particularly with respect to designing the mutual safeguards system, including the information to be verified and the nature of inspections. As Argentine Ambassador Pedro Villagra-Delgado, former head of the Division of International Security, Nuclear and Space Affairs at the Legal Advisor's Office in the Argentine Foreign Ministry (1996–2001), explained, "On how to implement these new policies of openness [opening up nuclear facilities to the other for inspection], the 'epistemic community' played a key role by analyzing different alternatives and eventually designing ABACC and the Quadripartite Safeguards Agreement, as well as the ratification of both the Treaty of Tlatelolco and NPT."

Acceptance of the epistemic community's expertise is facilitated when community members share common understandings of the policy issue in question. The scientists involved in setting up the mutual inspections regime shared and disseminated collective knowledge through an intensive period of engagement, including discussions in the JWG and PCNA. In an interview, Dr. Marco Marzo reported that the epistemic community sought to develop collective knowledge about how to verify that Argentine and Brazilian nuclear facilities were of a peaceful nature. This would ultimately be validated through the creation of a common system of safeguards and a verification system. These were both established in November 1990, under the Foz de Iguaçu Declaration, which created the common system for accounting and control of nuclear materials (SCCC). After the declaration, Argentina and Brazil exchanged lists of all their relevant facilities (including descriptions of each facility) and an inventory of nuclear materials, as a way to facilitate verification that their nuclear programs were of a peaceful nature.

Dr. Paulo Wrobel credited the emergence of the mutual inspections regime to the "crucial influence of the scientists." They enjoyed this influence, he explained, because "they knew what to do"—that is, to use joint safeguards to create mutual confidence—and "they knew how to do it." The epistemic community sought to develop greater collective knowledge over time. Sonia Fernández-Moreno, an Argentine representative from the PCNA, noted that the expert technical groups within the PCNA "shared inventories, learnt lessons, to try to make their systems compatible." Similar to other interviewees, Ambassador Roberto Garcia Moritán, an Argentine career diplomat and former secretary for foreign affairs (2003–9), concurred that the scientists "played a very important role from the technical point of view" in establishing ABACC.

Members of the epistemic community both developed and diffused technical knowledge, particularly through their communication within the JWG/PCNA setting. These bodies met every 120 days, alternating between venues in Argentina and Brazil (as mandated in the nuclear agreements). In these meetings, the Argentine and Brazilian participants exchanged technical information and assured each other that their respective nuclear programs were only for peaceful purposes. In particular, they developed specific measures on notification and assistance in all areas of nuclear safety, exchanged information on the security of nuclear installations, and began joint research and information exchange relating to safeguards—all of which required extensive knowledge and expertise.[18] As Argentine Ambassador Vicente Espeche Gil explained, "We had very frequent encounters with our Brazilian counterparts, and we even integrated a joint binational delegation to negotiate with the IAEA. Both national delegations were headed by diplomats with the technical support from the respective nuclear agencies."

The reciprocal visits, public declarations, and ongoing dialogue through the PCNA all provided a structural space for experts to diffuse their knowledge and ideas. These activities served as reassurance to the international community (as well as to each other) that the Argentine and Brazilian nuclear programs were of a peaceful nature. In addition, they also served as a precursor to establishing the mutual safeguards inspection regime. Over time, the regular technical and political exchanges under the remit of the PCNA contributed to the transformation of Argentina and Brazil's nuclear policy from one of technology cooperation to one of verification. Marco Marzo made an important observation about how this process unfolded:

> The way in which Argentina and Brazil came together in the nuclear field is astounding.... If you said to me at that time, in 1984 or 1985, that there would be a rapprochement between Argentina and Brazil, that the Bilateral Agreement would be signed in ten years, I would have said that you were crazy.... The first steps were very small steps. The rapprochement did not start with visits to secret enrichment plants. We started with small working groups in various areas.... At the beginning, we never discussed secret facilities, enrichment, or reprocessing.[19]

Consistent with a theme raised by Knopf in chapter 1, Marzo's observation suggests that working-level relationships played a major role in fostering cooperation. The epistemic community did not gain influence solely because of the persuasiveness of its ideas or knowledge; the PCNA was also responsible for turning ideas into concrete measures. Even before it designed ABACC, the PCNA engaged in other practical activities such as organizing the reciprocal visits, maintaining steady contacts at the political and technical levels, and engaging in consultations to increase mutual knowledge of each side's respective nuclear programs.[20] In an interview, Sonia Fernández-Moreno, an Argentine representative from the JWG/PCNA, confirmed that the PCNA "helped facilitate the joint visits and increased transparency mechanisms." Without the constant attempts by diplomats, scientists, and government officials to work on cooperative projects, and to maintain that commitment over a number of years, establishing the mutual safeguards inspection regime would not have been possible.

The work carried out by the PCNA facilitated political support in favor of progress toward mutual and, eventually, international inspections. When the political decision to establish ABACC was taken, two respected and experienced nuclear physicists, Jorge Coll from the CNEA representing Argentina and Carlos Feu Alvim, a professor of physics, representing Brazil, became the director and deputy director, respectively, of ABACC.

Access to Decision Makers

The extent of expert access to decision makers served as another crucial factor in the creation of ABACC. The JWG/PCNA, created through the 1985 and 1988 nuclear agreements, proved to be a key avenue of access. Representatives to these bodies from the foreign ministries and the scientific community of both countries were tasked to explore all avenues for nuclear cooperation. In doing so, they helped further negotiations and proposed directions for additional nuclear collaborative projects.[21] Given the origins of the JWG/PCNA in presidential agreements and the fact those bodies included officials from the foreign ministries, it seems likely that those within the JWG/PCNA would have had access to decision makers. Additional evidence supports such an inference. For example, the Collor administration hired one key member from the JWG/PCNA—a scientist—to implement the mutual inspections regime. From 1990 to 1992, Professor José Goldemberg held the post of Brazilian minister of science and technology. A nuclear physicist, Goldemberg was formerly the president of SBPC (1975–79). In addition, he himself remarked in an interview, "The president at the time, Fernando Collor, was a rather inquisitive mind and developed a good relationship with me asking frequently questions about science and technology."

According to Adler and Haas, the extent of an epistemic community's role in policy selection involves two factors: decision makers' unfamiliarity with policy issues and the timing of policy choice.[22] The foregoing has made it clear that political leaders lacked familiarity with the scientific and technical issues involved in safeguards and how to verify each country's non-nuclear-weapon status. This explains why they sought out expert advice through the step of creating the JWG and PCNA.

The second factor in assessing an epistemic community's role in policy selection involves timing. It may be easier for decision makers to accept ideas and advice from epistemic communities after political, military, or economic conditions have changed.[23] In the case of ABACC, timing was important, especially the transition to democracy. After 1985—once both states had become democracies—there was a greater exchange of information, leading to nine joint nuclear declarations. However, in terms of selecting the policy of mutual safeguards, Argentina played an especially important role. Argentine representatives took the initiative on promoting a collaborative nuclear partnership. In fact, according to Resende-Santos, who conducted extensive archival research in Brazil, the initiative for the first nuclear accord—that of May 1980—originated with Argentina.[24] Furthermore, as Argentine Ambassador Roberto Garcia Moritán explained, "The first move toward ABACC [was] started by us when President Alfonsín met President Sarney. We invited them to our enrichment plant in Pilcaniyeu. From there on, we started a process of conversation toward the acceptance of full-scope safeguards with the IAEA. We started to be satisfied with the bilateral reciprocal visits to each other's sensitive facilities. The evolution was part of a natural process where we both discovered the advantages of a bilateral mechanism."

Official negotiations on a mutual safeguards inspection regime began in 1987. However, the Argentines first put forward the idea of a bilateral or common system of nuclear inspections in 1985. Argentine president Alfonsín proposed to Brazilian president Sarney that they should negotiate a bilateral system of control of nuclear materials and installations and a bilateral verification system of nuclear facilities.²⁵ As Dr. Marco Marzo, a Brazilian representative of the PCNA explained, "Brazil did not [at first] accept Argentina's proposal because Brazil wanted to cooperate and not be controlled." In other words, Brazil still sought joint technology development rather than safeguards. Nevertheless, soon after Alfonsín's proposal, Brazil agreed in November 1985 to create the JWG to discuss nuclear issues. Three years later, its institutionalization—as the PCNA—not only furthered nuclear negotiations but also facilitated the presidential and technical nuclear installation visits. These visits gradually strengthened the case for the idea of bilateral inspections, helping persuade Brazil to become more willing to participate in bilateral nuclear initiatives.

In sum, all the factors that have been identified as necessary for epistemic community influence eventually fell into place. Once they did so, it did not take long for expert advice to lead to the setting up of ABACC. Because certain conditions had to be in place to facilitate a policy impact, the role of the epistemic community must be seen in the context of other explanatory factors. The next section takes up this task.

EXPLAINING COOPERATION

In relation to the seven possible factors for explaining cooperation outlined by Knopf in chapter 1, this chapter emphasizes the role of an epistemic community in the creation of ABACC and the importance of ABACC in enabling Argentina and Brazil's nonproliferation outcome. The epistemic community approach fits under Knopf's category of ideas, learning, and transnational networks. The case also supports some of Knopf's suggestions about how this factor might operate. The epistemic community behind ABACC did not influence policy solely through the persuasiveness or authority of its ideas. Direct communication and working-level relationships also fostered cooperation. The path to ABACC began with small, practical steps that helped demonstrate the feasibility and desirability of moving to a bilateral safeguards organization. These features of the case are consistent with chapter 1's observations that nonproliferation cooperation is sometimes built via operational activities. However, while the epistemic community explanation works well in the case of Argentina and Brazil, it is by no means the sole explanation. Other factors to consider in this case include self-interest and domestic political change.

Self-Interest

A self-interest argument can be applied to the case of Argentina and Brazil, though not precisely in the way Knopf summarizes self-interest explanations for cooperation on nonproliferation. The two states were not motivated by a shared proliferation threat posed by a third party. Instead, the two nations came together because of their common opposition to the international nuclear nonproliferation regime—particularly the NPT and the Tlatelolco Treaty—throughout the 1960s and 1970s. They viewed these international nonproliferation agreements as violations of their national interests and national sovereignty. In particular, Argentina and Brazil feared nonproliferation arrangements would restrict their autonomous efforts at technology development. Consequently, both states perceived it as in their respective state interests to *not* cooperate within the international nonproliferation regime framework.

Hence, in spite of their rivalry, they found common ground in relation to these nonproliferation agreements. This gave them reason to cooperate with each other to coordinate their objections to the nonproliferation regime and seek to overcome its potential restrictive effects on their development of nuclear technology. It can therefore be argued that the Treaty of Tlatelolco and the negotiations surrounding the NPT set the political context for the Argentine-Brazilian nuclear rapprochement and agreements of twenty years later. As John Redick notes,

> For the first time during the negotiations of the Latin American Treaty, these two suspicious rivals began to talk about these sensitive nuclear issues and *develop common positions*. The Tlatelolco negotiations became the first step in a long confidence-building process between Argentina and Brazil. The two countries were *now on the same side* of this nuclear policy issue. They saw themselves as pitted against the nonproliferation regime, which they viewed as insidiously trying to prevent the development of their nuclear programs. They viewed the nonproliferation regime as highly discriminatory. They viewed their *shared interest* as extending into common positions in opposition to the NPT, and this evolved into *common support* for each other's nuclear export policies.... Their... traditional animosity became muted into a sense of *shared victimization* by the advanced nations.[26]

What began as a largely reactive policy to perceived foreign pressure developed over time into a more active, bilateral nuclear cooperation, which then led to eventual involvement within the nuclear nonproliferation regime.

Argentina and Brazil felt marginalized from the nuclear-weapons club and the international order, and wanted to become global powers. At that time, power was synonymous with technological autonomy, which both nations desired to acquire. Against the backdrop of their intense nuclear rivalry, common positions taken against the nonproliferation regime began to emerge. In this context, the two countries started to see themselves not solely as competitors, but as also having shared interests and even a degree of shared identity as developing countries discriminated against by the global nuclear order. The developing sense of shared interests paved the way for the emergence of an epistemic community. As the epistemic community developed, it facilitated a further evolution in understandings of state interests. Guided in part by the epistemic community, Argentina and Brazil moved from giving priority to technological autonomy to a view that their interests would be served by making mutually verifiable nonproliferation commitments to each other.

While both nations were initially hostile to the nonproliferation regime, it is interesting to note that after their rapprochement, and *after the institutionalization of ABACC*, Argentina and Brazil became fully integrated within the nonproliferation regime. First, they signed the Quadripartite Agreement between themselves, ABACC, and the IAEA in December 1991; second, they acceded to the Tlatelolco Treaty in 1994; third, they joined the NSG in 1994 (Argentina) and 1996 (Brazil); and last, they acceded to the NPT (Argentina in 1995 and Brazil in 1998). They took these steps because key outside powers did not view ABACC as sufficient to prove Argentina and Brazil's nonproliferation credentials. Without their prior experience with ABACC, however, it is unlikely the two countries would have achieved the comfort level necessary to take the final step of joining the NPT.

Domestic Political Change

As Knopf states in chapter 1, domestic politics can be an important factor to consider in explaining cooperation. Many studies credit the transitions to democracy with a crucial role in explaining the nonproliferation outcomes in Argentina and Brazil.[27] The new democracies had an interest in reducing their military rivalry, including in the nuclear sphere, to remove a potential pretext for the military to once again intervene in domestic politics. However, it is important to note that although their efforts to develop a nuclear weapons option ceased after they became democracies, negotiations on nuclear issues between the two states had already begun in 1980, when both nations were ruled under military leaderships. The transitions to democracy were hence not the only factor involved. They still made an important contribution to the eventual outcome, however, because the new democratic governments continued and strengthened the initial steps taken by the military governments of President Videla of Argentina and President Figueiredo of Brazil. In the period soon after both countries transitioned to democracy—1983–89—five joint nuclear cooperation agreements were signed between President Alfonsín of Argentina and President Sarney of Brazil. As part of these agreements, the two presidents created the JWG, which later became the PCNA. The JWG/PCNA institutionalized the epistemic community and ensured its access to policy makers.

The epistemic community explanation interacts with the factor of domestic political change. The existence of democracy was not alone sufficient to ensure renunciation of nuclear weapons. The two sides had to find a practical way to get there.²⁸ The members of the JWG/PCNA led the way in finding this path. Over the years, they stressed the importance of a bilateral mutual inspections regime, which would verify Argentina and Brazil's non-nuclear-weapon status. Their proposals were adopted and implemented by the presidents of both Argentina and Brazil (Menem and Collor, respectively), culminating in the establishment of ABACC in 1991. Transitions to democracy served as a background factor that gave the epistemic community greater access to policy makers, but without the work performed by the epistemic community a nonproliferation outcome would have been much less likely.

LESSONS LEARNED

ABACC is the world's only binational safeguards agency responsible for verifying that the nuclear materials existing in both countries are being used exclusively for peaceful purposes. It is vested with the power to designate inspectors, carry out and evaluate inspections, and take legal action. It is made up of an equal number of Argentines and Brazilians. Dr. Marco Marzo, a former ABACC senior planning and evaluation officer, described everything in ABACC as "symmetric, with a Brazilian and Argentine counterpart."²⁹

Today, Argentine and Brazilian nuclear physicists continue to conduct mutual inspections at nuclear facilities on a cross-national basis through ABACC.³⁰ These inspections include verification of inventories of nuclear materials, unannounced and short-notice inspections, and inspections carried out along with the IAEA.³¹ Since its establishment in late 1991, ABACC has performed more than 1,200 inspections in seventy-five Argentine and Brazilian nuclear facilities, representing a total inspection effort of over 4,400 inspectors' days.³²

While the creation of ABACC helped verify Argentina and Brazil's non-nuclear-weapon status, it is worth bearing in mind ABACC's limitations insofar as keeping the two nations locked into the international nuclear nonproliferation regime. Twenty years since its inception, there is some concern over ABACC's effectiveness, particularly with regard to whether Brazil's nuclear submarine program could be used to give that country a mechanism to stockpile enriched uranium outside of safeguards.³³ In addition, neither Argentina nor Brazil has signed the Additional Protocol (AP), an agreement that bolsters the IAEA's ability to detect undeclared nuclear activities, which calls into question their position within the nuclear nonproliferation regime. Brazil more so than Argentina categorically refuses to enter into negotiations with the IAEA regarding the AP. Its reluctance to sign is based on two reasons: (1) the lack of progress toward disarmament by the nuclear weapon states and (2) the fact that further powers for international inspectors are deemed too intrusive. Brazil does not want to open up its nuclear installations in its universities for reasons of independence, autonomy, and academic freedom.[34] Argentina's noncommittal stance on the AP likely reflects Brazil's reluctance to accept it (given their former rivalry in the nuclear sphere) as well as the fact that the AP itself is of a voluntary nature.[35] Brazil and Argentina have argued that the existence of ABACC renders their acceptance of the AP unnecessary, and in 2011 the NSG agreed to recognize the Quadripartite Agreement as an alternative to the AP in qualifying countries to have access to sensitive nuclear technology.[36]

Although it has limitations, ABACC has performed a crucial function in helping Argentina and Brazil verify one another's non-nuclear-weapon status and move to policies officially renouncing any interest in nuclear weapons. As one of the most successful examples of bilateral cooperation on nuclear nonproliferation, it is important to pull out the "lessons learned" from its creation and subsequent impact. This section highlights three key lessons, concerning dialogue, trust building, and political leadership.

The Importance of Dialogue

The ABACC case demonstrates the value of establishing and maintaining a dialogue. Indeed, the main activities of the JWG/PCNA working group—the epistemic community—involved dialogue, information exchange, and consultation.[37] Meeting every 120 days alternately in Argentina and Brazil allowed the group to engage in discussions about the potential value and technical details of establishing a joint inspection regime. These discussions created opportunities to consider other topics of mutual interest in the nuclear field. Diplomats and technical experts assigned to the JWG/PCNA were tasked to explore all avenues for nuclear cooperation, including collaboration, safety measures, a data bank for information exchange, and application of safeguards to the two states' nuclear activities. For them to make progress in these tasks required ongoing dialogue.[38]

As chapter 1 reports, research has shown the value of communication in fostering cooperation. But dialogue, as reflected in the ABACC case, involves more. It includes an openness to two-way interaction and a sense of being involved in a common enterprise directed toward problem solving. One lesson of the ABACC case, therefore, is that establishing a forum for dialogue can enhance the impact of communication on the prospects for cooperation

Trust/Confidence Building

The ABACC case also supports the notion that confidence-building measures can help build a necessary element of trust. In the process of creating ABACC,

Argentina and Brazil embarked on a number of confidence-building measures. These helped them provide assurances to each other and to the international community that neither country was pursuing nuclear weapons. The high-level presidential and technical reciprocal visits to unsafeguarded and sensitive nuclear facilities represented the most important confidence-building steps paving the way for ABACC. In July 1987, Argentine president Alfonsín invited Brazilian president Sarney to tour the unsafeguarded Pilcaniyeu pilot uranium enrichment facility. Until that point, Argentina had not publicly admitted that this facility existed. In response, nine months after Alfonsín's invitation, President Sarney invited Alfonsín to the navy-controlled Aramar uranium enrichment facility in the Iperó nuclear complex. Similar to the Pilcaniyeu facility in Argentina, the Aramar facility had served as a secret nuclear installation.[39] Because it made Argentina's president the first foreigner to visit the plant, this invitation was highly symbolic. President Sarney made the final of the presidential visits to the Ezeiza nuclear facility in November 1988.

These mutual visits to hitherto secret and unsafeguarded nuclear installations created an atmosphere of trust, "a necessary precondition to on-site inspections of the respective nuclear activities."[40] In addition, they propelled further declarations encouraging deeper bilateral nuclear cooperation. In the words of Wrobel, "Opening the [Pilcaniyeu] facility to the scrutiny of a delegation headed by the Brazilian president allowed both leaders to end secrets and mistrust, and announce a new policy based on openness in nuclear matters."[41]

In addition, it is important to note that "while the presidents were publicly meeting and announcing fresh joint initiatives, the diplomats and scientific experts worked behind the scenes to transform trust and confidence into concrete measures."[42] The process of building confidence hence mattered both as a way to increase trust and because it facilitated working relationships that were helpful in finding ways to turn goodwill into practical steps, such as the creation of ABACC.

Political Will

The final lesson from this case concerns the political will of the Argentine and Brazilian leaderships. The idea of a mutual safeguards inspection regime, while formulated by an epistemic community, could not have been realized in the absence of strong political support from Argentine and Brazilian leaders. The reemergence of civilian leadership in both countries in the mid-1980s hastened and consolidated the confidence- and trust-building process between the two states. Under the civilian leadership, the bilateral nuclear agreements—while fostered under a military leadership in the 1980s—assumed a larger position in the rapprochement process because the democratically elected presidents also wanted to foster a cooperative relationship. The countries' first democratic governments (led by Alfonsín of Argentina and Sarney of Brazil) strengthened their nuclear partnership and established a common nuclear policy with the signing of five nuclear cooperation agreements. Through these agreements, both presidents were keen to prove to each other and to the rest of the international community that their nuclear programs were of a peaceful nature. Even after both countries underwent a change in the presidential leadership with the elections of President Carlos Menem of Argentina (elected in 1989) and President Fernando Collor de Mello of Brazil (elected in 1990), the new leaders continued the nuclear legacy of their predecessors with the signing of four nuclear cooperation agreements, which included the decision to implement ABACC. An epistemic community did much of the work to figure out how to cooperate in practical terms, but it required the support and political will of the political leadership to put the epistemic community in a position to turn its ideas into reality.

CONCLUSION

This chapter has traced the evolution from uncertainty over Argentina and Brazil's nuclear intentions to their creation of a mutual inspection safeguards regime. It has argued that an epistemic community acted as an important factor in the creation of ABACC. This bilateral policy coordination effort proved effective in its primary purpose, which was to verify the non-nuclear-weapon status of Argentina and Brazil to the satisfaction of both parties. Some important outside parties did not view ABACC as sufficient proof of nonproliferation commitments, but without their experience with ABACC it is hard to imagine Argentina and Brazil would have taken the subsequent steps of signing a safeguards agreement with the IAEA and joining the NPT.

This chapter's investigation of the role of epistemic communities in the creation of nuclear nonproliferation policies takes the epistemic community framework into a hitherto unexplored area. One of the main strengths of the epistemic community framework is to draw attention to the sources of the ideas behind implemented policies. As such, the framework calls attention to the relevance of thought leaders and expert communities. Consistent with a theme in the rest of this volume, the ABACC case also shows the value of looking not just at ideas but also at the working-level relationships that help translate ideas into concrete, operational activities and institutions. Given that research within the field of international security has traditionally been dominated by state-centric approaches, the epistemic community framework provides a useful

Bilateral Cooperation [247]

lens through which to understand the internal and transnational dimensions of policy making in international security.

Notes

This chapter draws in part upon material from Sara Z. Kutchesfahani, *Politics & the Bomb: The Role of Experts in the Creation of Cooperative Nuclear Non-Proliferation Agreements* (New York: Routledge, 2014), reproduced with permission.

1. Virginia Gamba-Stonehouse, "Argentina and Brazil," in *Security with Nuclear Weapons? Different Perspectives on National Security*, ed. Regina Cowen Karp (New York: SIPRI and Oxford University Press, 1991), 229–57; Ruth Stanley, "Cooperation and Control: The New Approach to Nuclear Nonproliferation in Argentina and Brazil," *Contemporary Security Policy* 13, no. 2 (Fall 1992): 191–213; John R. Redick, Julio C. Carasales, and Paulo S. Wrobel, "Nuclear Rapprochement: Argentina, Brazil, and the Nonproliferation Regime," *Washington Quarterly* 18, no. 1 (January 1995): 107–22; Michael Barletta, "Ambiguity, Autonomy, and the Atom: Emergence of the Argentine-Brazilian Nuclear Regime" (Ph.D. diss., University of Wisconsin-Madison, 2000); T. V. Paul, *Power versus Prudence: Why Nations Forgo Nuclear Weapons* (Montreal: McGill-Queen's University Press, 2000), chap. 6.

2. Mitchell Reiss, *Bridled Ambition: Why Countries Constrain Their Nuclear Capabilities* (Washington, D.C.: Woodrow Wilson Center Press, 1995), chap. 3; Paul, *Power versus Prudence*; Ariel E. Levite, "Never Say Never Again: Nuclear Reversal Revisited," *International Security* 27, no. 3 (Winter 2002–3): 59–88.

3. Peter M. Haas, "Do Regimes Matter? Epistemic Communities and Mediterranean Pollution Control," *International Organization* 43, no. 3 (Summer 1989): 377–403; Peter M. Haas, "Introduction: Epistemic Communities and International Policy Coordination," *International Organization* 46, no. 1 (Winter 1992): 1–35.

4. Haas, "Introduction: Epistemic Communities," 3.

5. "Knowledge, Power, and International Policy Coordination," ed. Peter M. Haas, special issue, *International Organization* 46, no. 1 (Winter 1992).

6. Haas, "Introduction: Epistemic Communities"; Emanuel Adler and Peter M. Haas, "Conclusion: Epistemic Communities, World Order, and the Creation of a Reflective Research Program," *International Organization* 46, no. 1 (Winter 1992): 367–90.

7. Etel Solingen, "The Political Economy of Nuclear Restraint," *International Security* 19, no. 2 (Fall 1994): 126–69; Jeffrey W. Knopf, "The Importance of International Learning," *Review of International Studies* 29, no. 2 (April 2003): 187–209; Jacques E. C. Hymans, *The Psychology of Nuclear Proliferation: Identity, Emotions, and Foreign Policy* (Cambridge: Cambridge University Press, 2006), chap. 6; Nicholas J. Wheeler, "Beyond Waltz's Nuclear World: More Trust May Be Better," *International Relations* 23, no. 3 (September 2009): 428–45; Harald Müller and Andreas Schmidt, "The Little Known Story of Deproliferation: Why States Give Up Nuclear Weapons Activities," in *Forecasting Nuclear Proliferation in the 21st Century, Vol. I: The Role of Theory*, ed. William C. Potter with Gaukhar Mukhatzhanova (Stanford, Calif.: Stanford University Press, 2010), 124–58; Paul, *Power versus Prudence*; Levite, "Never Say Never Again"; Reiss, *Bridled Ambition*.

8. In addition, the resolution of territorial disputes in the late 1970s assisted the rapprochement. John R. Redick, "Nuclear Illusions: Argentina and Brazil" (Occasional Paper 25, Henry L. Stimson Center, Washington, D.C., December 1995); João Resende-Santos, "The

Origins of Security Cooperation in the Southern Cone," *Latin American Politics and Society* 44, no. 4 (Winter 2002): 89–126; Charles A. Kupchan, *How Enemies Become Friends: The Sources of Stable Peace* (Princeton: Princeton University Press, 2010).

9. The 1980–83 period was marked by a lull, given other problems facing the two states. Argentina was preoccupied with the Malvinas/Falkland Islands War against the United Kingdom in 1982, and, at the same time, the Brazilian economy suffered a crisis.

10. Marco A. Marzo, "Origin and Role of Argentina's and Brazil's Nuclear Programs, and the Role of the Military and Non-governmental Scientists in Changing the Climate on Nuclear Development" (presentation, "Regional Safeguards in Latin America: Implications for the Middle East?" seminar, Institute for Science and International Security [ISIS] and the National Center for Middle East Studies, Cairo, October 27, 1997).

11. Paulo S. Wrobel and John R. Redick, "Nuclear Cooperation in South America: The Role of Scientists in the Argentine-Brazilian Rapprochement," *Annals of the New York Academy of Sciences* 866, no. 1 (December 1998): 176.

12. Quoted in Claudia M. Fabbri, "Social Constructivism and the Role of Ideas: The Construction of Argentine-Brazilian Nuclear Cooperation, 1979–1991" (Ph.D. diss., University of Warwick, 2005), 175.

13. It should be noted though that the Brazilian military opposed initial Argentine suggestions for establishing bilateral nuclear initiatives. Furthermore, the support for bilateral inspections grew in Brazil among the nonmilitary sectors in part due to the Vargas Commission— an interministerial committee composed of government officials set up by the Brazilian government in September 1985 (Fabbri, "Social Constructivism and the Role of Ideas," 148). The commission carried out an internal review of Brazil's nuclear policy and in April 1986 endorsed the idea of gradual establishment of a mutual inspections system with Argentina (Leonard S. Spector and Jacqueline R. Smith, *Nuclear Ambitions: The Spread of Nuclear Weapons 1989–1990* [Boulder, Colo.: Westview, 1990], 225 and 398n26).

14. Unless otherwise documented, quotations in the rest of this chapter come from these interviews.

15. The Brazilian Physics Society is a translation of the Portuguese Sociedade Brasileira de Física (SBF), the Brazilian Society for the Advancement of Science is a translation of the Portuguese Sociedade Brasileira para o Progresso da Ciência (SBPC), and the Argentine Physics Association is a translation of the Spanish Asociación Física Argentina (AFA). See Wrobel and Redick, "Nuclear Cooperation in South America," 174, 176.

16. Bradley Graham, "Argentine Nuclear Effort Running Out of Steam," *Washington Post*, August 14, 1987, A18.

17. Adler and Haas, "Conclusion: Epistemic Communities."

18. John R. Redick, "Nuclear Restraint in Latin America: Argentina and Brazil" (Programme for Promoting Nuclear Non-Proliferation Occasional Paper No. 1, Southampton, U.K., 1988), 5–9.

19. Marzo, "Origin and Role of Argentina's and Brazil's Nuclear Programs," 33–34.

20. Fabbri, "Social Constructivism and the Role of Ideas," 173.

21. Wrobel and Redick, "Nuclear Cooperation in South America," 169.

22. Adler and Haas, "Conclusion: Epistemic Communities," 381–83.

23. Ibid., 383.

24. Resende-Santos, "Origins of Security Cooperation," 116.

25. A *Washington Post* editorial remarks specifically that "the initiative has come from Argentina." "South America's Nuclear Security" (editorial), *Washington Post*, March 28, 1985, A26.

26. John R. Redick, "The Evolution of the Argentine-Brazilian Nuclear Rapprochement" (presentation, Argentina and Brazil: The Latin American Rapprochement seminar, Soreq Nuclear Research Center, Israel, May 16, 1996), emphasis added.

27. Georges Lamazière and Roberto Jaguaribe, "Beyond Confidence-Building: Brazilian-Argentine Nuclear Cooperation," *Disarmament* 15, no. 3 (1992): 102–17; José Goldemberg and Harold A. Feiverson, "Denuclearization in Argentina and Brazil," *Arms Control Today* 24, no. 2 (March 1994): 10–14; Solingen, "Political Economy of Nuclear Restraint"; Julio C. Carasales, *National Security Concepts of States: Argentina* (New York: United Nations Institute for Disarmament Research, 1992).

28. Knopf, "Importance of International Learning," 201–6.

29. Marzo, "Origin and Role of Argentina's and Brazil's Nuclear Programs," 62.

30. These inspectors render their services to ABACC only during the periods encompassed by the missions for which they are appointed. Brazilian inspectors verify the Argentine facilities, and Argentine inspectors verify the Brazilian facilities. According to ABACC's website, there are eighty-six Argentine and Brazilian inspectors, in exactly equal proportions.

31. Paul, *Power versus Prudence*, 103.

32. Nuclear Threat Initiative (NTI), "ABACC," www.nti.org/treaties-and-regimes/brazilian-argentine-agency-accounting-and-control-nuclear-materials-abacc/.

33. Brazil is reportedly in discussions to find a way for IAEA safeguards to apply to nuclear submarine fuel. See Togzhan Kassenova, *Brazil's Nuclear Kaleidoscope: An Evolving Identity* (Washington, D.C.: Carnegie Endowment for International Peace, 2014), 38–39.

34. Odair Dias Gonçalves, president of Brazil's National Nuclear Energy Commission (CNEN), explained, "The AP requires many new inspections. The universities are subject to safeguards and inspections. Universities in Brazil are proud and jealous of their independence, autonomy, and academic freedom." Frank Braun, "Analysis: Brazil and Additional Protocol," *Terra Daily*, July 1, 2005, www.terradaily.com/news/nuclear-civil-05zp.html.

35. John Carlson, "IAEA Safeguards Additional Protocol" (paper, International Commission on Nuclear Non-proliferation and Disarmament, January 20, 2009), icnnd.org/documents/iaea_additional_protocol.doc.

36. NTI, "ABACC."

37. Paulo S. Wrobel, "From Rivals to Friends: The Role of Public Declarations in Argentina-Brazil Rapprochement," in *Declaratory Diplomacy: Rhetorical Initiatives and Confidence Building*, ed. Michael Krepon, Jenny S. Drezin, and Michael Newbill (Washington, D.C.: Henry L. Stimson Center Report No. 27, May 1999), 142.

38. Wrobel and Redick, "Nuclear Cooperation in South America," 169.

39. Marzo, "Origin and Role of Argentina's and Brazil's Nuclear Programs," 36.

40. Wrobel and Redick, "Nuclear Cooperation in South America," 168.

41. Wrobel, "From Rivals to Friends," 143.

42. Wrobel and Redick, "Nuclear Cooperation in South America," 168.

CHAPTER TWELVE

Understanding the "Proliferation" of Nuclear Cooperation
An Alternative Theoretical Framework and Its Implications for Regional Efforts

FRANCESCA GIOVANNINI

AFTER A PERIOD OF intellectual dormancy, studies of nuclear weapons and proliferation are enjoying a comeback within the field of international security. The current wave of nuclear studies is characterized by theoretical eclecticism and the absence of a dominant research theme, with, instead, an impressive array of topics being explored and debated. The present volume represents a good example. It seeks to better our understanding of the institutional dimension of nuclear governance, which, as a topic of academic inquiry, has been largely neglected in past years.

In chapter 1, Jeffrey Knopf frames the role of institutions as a puzzle by noting that "the range of cooperative nonproliferation arrangements . . . is more extensive than literature in the field of international relations (IR) might lead one to predict." In particular, the existence of numerous nuclear multilateral institutions constitutes an empirical refutation to the neorealist expectation that, in the realm of international security, cooperation is ephemeral and ultimately unsustainable because of the anarchical nature of international politics and the presence of endemic mistrust and opportunism among states. In the nuclear sphere, according to the neorealist theoretical paradigm, cooperation should be even more elusive because of the potential cost that a country could incur should its cooperating partner defect from a nuclear agreement. Yet, history shows that states have cooperated rather extensively on nuclear issues, and they continue to do so in growing numbers. This flourishing of multilateral nuclear institutional arrangements presents an interesting puzzle that this volume aims to unravel.

This chapter presents some critical reflections on and a partial alternative to the theoretical framework developed by Knopf for this project. The analysis of this chapter fully supports the main argument of the book for it argues, in line with Knopf's findings, that nuclear cooperation has not only increased but has also deepened and matured remarkably over time. Knopf's approach remains incomplete, however, for at least two reasons. First, the volume focuses on explaining the genesis of nuclear *hegemonic regimes*, that is, nuclear multilateral institutions established as a result of the leadership provided by the United States. By using this lens, the volume fails to account for the significant role played by countries other than the United States in past and current nuclear institution-building processes. Second, the book adopts a functional logic and claims that multilateral nuclear cooperation is driven by a collective desire to respond to emerging nuclear risks in a context where existing global institutions are inadequate to provide for an effective solution. This argument underestimates how calculations over power and prestige equally impinge on the process of nuclear institution-building and multilateral cooperation.[1]

This chapter shares with Knopf the understanding that nuclear cooperation has been instigated in part by the need to respond to nuclear risks; however functional reasons are only one of the factors responsible for nuclear cooperation around the world. Along with functional considerations, nuclear institution-building processes have been driven by the interests that strong states, such as regional and great powers, harbor to influence and lead nuclear cooperation. By focusing on regional nuclear institution-building processes, this chapter concludes that many of the existing nuclear institutions at the regional level have been established due to the proactive role played by regional powers seeking to satisfy two fundamental interests: (1) to respond to localized nuclear risks and (2) to influence the global nuclear agenda designed and enforced by the United States.

EXPLAINING INCREASING NUCLEAR COOPERATION

The present volume has an ambitious agenda that seeks to deepen our understanding of the origins, growth, and impact of institutions relevant to combating WMD proliferation, especially in the nuclear realm.[2] With these goals in mind, the volume aims to address a set of related questions: (1) Under what conditions do states successfully cooperate to create institutions in the nuclear realm? (2) Why has nuclear cooperation evolved over time from negative cooperation (abstaining from doing something) to mature cooperation (actively collaborating)? and (3) Are newly established institutions effective in the fight against nuclear proliferation?

The central argument of the volume is that nuclear cooperation has changed over time in two significant ways: the number of nuclear institutions has steadily increased and nuclear cooperation has deepened significantly. Knopf writes, "The [earlier] core [nonproliferation] treaties all involve a commitment to self-restraint by each signatory. As such, they are primarily about policy coordination. In contrast, many of the cooperative efforts that have emerged since involve greater degrees of working together collaboratively." As a result, cooperation involves more than states agreeing not to do something, such as not to build certain weapons; it increasingly involves states acting together. Therefore, he concludes, "Since the NPT entered into force, additional nonproliferation activities have tended to move from simple coordination to involve greater elements of collaboration."

These important observations beg two additional questions: Where does the incentive for new nuclear cooperation originate from? And are these incentives responsible for both instigating cooperation and for driving it to its mature, collaborative form?

According to Knopf, nuclear institution-building has been spurred by the inadequacy of previously existing global institutions to respond to emerging and new nuclear problems. As Knopf argues, the global nonproliferation treaties "have not by themselves, however, removed every possible risk of proliferation. As a result, states have launched a variety of other efforts to address some of the remaining proliferation problems as well as new problems." The main driver of institutional proliferation in the nuclear realm is, in this argument, the functional inadequacy of global institutional infrastructures to respond to ever-evolving nuclear proliferation risks.

But why are states designing more proactive and mature institutions? The volume seems to suggest a "norm-cascade" element in explaining the formation of more demanding nuclear institutions. Knopf writes, "If the role of collaboration is in fact growing over time, this might also be helpful for explaining the patterns of cooperation observed in the nonproliferation arena. Because collaboration requires working together, it might serve as a conduit or a catalyst for the expansion of cooperation." The basic point here is that the continuous expansion of nuclear cooperation and the flourishing of multilateral arrangements may provide a springboard for more ambitious forms of cooperation in the future. But the reasons why or how this ratcheting up in the nature of cooperation might take place are not as well articulated as one might hope. The next section of this chapter proposes some alternative sources for the growth and deepening of cooperative arrangements.

MISSING DIMENSIONS IN THE PROPOSED EXPLANATION

There are two dimensions of nuclear institution-building that, although pivotal in explaining the continuous and impressive rise of new nuclear institutions and the coming to maturity of nuclear cooperation, seem to be missing in the theoretical framework presented in chapter 1. These two dimensions are (1) the type of nuclear risk that has prompted a renewed demand for nuclear cooperation and (2) the interests and nuclear preferences of countries other than the United States in instigating and facilitating nuclear institution-building processes.

Sources of the Demand for Nuclear Institution-Building

The list of factors that this book examines in attempting to explain the intensifying of nuclear cooperation is broad, ranging from power to interests to norms. Nevertheless, the theoretical framework as it currently stands is skewed in favor of emphasizing the U.S. role in both the demand for and supply of institution-building processes that lead to new nuclear arrangements. One finds very little in the theoretical framework on the factors that might be driving the demand for cooperation among other states. Furthermore, analysis of the types of risks prompting states to invest in nuclear cooperation is almost entirely omitted. Knopf suggests that the inadequacy of old institutions to deal with new and emerging nuclear risks is a triggering factor for additional cooperation. But how much inadequacy has to exist in order for states to initiate a new, costly process of institution-building when nuclear institutions already exist? And more important, are certain types of risks more likely to instigate a specific institutional response? Exploring more fully the demand side of nuclear cooperation and, specifically, the nature of the risks and the institutional inadequacies of old institutions is a critical element to complete Knopf's argument. As Robert Keohane has noted, it is only by understanding the demand side of regime building that we can fully appreciate both the origins of regimes and their effectiveness and longevity once they are established.[3]

The Possibility of Leadership by Other Countries

In the way Knopf sets out the explanatory framework for this volume, the United States is explored under its willingness to "lead," whereas *all* other countries are examined only in terms of their self-interest to cooperate or their willingness to coerce others to do so. This view of nuclear institution-building is an oversimplification, as it seems to suggest that in nuclear governance there are only two options: either institutions are designed hegemonically by the United States or else institutions result from the collective effort of like-minded countries in the absence of a country "willing to lead."

This dichotomy misses the institution-building processes that occur in the absence of the United States but with the leadership provided by other countries. Why is this point important? Because being willing to cooperate and being willing to lead are two very distinct things. The first simply acknowledges the intention of (or the obligation for) a country to accept and operate based on multilateral consensus. But in this act, a lot of delegation is done to the strongest country to define the rules through which cooperation occurs and to shape ultimately what the global nuclear order ought to be like. The second act instead identifies the intent of a country to shape, direct, and possibly alter existing institutions by manipulating material incentives (including possibly in the form of threats) and providing resources to other countries in order to achieve a specific idea of cooperation and through that an ideal global nuclear order.

If Knopf is correct that nuclear cooperation has evolved from mere abstaining to active participation, such a qualitative shift in the way in which countries see and approach nuclear cooperation cannot be solely attributed to the presence and leadership of the United States. In fact, it is quite the opposite, as I outline in the following section. The presumed maturity achieved by nuclear cooperation in recent years is largely ascribable to the fragmentation of power to multiples centers, which has resulted in the emergence of new centers of gravity for nuclear decision making at the subglobal level and the willingness of many other countries, outside of the United States, to take the lead in shaping and formulating nuclear policies.

AN ALTERNATIVE EXPLANATION FOR INCREASING (REGIONAL) NUCLEAR COOPERATION

This section advances a complementary explanation to the one offered in chapter 1. The argument is not necessarily an alternative theory. Many assumptions and theoretical claims proposed in this volume are also validated by my own research. However, because the focus of this volume is on global arrangements, the goal here is to articulate a framework that can explain in particular the evolution of nuclear institutions at the regional level. The process of nuclear institution-building has been ubiquitous, occurring at virtually all governance levels, but the development of regional nuclear institutions has been both rapid and distinct, and the distinctive features of regional governance have not received sufficient attention in studies of the nuclear issue area.

Regional efforts began at the height of the Cold War when, concurrently with the initial efforts conducted by the United States in the 1950s and 1960s to prevent nuclear proliferation, several groups of states began to cooperate on the establishment of nuclear-weapon-free-zone treaties. Their goal was to insulate their regions from the mounting rivalry between the United States and the Soviet Union, and from the risks arising from a global nuclear standoff between the two.[4]

More recently, new regional cooperative endeavors have sprung up in response to the threat posed by global terrorism. Regional cooperation has led to new agreements such as the European Strategy against the Proliferation of

Weapons of Mass Destruction (2003) and the ASEAN Convention on Counter Terrorism (2007) in Southeast Asia. These arrangements are regional and are designed to offer solutions to nuclear terrorism that are highly tailored and context specific. Nevertheless, these subglobal institutions indirectly affect more global nuclear governance processes and the interests of countries such as the United States, which has been the primary architect of global nuclear institutions. As nuclear institutions emerge at the regional and transnational levels, they embrace and pursue values, principles, and goals that may or may not be aligned with the ones that are upheld at the global level, therefore significantly affecting the implementation of the broader nuclear security agenda at the global level.

Factors Underpinning Regional Nuclear Institution-Building

Based on my previous research looking at empirical cases from different regions, I find that two factors can be evinced as indispensable for regional nuclear cooperation and institution-building to materialize successfully: (1) the presence of nuclear risks that global nuclear institutions are unable to tackle (demand side) and (2) the presence of a regional power willing and capable of providing leadership in the establishment of regional nuclear institutions (supply side). My framework starts from a point of agreement with Knopf's argument that the increase in the number of nuclear institutions and the overall changing nature of nuclear cooperation can be largely credited to functional reasons. If we look at regional dynamics, many of these regions have developed regional nuclear cooperation in parallel or, more accurately, in conjunction with the nuclear institution-building process that was going on at the global level. What propelled regional nuclear entrepreneurship was the exposure of these regions to nuclear risks, resulting from global dynamics, and the inability of global nuclear institutions to produce an appropriate response to such challenges.

For instance, the decision by Brazil, supported by Mexico, to promote a regional nuclear mechanism aimed at isolating and protecting the region of Latin America from the nuclear standoff between the two superpowers was prompted by the Cuban Missile Crisis of 1962. This led to the 1967 Tlatelolco Treaty, creating the world's first regional nuclear-weapon-free zone. Similarly, the decision by Indonesia to embark on a long-lasting negotiation for the adoption of the Bangkok Treaty, which resulted in the Southeast Asian Nuclear-Weapon-Free-Zone Treaty (1995), originated from concerns such as the successful development of the atomic bomb by China in 1964, escalation of the Vietnam War, and that war's expansion into Cambodia. The increasing involvement of Russia, China, and the United States created a desire in Jakarta to prevent the possibility for the region to become the chessboard for a proxy conflict among the great powers.

Yet, despite widespread nuclear risks and the significant incapacity of global institutions to respond to more localized risks, not all regions have been able to produce regional nuclear institutions. This suggests that the functional argument that regional nuclear cooperation has been prompted by local risks and the inadequacy of global institutions has to be further nuanced. To understand the ways in which "risks" play a role in instigating demand for nuclear cooperation, it is useful to distinguish them conceptually from "threats." Threats pertain to situations in which "there are actors that have the capabilities to harm the security of others and that are perceived by their potential targets as having intentions to do so."[5] Risks, however, emerge in the absence of direct threats and as negative externalities from other states' behaviors. The classic example of an externality that produces risk is the well-known security dilemma, in which one state's decision to build up arms for defensive purposes produces insecurity that prompts its neighbors to arm as well, triggering an arms race.[6]

Only in a situation characterized by the presence of nuclear risks, and the concurrent absence of nuclear threats, is it likely that a collectivity of states will demand new nuclear cooperation. In the face of a nuclear threat, states often prefer to adopt unilateral solutions (normally by boosting their defenses), and if there is a cooperative response it will be in the form of a military alliance against the threat rather than a new multilateral institution. Risks, as well as threats, can result in harm, but they invoke a different response and favor a collective institutional solution intended to help states manage the risk.[7] Nuclear risks can originate in a diverse range of factors, some of which are specific to the regional context in which they emerge, and others more properly linked to global factors. In the regional context, because of the geographical proximity among regional member states, the decision by one country to initiate a civilian nuclear energy program can upset the fragile equilibrium within the corresponding region and result in negative externalities for neighboring countries, which must estimate whether a civil nuclear program could be used to pave the way for a later military program. Terrorist activities can be another source of negative externalities if a state cannot adequately prevent domestic groups from operating outside its borders or keep its territory from being exploited by groups seeking to obtain or transship WMD-related materials.

As the Cold War ended, nuclear threats declined sharply, allowing for an intensification of nuclear cooperation initiatives all over the world. The institutions that have been created in recent decades have been designed to deal with nuclear risks and to mitigate negative externalities resulting mostly from the diffusion of nuclear technology for peaceful purposes. These institutions fulfill their mandates by facilitating information sharing and communication, harmonizing policies and regulations, and identifying possible new areas for cooperation among their member states. Recent cooperative efforts have focused especially on a nuclear security agenda intended to keep nuclear materials out of the hands of non-state terrorist actors.

Presence of a Regional Power

The presence of risks would not per se spark the ability of countries to generate new nuclear institutions. Rather, the presence of global institutions functions as a major disincentive to create costly new institutions. In addition, nuclear risks can affect countries to different degrees and create incentives for countries not directly affected to free ride and rely on others to support and sustain institutional solutions.

In such situations, the presence of a country that has powerful incentives to favor institutions is the key to materialize such cooperation. It is reasonable to believe that, among such countries, regional powers have the greatest incentive to promote regional cooperation.[8] Nuclear cooperation is an essential component of any regional security architecture and, as the main country in their region, regional powers have not only enormous resources but also powerful interests to protect. Regional powers constitute an important source of interdependence in a region and can, for example, offer side payments to other regional states that fear being relatively disadvantaged by participation in a new regional cooperative arrangement.[9]

Regional powers can be effective and credible leaders at the regional level because they share with their neighbors much the same identity, culture, and resources.[10] At the same time, this interdependence makes regional powers not only less threatening and more credible than the United States or other great powers in the eyes of other regional players, but also more vested in peace and stability in areas where their main interests lie.[11] At the same time, in spite of their relatively abundant resources, regional powers are not completely autonomous in the design of their policies, as their interests are intertwined with those of their region.[12]

All the aforementioned attributes of regional powers make them suitable leaders of regional nuclear institution-building. Nevertheless, to argue that regional powers lead simply because they can, although true, is a rather reductive proposition. There are several reasons behind regional powers' interest in leading the costly undertaking of nuclear institution-building. Thomas Pedersen has explained that "regional institutionalization is a typical product of the grand strategy pursued by regional powers" to establish and maintain primacy within their corresponding regional grouping.[13] According to Pedersen, regional powers aim to rule through "cooperative hegemony," that is, through regional governance institutions. The resulting "aggregation of power is of particular importance to a regional power aspiring to a global role because it enables it to use its region as a basis of projecting power in world affairs."[14]

In the nuclear realm, leading and shaping the formation of nuclear institutions is instrumental for regional powers that seek to relate to and influence significantly the nuclear agenda that has been built at the global level, predominantly by the United States. By leading in the design of regional institutions that can either align with or reject some of the goals that other nuclear institutions are pursuing at the global level, regional powers use regional institution-building processes as a critical political instrument for either reinforcing or alternatively soft-balancing against American nuclear interests at the global level. Efforts at the regional level to align with and reinforce global institutions can be described as integrative leadership, as exemplified by France in the example that follows. Efforts to resist global institutions involve either strategic or hedging leadership, as illustrated by Indonesia's spoiler role in the following example.

EMPIRICAL EXAMPLES: THE CONTRASTING CASES OF FRANCE AND INDONESIA

To briefly illustrate my argument, I consider two empirical cases of regional nuclear institution-building and the leadership provided by regional powers in each of them. The first case has to do with the role of France as regional leader in the establishment of the EU Strategy Against Proliferation of Weapons of Mass Destruction (henceforth EU WMD Strategy) in 2003 and the adoption, in 2008, of New Lines for Action to Combat the Proliferation of Weapons of Mass Destruction and Their Means of Delivery (henceforth New Lines for Action), which further deepened and widened the EU WMD Strategy. The second case investigates the role of Indonesia acting as a spoiler to try to halt the establishment and entering into force in 2007 of the ASEAN Convention on Counter Terrorism, a convention that was supported by other Southeast Asian countries, especially Singapore.

The two cases have been chosen for their commonalities as well as their differences. Both cases show how the presence of nuclear risks prompted demand for new nuclear cooperation at the regional level and illustrate how the presence and role of the regional power (either as leader or spoiler) has been pivotal in influencing the kind of regional nuclear institution that is created. The case of France is one of positive leadership, whereby the country engages with regional institution-building and leads proactively in the establishment of European nuclear institutions that simultaneously satisfy regional nuclear cooperation demands while also embracing the global nuclear security agenda as proposed by the United States. The case of Indonesia, in contrast, presents an example of a regional power that plays the role of spoiler in an institution-building process initiated by another regional player, Singapore. Ultimately Indonesian efforts forced ASEAN to settle for a compromise solution that left the newly formed institution much weaker and less effective than what was originally conceived by its architect, thereby impeding the ability of countries in the region to take credible action to fight terrorism or support the global nuclear security agenda.

This second case does not contradict my argument that in order to form nuclear institutions at the regional level, the presence and leadership of the regional power are pivotal. Quite the opposite, it reinforces it by showing that for a successful regional institution-building process to take place, particularly in a sector as sensitive as the nuclear one, the involvement and support of the leading regional power are indispensable.

France and the Development of the European Strategy against WMD Proliferation

With its independent nuclear deterrent force, the second largest nuclear energy industry in the world, and its long-standing history of using its military, France has played a natural leading role in shaping European thinking and policy formulation in matters related to security. France has been able to exercise leadership in the European context in ways that the other two regional powers, Germany and the United Kingdom, have not. In the case of the United Kingdom, its "special relationship" to the United States has largely prevented it from adhering wholeheartedly to the EU integration project and has frequently called into question its own independence in decision making, thereby reducing the ability—and willingness—of the United Kingdom to exercise leadership in the European Union context. Germany, on the other hand, deeply affected by the reputational costs of its past, long adopted a low-profile position on political and security matters, allowing France to seize the institutional vacuum left by German near-invisibility within European security affairs.[15]

Yet, the willingness and commitment of France to "lead" toward the formulation of cohesive European security and defense policies have not always been straightforward. Historically, France's relation to the project of European collective security had been ambivalent and pragmatic, embracing it when it favored French national interests and rebuking it when it claimed costs that the French Republic was unwilling to sustain. During the Cold War, France began to lobby for a more cohesive European Security and Defense Strategy, more autonomous from the American agenda, but for years France simultaneously resisted the call for negotiating a regional export control policy that could provide the European Union with a coherent strategy for governance of dual-use technology. And in the nuclear sphere, France was the last among the founders of the European Union to ratify the Nuclear Non-Proliferation Treaty (doing so only in 1992), thereby impairing the development of a common European approach to nonproliferation for several decades. In addition, it has systematically rebuffed the demand among powerful European neighbors, including Germany, for a collective discussion over nuclear disarmament, including the possible removal of NATO nuclear warheads from European soil.

Things have changed in recent years. With the outbreak of the First Gulf War and the discovery of the secret military program of Saddam Hussein, France became more open to the idea of collective nonproliferation and more supportive of regional nuclear nonproliferation cooperation. Such a trend has been further reinforced since 9/11, as France has taken a more active role in fostering regional nuclear institutions.

Although 9/11 did not directly impact the security of Europe, it altered European security perceptions in at least two ways. First, 9/11 highlighted the global dimension of terrorism in the twenty-first century and the technological sophistication of the new terrorist movements. This raised the issue within Europe and NATO of how to best secure and protect the many nuclear weapons, as well as the nuclear technology, situated in the EU area. For instance, NATO allies collectively have stationed on their territory 150 to 250 U.S. nuclear warheads,[16] which need to be properly secured through the enhancement of intelligence gathering and physical protection in concerned countries.[17] The necessity of securing highly sensitive material put a spotlight on the inadequacy and lack of cohesiveness of existing EU antiterrorist policies. In fact, until 2001, the EU had chosen to treat antiterrorism policies as an issue for the national domain in which it had no specific authority, although several European countries had fought domestic terrorist organizations in the recent past.[18]

Second, 9/11 brought about a deep crisis concerning the credibility and influence of the multilateral governance architecture, including international organizations. As the United States chose to operate unilaterally or by forming ad hoc coalitions of like-minded states, the multilateral nuclear order was called into question. For many European countries, this turn back toward the practice of power politics brought about significant political uneasiness that was partly managed through the reinforcement of regional structures of cooperation.[19] As one report claimed, with 9/11, the United States "effectively relinquished its leadership in arms control and adopted alternative methods to avert the spread of WMD. This makes it necessary for other actors willing to uphold the existing regime to upgrade their efforts."[20]

This interest in upholding multilateral approaches is clearly reflected in the EU WMD Strategy adopted by the European Council in December 2003. The EU strategy had two substantive goals: (1) to enhance EU security in a post-9/11 world and (2) to strengthen global nuclear institutions, even in the absence of U.S. leadership, by embracing goals that reiterate and reproduce goals of global nuclear governance. Although the document as it was conceived in 2003 marked an important step in the assumption of EU responsibilities in the fight against nuclear proliferation, it remains comfortably within the EU approach to foreign policy. The document states, on the one hand, that "the proliferation of weapons of mass destruction and their means of delivery such as ballistic missiles are a growing threat to international peace and security" and "the European Union cannot ignore these dangers.... Meeting this challenge must be a central element in the EU's external action." On the other hand, it largely dismisses the possibility of using coercive measures and simply calls for effective multilateralism without ever defining what "effective" means in the context of regional and global cooperation.[21]

When Europe experienced its own versions of 9/11 in the form of terrorist attacks in Madrid in 2004 and London in 2005, this created additional motivation for stronger European action. However, it was only in 2008, with the French presidency of the EU, that the EU began to review and enhance both border control and export control policies. Under French president Nicolas Sarkozy's rotation as president of the EU Council, the EU adopted the "New Lines for Action."[22] In contrast to the EU WMD Strategy, this later document embraced a more proactive approach to the fight against nuclear terrorism. In particular, the New Lines for Action ensured a more robust response to the threat of nuclear terrorism by listing a set of specific actions for member states to undertake. These included measures to prevent transfers of technology or know-how, to block terrorist financing, and to tighten reviews and mutual notifications concerning visa applications, particularly for scientists coming from rogue states (such as North Korea), unstable countries (such as Pakistan), or threshold countries (such as Iran).

The changes to the strategy made under the French presidency were significant because they served to strengthen the enforcement commitment of the EU in dealing with nuclear proliferation risks and, albeit indirectly, aligned more explicitly EU regional nuclear nonproliferation policies to the U.S. global nuclear agenda. This alignment between the EU and the United States in matters related to nuclear affairs is something that France has long aspired to achieve. In spite of the long-standing differences between Paris and Washington in other matters, the nuclear policies of the two countries have often been quite similar.[23]

During the George W. Bush administration in particular, despite the rift between the two countries over the Iraq war, France consistently aspired to identify ways to maintain, and possibly to strengthen, its ties with the United States on nuclear issues. For example, France was one of the first countries that the United States consulted on the establishment of the Proliferation Security

Initiative (PSI) and one of the first to lend its support. France also exercised leadership when, in September 2003, in part to respond to the uneasiness of some European countries over PSI, it hosted a meeting on the PSI during which the "statement of interdiction principles," also known as the Paris Principles, was approved. The statement helped to address European reservations that PSI might permit the unilateral use of force.[24]

Furthermore, France, similarly to the United States, has made nuclear terrorism one of its top priorities, in line with the U.S. approach at the global level. In the landmark speech of President Jacques Chirac in 2006, and in the subsequent 2008 Defense White Paper issued by President Nicolas Sarkozy, France clearly elaborated its national view on the terrorist threat. According to the White Paper, "the most serious currently identified scenario is the combination of a major terrorist attack on European soil, using non-conventional nuclear, chemical or biological-type means, together with a war situation in one of the strategically important zones for Europe."[25] In its bilateral cooperation with the United States, therefore, France has been supportive of coercive diplomacy as a potential instrument of WMD nonproliferation and has cosponsored UN Resolution 1540 with the United States.

The strengthening of the EU's approach to nuclear nonproliferation and nuclear security allowed France to further its influence over European nuclear affairs while also strengthening its bilateral relations with the United States. The French case is hence an example of leadership by a regional power that produced new regional cooperation that aligned with developments at the global level.

Indonesia and the ASEAN Convention on Counter Terrorism

Southeast Asia has a very dense nuclear regional infrastructure. This may seem paradoxical in a region where none of its members has yet developed a full-fledged nuclear energy program. Yet because of its geostrategic location, Southeast Asia has been exposed to nuclear risks and threats since the 1950s, and regional cooperation has been cemented because of the collective need of Southeast Asian countries to provide for their security. The region has shown an interest in nuclear institutions since the 1960s, when the conflicts in Vietnam and Cambodia created the potential for the United States, the Soviet Union, or China to get involved in a nuclear standoff with one of the other two. Fear of such a scenario prompted Indonesia as the regional leader to suggest the formation of a nuclear-weapon-free-zone treaty in the region as a safeguard against the interference of nuclear weapons countries.

Institution-building then went through several phases, the last of which began almost immediately after 9/11. In the aftermath of 9/11 and the October 2002 terrorist attack in Bali,[26] the United States chose to reengage heavily with Southeast Asia, both politically and militarily. These developments, not surprisingly, also affected the intraregional equilibrium among countries in Southeast Asia. From the U.S. perspective, Southeast Asia began to be cast by American media and policy makers alike as a region in which terrorism was largely endemic, leading U.S. commentators to start describing Southeast Asia as the "the second front in the global war on terror."[27] As summarized by Mauzy and Job, reports issued by the U.S. Congressional Research Service noted with apprehension that "Southeast Asia with its combination of large Muslim populations; dissident and separatist movements; porous borders and easy transnational communication; [and] under-resourced ... intelligence ... services ... [is] a 'fertile breeding ground for terrorist operations.'"[28] As a clear indication of the official U.S. government perspective, at a congressional hearing in 2004, the U.S. assistant secretary of state for East Asia and Pacific affairs, James Kelly, described it as "a time of transition" in the region and added that "at the top of our policy priorities is waging the war against terrorism."[29]

The United States sought to reengage with Southeast Asia in two ways. It primarily pursued the strengthening of military partnerships with traditional allies such as the Philippines and Singapore.[30] In addition, Washington explored new opportunities for cooperation with countries that were highly strategic but did not normally align with the United States, such as Indonesia.[31] The United States deployed troops to assist the Philippines in the fight against terrorism, while providing other regional states with financial resources for military and counterterrorism operations. Concurrently, the United States sought to influence the ASEAN security agenda by lobbying ASEAN, although unsuccessfully, to create binding institutions that were more directly oriented toward the fight against terrorism. Outcomes included the nonbinding ASEAN-U.S. Joint Declaration for Cooperation to Combat International Terrorism (August 2002) and the launch (starting in 2009) of the ASEAN Regional Forum Inter-Sessional Meeting on Nonproliferation and Disarmament to facilitate coordination with ASEAN member states. According to a U.S. official, "the choice of pursuing multilateral cooperation allowed us to strengthen regional cooperation and overcome the resistance of individual ASEAN countries to lend support towards specific counterterrorism policies."[32]

The reengagement of the United States in Southeast Asia had dramatic repercussions at the ASEAN level in regard to the evolution of the regional nuclear agenda and, more important, the position of leadership historically held by Indonesia in its formulation. The revived U.S. presence and the U.S. agenda in the region had distinctly different implications for countries allied to the United States, such as Singapore, and countries, such as Indonesia, that have traditionally resisted U.S. influence in the region. For Singapore, the presence of the

United States served as an important empowerment mechanism to raise new demands for cooperation in areas such as the fight against terrorism, into which ASEAN member states had historically been reluctant to venture. Conversely, the reconfiguration of power and influence in Southeast Asia seriously undermined the ability of Indonesia to lead in a region of states far less amenable to follow Jakarta. This sparked efforts by Indonesia to put in place institutional mechanisms at the regional level to lessen U.S. influence and resist its attempts to dominate the ASEAN security and nuclear agendas.

The Bali bombing in 2002, which killed 202, also triggered rather distinct reactions within the region. For Singapore, the Bali bombing was an additional reason to join the U.S. fight against terrorism (including nuclear terrorism), but it also provided an important incentive for the country to lead the regional efforts within ASEAN. Besides the obvious security preoccupations, Singapore had been increasingly concerned that the reputation of Southeast Asia as a region with an endemic terrorism problem would affect its economy. As Prime Minister Goh pointed out in the aftermath of 9/11, 70 percent of the Singaporean economy is based on providing services to external countries.[33] The government thus had a significant incentive to take decisive security measures in order to preserve the country's reputation as a safe destination for foreign direct investment and a hub for security or intelligence exchange in Southeast Asia. It also began to demand a more serious commitment from neighboring countries within ASEAN, particularly Indonesia,[34] which Singapore has always perceived as too lenient in tolerating rebel groups and terrorist organizations. For Indonesia, in contrast, the Bali bombing was a painful reminder that any support that the government would have extended to a U.S. or ASEAN initiative against terrorism could have served to further radicalize part of its vast Muslim population. The Bali attack hence implicitly triggered an even more cautious and critical approach to the U.S.-led war on terror.

The way in which Indonesia decided to exercise leadership on the development of a regional nuclear security architecture can be described as one of a regional spoiler. Indonesia's fear that the political closeness of Singapore to the United States would increase U.S. interference in ASEAN affairs prompted Indonesia to devise a strategy to counterbalance the increasing assertiveness of Singapore within the realm of security (and nuclear) cooperation. In 2003, Jakarta proposed a further deepening of the regional security integration process through the formation of the ASEAN Community, which in the view of Indonesia would consist of three main pillars: a political-security agenda to be designed by Indonesia, an economic agenda to be developed by Singapore, and a sociocultural cooperation agenda to be drawn up by Malaysia. Indonesia viewed stronger regional cooperation as critical to maintaining the relevance of Southeast Asia in an increasingly globalized world, yet an equally significant underlying motive was to "reduce U.S. hegemonic interference, particularly in issue-areas that Indonesia perceives as extremely sensitive to its own national security interests politics."[35]

Implicitly, the ASEAN Political-Security Community Blueprint prepared by Indonesia confirms this motive. It states that "conscious that strengthening of ASEAN integration through accelerated establishment of an ASEAN Community will reinforce ASEAN's centrality and role as the driving force in charting the evolving regional architecture ... the ASEAN leaders decided to accelerate the establishment of an ASEAN Community by 2015."[36] Among the proposals to strengthen political and security cooperation, Indonesia recommended the implementation of the Southeast Asian Nuclear-Weapon-Free-Zone Treaty and its related plan of action;[37] promotion of ASEAN maritime cooperation, with the establishment of a regional forum for maritime security;[38] and the strengthening of cooperation in addressing nontraditional security issues.[39]

When that comprehensive proposal received a lukewarm reaction from Singapore and other countries, Indonesia began to display a more passive resistance to the undertaking of nuclear policies that ran counter to its own interests. While Singapore lobbied for completing the ASEAN Convention on Counter Terrorism (signed in January 2007) and became the first country to ratify it, Indonesia dragged its feet due to concerns about "the interests of Western countries which might use their diplomatic ties with some ASEAN members to interfere with our counterterrorism efforts."[40] For years the convention was kept in limbo while the negotiations between Singapore (supported by the United States) and Indonesia stalled.

In order to overcome the resistance of Indonesia, the two countries reached a political compromise, but the results severely undermined the effectiveness of the convention. Although the convention is binding and contains a list of concrete steps and operational measures to reinforce ASEAN's response to terrorist threats, it emphasizes the principle of sovereignty so strongly that a regime can define a national conflict as a purely domestic issue, thus impairing ASEAN from interfering.[41] In this regard, Alfred Gerstl notes, "Even after a successful ratification process, the instruments identified in the ACTC to deepen regional cooperation, e.g. mutual legal assistance in criminal matters and even the possible extradition of terrorist suspects (Art. XIII), are not strong enough to prevent and suppress terrorist acts."[42]

The Convention on Counter Terrorism as it currently stands resulted from a protracted and painstakingly difficult negotiation between Singapore and Indonesia that dramatically weakened the ability of the convention to effectively deliver on the mandate of preventing terrorism in Southeast Asia. This outcome demonstrates how a regional power can use its leading role to act as a spoiler on regional cooperation processes when it expects that regional institutions will not sufficiently constrain U.S. influence in the region. This again shows the importance of a proactive regional leader for the successful creation of strong regional cooperative institutions.

CONCLUSION

Regional nuclear regimes are an essential component of global nuclear governance, and they have historically played a critical role in the advancement of the global nuclear agenda. Yet the interlinkage between global and subglobal nuclear institutions, particularly operating at the regional level, is complex and ever changing. On the one hand, regional processes are influenced by global processes. For instance, systemic implications of the nuclear rivalry between the United States and the Soviet Union during the Cold War, as illustrated by events like the Cuban Missile Crisis, prompted the creation of nuclear-weapon-free-zone treaties.

On the other hand, advancements in regional nuclear cooperation can provide an important incentive for new global processes of cooperation to emerge. Regional nuclear cooperation can bring new ideas and norms to life. In contrast to global nuclear cooperation, which is designed to operate as a minimum common denominator among countries with widely disparate ranges of capabilities and values, regional nuclear cooperation may benefit from an ongoing process among states that are both geographically proximate and connected by a complex interdependence of culture, economics, politics, and security. For this reason, regional nuclear cooperation can be more ambitious in what it seeks to accomplish. As Hurrell has argued, there is a long history behind the idea of regions as "harbingers of change and possible transformation."[43]

Finally, regional nuclear governance processes can serve as mechanisms for the projection of power by countries that in global contexts would play a more marginal role. Regional nuclear regimes empower states other than great powers to play a lead role in nuclear governance and to be involved in nuclear institution-building. The partial autonomy of regional nuclear cooperation from global dynamics presents states with an important setting in which to exercise power and leadership away from global processes and institutions led by the United States. The incentives for regional powers to take the lead in localized nuclear cooperation reside not only in being able to exercise power in the corresponding region, but also in the consequences that such regional processes may bear at the global level. Institution-building could be pursued by regional powers as a strategy to indirectly acquire greater influence and greater visibility on the global stage, without bearing the costs of directly challenging the hegemonic interests of the United States.

Regional powers do not possess adequate resources to resolve a global nuclear governance impasse, but they do possess adequate resources to move the process forward at the regional level. When they experience high dissatisfaction with the global status quo, regional powers can exercise a strategy to sidestep those global policies they oppose. In cases where they are satisfied with current global norms, they may still resort to regional nuclear processes in order to strengthen and consolidate the nuclear status quo. Whether they compete with or reinforce global nuclear governance, it is important to pay attention to regional nuclear institutions and the regional powers that shape them as distinct elements of international cooperation on nonproliferation.

Notes

The theoretical framework and the empirical material presented in this chapter are drawn from the dissertation that I completed at Oxford University. That thesis explores the role of regional powers in designing regional nuclear policies as a mechanism for soft-balancing against global nuclear institutions that regional powers perceive as skewed in favor of American interests. The thesis reviews three cases of leadership by regional powers in regional nuclear governance: the case of Brazil in Latin America (defined as hedging leadership), the case of Indonesia in Southeast Asia (characterized as strategic leadership), and the case of France in the European Union (depicted as integrative leadership). Two of the case studies, Indonesia and France, are briefly examined in this chapter.

1. Two key questions that the volume does not necessarily address are these: Who stands to gain, in terms of power and prestige accumulation, from the proliferation of these new nuclear institutions? And how does the creation of new nuclear institutions affect the current power distribution at the international level?

2. Many studies of proliferation comment on whether or not the NPT has an impact on proliferation dynamics, but few make the role of institutions their central focus. As William Potter and Gaukhar Mukhatzhanova point out, "A neo-liberal institutionalist might be expected to argue that countries join non-proliferation institutions to address immediate and projected security concerns or to derive economic benefits such as access to peaceful nuclear energy. Although intuitively plausible, in practice this proposition tends to be more implied than rigorously tested and relatively few studies have sought to demonstrate the influence of non-proliferation institutions on nuclear weapons restraint." William Potter and Gaukhar Mukhatzhanova, "Divining Nuclear Intentions: A Review Essay," *International Security* 33, no. 1 (Summer 2008): 155.

3. Robert Keohane, "The Demand for International Regimes," *International Organization* 36, no. 2 (Spring 1982): 326.

4. For more on nuclear-weapon-free zones, see chapter 10 in this volume by Michael Hamel-Green.

5. Helga Haftendorn, Robert Keohane, and Celeste Wallander, eds., *Imperfect Unions: Security Institutions over Time and Space* (Oxford: Oxford University Press, 1999), 25.

6. Robert Jervis, "Cooperation under the Security Dilemma," *World Politics* 30, no. 2 (January 1978): 167–214.

7. Haftendorn, Keohane, and Wallander, *Imperfect Unions*.

8. Regional powers are countries that are "economically, politically and culturally interconnected to a region, are ready to assume leadership in their regions, display the necessary

material and ideational capacities for leadership and are highly influential in regional affairs." Daniel Flemes, ed., *Regional Leadership in the Global System: Ideas, Interests and Strategies of Regional Powers* (Farnham, U.K.: Ashgate, 2010), 323.

9. It has been noted that "while a global power can be any state in the system, a regional power must be embedded geographically within its region. And while a global power must have opportunity and willingness above and beyond other states in the system, regional powers must be strong and active relative to the region." Kirssa Cline et al., "Identifying Regional Powers and Their Status," in *Major Powers and the Quest for Status in International Politics: Global and Regional Perspectives*, ed. Thomas Volgy, Renato Corbetta, and Keith Grant (New York: Palgrave MacMillan, 2011), 140.

10. Embeddedness in a given geographical area makes regional powers more suitable to instigate and support regional institution-building processes than middle powers. While middle powers are interested in simply supporting multilateral processes of cooperation, regional powers have direct interests in their region, making them more credible leaders. The distinction between middle powers and regional powers is presented in Flemes, *Regional Leadership in the Global System*, 322.

11. The point about regional states being seen as less threatening than outside powers is articulated by Richard Higgott and Kim Richard Nossal in reference to the hegemonic aspirations of China. The authors argue that many states in Southeast Asia are reasonably concerned about the rise of China, which, in contrast to regional powers such as Indonesia, cannot be constrained by regional institutions and therefore poses a far greater threat. See Richard Higgott and Kim Richard Nossal, "Australia and the Search for a Security Community in the 1990s," in *Security Communities*, ed. Emanuel Adler and Michael Barnett (Cambridge: Cambridge University Press, 1998), 286–87.

12. Several scholars have underlined how regional powers, although powerful, remain largely constrained by the regional context in which they operate. And although regional powers have a special role to play in supporting and sustaining processes of regional institution-building, in order to succeed in the exercise of their leadership, they need to gather political consensus and befriend followers. See David Lake and Patrick Morgan, eds., *Regional Orders: Building Security in a New World Order* (University Park: Pennsylvania State University Press, 1997); Flemes, *Regional Leadership in the Global System*.

13. Pedersen's contribution to the understanding of regional institution-building is discussed in Daniel Flemes and Thorsten Wojczewski, "Contested Leadership in International Relations: Power Politics in South America, South Asia, and Sub-Sahara Africa" (German Institute of Global and Area Studies Working Paper No. 121, February 2010), 9.

14. Flemes and Wojczewski, "Contested Leadership in International Relations," 9. The concept of "cooperative hegemony" is developed in Thomas Pedersen, "Cooperative Hegemony: Power, Ideas and Institutions in Regional Integration," *Review of International Studies* 28, no. 4 (October 2002): 677–96.

15. Jan Techau, "No Strategy, Please, We're German—The Eight Elements that Shaped German Strategic Culture," in *Towards a Comprehensive Approach: Strategic and Operational Challenges*, ed. Christopher Schnaubelt (NATO Defense College Forum Paper no. 18, 2011), 69–93.

16. Malcolm Chalmers, *NATO's Tactical Nuclear Dilemma* (Washington, D.C.: Royal United Services Institute, March 2010), 1–2.

17. Steve Andreasen and Isabelle Williams, eds., *Reducing Nuclear Risks in Europe: A Framework for Action* (Washington, D.C.: Nuclear Threat Initiative, 2011), 17–18. The authors underscore that tactical nuclear weapons are a NATO possession and therefore NATO respon-

sibility, but nonetheless the European Union had significant stakes in ensuring that each relevant NATO member (most of which—Turkey being the exception—were also EU member states) took the necessary steps to secure their nuclear capabilities and prevent non-state actors from having access to them.

18. Many EU member states had experienced in the past domestic and politically driven terrorism, of the type practiced by groups like the IRA, ETA, and the Red Brigades, to name a few.

19. Bruno Tertrais, "The European Union and Nuclear Non-proliferation: Does Soft Power Work?," *International Spectator: Italian Journal of International Affairs* 40, no. 3 (2008): 45–57; Ian Manners, "Normative Power Europe: A Contradiction in Terms?," *Journal of Common Market Studies* 40, no. 2 (June 2002): 235–58.

20. Clara Portela, *The Role of the EU in the Non-proliferation of Nuclear Weapons: The Way to Thessaloniki and Beyond* (Peace Research Institute–Frankfurt Reports No. 65, December 2003), 1.

21. Council of the European Union, "EU Strategy against Proliferation of Weapons of Mass Destruction" (Brussels, December 2003), 2.

22. Council of the European Union, "New Lines for Action by the European Union in Combating the Proliferation of Weapons of Mass Destruction and Their Delivery Systems" (Brussels, December 2008).

23. Bruno Tertrais notes that "if there is a domain in which one cannot radically contrast Paris and Washington, it is surely nuclear policy. The only difference that can be noted is that nuclear weapons hold a more central place in the defense policy of France than for the United States. The French doctrine is much closer to U.S. (and UK) doctrine than generally thought. Washington and Paris share a common view about the fundamentally political role of nuclear weapons, which are identified as an instrument of deterrence rather than a warfighting tool. The countries oppose a no-first-use doctrine as they believe it would weaken deterrence by allowing an adversary to calculate the risks inherent in his aggression." Bruno Tertrais, "La dissuasion revisitée" (Notes de la FRS, Fondation pour la Recherche Stratégique, Paris, January 23, 2006), 4.

24. EU official, interview, Brussels, May 15, 2012.

25. *The French White Paper on Defense and National Security* (2008), 38.

26. Amitav and Arabinda Acharya have defined Southeast Asian domestic terrorism as "the most serious security threat in the region since the Indochina conflict," in Amitav Acharya and Arabinda Acharya, "The Myth of the Second Front: Localizing the 'War on Terror' in Southeast Asia," *Washington Quarterly* 30, no. 4 (Autumn 2007): 75.

27. Amitav Acharya, "Terrorism and Security in Asia: Redefining Regional Orders?" (Asia Research Centre Working Paper No. 113, 2004), 2.

28. Diane K. Mauzy and Brian L. Job, "U.S. Policy in Southeast Asia: Limited Reengagement after Years of Benign Neglect," *Asian Survey* 47, no. 4 (2007): 635.

29. James Kelly, testimony before the United States House of Representatives, International Relations Committee, June 2, 2004.

30. In January 2002, the United States formed the Joint Special Operations Task Force–Philippines to help the country fight transnational and domestic terrorists. One operation led to the deployment of 660 U.S. Marines in the southern Philippines to fight against the terrorist group Abu Sayyaf. Data related to Philippine-U.S. cooperation in the war on terror can be found in James Putzel, "Political Islam in Southeast Asia and the U.S.-Philippines Alliance," in *Global Responses to Terrorism: 9/11, Afghanistan and Beyond*, ed. Mary Buckley and Rick Fawn (London: Routledge, 2003), 176–87.

31. Indonesia became a top priority for the Bush administration due to its huge Muslim population and its strategic regional relevance. In 2005–6, the country received approximately seven hundred million dollars for counterterrorism measures, and an additional seventy-four million in development aid. Alice Ba, "China and ASEAN: Re-navigating Relations for a 21st Century Asia," *Asian Survey* 43, no. 4 (2003): 644.

32. U.S. official, interview, Jakarta, Indonesia, October 18, 2011.

33. The high dependence of Singapore on external demand for services is perceived as a great source of vulnerability for the country, while also constituting its largest source of revenue. The most relevant speech by a Singaporean official on the economic impact of terrorism was delivered by Prime Minister Goh Chik Tong at the Dialogue Session with Union Leaders/Members and Employers (October 14, 2001).

34. Senia Febrica, "Securitizing Terrorism in Southeast Asia," *Asian Survey* 50, no. 3 (May–June 2010): 580.

35. Professor Makmur Keliat, Indonesia University, interview, Jakarta, October 4, 2011. The opinion expressed by Professor Keliat was his own and did not represent the view of his academic institution.

36. *ASEAN Political-Security Community Blueprint* (Jakarta: ASEAN Secretariat, June 2009), introduction, point 3.

37. Ibid., point A.2.4.

38. Ibid., point A.2.5.

39. Ibid., points B.4.1 and B.4.2.

40. Ezra Sihite, "Indonesia Accused of Dragging Feet on ASEAN Terror Pact," *Jakarta Globe*, March 6, 2012; Yusuf Al Muzzammil, reported by Margareth. S. Aritonang, "Indonesia Set to Ratify ASEAN Anti-Terror Pact," *Jakarta Post*, March 9, 2012.

41. Article III of the convention states, "The Parties shall carry out their obligations under this Convention in a manner consistent with the principles of sovereign equality and territorial integrity of States and that of non-interference in the internal affairs of other Parties." Article IV claims, "Nothing in this Convention entitles a Party to undertake, in the territory of another Party, the exercise of jurisdiction or performance of functions which are exclusively reserved for the authorities of that other Party by its domestic laws."

42. Alfred Gerstl, "The Depoliticisation and 'ASEANisation' of Counter-terrorism Policies in South-East Asia," *ASEAS* 3, no. 1 (2010): 65.

43. Andrew Hurrell, *On Global Order: Power, Values and the Constitution of International Society* (Oxford: Oxford University Press, 2007), 253.

CHAPTER THIRTEEN

European and P5 Responses to Iran's Nuclear Program

DAVID SANTORO

MULTILATERAL EFFORTS TO ADDRESS recent proliferation crises have consistently involved five states: the permanent members of the United Nations Security Council (UNSC), known as the "Permanent Five" or P5 (the United States, the United Kingdom, France, Russia, and China). This is because the Nuclear Non-Proliferation Treaty (NPT) makes the UNSC the final arbiter of issues of enforcement. If other actors or processes cannot resolve compliance concerns, the responsibility falls on the UNSC to act, potentially through authorizing the imposition of sanctions or the use of force. Not surprisingly, as members with permanent seats and veto power, the P5 have been central to all multilateral efforts to address proliferation crises. This makes the extent of cooperation among these states relevant to any assessment of international cooperation on behalf of nonproliferation.

This chapter focuses on cooperation among the P5, along with Germany, on efforts to address Iran's suspected nuclear weapon program. The issue has been a high-profile concern since 2002, when the world learned of Iranian efforts to develop key aspects of the nuclear fuel cycle, including uranium enrichment and activities relevant to producing plutonium. Although Iran claims its program is peaceful, concern about Iran's activities has led to multilateral efforts to persuade Iran to restrict those aspects of its nuclear program that could help it build a nuclear bomb. The first initiatives were launched by three European states, the United Kingdom, France, and Germany, which came to be known as the "European Three" or E3. These states were later joined by the United States, Russia, and China, turning E3 efforts into "E3+3" or "P5+1" initiatives.

This chapter covers the period up to the June 2013 election of Hassan Rouhani as Iran's president. In November 2013, the new Iranian government reached an interim agreement with the P5+1 to institute a six-month freeze on some of Iran's nuclear activities in return for the easing of some sanctions. The parties said they would use the time provided by this agreement to negotiate a resolution of the nuclear issue. After they were unable to reach a longer term deal in six months, the parties agreed several times to extend the interim deal and talks. In July 2015, the parties announced a deal that would ease sanctions on Iran in return for constraints on Iran's nuclear activities. As of this writing, it remains unknown whether the deal will be implemented successfully, so this chapter's conclusions are mainly based on developments prior to the November 2013 interim agreement.

A review of E3 and P5+1 cooperation in the first part of this chapter shows that this cooperation was motivated by two goals: to solve the Iranian nuclear puzzle and to show that multilateralism could work as a basis for addressing proliferation crises. The chapter then assesses effectiveness. It argues that multilateralism was successfully achieved, but that the extent of cooperation did not grow as much as advocates of multilateralism would have hoped. The chapter also finds that although the E3 and P5+1 efforts had failed as of 2014 to solve the Iranian nuclear puzzle, their role was critical in limiting the development of Tehran's nuclear program and managing its consequences. The chapter concludes that E3 and P5+1 efforts have had a net positive effect on nonproliferation.

THE EVOLUTION OF EUROPEAN AND P5 COOPERATION

This section first discusses interactions with Iran by the E3 and then the efforts of the P5+1. This review shows that, prior to the November 2013 interim deal, Iran moved from a degree of cooperation to increasingly defiant responses.

Efforts of the E3

Iran has been a member of the NPT since the time of the Shah and signed a safeguards agreement with the International Atomic Energy Agency (IAEA) in 1974. Although there have long been suspicions that, despite its NPT membership, Iran is interested in nuclear weapons, multilateral efforts to address the issue have their origins in August 2002. That month, an exiled Iranian opposition group revealed the existence of an underground uranium enrichment facility under construction at Natanz and a heavy water production facility (which could be a potential building block in a program to obtain plutonium) at Arak.[1] These revelations raised suspicions about Iran's intentions at a time when concerns about proliferation had been accentuated by the 9/11 attacks. To reduce suspicions, Iran sought to provide assurances by acknowledging the existence of the projects, promising cooperation with the IAEA, and stating that it would consider adopting the Additional Protocol (AP).[2]

For a brief time, the George W. Bush administration secretly reached out to Tehran in a bid to normalize relations. Yet, after attacks in May 2003 against U.S.

targets in Saudi Arabia, which the United States traced back to al-Qaeda members living in Iran, the administration decided to abandon engagement and increase pressure against Tehran. On the basis of an IAEA report to the thirty-five member states on the Board of Governors (BOG) in June 2003, which found that Iran had "failed to meet its obligations under its Safeguards Agreement," the Bush administration argued that Iran should be found in noncompliance with its safeguards obligations and reported to the UNSC.[3] But other BOG members argued that Iran should be given time to correct its violations. Some feared that UNSC referral could give the United States a potential justification to invade Iran; the United States had just invaded Iraq over alleged proliferation activities, and President Bush had included Iran (along with Iraq and North Korea) on the "Axis of Evil" list in his 2002 State of the Union address. As a result, the BOG issued only a chairman's statement expressing concern about Iran's past reporting failures and urging it to cooperate with the IAEA, implement the AP, and refrain from introducing nuclear material at Natanz.[4]

With Washington refusing to engage Tehran, the United Kingdom, France, and Germany saw an opportunity for a joint European approach. The E3, which would later be represented by Javier Solana, the European Union's high representative for common foreign and security policy,[5] were partly motivated by a desire to restore international cooperation after divisions over the invasion of Iraq. While the United Kingdom had joined the U.S.-led coalition, France and Germany had opposed the invasion, creating tensions in transatlantic relations. At a time when the U.S. government was signaling its willingness to act unilaterally if necessary, the three European powers sought to prove that multilateral diplomacy could work. Moreover, the E3 wanted to show that the European Union was capable of solving "hard" international issues.[6]

In August 2003, the E3 sent a letter to Iran urging it to adopt the AP, cooperate with the IAEA to resolve concerns, suspend activities related to the production of fissile materials, and initiate negotiations for a "permanent cessation" of its fuel cycle program, in exchange for various incentives. Iran did not immediately respond. Meanwhile, new revelations surfaced about its nuclear activities and the IAEA reported that Tehran had begun to introduce nuclear material into some machines at Natanz, despite the recommendation of the chairman's statement.[7] At the BOG meeting of September 2003, the Bush administration pressed its case for Iran to be found in noncompliance with its safeguards obligations and reported to the UNSC. But many BOG members wanted to give Iran a chance to accept the E3 offer to negotiate. The E3 stressed that if Iran were not given this chance, it would be difficult to gain agreement that the time had come for UNSC action.[8] This led to the unanimous adoption of a BOG resolution calling on Tehran to endorse the AP and suspend all activities related to uranium enrichment and potential future plutonium reprocessing.⁹ The resolution implicitly suggested that unless Iran complied with these demands, the matter would be referred to the Security Council.

These developments brought Iran to the negotiating table with the E3 and led to the Tehran Agreement in October 2003. Iran agreed to cooperate with the IAEA, endorse the AP (and observe its requirements pending ratification), and voluntarily suspend its enrichment- and reprocessing-related activities. In exchange, in addition to promising negotiations for longer-term cooperation, the E3 recognized Iran's right to peaceful nuclear uses, as enshrined in NPT Article IV, and stated that "the full implementation of Iran's decisions . . . should enable the immediate situation to be resolved by the IAEA Board."¹⁰ This implied that full cooperation by Iran would enable it to avoid referral to the UNSC.

Implementation of the Tehran Agreement ran into problems because it did not specify the scope of the suspension. Iran embraced a narrow definition, allowing it to pursue some activities, whereas the E3 understood the agreement to require "full suspension" of fuel-cycle-related activities. Meanwhile, the IAEA also raised new questions about Iran's past activities. To restore full suspension, the E3 met with Iran in Paris in July 2004, warning that they would support a BOG resolution threatening to report Iranian noncompliance to the UNSC. Tehran indicated that it was prepared to consider a temporary suspension, but proceeded with some nuclear activities, prompting the adoption of a BOG resolution calling on Iran to restore full suspension.¹¹

Seeking to defuse the crisis, the E3 hashed out a new agreement with Iran. Concluded before the November 2004 BOG meeting, the Paris Agreement stressed that Iran was required to "continue and extend its suspension to include *all* enrichment-related and reprocessing activities."¹² Although the scope of the suspension was now specified, the E3 accepted Iran's demand that it be a "voluntary confidence-building measure, not a legal obligation." Moreover, the duration of the suspension was left ambiguous; it would be "sustained while negotiations proceed on a mutually acceptable agreement on long-term arrangements."

The Paris Agreement established the basis for negotiations between the E3 and Iran on a long-term agreement meant, as the accord put it, to "provide objective guarantees that Iran's nuclear program is exclusively for peaceful purposes." A steering committee was established, but little progress was made. The E3 insisted that Iran should not develop or operate facilities to produce fissile material, including any enrichment and reprocessing technology. In contrast, Tehran argued that it had accepted stronger inspections and cooperated with the IAEA to correct its past "mistakes," and that it could now resume its program, including fuel cycle activities. In the words of Seyyed Hossein Mousavian, one of the Iranian representatives to the Paris Agreement negotiations, "The Iranians made it clear to their European counterparts that if the latter sought a complete termination of Iran's nuclear fuel-cycle activities, there would be no negotiations."[13] In sum, while the E3 sought to turn the "temporary suspension" into a "permanent cessation," Tehran insisted that such suspension was only a temporary confidence-building measure.[14]

From the E3 to the P5+1

In 2005-6, it became apparent that E3 efforts would not elicit the hoped-for response from Iran. This led the other three members of the P5 to become involved, broadening cooperation from the E3 to what became known as the P5+1. This did not, however, produce better results. Instead, the ensuing years saw increasing confrontation with Iran.

The United States, Russia, and China all took different routes to adding their voices to the E3, with the U.S. position shifting first. During the E3-Iran negotiations, the United States had remained a bystander, frustrated by European refusals to support a BOG resolution referring Iran to the UNSC.[15] Unlike the E3, which sought the "permanent cessation" of Iranian enrichment and reprocessing facilities, Washington in 2003-4 demanded their *dismantlement*, rejecting any nuclear power program in Iran. It also refused to offer any inducements. The U.S. government believed that the E3 efforts would fail and the issue would end up in the UNSC, where sanctions would be imposed.

In early 2005, however, the United States began to support the E3. This was motivated by an effort to improve transatlantic relations after President Bush's reelection in November 2004. Washington also determined that U.S. support would guarantee that, if negotiations collapsed, the blame would fall on Iran, not the United States. This would help to rally support for sanctions at the UNSC. As Secretary of State Condoleezza Rice put it, "What we're looking at here is helping the Europeans in their diplomacy, not shifting policy toward Iran."[16] In return, the E3 agreed that they would support referral to the UNSC if Iran broke its suspension agreement.

To regain the diplomatic initiative, Iran made a proposal to the E3 in March 2005. The proposal included the phased resumption of enrichment under inspections, but made no concession on plans to complete a heavy water research reactor other than a political pledge not to build reprocessing facilities.[17] The E3 resisted the offer and warned that even a partial break in the suspension would lead to a referral to the UNSC. Iran backed down and accepted continued suspension in exchange for E3 agreement to present a comprehensive proposal in the summer. This constituted a victory for the E3, which had sought to delay the negotiations until after the Iranian presidential elections of June 2005. The hope was that moderate Akbar Hashemi Rafsanjani would win and be more amendable to compromise.[18]

The surprise election of Mahmoud Ahmadinejad dashed hopes of finding common ground on an agreement. Ahmadinejad had no intention of compromising with the West and showed strong hostility toward Israel, reportedly stating that it should be "wiped off the map."[19] Not surprisingly, when the E3 made their proposal in August 2005, Ahmadinejad rejected it. The proposal called for a binding agreement by Iran (reviewable after ten years) not to pursue fuel-cycle activities other than the construction and operation of light water and research reactors, in exchange for incentives, including support (with Russian cooperation) for Iran's civilian nuclear program.[20] Iran considered that the proposal denied its right to enrichment and doubted that the Europeans would be able to provide the incentives because they would require the support of United States, which was not a party to the offer.[21]

After Iran's rejection of the E3 proposal, the September 2005 BOG meeting found Iran to be in noncompliance with its safeguards obligations, both on the basis of its recent violations and its history of concealment of enrichment-related activities.[22] However, due to opposition from Russia and China and the majority of the members from the Non-Aligned Movement (NAM), which all abstained from the vote, reporting to the UNSC was deferred. The NAM states were reluctant to condemn Iran, a fellow member, and they have been sympathetic to claims that Iran has the right under NPT Article IV to develop fuel cycle activities.[23]

For their part, Russia's and China's resistance to condemning Iran was (and remains) the direct consequence of commercial and geopolitical interests. Although both Russia and China would prefer Iran not to go nuclear, they have been mindful to maintain good relations with this country because they supply it with weapons and have strong trade ties with it, notably in the oil and gas sectors, and, in the case of Russia, in the nuclear power sector. Moreover, Russia and China resisted upping the pressure on Iran for fear of setting a precedent that would jeopardize their own sovereignty in other contexts. They were particularly concerned after the Iraq war that sanctions on Iran would give the United States a pretext for another military intervention in the Persian Gulf.[24]

After the BOG resolution, Russia sought to defuse the crisis by proposing a joint venture to Iran to use its converted uranium to produce enriched-uranium fuel on Russian soil.[25] The E3 and the United States supported the proposal, but in early 2006 Tehran rejected the Russian proposal and announced that it was resuming work on enrichment. The E3 and Solana labeled Iran's decision to restart enrichment a "clear rejection of the process the E3/EU and Iran have been engaged in for over two years" and now called for Security Council action.[26]

Soon after, the E3 foreign ministers met in London with their counterparts from the United States, Russia, and China, marking the effective emergence of the P5+1, and the group agreed that Iran's noncompliance should be reported to the UNSC. Henceforth, the circle of cooperation would involve this wider set of six powers and their efforts would gradually switch to a more coercive approach. In February 2006, a BOG resolution—supported by Russia, China, and half of the NAM members—instructed the IAEA director-general (DG) to report Iran's noncompliance to the UNSC. The resolution specified that Iran would have to suspend all enrichment-related and reprocessing activities, abandon the construction of a heavy water reactor, ratify the AP, and implement transparency measures.[27]

When the BOG met a month later, Iran had not met any of these conditions. An IAEA report also provided evidence of Iran's work to develop nuclear weapons.[28] The UNSC issued a presidential statement, giving Tehran thirty days to comply.[29] Tehran ignored the deadline and responded by stopping AP implementation and all non–legally binding cooperation with the IAEA, and by resuming enrichment.

The P5+1 in Action

The P5+1 were divided over how to respond to Iran's defiance. While the United States, the United Kingdom, France, and Germany all sought the imposition of sanctions, Russia and China argued that such measures would make Tehran more obstinate. There were also divisions among the Western powers. While the United States and United Kingdom strongly supported sanctions, Germany and France were more circumspect.[30] Following the election of French president Nicolas Sarkozy to succeed Jacques Chirac in May 2007, however, Paris would strongly favor the strengthening of sanctions, leaving Germany, the country with the most extensive economic ties with Iran, as the most cautious Western power.

Maintaining cooperation among the P5+1 required accommodating the states most hesitant to increase confrontation with Iran. The P5+1 thus first agreed to offer Iran an updated incentives package. Presented by Solana in Tehran in June 2006, the proposal required Iran to suspend its fuel-cycle activities during the negotiations. Unlike the 2005 proposal, which asked Iran to make a binding commitment not to pursue fuel-cycle activities in return for incentives, under the new proposal the suspension would be reviewed once there was confidence that the Iranian program was exclusively for peaceful purposes.[31]

Iran rejected the proposal, mainly because it did not believe that Washington would ever agree that it had restored confidence. The stage was now set for UNSC action. In July 2006, the UNSC adopted Resolution 1696 under Article 40 of Chapter VII of the UN Charter, demanding Iranian suspension of all enrichment-related and reprocessing activities and requiring Tehran to cooperate with the IAEA.[32] Although Article 40 does not involve sanctions or the threat or use of military force, by acting under Chapter VII the Security Council made the suspension requirement legally binding. If Iran failed to meet these requirements within thirty days, sanctions would be imposed. Iran indicated that it was prepared to discuss suspension, but only while negotiations were under way. Iran also stressed that the discussion should be taken out of the UNSC and aimed only at providing assurances of the peaceful nature of its program, not at limiting it. When the thirty-day deadline passed, because Russia and China balked at imposing sanctions, the three Western powers agreed to explore Iran's position and set a new deadline for early October.

When the second deadline passed without Iranian compliance, the UNSC in December 2006 imposed sanctions through Resolution 1737. This resolution was adopted under Article 41 of Chapter VII of the UN Charter, allowing for economic sanctions but not the use of force. Resolution 1737 gave Tehran sixty days to suspend enrichment.[33] In deference to Russia and China, the resolution was weaker than the E3 had proposed. But it was significant because it was the first set of sanctions imposed unanimously by the UNSC against Iran. When the deadline passed and no progress had been made (in fact, the day the resolution was adopted Iran had announced that it would install centrifuges at Natanz and reduce its cooperation with the IAEA), a second sanctions resolution was reached unanimously. Resolution 1747 of March 2007 upped the pressure by targeting officers of the Iranian Revolutionary Guard Corps, who control significant economic resources in Iran.[34] Tehran responded by further restricting its cooperation with the IAEA.

Once the sixty-day deadline set by Resolution 1747 passed, the three Western powers hoped to keep building pressure on Iran. But Russia and China were reluctant to do so because, starting in June 2007, chief Iranian negotiator Ali Larijani initiated negotiations with the IAEA. The United States and the E3 expressed concerns that IAEA DG Mohamed ElBaradei's involvement in resolving political differences could derail P5+1 unity and allow Iran to sidestep sanctions.[35] IAEA-Iran negotiations proceeded nonetheless, and at the same time Larijani and Solana explored the idea of a "freeze-for-freeze," whereby Iran would agree not to expand enrichment in exchange for the UNSC refraining from imposing new sanctions. While Germany and Russia supported the idea, the United States, France, and the United Kingdom rejected it, demanding full suspension as a condition for negotiations on a long-term arrangement. Russian attempts to sell the idea to Iran failed and led to Larijani's replacement by hardliner Saeed Jalili.[36]

The Western-led campaign to pressure Iran was further hampered in December 2007, when Washington declassified the findings of a National Intelligence Estimate (NIE) that Iran had halted its nuclear-weapon-related work in late 2003.[37] According to a December 6, 2007, cable from the U.S. embassy in Beijing, China's assistant foreign minister said that "the general view of the international community is that the [NIE] report casts doubts on the need for an additional UNSC resolution."[38]

Unresolved concerns about Iran's alleged past weaponization studies and reported tests of a new generation of centrifuges, however, provided a basis for a third sanctions resolution. Resolution 1803, adopted in March 2008, marginally increased pressure on Iran, which responded by announcing the installation of additional centrifuges at Natanz.[39] Chinese efforts to balance the new sanctions with incentives were initially rejected by the other P5+1. Yet, in June 2008, the P5+1 agreed on repackaging their 2006 proposal with additional incentives, including a promise to give Iran its rightful place in the world. In exchange, there would be a "freeze-of-enrichment for freeze-of-sanctions" followed by a full suspension of both enrichment and sanctions.[40] Although Tehran initially suggested that it would accept the offer, it ended up proposing a protracted round of "pre-talks" and ignored the call for a reciprocal freeze and then suspension. This led to Resolution 1835 in September 2008, which reaffirmed UNSC support for the four prior resolutions concerning Iran's nuclear activities.[41] Because it came after the Georgia-Russia war, which led to high tensions between the West and Russia, the ability of the P5 to cooperate on the Resolution was significant even though it did not lead to any change in the Iranian position.

A New U.S. Administration

In the 2008 U.S. presidential campaign, candidate Barack Obama promised engagement with Iran without preconditions.[42] Once in office, the Obama administration adopted a two-pronged strategy meant to persuade the P5+1 to up the pressure on Iran if engagement failed.

The new U.S. approach prompted concerns among the E3 that Washington might concede that Iran be allowed to conduct some enrichment activity. France under Sarkozy insisted that the goal of zero enrichment should be kept.[43] Similarly, for the U.K., Minister of State for Foreign and Commonwealth Affairs Bill Rammell explained that the United Kingdom welcomed engagement but stressed that it was "not an open-ended offer" and that if Tehran did not deliver, the coalition would need to be "much tougher" on sanctions.[44]

Obama's strategy was put on hold, however, after Iran's June 2009 elections, when three million people took to the streets to protest against what they considered a fraudulent reelection of Ahmadinejad. The Obama administration finally put forward a new proposal in October 2009. It offered to exchange the bulk of Iran's low-enriched uranium (LEU) stockpile for replacement fuel for the Tehran Research Reactor (TRR), which produces medical isotopes and utilizes 19.75-percent-enriched uranium.[45] In June 2009, Iran had made a request to the IAEA for assistance in obtaining replacement fuel for the TRR (probably knowing that this would be denied and hoping to justify its own production of 19.75-percent-enriched uranium).

The U.S. offer called Iran's bluff, inviting Tehran to send its LEU to Russia for enrichment to 19.75 percent and then to France for fabrication into fuel assemblies. The goal was to keep Iran's stockpile of enriched uranium below a weapon's worth, providing diplomatic space to negotiate a long-term solution. The proposed deal also offered Iran an opportunity to legitimize its enrichment program (hence France's, the United Kingdom's, and especially Israel's skepticism), provided that Iranian uranium would be enriched outside of Iran.[46] Because fabrication into fuel assemblies would take France a year to complete, the proposal required Iran to send its LEU abroad before receiving the fuel. Tehran initially accepted, but political battles at home led it to insist that the exchange be simultaneous. The P5+1 refused because, after a year, Iran's continued LEU production would have replaced—and exceeded—the amount to be transferred.

The failure of the deal, when combined with revelations of a secret enrichment plant at Fordow, the persistence of unresolved issues with the IAEA, and Iran's decision to enrich small quantities of uranium to a 19.75 percent level (officially for the TRR), gave an impetus for fresh sanctions. Yet, in mid-May 2010, as the UNSC neared action on a new resolution, Iran agreed to a refashioned fuel-swap deal brokered by Brazil and Turkey. This deal, however, offered fewer nonproliferation benefits than the original one: it was silent about Iran enriching to higher levels and did not address its further accumulation of LEU since the first fuel-swap deal was proposed.[47] The P5+1 therefore shunned the deal and introduced new sanctions.

Although Russia and China watered down the initial draft, Resolution 1929 in June 2010 imposed strong sanctions on Tehran.[48] It also established a basis for unilateral sanctions. The United States and the European Union, which had taken such measures over the years, upped the pressure further. Australia, Canada, Japan, and South Korea also imposed sanctions beyond those required by the UNSC, and Russia interpreted the Resolution as prohibiting its controversial planned sale of S-300 antiaircraft missiles to Iran.[49] Finally, both Russia and China, which had given Iran an observer status at the Shanghai Cooperation Organization in anticipation of granting it full membership, have since made it clear that they will not support its accession while Iran is under UN sanctions.[50]

Iran responded defiantly, threatening economic reprisals against countries that would implement sanctions and stating that enrichment would continue.

Although Tehran eventually agreed to meet with the P5+1, the talks, which took place in Turkey in January 2011, did not produce results. The situation deteriorated further after a November 2011 IAEA report stating that "Iran has carried out activities relevant to the development of a nuclear explosive device," which led to a BOG resolution requiring Iran to provide additional information and access to the agency.[51] Because Russia and China resisted adding new international sanctions, the United States adopted unilateral sanctions targeting Iran's financial sector and its nuclear, petrochemical, and oil industries, and the European Union announced a ban on Iranian oil, along with sanctions against Iran's Central Bank. Israel, for its part, signaled its readiness to attack Iran's facilities, forcing the United States and the European Union to engage Israeli authorities. U.S. officials, including President Obama, assured Israel they remained willing to take military action if necessary to prevent Iran from acquiring the bomb.[52]

Iran dismissed the weaponization allegations, reiterating a claim that it viewed nuclear weapons as "a great sin."[53] But Tehran also resisted greater verification of its activities and announced new advances, including new centrifuges able to enrich uranium faster. Moreover, it responded to the West's unilateral sanctions with a threat to shut the Strait of Hormuz, a vital oil transit point. In early 2012, the possibility of war felt real. Covert operations multiplied including cyber attacks, and targeted assassinations. Negotiations resumed in spring 2012, but proved inconclusive, and meanwhile Tehran continued to press ahead with its enrichment program and to resist full cooperation with the IAEA.

Subsequently, however, the June 2013 election of the relatively moderate candidate Hassan Rouhani to succeed Ahmadinejad as president raised hopes that Iran might become willing to negotiate. In November, Iran and the P5+1 agreed on a "Joint Plan of Action" under which Iran would freeze some of its nuclear activities for six months in return for an easing of sanctions, with the idea that the parties would use this time to negotiate a more permanent agreement. When no agreement was reached after six months, the parties extended the arrangement several times. In July 2015 they announced a deal that will cut back but not eliminate Iran's nuclear activities. As of this writing, it is uncertain whether the deal will be implemented or will lead Iran to foreclose the nuclear weapons option. Also uncertain is what will happen to cooperation among the P5+1 in the aftermath of Russia's annexation of the Crimean Peninsula in February 2014 and subsequent unrest in eastern Ukraine. These events chilled relations between the West and Russia and led to Western sanctions against Moscow. Despite the worsening relations with the West, Russia maintained cooperation with the P5+1 in the negotiations with Iran, but it is hard to predict whether this will continue.[54]

This foregoing review has shown that the P5+1 achieved a good though far from perfect level of cooperation, but did not succeed in convincing Iran to address all of the issues of concern about its nuclear program. Subsequent sections of this chapter explain the international cooperation observed and more fully assess the effectiveness of these efforts through 2014.

EXPLAINING COOPERATION

Several factors identified by Knopf in chapter 1 had a bearing on this case. The E3 joined together partly out of self-interest: to prevent Iran from going nuclear, which they saw as a threat, and to prove that the European Union was a relevant actor on the international stage. Upholding norms was also a key driver. EU members have been developing a security culture that favors multilateralism. After the Iraq episode, the United Kingdom, France, and Germany all wanted to restore international cooperation and prove that multilateral diplomacy could work. This case also shows that U.S. leadership is not always necessary. E3 cooperation emerged because Washington refused to lead the negotiation process and because the E3 had enough diplomatic capital to fill the gap.

Self-interest also largely explains why the United States joined the E3. Washington wanted to solve the Iranian problem, which it considered a serious threat. An element of learning also played a role. The realization that supporting the E3 approach (and international norms and rules) was in U.S. interests came only with time. The United States eventually determined that garnering international support for stronger measures against Iran would require working through existing mechanisms, as a way to show U.S. willingness to exhaust other alternatives.

Domestic politics also had an impact in this case. Shifts in the U.S. approach coincided with domestic political changes following Bush's reelection in 2004 and Obama's election in 2008. Domestic politics also affected French policy, which favored a harder line after Sarkozy succeeded Chirac.

The reasons why Russia and China opted to cooperate with the E3 and the United States are more complex. They joined partly because they did not want to be left out and yield to other powers a free hand to determine the course of action. Russian and Chinese decisions to cooperate with the four Western states also reflected a significant behind-the-scenes persuasion (pressure?) campaign from the West. Russian and Chinese cooperation has been also partly self-interested and motivated by a genuine willingness to solve the Iranian problem. But self-interest also explains the limits of Russian and Chinese cooperation. These two powers wanted to restrain "U.S. hegemony" and avoid further precedents for "regime change." The conflicting interests of Russia and China explain why the extent of their cooperation with the rest of the P5+1 was so carefully calibrated.

Finally, transnational, working-level relationships did not play as prominent a role as in other cases. Instead, high-ranking diplomats and national leaders determined the extent of cooperation to pressure Iran.

ASSESSING EUROPEAN AND P5 EFFECTIVENESS

The Goals of Cooperation

Having reviewed E3 and then P5+1 cooperation, it is now critical to assess how successful it has proved. To do so, it is first necessary to understand the goals of E3 and P5+1 cooperation. In the above analysis, two key goals stand out: (1) making multilateralism effective and (2) solving the Iranian nuclear puzzle.

The E3 and then P5+1 joined together to address the Iranian nuclear crisis. Ending possible Iranian nuclear weapon development has been their overarching goal. If their multilateral efforts were to achieve a definitive solution to the Iranian nuclear puzzle, E3 and P5+1 cooperation would be considered a success because the problem would no longer exist.

However, success should not be measured solely against this yardstick. After the divisions among major powers generated by the Iraq invasion, a key goal of the E3 was to repair these relations. The Europeans took it upon themselves to play the multilateral diplomacy card and demonstrate that it can function. Subsequently, the P5+1 were driven by a similar goal: to make multilateralism work. After all, multilateral approaches involving the IAEA and UNSC are—and always have been—the default strategy to respond to proliferation crises.

Beyond merely resolving the Iranian nuclear crisis, therefore, another central goal of E3 and then P5+1 cooperation has been to show that the institutions that are supposed to tackle proliferation crises are relevant and can be effective. Going through the proper processes and making them work should hence also be considered a form of success. This approach has shaped E3 and P5+1 initiatives toward Iran. Have they proved successful, either in making multilateralism effective or in solving the Iranian nuclear crisis?

Making Multilateralism Effective

Based on Article XII.C of the IAEA Statute,[55] there is a standard multilateral process for responding to suspected nuclear proliferation by an NPT member state, which consists of four main stages. In stage 1, IAEA inspectors determine whether states are in compliance with their safeguards agreements and report "any noncompliance to the Director General who shall thereupon transmit the report to the Board of Governors." Upon receiving the report transmitted by the DG, the thirty-five-member-state BOG, in stage 2, "shall call upon the recipient State or States to remedy forthwith any noncompliance which it finds to have occurred." There is no specification of the criteria that the BOG should use to reach a finding about compliance. If no solution can be found and the issues remain unresolved, the BOG, in stage 3, "shall report the noncompliance to all members and the Security Council and General Assembly of the United Nations." Although the BOG is obliged to report the noncompliance, the IAEA Statute does not specify a time limit for doing so. Such reporting takes place through the DG transmitting a BOG resolution to the UNSC.

The final stage of the process consists of the UNSC (in practice, led by the P5) deciding, after considering the report(s) transmitted by the DG, to act either through a presidential statement or through a resolution adopted under Chapter VI or Chapter VII of the UN Charter. Chapter VI authorizes the UNSC to issue recommendations to promote the peaceful settlement of disputes, but does not give it the power to make binding resolutions.[56] Chapter VII goes further, allowing the UNSC to determine threats to or breaches of the peace, and to impose sanctions or authorize military action to "restore international peace and security."[57] Under Chapter VII, the resolutions adopted by the UNSC are binding on all UN member states.

In short, a standard process for dealing with suspected NPT violations involves four stages: (1) IAEA inspectors report noncompliance, (2) the BOG requests the state to remedy the situation, (3) the BOG refers the situation to the UNSC if no remedy is forthcoming, and (4) the UNSC takes action under the UN Charter.

With this framework as a backdrop, have E3 and then P5+1 efforts helped to make this multistage process effective? On the surface, the answer is an unambiguous yes. E3 initiatives were pivotal to generating broad international support to confront Iran's nonproliferation violations and find it in noncompliance with its safeguards obligations. When the problem first emerged in 2002–3 (stage 1), most states recognized that Tehran had to come clean about its activities, but there was little enthusiasm to be proactive about it because the issue arose shortly after the U.S. invasion of Iraq. To the great displeasure of the United States, most BOG member states refused at that point to find Iran to be in noncompliance. Moreover, even had a noncompliance finding been reached in 2003, it is unlikely that any agreement would have been reached in the UNSC on subsequent enforcement actions because neither Russia nor China was prepared to support them. The process created by the E3, which sought negotiations with Iran, proved critical in gradually rallying support from Russia, China, and key NAM members on a noncompliance finding, which was eventually achieved in September 2005 (stage 2). Russia, China, and most NAM members abstained on this vote, but the fact they did not actively oppose it meant that this stage of the process was nevertheless reached successfully.

Finding Iran in noncompliance with its safeguards agreement set the stage for Iran's referral to the UNSC (stage 3), which took place in a February 2006 BOG resolution that received the support of Russia, China, and half of the NAM members. After issuing a presidential statement giving Tehran a thirty-day deadline to comply with the requirements of the resolution (on which Tehran did not deliver), the UNSC duly took action (stage 4). While always keeping the negotiation route open, the P5 began by supporting Resolution 1696 in July 2006 demanding Iranian suspension of all enrichment-related and reprocessing activities and requiring Tehran to cooperate with the IAEA. When this did not produce results, the P5 supported a resolution under Chapter VII of the UN Charter (Resolution 1737, March 2007) boosting the pressure on Tehran by making their demands legally binding and by imposing sanctions. Subsequently, the P5 advanced four other sanctions resolutions, gradually increasing pressure, with the latest one, Resolution 1929 of June 2010, imposing strict penalties on Tehran.

On one level, therefore, E3 and P5+1 efforts have made the multilateral process in place "effective." There was cooperation among key partners, and all stages of the enforcement process were reached. This is significant and a form of success.

Nonetheless, below the surface, E3 and P5+1 efforts have *not* been an unqualified success, mainly because getting from one stage of the enforcement process to the next has been a lengthy endeavor. After the allegations of Iranian nuclear activities were first made in August 2002, it took nearly a year for the IAEA to establish Iran's violations: the agency did so in its June 2003 report (stage 1). It then took much longer for the BOG to find that Iran was in noncompliance with its safeguards obligations, which did not happen until September 2005 (stage 2). Paradoxically enough, although the process created by the E3 was essential in rallying the necessary international support to confront Tehran, it may also have played some role in delaying a noncompliance finding. Many states hoped that the E3 could resolve the problem through negotiations and seem to have feared that upping pressure on Tehran by proceeding through the stages of the enforcement process would ruin that prospect, making them reluctant to do so.

After the IAEA resolution on noncompliance, it took another five months for the BOG to report the matter to the UNSC, which it did in February 2006 (stage 3). The UNSC issued a presidential statement only a month later, in March 2006, but because of divisions among the P5+1 and the decision to try to solve the problem through an offer of new incentives, no resolution was adopted before Resolution 1696 of July 2006 (stage 4). The first sanctions resolution was adopted only five months later, in December 2006 (Resolution 1737), meaning that Security Council enforcement action did not come until three and a half years after the IAEA first established Iran's violations. After Tehran failed to honor the resolution's deadline for compliance, a second one followed expeditiously (Resolution 1747 of March 2007), amplifying the pressure further. Yet, the enforcement process then stalled again because of Iran's apparent willingness to negotiate (and because of the release of the U.S. NIE). Although Iran continued to proceed with nuclear development without any interruptions, it took a year for the P5 to agree on a third sanctions resolution (Resolution 1803 of March 2008).

After the U.S. presidential election, the Obama administration's efforts to "extend a hand to Iran" to either reach a negotiated solution or rally international support for strict sanctions if engagement failed had the desired effects. Negotiations failed and the P5 agreed on a strict sanctions resolution. But this resolution (Resolution 1929) was adopted only in June 2010, more than two years after the previous round of sanctions. After that, because of Russian and Chinese resistance, no new Security Council resolution could be negotiated.

The bottom line is that E3 and then P5+1 efforts *have* made multilateralism effective because each stage of the enforcement process has been reached. This is a form of success because it was one of the original goals of E3 cooperation. Yet, this process was not a smooth ride. It proved difficult and, to this day, has remained limited because of resistance from Russia, China, and states such as Brazil, Turkey, and others, notably NAM members. Only time will tell if the P5+1 can continue to prove multilateralism's effectiveness in the aftermath of the crisis in Ukraine.

Solving the Iranian Nuclear Puzzle

In addition to showing that multilateralism could work, the second and more important goal for the E3 and then P5+1 was to solve the Iranian nuclear puzzle. Although there is no standard definition, solving proliferation crises is usually understood as preventing the development of nuclear weapons by the state in question. Increasingly, however, solving proliferation crises has also come to be seen as preventing the development of a nuclear weapon *capability*, that is, the development of the building blocks necessary to manufacture nuclear weapons.

The traditional metric to determine if states have developed nuclear weapons (and become nuclear weapon states) has been their first nuclear tests. Yet, in an attempt to address the problem of nuclear weapon capabilities, the demarcation line has been moved back to an earlier step on the proliferation ladder: the accumulation by states of enough fissile material to manufacture nuclear weapons, known as a significant quantity (SQ).[58] This has led many to argue that there should be restrictions (even bans) on facilities that can produce an SQ expeditiously, that is, uranium enrichment and spent fuel reprocessing plants.[59]

In reality, both metrics are flawed. The explosion of a nuclear device by a state does not mean that it automatically possesses an operational nuclear arsenal. Similarly, as the first North Korean nuclear test has shown, there is a major difference between having an SQ and being able to explode a nuclear device at the expected yield. Still, currently, nonproliferation policy focuses predominantly on these two metrics to assess how close states are to achieving nuclear weapon status.[60]

With this in mind, have E3 and then P5+1 efforts helped to solve the Iranian nuclear puzzle? At the outset, E3 negotiations appeared productive. With the prospect of future negotiations for a long-term arrangement (as described in both the Tehran and Paris Agreements) and desire to avoid referral to the UNSC and imposition of sanctions, Iran responded positively to E3 efforts. As required by the E3, Tehran provided significant, although not full, cooperation with the IAEA. It also agreed to endorse the AP and observe its requirements pending ratification (but then never ratified it). More significant is that Tehran agreed to a temporary suspension of various enrichment-related activities—the key method to develop an SQ. These steps are all noteworthy achievements that should be regarded—while they lasted—as unambiguous successes.

However, subsequent E3 and P5+1 negotiations with Iran seeking satisfactory assurances of the peaceful nature of the Iranian nuclear program failed. Tehran rejected E3 demands that it accept a permanent cessation of its enrichment and reprocessing programs and abandon its heavy water research reactor project. With the arrival in power of Ahmadinejad in June 2005, Tehran then rejected any negotiated solution and, in response to the September 2005 BOG resolution on noncompliance and its subsequent referral of the Iran file to the UNSC (in February 2006), Iran decided to stop implementing the AP and all non-legally binding cooperation with the IAEA, and to resume its enrichment activities. Subsequently, it responded to each UN sanctions resolution by accelerating the development of its sensitive nuclear activities and restricting its cooperation with the IAEA. In short, over time, Iran continued slowly but steadily moving toward a nuclear weapon capability.[61]

So far, Tehran has stopped short of developing nuclear weapons. As of this writing, according to U.S. intelligence estimates, Iran has not made the political decision to move from capability to production (of an SQ), let alone to nuclear testing.[62] But it has moved closer to having the option to become a nuclear weapon state. The implications of Iran's nuclear development have already been felt. Several states in the greater Middle East have initiated or revived plans to develop civilian nuclear energy, perhaps in part to give themselves a foundation for a potential future weapons program.[63] Episodically, experts in the West and Israel have also suggested preemptive military strikes to end or at least delay Iran's nuclear program.[64] Although these developments have so far been contained (at least partly thanks to the sustained P5+1 efforts to deal with the problem), they are symptomatic of the fact that up to 2014 the Iranian nuclear puzzle was unresolved and had mostly been getting worse. Although the July 2015 deal might change this outcome, this is evidence that the P5+1 have so far failed in their efforts.

Nevertheless, the P5+1 *have* had a useful impact on Iran's nuclear program. Although sanctions have not achieved their strategic goal of changing Iran's behavior and ending its program, they have had an impact. As Dina Esfandiary and Mark Fitzpatrick note, "Iran does not have to surrender its enrichment programme for sanctions to be judged successful."[65] As these two analysts demonstrate, sanctions *have* worked in helping to limit Iran's ability to obtain what it needs to quickly assemble a nuclear arsenal. Moreover, sanctions helped to create the conditions for the 2013 interim agreement: they gave Tehran reasons to come to the bargaining table. Another essential point is that sanctions are, as George Perkovich has put it, the "least bad option" because they stand between acquiescence to Iran's nuclear activities, which would be detrimental to the NPT, and military strikes (or war), an option that most analysts agree has little prospect of truly stopping Iran's nuclear program.[66]

To date, the question of whether E3 and then P5+1 efforts have helped to solve the Iranian nuclear puzzle must mostly be answered in the negative. After initial E3 successes in stemming the program, the P5+1 for many years failed to prevent Iran's march toward a nuclear weapon capability. Still, the E3 and P5+1 played an important role in helping to slow this development and limit its consequences, and they brought Iran into negotiations starting in late 2013 that produced a deal in July 2015. Their efforts also sent a signal to would-be future proliferators that the P5 are willing to act to raise the economic and diplomatic costs of clandestine attempts to develop a nuclear weapon capability.

CONCLUSION

Conventional wisdom holds that the E3 and then P5+1 have failed. The ubiquitous argument goes as follows. E3 and P5+1 cooperation has been motivated by a shared goal to solve the Iranian nuclear puzzle. These efforts have not prevented Iran from moving toward developing nuclear weapons (or at least a nuclear weapon capability). Therefore, the E3 and P5+1 have proved unsuccessful.

As this chapter demonstrates, however, the E3 and even the P5+1 have been motivated by more than an attempt to end Iranian progress toward a nuclear weapon option. Although finding solutions to this problem has been paramount, another goal has been making multilateralism a meaningful option to address proliferation crises. As it turns out, the E3 and P5+1 have had much success in this endeavor. It proved difficult and cooperation remained more limited than many had hoped, but the key players did sign on to the multilateral approach and followed it step by step through several UNSC resolutions imposing sanctions. Similarly, although the E3 and P5+1 have so far failed to stop Iran's nuclear ambitions, they have helped to limit its progress and reduce negative spillover effects. Assuming that E3 and P5+1 efforts have bluntly failed is thus incorrect.

What are the key takeaways for policy? The Iranian experience suggests that proliferation crises can act as a catalyst for major-power cooperation. Driven by a mix of self-interest and norms, substantial cooperation can emerge without always requiring U.S. leadership, at least in its initial stages. Learning is also important, as the United States, Russia, and China all concluded that it would be better to work with the E3 in established multilateral channels if they wanted to shape the international response to Iran's nuclear activities. Among these sources of cooperation, norms turn out to be especially important. However long and difficult it may be to build cooperation, the establishment of a negotiating process based on respect for norms and rules is critical to success. Self-interest, in contrast, proved to be more of a double-edged sword, as the conflicting interests at stake for Russia and China limited how fast and how far they were willing to go. Because self-interest can hamper cooperation over enforcement efforts, the multilateral process could be made more effective if, as some have proposed, the Security Council were to adopt a generic, legally binding resolution specifying *automatic* consequences for any state found in noncompliance with its safeguards agreement.[67]

Finally, this chapter's findings suggest that although it may not always be possible to prevent a state from going nuclear (or almost nuclear), much can be done to slow the process and "buy time." Buying time is essential because, if properly managed, it can make room for a negotiated solution. As of this writing, there remains an opportunity for the P5+1 to achieve a diplomatic success. One hopes, therefore, that the end of the story of P5+1 interaction over Iran is yet to be written.

Notes

1. For a history (through early 2011) of key diplomatic developments regarding Iran's nuclear program, see *Iran's Nuclear, Chemical, and Biological Capabilities: A Net Assessment* (London: International Institute for Strategic Studies, 2011), 7–46.

2. The Additional Protocol is a voluntary supplement to a country's safeguards agreement with the IAEA, granting the IAEA expanded inspection powers. It is intended to improve the IAEA's ability to detect clandestine nuclear activities.

3. IAEA Board of Governors (BOG), "Implementation of the NPT Safeguards Agreement in the Islamic Republic of Iran, Report by the Director-General" (GOV/2003/40, June 6, 2003).

4. IAEA Media Advisories, "Statement by the Board" (June 19, 2003).

5. A process of cooperation between the E3 and the European Union was set up and has remained in place ever since. In December 2009, Solana was succeeded by Catherine Ashton in an expanded version of the EU High Representative post, and she took over his role as the lead European negotiator with Iran. On the EU role, see Oliver Meier, "European Efforts to Solve the Conflict over Iran's Nuclear Programme: How Has the European Union Performed?" (EU Nonproliferation Consortium, Nonproliferation Papers No. 27, February 2013), 4.

6. Alyson Bailes, "Europeans Fighting Proliferation: The Test-Case of Iran," *Sicherheit und Frieden* 24, no. 3 (2006): 129–34; Oliver Meier and Gerrard Quille, "Testing Time for Europe's Nonproliferation Strategy," *Arms Control Today* 35, no. 4 (May 2005): 4–12.

7. IAEA BOG, "Implementation of the NPT Safeguards Agreement in the Islamic Republic of Iran, Report by the Director-General" (GOV/2003/63, August 26, 2003).

8. U.S. Ambassador Kenneth Brill explained that the United States would go along with this approach because it had "taken note . . . of the desire of other member states to give Iran a last chance to stop its evasions." "Statement by U.S. Ambassador Kenneth Brill" (IAEA Board of Governors Meeting, Vienna, September 8, 2003).

9. IAEA BOG, "Implementation of the NPT Safeguards Agreement in the Islamic Republic of Iran, Resolution Adopted by the Board on 12 September 2003" (GOV/2003/69).

10. "Statement by the Iranian Government and Visiting EU Foreign Ministers" (October 21, 2003).

11. IAEA BOG, "Implementation of the NPT Safeguards Agreement in the Islamic Republic of Iran, Resolution Adopted by the Board on 18 September 2004" (GOV/2004/79).

12. "Iran-EU Agreement on Nuclear Programme" (November 14, 2004), emphasis added.

13. Seyyed Hossein Mousavian, "Iran and the West: The Path to Nuclear Deadlock," *Global Dialogue* 8, nos. 1–2 (Winter–Spring 2006): 77.

14. According to a December 22, 2004, cable released by WikiLeaks, negotiators for the E3 were aware of the incompatibility of the two sides' positions. Written by Annalisa Giannella, who was Solana's personal representative, the cable titled "EU/Iran: WMD Rep Giannella Readout on Talks, Path Ahead for EU3-Iran Dialogue" is available at www.wikileaks.org/plusd/cables/04BRUSSELS5396_a.html.

15. Christopher Ford, "A New Paradigm: Shattering Obsolete Thinking on Arms Control and Nonproliferation," *Arms Control Today* 38, no. 9 (November 2008): 12–19.

16. Condoleezza Rice, "Interview with Reuters News Agency" (Washington, D.C., March 11, 2005).

17. "Elements of Objective Guarantees" (Presented by Iran in the Meeting of Steering Committee, Paris, March 23, 2005).

18. Farideh Farhi, "'Atomic Energy Is Our Assured Right': Nuclear Policy and the Shaping of Iranian Public Opinion," in *Nuclear Politics in Iran*, ed. Judith Yaphe (Washington, D.C.: Institute for National Strategic Studies, 2010), 10.

19. "Ahmadinejad: Israel Must Be Wiped Off the Map," *IRIB News*, October 26, 2005.

20. IAEA, INFCIRC/651, "Communication Dated 8 August 2005 Received from the Resident Representatives of France, Germany and the United Kingdom to the Agency" (Vienna, August 8, 2005).

21. Mohammed Saeedi, the deputy head of Iran's atomic energy organization, reportedly said that "the EU proposal was very insulting and humiliating." Quoted in Rosalind Ryan, "Iran Resumes Uranium Enrichment," *Guardian*, August 8, 2005.

22. IAEA BOG, "Implementation of the NPT Safeguards Agreement in the Islamic Republic of Iran, Resolution adopted on 24 September 2005" (GOV/2005/77).

23. On the role of the NAM in nuclear politics, see William Potter and Gaukhar Mukhatzhanova, *Nuclear Politics and the Non-Aligned Movement: Principles vs. Pragmatism*, Adelphi Series 427 (London: Routledge, 2012).
24. John Parker, *Russia and the Iranian Nuclear Program: Replay or Breakthrough?* (Washington, D.C.: Institute for National Strategic Studies, 2012); Richard Weitz, "Why China and Russia Help Iran," *Diplomat*, November 19, 2011.
25. Paul Kerr, "New Iran Talks Set, but Prospects Gloomy," *Arms Control Today* 36, no. 1 (January–February 2006).
26. Council of the European Union, "Statement by Germany, United Kingdom, France, and EU High Representative on Iranian Nuclear Issue" (Berlin, January 12, 2006).
27. IAEA BOG, "Implementation of the NPT Safeguards Agreement in the Islamic Republic of Iran, Resolution Adopted on 4 February 2006" (GOV/2006/14).
28. IAEA BOG, "Implementation of the NPT Safeguards Agreement in the Islamic Republic of Iran, Report by the Director General" (GOV/2006/15, February 27, 2006).
29. UNSC, "Statement by the President of the Security Council" (S/PRST/2006/15, March 29, 2006).
30. Paul Kerr, "Iran, EU Struggle to Start Nuclear Talks," *Arms Control Today* 36, no. 8 (October 2006).
31. "Elements of a Proposal to Iran, as Approved on 1 June 2006 at the Meeting in Vienna of China, France, Germany, the Russian Federation, the United Kingdom, the United States of America and the European Union" (S202/06).
32. UNSC, "Resolution 1696 (2006) Adopted by the Security Council at its 5500th Meeting, on 31 July 2006" (S/RES/1696, 2006).
33. UNSC, "Resolution 1737 (2006) Adopted by the Security Council at its 5612th Meeting, on 23 December 2006" (S/RES/1737, 2006).
34. UNSC, "Resolution 1747 (2007) Adopted by the Security Council at its 5647th Meeting, on 24 March 2007" (S/RES/1747, 2007).
35. Peter Crail, "Iran Agrees on Work Plan with IAEA," *Arms Control Today* 37, no. 7 (September 2007).
36. Anne Penketh, "Iran's New Hardline Nuclear Envoy Causes Jitters in West," *Independent*, October 22, 2007.
37. National Intelligence Council, National Intelligence Estimate, "Iran: Nuclear Intentions and Capabilities" (November 2007).
38. Linda Pearson, "WikiLeaks and the 2007 Iran NIE—Part 1," ZNet, April 13, 2013, http://zcomm.org/znetarticle/wikileaks-and-the-2007-iran-nie-part-1-by-linda-pearson/.
39. UNSC, "Resolution 1803 (2008) Adopted by the Security Council at its 5848th Meeting, on 3 March 2008" (S/RES/1803, 2008).
40. U.S. Department of State, Office of the Spokesman, "P5+1 Updated Incentives Package" (Washington, D.C., June 17, 2008).
41. UNSC, "Resolution 1835 (2008) Adopted by the Security Council at its 5984th Meeting, on 27 September 2008" (S/RES/1835, 2008).
42. "The First Presidential Debate" (Transcript), *New York Times*, September 26, 2008.
43. Trita Parsi, *A Single Roll of the Dice: Obama's Diplomacy with Iran* (New Haven, Conn.: Yale University Press, 2012), 57.
44. Jeff Abramson and Daniel Horner, "Interview with British Minister of State for Foreign and Commonwealth Affairs Bill Rammell," *Arms Control Today* 39, no. 5 (June 2009).
45. For an analysis, see Mark Fitzpatrick, "Iran: The Fragile Promise of the Fuel-Swap Plan," *Survival* 52, no. 3 (June–July 2010): 67–94.

46. Mark Fitzpatrick, "Containing the Iranian Nuclear Crisis: The Useful Precedent of a Fuel Swap," *Perceptions* 16, no. 2 (Summer 2011): 31.
47. Fitzpatrick, "Iran: The Fragile Promise."
48. UNSC, "Resolution 1929 (2010) Adopted by the Security Council at its 6335th Meeting, on 9 June 2010," S/RES/1929 (2010).
49. "On Measures to Implement Resolution 1929 of June 9, 2010 of the UN Security Council" (Presidential Decree by Dmitry Medvedev, September 22, 2010).
50. Wu Jiao and Li Xiaokun, "SCO Agrees Deal to Expand," *China Daily*, June 12, 2010.
51. IAEA BOG, "Implementation of the NPT Safeguards Agreement and Relevant Provisions of Security Council Resolutions in the Islamic Republic of Iran" (GOV/2011/65, November 8, 2011), 10.
52. Jeffrey Goldberg, "Obama to Iran and Israel: 'As President of the United States, I Don't Bluff,'" *Atlantic*, March 2, 2012.
53. "Statement by H. E. Dr. Ali Akbar Salehi" (Conference on Disarmament, Geneva, February 28, 2012).
54. Mark Fitzpatrick, "Russia's Solidarity with the West in the Iran Nuclear Talks," Politics and Strategy: The *Survival* Editors' Blog, June 26, 2014, https://www.iiss.org/en/politics%20and%20strategy/blogsections/2014-d2de/june-cf18/iran-russia-do3b.
55. Statute of the IAEA, Article XII.C.
56. Charter of the United Nations, "Chapter VI: Pacific Settlement of Disputes."
57. Charter of the United Nations, "Chapter VII: Action with Respect to Threats to the Peace, Breaches of the Peace, and Acts of Aggression," Article 39.
58. The IAEA defines an SQ as "the approximate amount of nuclear material for which the possibility of manufacturing a nuclear explosive device cannot be excluded." This corresponds to eight kilograms of plutonium or twenty-five kilograms of highly enriched uranium. See *IAEA Safeguards Glossary* (Vienna: International Atomic Energy Agency, 2002), 23. Many experts, however, have argued that the IAEA should lower these amounts. See, for instance, Thomas B. Cochran and Christopher E. Paine, *The Amount of Plutonium and Highly Enriched Uranium Needed for Pure Fission Nuclear Weapons* (New York: Natural Resources Defense Council, 1995).
59. For instance, Henry D. Sokolski, ed., *Falling Behind: International Scrutiny of the Peaceful Atom* (Carlisle, Pa.: U.S. Army War College Strategic Studies Institute, 2008).
60. For a discussion, see Jacques E. C. Hymans, "When Does a State Become a 'Nuclear Weapon State'? An Exercise of Measurement Validation," *Nonproliferation Review* 17, no. 1 (March 2010): 161–80.
61. Experts disagree over how close Iran is to achieving that capability, but not on the fact it has been making progress toward the ability to produce fissile materials that could be used in a bomb. See *Iran's Nuclear, Chemical, and Biological Capabilities*.
62. James R. Clapper, director of national intelligence, Statement for the Record, "Worldwide Threat Assessment of the U.S. Intelligence Community" (Senate Select Committee on Intelligence, March 12, 2013).
63. For an analysis, see *Nuclear Programmes in the Middle East: In the Shadow of Iran* (London: International Institute for Strategic Studies, 2008).
64. See, for instance, Matthew Kroenig, "Time to Attack Iran—Why a Strike Is the Least Bad Option," *Foreign Affairs* 91, no. 1 (January–February 2012): 76–86, which was later expanded into a book, *A Time to Attack: The Looming Iranian Nuclear Threat* (New York: Palgrave Macmillan, 2014).

65. Dina Esfandiary and Mark Fitzpatrick, "Sanctions on Iran: Defining and Enabling 'Success,'" *Survival* 53, no. 5 (October–November 2011): 147. See also "Iran: Sanctions Halt Long-Range Ballistic Missile Development," *IISS Strategic Comments* 18, no. 22 (July 2012).

66. George Perkovich, "Sanctions on Iran—The Least Bad Option" (Carnegie Endowment for International Peace, June 28, 2010).

67. Pierre Goldschmidt, "IAEA Safeguards: Dealing Preventively with Noncompliance" (Belfer Center for Science and International Affairs, July 12, 2008).

CHAPTER FOURTEEN

Conclusions

JEFFREY W. KNOPF

INTERNATIONAL COOPERATION to prevent and reverse the spread of nuclear, biological, and chemical (NBC) weapons has expanded over time. These nonproliferation efforts rest on a set of global treaties: the Nuclear Non-Proliferation Treaty (NPT), the Biological Weapons Convention (BWC), and the Chemical Weapons Convention (CWC). The global treaties, however, do not exhaust the range of cooperative endeavors. States have added a diverse array of other cooperative initiatives to the nonproliferation tool kit. A starting goal for this volume was to draw attention to how extensive the range of cooperative nonproliferation activities has become. The research for this volume also aimed to provide insight into how nonproliferation cooperation is evolving over time, to examine possible explanations for the patterns of cooperation observed, and to assess the effectiveness of the cooperative arrangements that have arisen in addition to the global treaties.

In the preceding chapters, a dozen subject-matter experts have examined different cases of nonproliferation cooperation. The cases include efforts that are both global and regional, both formal and informal, and drawn from the Cold War, post–Cold War, and post-9/11 periods. As outlined in chapter 1, the case study authors were asked to consider a list of factors that might be relevant for explaining cooperation and to evaluate the effectiveness of each cooperative endeavor. This concluding chapter considers what the findings from the individual cases add up to collectively. The chapter begins with findings about the nature of nonproliferation cooperation and ends with a summary of the policy implications of the research presented in this volume.

THE BIG PICTURE: COOPERATION IS EXPANDING AND EVOLVING

The case studies paint a picture of growing international cooperation in support of nonproliferation and nuclear security. First, states continue to launch new cooperative initiatives. As Francesca Giovannini observes in her chapter on regional institutions, we have witnessed a "proliferation" of nonproliferation efforts. Treaties and other legally binding measures remain part of this effort, as can be seen in regional nuclear-weapon-free-zone (NWFZ) agreements and the International Convention for the Suppression of Acts of Nuclear Terrorism. Alongside these formal measures, however, informal initiatives have become increasingly prominent. Informal arrangements launched by small groups of like-minded states include the multilateral export control regimes (MECRs) and the Proliferation Security Initiative (PSI). One should not infer from this that formal approaches lack value; rather, the relevant point is that any analysis has to recognize the presence of many non-treaty-based arrangements in the landscape of international cooperation on nonproliferation.

Cooperation is also expanding in a second way: participation in almost all the endeavors studied in this volume has increased over time. In his chapter on the MECRs, Scott Jones points out that they mostly began as efforts by a little more than a half dozen states, but have all grown to memberships of around forty or more countries. Involvement in threat reduction activities has also grown. Wyn Bowen and Alan Heyes note that the Global Partnership (GP) was essentially a mechanism for other G8 countries to contribute to efforts first initiated by the U.S. Cooperative Threat Reduction (CTR) program. Other states have since joined in, and—notwithstanding Russia's ouster from the G8 after its annexation of Crimea in 2014—the GP continues to function and now has twenty-five members. Even efforts that initially encountered resistance have gained support. Many states were initially critical of George W. Bush administration initiatives such as PSI and UN Security Council Resolution (UNSCR) 1540. These initiatives have since become more widely accepted as legitimate, with more than one hundred states, for example, now participating in PSI.

Participation is not uniform across the different initiatives, however, and cooperation is not universal. Some key states remain holdouts with respect to some of the initiatives. China, for example, was slow to join many of the nonproliferation instruments, and it remains unwilling to participate in some such as PSI. In other cases, such as India's desire to join the Nuclear Suppliers Group (NSG), existing members remain divided on whether to accept the country as a member. Finally, as Giovannini points out in her analysis of Indonesia, regional powers sometimes join a cooperative arrangement but act as spoilers in the sense that they water down and thereby limit the effectiveness of the regional mechanism in question. Figuring out how to encourage buy-in among reluctant parties remains an important challenge, but this should not obscure the overall trend toward increasing participation in cooperative nonproliferation efforts.

This conclusion stands in contrast to other studies that emphasize "gridlock" in multilateral institutions, including those dealing with WMD proliferation. The authors of *Gridlock* argue that decision making in formal institutions often ends in stalemate; the failure of the 2015 NPT Review Conference to reach consensus on a final document is a case in point. From this, *Gridlock* concludes that international institutions are increasingly incapable of solving global problems.[1] The different conclusions reflect different yardsticks for evaluating international cooperation. *Gridlock* focuses on how global institutions fall short of achieving ideal outcomes. This volume focuses instead on trends in the number of states participating in cooperative endeavors and whether these make a difference at the margins. The problems posed by NBC weapons are still far from being solved, but the cases in this volume reveal areas of progress. Both studies share an interest in making international cooperation more effective, and it is hoped that the policy lessons summarized below will contribute toward that goal.

From Coordination to Collaboration?

The nature of nonproliferation cooperation has also changed over time. Chapter 1 suggested an overarching hypothesis that cooperation has evolved from "coordination" toward "collaboration."[2] The foundational nonproliferation treaties mainly involve coordination: under them, states coordinate their policies around pledges of mutual self-restraint, such as pledges not to transfer or acquire NBC weapons. Many of the post–Cold War and post-9/11 initiatives, in contrast, have required active collaboration, in the sense of states working together to implement programs or operations.

The case study chapters provide substantial though not complete support for this broad hypothesis. Many of the initiatives do require states to work together. The Brazilian-Argentine Agency for Accounting and Control of Nuclear Materials (ABACC), which was analyzed by Sara Kutchesfahani, provides one example. Under ABACC, participants from Argentina and Brazil participate jointly in various forms of training and technical cooperation. Other cases also fit this pattern. Cooperative threat reduction activities have brought together personnel from different countries to dismantle nuclear warheads, build chemical weapon destruction facilities, or install better fences and locks at facilities that store WMD-related materials. And PSI encourages states to share intelligence and could lead to joint interdiction operations.

Despite the increased role of collaboration, however, coordination also remains important. The export control regimes fundamentally involve an effort to coordinate national export polices. UNSCR 1540 similarly mandates policy coordination through its requirements that states implement certain domestic laws and regulations intended to prevent WMD proliferation and keep such weapons out of the hands of non-state actors. Because many states seek assistance in meeting the burdens imposed by 1540, the resolution has also made another type of coordination necessary. As Tanya Ogilvie-White points out in her analysis of 1540, uncoordinated offers of assistance from donor states proved inefficient, and the 1540 Committee created by the resolution has gained the important task of helping to coordinate offers of assistance and match them to appropriate recipients.

Even these examples of coordination, however, involve elements of collaboration. To update the guidelines and control lists of the MECRs requires holding regular meetings at which officials must work together to make decisions about how to update the relevant export controls. The work of coordinating 1540 assistance likewise leads to a certain amount of collaboration. The small staff of the 1540 Committee must work with Security Council members as well as relevant regional organizations to match requests for assistance with appropriate providers.

The nuclear security summit process, which is the subject of Libby Turpen's chapter, also shows how coordination can take on collaborative aspects. At the first summit, in 2010, participating states brought "house gifts." These were pledges by individual states to carry out some action that would enhance nuclear security. Separate pledges of this type can be seen as an example of policy coordination. The second summit in 2012 involved a new innovation, however, called the "gift basket." Gift baskets involve promises by groups of states to work collectively on some effort that will advance nuclear security. As an example, Belgium, France, South Korea, and the United States pledged a joint effort to develop a high-density low-enriched uranium (LEU) fuel that could replace the weapons-grade highly enriched uranium (HEU) fuel in certain types of nuclear reactors.[3] This gift basket involved a move from simply coordinating policy to actually collaborating on a joint project. Policy coordination remains an important aspect of cooperation on behalf of nonproliferation, but a trend toward greater levels of active collaboration is also apparent.

Explaining the Big Picture: A First Cut

Nonproliferation cooperation is expanding. New initiatives have been added over time, and many of these involve an evolution toward active collaboration. Several factors appear relevant to explaining these developments.

First, key treaties are already in place. Global conventions exist that outlaw biological and chemical weapons. In the nuclear realm, the NPT and Comprehensive Test Ban Treaty aim to prevent new states from acquiring nuclear weapons while limiting the programs of the existing nuclear-armed states and pushing them to make good-faith efforts to negotiate nuclear disarmament. There is support for further measures such as a fissile material cutoff treaty and perhaps one day a nuclear weapons convention along the lines of the BWC and CWC, but prospects for negotiations on these proposals are presently dim.

In these circumstances, there might not be much more that can be achieved, at least in the short run, through global treaty negotiations. Yet there have still been steps that states can take to reduce the chances of WMD proliferation to both states and non-state actors. It has hence made sense to seek new forms of international cooperation that can be established without negotiating new global treaties. Some observers may interpret this as an argument against or a move away from treaties, but this is not correct. The global treaties provide the legal and normative foundations that make other cooperative efforts possible. It would be hard to enlist state support for interdicting WMD shipments, for example, if there were not treaties in place that prohibit assisting other states in acquiring NBC weapons. But not every proliferation risk can be addressed through existing treaties, and this creates an opening for developing other kinds of cooperative arrangements.

This means that a part of the explanation is functional. Events have revealed new problems and risks that need to be addressed if states seek to minimize proliferation. India's 1974 nuclear test used plutonium from a Canadian-supplied research reactor. This revealed a need to manage nuclear exports more carefully, leading to creation of the NSG. The collapse of the Soviet Union created a fear of "loose nukes," which motivated setting up the CTR program. And the combination of 9/11 and discovery of the A. Q. Khan network showed that illicit trafficking might enable a terrorist group to obtain WMD. This helped spur a whole series of initiatives.

A functional explanation suggests that new transnational problems create an interest in new cooperative responses. However, the steps from new danger to new initiative are not always direct. States can perceive and interpret their interests differently. For this reason, ideas and the advocates of those ideas can have an impact on whether states decide that they have an interest in setting up or joining a new cooperative nonproliferation arrangement. Transnational networks are especially likely to play a role in promoting understandings that favor cooperation. Individuals participating in transnational networks will interact with other individuals who advocate cooperative approaches. If their experiences are positive, they may themselves become advocates at home for participating in cooperative arrangements. The more support there is for cooperative efforts, the stronger the transnational networks are likely to become. In short, cooperative nonproliferation arrangements have grown in number and diversity in part because new problems reveal functional reasons to create them, in part because they cannot always be addressed through existing or proposed global treaties, in part because an understanding that transnational problems require cooperative responses has become widely embraced, and in part because these dynamics are amplified by the progressive building up of transnational networks.

This broad-brush account can explain why there is a trend toward greater interest in international cooperation on WMD nonproliferation. It is not fine grained enough, however, to provide much leverage on individual cases. To explain why states first propose new cooperative initiatives and other states choose whether or not to participate, chapter 1 proposed seven potentially relevant factors: self-interest, U.S. leadership, norms and identity, ideas and learning, inducements and persuasion, domestic politics, and capabilities. The next section reviews the findings across the case studies with respect to these seven factors.

EXPLAINING COOPERATION

Assessing the Roles of Seven Factors

Chapter 1 identified seven factors that might account for the patterns of cooperation observed in the cases. Reviewing the case findings, it is clear that no one factor can by itself explain cooperation across all the different nonproliferation initiatives. In most cases, cooperation (or its absence) arose from a combination of factors. The particular combination also varied across cases, and each hypothesized factor played a role in at least some cases. That said, however, some factors exerted more influence than others.

Self-interest tended to have the greatest impact. Across the various cases, national interests often emerged as the most important factor in explaining whether or not states embrace cooperation on behalf of nonproliferation. The states most likely to sponsor or join cooperative nonproliferation activities tend to be those that perceive the greatest threats from WMD proliferation, illicit trafficking networks, and poorly secured nuclear materials.

In some of the cases of regional cooperation, however, some of the perceived threats were posed by the existing nuclear weapon states. In his chapter, Michael Hamel-Green found this to be a major factor in several NWFZ negotiations. The Cuban Missile Crisis, for instance, served as a stark warning that states in Latin America and the Caribbean could become victims in a superpower nuclear war. This became the main motivation to negotiate the Treaty of Tlatelolco, establishing the Latin American NWFZ. Similarly, nuclear weapon testing and its legacies helped spur zones in other regions, including Central Asia and the South Pacific. When one focuses on regional institutions, it becomes apparent that not all nuclear dangers derive from proliferation, and some states also have an interest in constraining the actions of the NPT-recognized nuclear weapons states.

In addition, not all states participate in cooperative nonproliferation activities, and self-interest also helps explain these decisions. Some states, especially in the Global South, do not perceive proliferation or terrorism to be major threats to them and are reluctant to devote scarce resources to nonproliferation measures. In some cases, states also have other security or economic interests that lead them to refrain from joining certain initiatives.

The importance of national interests is a truism, but states' calculations of their interests are often complicated. Support for cooperation has not always derived from threat perceptions, but at times has reflected other interests. India, for example, has recently sought to join the NSG. By the terms of the NPT, India cannot join that treaty as a nuclear weapon state,[4] so it views membership in export control arrangements as a way to gain de facto acceptance of its status as a nuclear weapon possessor. The existence of multiple initiatives also creates a situation in which states might choose to join some as a way to deflect potential criticism about their nonparticipation in others. According to Gavin Cameron, China welcomed the Global Initiative to Combat Nuclear Terrorism (GICNT) because it was an alternative to PSI, which Beijing opposes.

States also often have conflicting interests, and international cooperation is sometimes calibrated to the balance between competing interests. Togzhan Kassenova's analysis of CTR provides a good illustration. She highlights how some officials in both Russia and the United States focused on potential security risks that could accompany CTR efforts: the Russians feared it was an attempt by America to spy and learn Russian military secrets, while some U.S. officials believed Russia would exploit CTR as a way to free up funds to devote to a new military buildup. These fears did not kill the program, but officials in both countries who saw CTR as contrary to the national interest were able to do things that slowed down or in other ways impeded program implementation.

It is also important to recognize that interests are not set in stone. Perceptions can change and interests can be reinterpreted. As a result, in some cases states that started out as critical of a nonproliferation initiative have eventually changed their minds. India, for example, began as the kind of country nuclear exporters intended to target when they set up the NSG, but now India wants to become a member. Similarly, in her chapter on PSI, Emma Belcher points out that Russia criticized the PSI at first but later joined the initiative.

U.S. leadership also played a significant role. Many of the global efforts resulted from a U.S. initiative, and it is hard to imagine them coming into being in the absence of U.S. leadership. At the same time, the U.S. role does not always have a positive impact. Some states express concern about the extent of U.S. reach as the world's sole superpower, which makes them reluctant to endorse U.S. proposals. The way in which the U.S. government handles its efforts to promote new nonproliferation initiatives can also make a difference. When officials take a heavy-handed approach, using harsh language and seeming to dismiss the concerns of other countries, this limits support for even those cooperative activities that U.S. officials want to promote. The fact that PSI was associated with the controversial John Bolton, for example, accounts for some of the skepticism that effort encountered. In contrast, when officials take a more diplomatic approach and seek creative solutions to other states' concerns, U.S. leadership is more effective in eliciting cooperation. As Ogilvie-White notes, evidence for this can be seen in the case of UNSCR 1540. The transition from the Bush to the Obama administration brought in a new team that set a different tone and engaged in more active diplomatic outreach, and this resulted in an increase in state efforts to fulfill the 1540 mandates.

The cases also revealed that leadership does not always come from the United States. As both Hamel-Green and Giovannini make clear, the theoretical framework for this project implicitly assumed that only the United States, as the hegemonic power, might play a leadership role. This is not true, however, and at the regional level it is often a regional power that takes the lead in promoting new regional arrangements.

Leadership can also be exercised jointly. The United States worked with Canada on the launch of the GP and with the United Kingdom on passing Resolution 1540. The GICNT, similarly, was a joint U.S.-Russia product.

In discussing state leadership, moreover, it is important not to assume this means a unitary state effort. Particular individuals sometimes play a critical entrepreneurial role in promoting a new initiative. There would have been no CTR without the efforts of Senators Nunn and Lugar, which is why CTR is also called the Nunn-Lugar Program. Hamel-Green likewise emphasizes the role of "advocate leaders" in key states in paving the way for many of the NWFZ treaties.

The cases also suggest that *norms* matter, but their impact does not appear to be quite as great as that of the first two factors. In general, participation in cooperative efforts is greater among states that already embrace nonproliferation and antiterrorism norms and that already favor international cooperation and multilateralism more generally. In his study of diplomatic engagement with Iran by the EU-3 and P5+1, for example, David Santoro observes that support for multilateralism was a major reason why the three EU powers launched their diplomatic initiative toward Iran.

New cooperative initiatives can also be effective in building up new norms and encouraging more states to embrace them. In some cases, this appeared to be where norms had the greatest effect. State interests and the presence of a leader may be crucial in establishing a cooperative effort, but norms often help account for the subsequent enlargement of participation. The Reduced Enrichment for Research and Test Reactors (RERTR) program fits this pattern. It began as a unilateral U.S. initiative to pressure other countries to convert certain reactors from use of bomb-grade HEU to proliferation-resistant LEU. In his chapter on RERTR, Alan Kuperman found that many nuclear operators eventually internalized nonproliferation norms, which made them more willing to accede to U.S. pressure to convert their plants from HEU to LEU fuel. Hamel-

Green likewise argues that initial holdout states in the regional NWFZs were later persuaded to ratify those treaties once the nuclear-free norm was established because they did not want to isolate themselves within the region.

The impact of norms can be complicated because of the presence of conflicting norms. Initiatives based on norms against proliferation or terrorism sometimes come into conflict with other norms that states embrace, such as those concerning sovereignty or freedom of the seas. Conflicting norms were especially prominent in the 1540 case. Because 1540 imposes legal obligations on all states, many capitals objected to the fact it was adopted by the Security Council rather than the full General Assembly, seeing this as a violation of their sovereign rights. When norms collide in this way, support for cooperative nonproliferation efforts is reduced.

The analytical framework summarized in the first chapter listed *ideas, learning, and transnational networks* as a linked set of factors to consider. This reflected the notion of epistemic communities as transnational networks that promote certain ideas.[5] A review of the cases, however, suggests the value of disaggregating these factors. Ideas and learning were not as prominent as some of the other factors considered in this study, but they did still sometimes make a difference. Jones, for example, concluded that social learning played a key role in helping the MECRs adapt and expand their memberships in response to changing circumstances. States also learned from the successes of earlier efforts. The lesson that cooperative threat reduction programs could make important contributions, for instance, was a key factor leading to the creation of the GP. And Kuperman notes that Russia and China both imitated the U.S. RERTR program, initially unbeknownst to U.S. officials.

Turning to transnational networks, they play a prominent role in several cases, in ways that both include and go beyond being a vehicle to transmit ideas. *Epistemic communities* were important in a few cases. Kutchesfahani shows how Brazilian and Argentine scientists put the idea of a joint inspection agency on the agenda and designed how ABACC would operate. In the RERTR case, research studies sponsored by the IAEA and visits by foreign scientists to work with their counterparts at the U.S. Argonne National Lab helped convince foreign reactor operators that conversion to LEU fuel was technically feasible and would not cost as much as they feared.

Relevant transnational relationships included more than epistemic communities however. *Working-level relationships, including but not only among scientific and technical experts, have become a crucial ingredient in many successful endeavors.* This is a function of the shift toward more actively collaborative forms of cooperation. Many cooperative nonproliferation efforts involve operational activities, such as dismantling a former chemical weapons production facility, or other actions that require a degree of knowledge and expertise, such as crafting laws to criminalize the financing of proliferation. Many of these efforts require personnel from different states to work together. The same point can be made about the many diplomatic meetings that take place under the umbrella of the various cooperative nonproliferation arrangements. In some cases, the same individuals represent their states in multiple forums. The quality of these various working-level relationships has hence become a crucial factor in the likelihood that cooperative programs will be successful.

Kassenova's analysis of CTR demonstrates this clearly. She compares different specific CTR efforts, showing that some were implemented more effectively than others. This comparison reveals that the quality of working-level relationships, as well as their ability to remain insulated from higher level politics, played a major role in the varying success levels of different CTR programs. The lab-to-lab component of material protection, control, and accounting and the effort to improve materials protection at Russian nuclear navy sites both involved good relations between U.S. and Russian personnel and hence proceeded more smoothly than many other CTR projects.

At the same time, the impact of working-level relationships should not be overstated. Not everything can be accomplished at the working level. Government leaders and high-ranking diplomats still play crucial roles. For instance, although implementation of PSI involves working-level cooperation, Belcher notes that it took the efforts of President Bush with the support of other heads of state to get this project off the ground. Likewise, in the ABACC case, Kutchesfahani concludes that the epistemic community could not have succeeded without the strong support it received from Brazilian and Argentine leaders. And the nuclear security summits, like all summits, by definition involve heads of state or other senior officials. Indeed, President Obama initiated the summits in part as a way to bring high-level political attention and urgency to issues that cannot necessarily be moved forward by personnel at lower levels of state bureaucracies. Once the summit process was under way, however, implementation of commitments and planning for subsequent summits has required a lot of efforts by personnel at lower levels of government. The greatest progress, this suggests, is likely to come when high-level interest empowers individuals at the working level to connect with their counterparts in other countries to figure out how to implement cooperative programs and activities.

Inducements and persuasion have not been as significant as chapter 1 surmised they might be. Positive inducements have been offered to individual states in an effort to lure them away from nuclear programs, as in the example of the 1994 Agreed Framework with North Korea. But such "carrots" have not been used as prominently in efforts to elicit participation in cooperative arrangements. Many of the cases involve transfers of aid or other types of assistance, but these are intended to help recipients build capacity; they are not side payments offered in exchange for a state agreeing to join a nonproliferation initiative. Turpen suggests, however, that inducements and persuasion have played a role in the nuclear security summits. States perceived a positive incentive to participate in the 2010 summit as a way to make a favorable impression on President Obama at the height of his global popularity, and the summits have also been an opportunity to persuade state leaders that nuclear security deserves to be taken more seriously.

Inducements can be negative as well as positive, and negative incentives were applied successfully in some cases. Kuperman in particular emphasizes the role of *coercion* in the RERTR program. The U.S. program deliberately targeted reactors that would require a resupply of fuel that was available only from the United States. This provided great leverage to persuade operators to convert from HEU to LEU fuel.

The impact of *domestic politics* was also clearly apparent in several cases. In some cases, domestic politics functioned as a constraint that limited cooperation. The "buy American" provision that Congress attached to CTR funding, for example, proved problematic because U.S.-made goods did not always work in Russian installations. Anti-U.S. sentiment in public opinion in certain developing countries has also sometimes constrained governments from joining U.S.-sponsored cooperative activities. At the same time, the creation of multilateral mechanisms can offer a way for governments to overcome domestic constraints. Bowen and Heyes report that the fact multiple states made funding pledges to the GP helped officials in some of those states convince their legislatures to finance threat reduction programs.

As a final factor to consider, the list given to case study authors included *capabilities*. State capacity affects not a state's preferences but rather its ability to participate in and implement cooperative nonproliferation efforts. Capacity issues proved important in several cases, especially those such as 1540 that impose significant burdens on developing states.[6] As discussed below, some of the most important policy questions raised by this study involve how best to bring in and assist countries that have limited capabilities to meet the requirements being created by some of the newer nonproliferation initiatives.

Other Factors Proved Relevant

The list of factors proposed in chapter 1 did not turn out to exhaust all the relevant variables. Some case studies identified other factors that helped explain what happened in the case but were not part of the original analytical framework. This section highlights three sets of factors that emerged in certain cases.

First, Kassenova pointed to a constellation of factors that played roles in the CTR case, including geopolitics, interagency coordination problems, and cul-

Conclusions [305]

tural differences. To start with geopolitics, CTR involved cooperation between states that had just recently been Cold War rivals. As such, cooperation had to contend with lingering mistrust on both sides, which acted to slow down or stall implementation of certain programs.

The importance of geopolitics has become all the more clear since the CTR chapter was first drafted. Worsening U.S.-Russian relations and events in Ukraine have reduced cooperation on nonproliferation. In particular, Russia's expulsion from the G8 has effectively ended its involvement in the GP, and in late 2014 Russia also ceased any further participation in CTR projects. At the same time, however, it is important to recognize that geopolitical differences do not always prevent cooperation. Although the two sides have very different approaches to the conflict in Syria, Russia and the United States worked together to bring about Syria's renunciation of chemical weapons, and Russia continued to support the P5+1 approach to Iran even while the Ukraine crisis got worse. The GP has also continued to operate without Russia's participation. In general, however, these observations make it clear that cooperative nonproliferation projects will be affected, sometimes profoundly, by the impact of broader geopolitical currents in international politics.

If cooperative nonproliferation efforts increasingly involve working-level relationships across national boundaries, it makes sense that they can also require significant interagency coordination within states. Shortcomings in interagency coordination handicapped the implementation of CTR programs.[7] In addition, cultural differences in how the United States and Russia think about government programs created misunderstandings and amplified mutual mistrust.[8] This further hampered CTR implementation. Both interagency coordination and cultural similarity or difference seem likely to be relevant in many other cases as factors that can affect the quality of working-level relationships.

A second observation that emerges from several case studies is the role of actors other than states and their officials. The research for this project focused on interstate cooperation, and this may have led to an overly narrow focus on national governments as the actors. In several cases, however, academics and NGOs played important roles, especially as sources of ideas. The suggestions that led to both CTR and the nuclear security summits were developed initially at academic research centers. International organizations were also important actors in several cases. Along with individuals at certain NGOs, officials with the UN or regional organizations helped facilitate many of the regional NWFZ treaty negotiations. The IAEA has also taken on an increasingly active role in the nuclear security sphere, as has the World Institute for Nuclear Security (WINS), a partnership among governments, international organizations, academic experts, and the nuclear industry.[9] The WINS example shows that private actors can also play a role, as was also the case with nuclear operators in the RERTR program. An appropriate question for future research would be the ways in which international organizations, NGOs, and industry affect international cooperation on nonproliferation.

As a third factor worth noting, several case studies drew attention to regime design. This issue dovetails with a series of long-running debates, especially within U.S. domestic politics. Is it better to keep membership small or to seek the widest participation possible? Are informal arrangements or formal treaties better?

Perhaps not surprisingly, the case studies suggest mixed conclusions on these questions. In his analysis of export control regimes, Jones argues that informality has been an advantage, but not exactly for the reasons that traditional critics of multilateralism might expect. According to Jones, consensus-based decision-making rules have reduced the risks for new states contemplating joining the MECRs, enabling the regimes to expand their membership.[10] At the same time, the requirement to achieve consensus among a larger and more diverse set of states has led the regimes to put in place regular meetings and consultations and to accept compromises that make it possible to still reach consensus. Informality works, in short, because it has been paired with elements of institutionalization.

PSI is the paradigmatic case for advocates of more informal approaches. Its designers wanted it to be "an activity, not an organization." In her analysis of PSI, Belcher concludes that an informal, nonbinding approach did not prove to be an obstacle to establishing a cooperative project that successfully expanded its membership and helped establish a new norm. At the same time, she observes, states need to be careful about whom they exclude from the invitation to be part of a new initiative. According to Belcher, much of Russia's initial criticism of PSI reflected its unhappiness at not being asked to be a founding member, and Russia's position changed once it had the opportunity to join PSI.

In sum, regime design questions are important. The cases do not suggest, however, a single, one-size-fits-all approach. Both formal and informal cooperative mechanisms have achieved positive results. This implies it would be useful to move beyond ideological debates over whether to emphasize formal multilateral institutions or instead work informally through "coalitions of the willing." Both approaches can be effective, and the two can complement each other; indeed, sometimes one approach can start to take on characteristics of the other. Many of the initiatives examined in this project began as informal efforts by small groups of like-minded states, but over time grew in membership and developed more institutionalized features. In other cases, a small, ad hoc group of states essentially functions as an intermediary on behalf of a formal element of the regime, as is the case in diplomatic efforts to persuade Iran and North Korea to come into compliance with the NPT. Moreover, many of the

Conclusions [307]

informal initiatives would not be viable without the prior existence of formal treaties to give them legitimacy. For these reasons, it makes sense to get away from prevailing ideological cleavages in favor of a more pragmatic approach that utilizes both informal and institutionalized forms of international cooperation on WMD nonproliferation.

To sum up, this section has reported the findings in this volume regarding the sources of international cooperation on nonproliferation. Self-interest proved especially prominent, but a wide range of other factors also play major roles. Among these, the cases have highlighted the importance of both high-level leadership and working-level relationships. The other major goal of this project was to assess the effectiveness of cooperative nonproliferation efforts. The next section summarizes the key findings in this area.

EVALUATING EFFECTIVENESS

Assessing the effectiveness of cooperative nonproliferation activities proved to be the most challenging aspect of the project. Despite this, it is possible to draw some conclusions.

Cooperative Nonproliferation Has a Mixed
Record but Includes Some Major Successes

Nearly all the authors conclude that the cases they studied were at least partially successful, and some of the programs were judged highly successful. None of them were deemed a complete success. The ability to assess effectiveness more precisely than this, however, varied across cases.

The main difficulty is that it is not always possible to obtain clear information about whether or not program objectives have been achieved. But evidence is not always so hard to obtain, and in some cases positive achievements are even officially reported. For example, the Nunn-Lugar CTR program has long maintained a "scorecard" that lists how many warheads, missiles, bombers, submarines, and production facilities have been dismantled with assistance from CTR.[11] But more intangible CTR goals, such as scientist "redirect" away from weapons-related work or building a lasting security culture at key facilities, are harder to assess and hence do not appear on the scorecard.

Some cooperative endeavors include reporting requirements that make it possible to track progress, though with some uncertainty due to the fact that state reporting might not always be accurate. Most countries, for example, have now filed at least one report on their implementation of UNSCR 1540. As Ogilvie-White observed, summary tallies of the collected country reports show significant progress in meeting some benchmarks set out by 1540 while also revealing that many states lag behind in other areas. Progress has been especially slow in areas such as improving bio-security, establishing financial controls, and enforcing relevant laws through criminal prosecutions. Based on reports issued by the officials who worked on the RERTR program, Kuperman was also able to provide a count that showed many facilities were successfully converted to use of LEU fuel at an overall modest cost.

Even where a quantitative measure is not possible, one can identify clear successes in some efforts. For example, no country within a region covered by an NWFZ treaty has ever acquired nuclear weapons. Similarly, although ABACC does not always function smoothly, it was successfully created, it still exists, and it contributed in obvious ways to helping Argentina and Brazil move away from potential nuclear weapons programs.

Finally, it also possible to identify some outcomes that appear to be program failures. Syria received significant assistance from North Korea in constructing a nuclear facility that was eventually destroyed by Israeli bombing. The lack of discovery and interdiction of North Korean shipments to Syria can be interpreted as a failure for PSI. Similarly, in the case of the P5+1 negotiations with Iran, at the time Santoro completed his case study, the effort had so far failed to stop Iran from making continued progress toward a nuclear weapon capability, although that outcome could change if the deal reached in July 2015 is implemented successfully.

Although the overall record is mixed, even partial success can represent a positive contribution to nonproliferation. As John Holmes and Andrew Winner have pointed out with respect to PSI, 100 percent effectiveness is not necessary for the program to be worthwhile. As they note, "stopping even one catastrophic terrorist event or deadly weapons-related cargo may be deemed a success if it averts devastating consequences."[12] In short, even partial success contributes to nonproliferation and nuclear security goals, and in this sense the cases in this volume demonstrate that cooperative approaches to nonproliferation have value.

Cooperative Efforts Have Helped to Raise Awareness and Promote Norms

Whether or not it is possible to document specific achievements, there are good reasons to believe that the ways governments think and act today are different because of the range of international nonproliferation initiatives that have been launched. The various high-level meetings and outreach and assistance efforts undertaken have created greater awareness of the dangers associated with WMD proliferation, poorly secured nuclear or chemical materials, illicit trafficking networks, and transnational terrorist organizations.[13] Several of the case studies display a similar pattern: a new effort was met with initial criticism or resistance, but later became more widely accepted. This happened in the cases of the export control regimes, PSI, and efforts to promote nuclear security. Despite the skepticism or even hostility expressed by some states at first, over time the number of participating states increased and the new norms these measures sought to promote came to be more widely accepted as legitimate.

New initiatives can be especially effective in this regard when they interact in productive ways with existing institutions. Turpen credits the 2010 Nuclear Security Summit with giving a boost to efforts to complete the fifth revision of the IAEA's Information Circular 225, which lays out standards and best practices for physical protection of nuclear materials and facilities. The increased role of the IAEA in this area, including as a potential source of assistance, in turn helped make the whole notion of nuclear security more legitimate to states that had not welcomed initial U.S. and U.K. efforts to promote nuclear security as an objective.[14]

Proliferation Problems Would Likely Be Worse in the Absence of Cooperative Nonproliferation Activities

In any program assessment, it can be useful to consider the counterfactual question of what would have happened if the programs had never existed.[15] Although this is necessarily a thought experiment, it is hard to imagine that the world would be safer today if countries had not acted to create the various mechanisms for international cooperation on nonproliferation considered in this study. In the absence of export control regimes, CTR, PSI, and various regional initiatives and antiterrorism efforts, the record of WMD proliferation and its attendant risks would almost certainly have been worse.

This is likely true even in cases that many observers would judge to be nonproliferation failures. The EU-3 and P5+1 talks with Iran, which after ten years still had not halted Iran's nuclear program, are a case in point. First, as Santoro points out, cooperative nonproliferation efforts can have other benefits even when they fall short of their nonproliferation objective. In this case, P5+1 efforts helped restore multilateral cooperation among major powers as a viable option in the nonproliferation tool kit. Second, Santoro argues, in the absence of the outside diplomatic efforts, Iran would probably have proceeded even further down the road toward nuclear weapons. The diplomatic engagement with Iran sometimes convinced that country to slow down its nuclear activities for a time, and when Iran behaved more defiantly, the prior diplomatic efforts made it easier for the P5 to agree on imposing UNSC sanctions. Overall, the P5+1 effort succeeded in buying time to see if other developments would create more favorable conditions for resolving the Iran situation.

In short, although it proved impossible to quantify exactly the level of success in achieving their objectives or the extent to which this has contributed to reducing threats associated with proliferation, the various cooperative endeavors studied in this project have clearly made positive contributions. This makes it important to sustain them and to utilize them where appropriate. It also makes it important to consider how their performance might be improved.

POLICY RECOMMENDATIONS

Some policy-relevant conclusions have already emerged in this chapter. First, and most basic, cooperative approaches to nonproliferation can make valuable contributions. When states and international organizations confront potential proliferation risks, they should continue to consider cooperative arrangements such as those studied in this volume as potential options. Second, it would be helpful to get away from polarized ideological debates over the respective merits of formal, multilateral approaches versus informal, ad hoc efforts. Both can have merits depending on the situation, and they can be complementary. It hence does not make sense to commit to only one approach to international cooperation to the exclusion of the other. Two other policy-related issues merit further discussion.

The Needs and Perceptions of Developing Countries Have Become More Important

Although not all of the activities studied in this project seek the participation of all states, many of them aspire to recruit a broad range of members. Moreover, some, such as UNSCR 1540, do apply to all states. As a result, developing nations find themselves being asked to take on significant new burdens. Many of them do not perceive the same level of threat from proliferation and terrorism that the United States does. They also have limited resources and government capacities to take on some of the tasks being requested of them, and they have competing priorities in the areas of public health, education, and economic development.

As a result, capacity-building has become a crucial aspect of international cooperation on nonproliferation. This has led to a greater commitment to provide international assistance to countries that need it and efforts to help match donors and recipients. These assistance programs are crucially important and need to continue. At the same time, however, as Turpen highlights in her chapter, the donor-recipient model has become something of a double-edged sword. To the extent that developing countries have an expectation that wealthier nations will provide what poorer countries need to meet NBC security obligations, developing nations may be tempted to free ride on the efforts of the developed world, which could make them less likely to sustain commitments once assistance ends. The donor-recipient approach can also echo the division between nuclear "haves" and "have-nots" in the NPT, a situation that has long been a source of complaints among developing countries.

There is a need for creative thinking about how to avoid reinforcing existing cleavages in world politics, because this could eventually undermine support for international cooperation on nonproliferation. The cases examined in this project suggest two possible ways to deal with this issue. One option would be to do more work via intermediary organizations. As Ogilvie-White points out, acceptance of UNSCR 1540 increased once the 1540 Committee started to function and also after regional and subregional organizations were given larger roles. The nuclear security summits held to date have similarly called for an enhanced IAEA role in nuclear security. Global and regional organizations have potential advantages in terms of their legitimacy with and acceptability to developing countries. Having such organizations function as intermediaries between donor states and recipients could reduce the likelihood of reinforcing some of the cleavages associated with the NPT.

A second possible response involves reconsidering the framing of cooperative initiatives. The United States and other leading countries tend to describe them as being a response to the dangers posed by WMD proliferation and terrorism. Yet this framing does not necessarily resonate with states that see little threat to themselves from such dangers. In addition, the term "threat reduction" can have the unfortunate consequence of making it appear that the recipient of assistance is regarded as a threat to be reduced. A process of dialogue about the larger purposes and underlying principles of the cooperative endeavors might enable them to be reinterpreted in a way that would make them more attractive to developing countries. Something that emphasizes security instead of threat and that highlights shared responsibilities among equals might elicit greater support. For these reasons, Turpen proposes describing the initiatives as efforts to promote collective or global security rather than framing them narrowly around a nuclear security agenda.

Ogilvie-White also suggests drawing attention to the nexus of development and security. Many of the actions called for by 1540 could have development benefits that go beyond their contribution to improving WMD-materials security. If states improve their export and border controls and financial monitoring systems, they will be in a better position to participate in global trade. Various measures called for by 1540 could also help states combat crimes such as human and drug trafficking. Giving more attention to how some of the actions called for under cooperative approaches could address development objectives would make them more attractive to recipients of assistance.

Finally, it is important to recognize the existence of multiple and sometimes competing norms in this area. Non-nuclear-weapon states, especially those affiliated with the Non-Aligned Movement (NAM), attach great importance to the pillars of the NPT that emphasize access to peaceful uses of nuclear technology and the goal of nuclear disarmament.[16] Initiatives that impose new obligations in support of nonproliferation or that suggest a need to make nuclear security a "fourth pillar" of the nonproliferation regime sometimes provoke an almost reflexive negative response in the developing world. They are seen as upsetting the balance of reciprocal obligations between nuclear haves and have-nots. If non-nuclear states are going to be asked to do more on behalf of nonproliferation and nuclear security, they are going to look for evidence that nuclear weapons states are upholding their end of the NPT bargain. For this reason, the nuclear weapon states (which are also the P5 in the Security Council) can help smooth the way for developing countries to support cooperative nonproliferation arrangements by taking steps to demonstrate their continuing commitment to peaceful use and eventual nuclear disarmament.[17]

There Is a Need to Improve Integration among the Different Elements of Nonproliferation Cooperation

It can be surprising to realize how many different cooperative activities and initiatives exist that deal with the proliferation of NBC weapons and their means of delivery. Although this is good news about the international community's desire to lessen the dangers posed by such weapons, the sheer number of cooperative endeavors also creates complications. To put it simply, it is far from clear how all these activities are supposed to fit together.[18]

One problem is that participants are not the same across the different initiatives. Even the different export control regimes have slightly different memberships. If countries belong to different subsets of the various arrangements, it can be hard for governments to coordinate with each other because they have made varying sets of commitments. It also makes it hard to integrate the various initiatives because some countries participate in many of them while others are active in just a few.

Beyond these issues of coordination, there may be deeper frictions between different cooperative arrangements. Giovannini suggests that regional institutions sometimes reflect efforts to constrain or even oppose U.S.-dominated global institutions. An external reviewer for this project also proposed that there may be divergences between traditional nonproliferation measures and efforts that deal with nuclear security. Some observers also view the more informal, voluntary measures championed by the Bush administration as being in conflict with the traditional, treaty-based elements of the nonproliferation regime.[19]

These observations capture part of reality. Different nonproliferation measures can embody different principles and approaches and be favored by different sets of actors. Hence, they are unlikely to fit together completely smoothly, and some friction between alternative measures should be expected. However, this represents only one side of the equation. In other ways, the efforts can be interpreted as all being part of a common enterprise. They all share the goals of preventing the spread of NBC weapons and improving the security of WMD-related materials and expertise.

In part, this reflects functional drivers of cooperation. Whenever events have drawn attention to potential holes in existing arrangements or to potential new threats, certain states have promoted initiatives intended to address the newly recognized problems. Hence, the various cooperative arrangements that have been added over time can be seen as supplementary measures intended to fill in gaps in the foundational treaties, rather than as measures intended to bypass the treaties.

This is not the whole story, and there are still potential frictions between different nonproliferation measures. But there does seem to be an underlying trend toward greater embrace of nonproliferation and nuclear security norms. This does not exclude disagreements about relative priorities among the norms of the core treaties, as when NAM states call for doing more to fulfill the peaceful use and disarmament pillars of the NPT. Yet, the fact there is a normative dimension to developments, in the sense that they involve movement toward shared understandings of key goals and principles, adds an element of coherence to the nonproliferation project. This is not solely a functional story of states acting out of self-interest. It is complemented by a trend toward the spread and deepening of certain norms. All of this is reinforced by the development of transnational, working-level relationships, which help give a concrete reality to more abstract interests and norms.

Different forms of international cooperation on nonproliferation, taken collectively, can be described as making up a "regime complex."[20] This term refers to the presence of multiple, partially but not perfectly overlapping regimes that apply to the same issue area. Because memberships and rules vary, clashes across elements of the regime complex become possible. However, there is also enough commonality in the norms and purposes of the different regime components to give them some coherence. Maintaining coherence could be challenging, however, given just how complex the nonproliferation regime has become.

For those who care about achieving nonproliferation goals and enhancing global security, the key question raised by the complexity of the nonproliferation regime is how best to integrate its different components.[21] There is a need to work on finding the most effective way possible of fitting the different pieces together. Rather than launching new cooperative initiatives, governments today might be better served by taking a pause. The pause would be used to enter into dialogue to discuss what states see as the connections among different cooperative nonproliferation measures and how these fit into the broader global security architecture. If serious thought is not given to integration of the various activities, there is a risk that cooperative efforts will become incoherent or even begin to work at cross-purposes with each other. While the effort to improve integration is under way, it will also be important to continue the work of the individual cooperative initiatives for the practical contributions they can make to reducing proliferation dangers.

CONCLUSION: BUILDING COOPERATION

The international regimes that seek to prevent WMD proliferation rest upon foundations provided by global treaties: the NPT, BWC, and CWC. These treaties have not, however, removed every possible risk of proliferation. As a result, states have launched a variety of other efforts to address some of the remaining proliferation problems as well as new problems, such as possible WMD acquisition by terrorist groups, that have grown in salience since the key nonproliferation treaties were concluded. Many of these newer efforts require cooperation, and often multilateral cooperation, to achieve their objectives.

This study has described and compared a wide range of the additional cooperative endeavors that have arisen alongside the core nonproliferation treaties. It has identified the sources of this cooperation and assessed the effectiveness of these cooperative activities. In addition, the research conducted for this project produced one broad observation about the nature of nonproliferation cooperation. The core treaties all involve a commitment to self-restraint by each signatory. As such, they are primarily about policy coordination. In contrast, many of the cooperative efforts that have emerged since involve greater degrees of active collaboration. To the extent this is true, implementation is likely to involve something more than merely not doing something, such as not building weapons; implementation may actually require carrying out certain operational activities. This, in turn, is likely to put a greater premium on working-level relationships than was necessary when the key treaties were being negotiated.

Existing theories of cooperation do not entirely capture the type of cooperative nonproliferation activity that has developed in practice. Mainstream theories focus on what might be called "agreeing to cooperate"; they are concerned with whether negotiations result in an agreement, whether international institutions will be created or sustained, and whether individual states will agree to comply with cooperative arrangements. Social constructivists, in turn, focus on "constructing cooperation"; what they mean by this, however, is not physical construction but rather developments in the realm of ideas, that is, whether states construct shared norms and identities that lead them to favor cooperation. This study, in contrast, identifies a need to pay attention as well to what might be called "building cooperation."

States have been building cooperation on nonproliferation in several ways. First, as states come to perceive gaps or shortcomings in the existing set of nonproliferation arrangements, they build on these by creating new cooperative activities to address new or unresolved problems. Hence, the nonproliferation regime is getting built up over time. Second, as states have to figure out how to turn a new idea into reality, they have to build working-level relationships and operational capacities necessary to carry out a planned activity. Hence, cooperation is also being built in the very prosaic sense of being put together, piece by piece. Third, as cooperative activities get off the ground, states sometimes seek additional participants, thereby building up the circle of cooperating parties. Thinking in terms of the metaphor of "building cooperation" highlights these practical and operational issues in international nonproliferation activities. Future efforts to reduce the dangers from NBC weapons will benefit from actions to consolidate and integrate the cooperative nonproliferation initiatives that have been created to date as well as from efforts to build upon them further.

Notes

1. Thomas Hale, David Held, and Kevin Young, *Gridlock: Why Global Cooperation Is Failing When We Need It Most* (Cambridge: Polity Press, 2013).

2. Arthur A. Stein, "Coordination and Collaboration: Regimes in an Anarchic World," in *International Regimes*, ed. Stephen D. Krasner (Ithaca, N.Y.: Cornell University Press, 1983), 115–40.

3. Duyeon Kim, "2012 Nuclear Security Summit: What It Was and Wasn't," *Bulletin of the Atomic Scientists*, March 30, 2012, http://thebulletin.org/2012-nuclear-security-summit-what-it-was-and-wasn%E2%80%99t.

4. Only states that tested a nuclear weapon prior to January 1, 1967, can sign the NPT as a nuclear weapon state. Because India had not tested by that date, rather than join as a non-nuclear state it chose to stay out of the treaty so it could pursue a nuclear option without violating a treaty commitment.

5. "Knowledge, Power, and International Policy Coordination," ed. Peter M. Haas, special issue, *International Organization* 46, no. 1 (Winter 1992).

6. For another study that reaches the same conclusion, see Douglas M. Stinnett, Bryan R. Early, Cale Horne, and Johannes Karreth, "Complying by Denying: Explaining Why States Develop Nonproliferation Export Controls," *International Studies Perspectives* 12, no. 3 (August 2011): 308–26.

7. This is also the conclusion in Sharon K. Weiner, *Our Own Worst Enemy? Institutional Interests and the Proliferation of Nuclear Weapons Expertise* (Cambridge, Mass.: MIT Press, 2011).

8. Kassenova points out that U.S. officials cared more than their Russian counterparts about accounting and legal liability provisions in the CTR agreement. Russians, in turn, greatly valued stable, long-term relationships and were puzzled by the U.S. practice of regularly rotating personnel.

9. I thank an external reviewer for suggesting the relevance of this case. For more about WINS, see https://www.wins.org/ or www.nti.org/about/projects/wins/.

10. In their analysis of the GP, Bowen and Heyes reach a conclusion contrary to that of Jones about consensus-based decision making, arguing that the need to operate by consensus prevented the GP from effectively setting strategic priorities.

11. A periodically updated tally is maintained by the U.S. Defense Threat Reduction Agency at www.dtra.mil/Missions/Nunn-Lugar/scorecards.aspx.

12. John R. Holmes and Andrew C. Winner, "The Proliferation Security Initiative," in *Combating Weapons of Mass Destruction: The Future of International Nonproliferation Policy*, ed. Nathan E. Busch and Daniel H. Joyner (Athens: University of Georgia Press, 2009), 149.

13. This is also a finding of the Nuclear Threat Initiative, *NTI Nuclear Materials Security Index* (Washington, D.C.: Nuclear Threat Initiative, 2012).

14. See also Wyn Q. Bowen, Matthew Cottee, and Christopher Hobbs, "Multilateral Cooperation and the Prevention of Nuclear Terrorism: Pragmatism over Idealism," *International Affairs* 88, no. 2 (2012): 349–68.

15. I thank Wade Huntley, who made this observation at a workshop to discuss preliminary drafts of the case studies.

16. William Potter and Gaukhar Mukhatzhanova, *Nuclear Politics and the Non-Aligned Movement: Principles vs. Pragmatism*, Adelphi Papers 427 (London: Routledge, 2012).

17. Jeffrey W. Knopf, "Nuclear Disarmament and Nonproliferation: Examining the Linkage Argument," *International Security* 37, no. 3 (Winter 2012–13): 92–132.

18. I thank Christine Wing, who called attention to this question at a workshop to discuss preliminary drafts of the case studies.

19. For example, Oliver Meier and Christopher Daase, eds., *Arms Control in the 21st Century: Between Coercion and Cooperation* (New York: Routledge, 2013).

20. I thank Scott Jones for suggesting this term. For other applications of the regime complex concept, see Kal Raustiala and David Victor, "The Regime Complex for Plant Genetic Resources," *International Organization* 58, no. 2 (Spring 2004): 277–310; Robert O. Keohane and David G. Victor, "The Regime Complex for Climate Change," *Perspectives on Politics* 9, no. 1 (March 2011): 7–23; Amandine Orsini, Jean-Frédéric Morin, and Oran Young, "Regime Complexes: A Buzz, a Boom, or a Boost for Global Governance?," *Global Governance* 19 (2013): 27–39.

21. This is also an important theme in Harald Müller et al., *Non-proliferation "Clubs" vs. the NPT* (Swedish Radiation Safety Authority, report 2014:04, January 2014).

CONTRIBUTORS

EMMA BELCHER is director of the International Peace and Security Program at the John D. and Catherine T. MacArthur Foundation. Prior to arriving at MacArthur in 2011, she was a Stanton nuclear security fellow at the Council on Foreign Relations. She has a Ph.D. and MALD from the Fletcher School of Law and Diplomacy, Tufts University. She has also worked as an advisor to the Australian prime minister and cabinet on national security and international affairs, and as a public affairs officer at the Australian embassy in Washington, D.C. Her chapter was written in her personal capacity and the views expressed therein are her own.

WYN Q. BOWEN is professor of nonproliferation and international security and head of the Defence Studies Department, King's College London, at the Joint Services Command and Staff College, Defence Academy of the United Kingdom. He is also codirector of the Centre for Science and Security Studies, King's College London. He has written widely on issues related to proliferation and terrorism, including a 2006 Adelphi Paper on *Libya and Nuclear Proliferation: Stepping Back from the Brink*.

GAVIN CAMERON is an associate professor of political science and fellow of the Centre for Military & Strategic Studies (CMSS) at the University of Calgary. He has written primarily on terrorism and counterterrorism, as well as on U.K. and Canadian foreign policy. His publications include *Nuclear Terrorism: A Threat Assessment for the 21st Century* (Macmillan, 1999). He is also a contributing editor to the journal *Studies in Conflict & Terrorism*.

FRANCESCA GIOVANNINI is staff director for the Global Security and International Affairs Program at the American Academy of Arts and Sciences. She is also an associate to the Project on Managing the Atom at Harvard's Belfer Center for Science and International Affairs and an affiliate to the Center for International Security and Cooperation (CISAC) at Stanford University, where she was previously a MacArthur nuclear postdoctoral fellow. She completed her D.Phil. at Oxford University in 2012 in the Department of Politics and International Relations. Previously, she served as a postconflict state-building consultant for the Crisis Prevention and Recovery Network program and the United Nations Regional Pacific Center, Suva—Fiji Islands, and as resident coordinator analyst and postconflict state-building specialist for the UN Development Program in Beirut, Lebanon. She also served in the Gaza Strip, Turkey, and Ghana.

MICHAEL HAMEL-GREEN is an emeritus professor in social inquiry in the College of Arts at Victoria University, Melbourne, Australia. He is the communications editor of the Routledge journal *Global Change, Peace and Security*. His recent publications include

Australia's Disarmament Dilemma: Nuclear Umbrella or Nuclear-Free (International Law and Policy Institute, 2014); "Peeling the Orange: Regional Paths to a Nuclear Free World," *Disarmament Forum* (UNIDIR, 2011); "Paths to Peace on the Peninsula: The Case for a Japan-Korea Nuclear Weapon Free Zone," coauthored with Peter Hayes, *Security Challenges* (2011); and "Atomwaffenfreie Zone Arktis: Vorbilder und Perspektiven," *Osteuropa* (2011).

ALAN HEYES, now retired, is a former senior visiting research fellow in the Centre for Science and Security Studies, King's College London. Up to the end of September 2008, he was programme director for the United Kingdom's Global Threat Reduction Programme, which implemented and managed a portfolio of nuclear nonproliferation, security, and nuclear safety projects in the former Soviet Union, Libya, and Iraq.

SCOTT A. JONES is the executive director of the Center for International Trade and Security at the University of Georgia. He received his Ph.D. in political science and philosophy at the University of Georgia and an MA at Lancaster University in the United Kingdom. He has previously held positions at the Delegation of the Commission for the EU in Washington, D.C., and at Los Alamos National Laboratory. He is the author of *The Evolution of the Ukrainian Export Control System: State Building and International Cooperation* (Ashgate, 2002).

TOGZHAN KASSENOVA is an associate in the Nuclear Policy Program at the Carnegie Endowment for International Peace. She serves on the UN secretary general's Advisory Board on Disarmament Matters. Prior to joining the Carnegie Endowment, she worked as a senior research associate at the University of Georgia's Center for International Trade and Security in Washington, D.C., as a postdoctoral fellow at the James Martin Center for Nonproliferation Studies, and as an adjunct faculty member at the Monterey Institute of International Studies. She is the author of *From Antagonism to Partnership: The Uneasy Path of the U.S.-Russian Cooperative Threat Reduction* (2007) and *Brazil's Nuclear Kaleidoscope: An Evolving Identity* (2014).

JEFFREY W. KNOPF is a professor in and program chair of the M.A. in Nonproliferation and Terrorism Studies at the Middlebury Institute of International Studies (formerly known as the Monterey Institute of International Studies). He is also a senior research associate at the institute's Center for Nonproliferation Studies. Before this volume, his most recent book was a volume he edited on *Security Assurances and Nuclear Nonproliferation* (Stanford University Press, 2012).

ALAN J. KUPERMAN is an associate professor at the LBJ School of Public Affairs, University of Texas at Austin, where he is also coordinator of the Nuclear Proliferation Prevention Project. His latest book is *Nuclear Terrorism and Global Security: The Challenge of Phasing out Highly Enriched Uranium* (Routledge, 2013). Prior to his academic career, he worked as a U.S. congressional staffer and at the nongovernmental Nuclear Control Institute. He holds a Ph.D. in political science from the Massachusetts Institute of Technology.

SARA Z. KUTCHESFAHANI is a senior research associate at the Center for International Trade and Security (CITS) at the University of Georgia (UGA) and a part-time instructor at UGA's School of Public and International Affairs. Before coming to CITS, she worked at Los Alamos National Laboratory (LANL), where she was the only political science research associate among a pool of 440 at the laboratory. She holds a Ph.D. in political science from University College London. She is the author of *Politics and the Bomb: The Role of Experts in the Creation of Cooperative Nuclear Non-proliferation Agreements* (Routledge, 2014).

TANYA OGILVIE-WHITE is associate professor and research director at the Centre for Nuclear Non-Proliferation and Disarmament, Australian National University. Previously, she was senior analyst at the Australian Strategic Policy Institute, Canberra; Stanton nuclear security fellow at the International Institute for Strategic Studies, London; and senior lecturer in international relations at the University of Canterbury, Christchurch, New Zealand. Her publications include the edited collection *On Nuclear Deterrence: The Correspondence of Sir Michael Quinlan* (IISS/Routledge, 2011).

DAVID SANTORO is a senior fellow at the Pacific Forum CSIS, where he works on nuclear policy issues with a regional focus on the Asia Pacific and Europe. He is the author of *Treating Weapons Proliferation* (Palgrave, 2010) and coeditor, with Tanya Ogilvie-White, of *Slaying the Nuclear Dragon* (University of Georgia Press, 2012). He was educated in France and Australia.

ELIZABETH (LIBBY) TURPEN is the executive vice president of Octant Associates, a small woman-owned consulting firm. Before taking this position, she was a lead associate at Booz Allen Hamilton, where she provided policy and technical expertise to the Defense Threat Reduction Agency and National Nuclear Security Administration. From 2001 to 2009, Libby was senior associate at the Stimson Center, where she was primary author of the task force report *Leveraging Science for Security: A Strategy for the Nuclear Weapons Laboratories in the 21st Century*. Prior to joining Stimson, she served in the Office of Senator Pete V. Domenici (R-N.Mex.) as a legislative assistant. She holds a Ph.D. from the Fletcher School of Law and Diplomacy at Tufts University.

INDEX

ABACC, 2, 17, 216, 223, 229–47 passim, 296, 302–3, 308
Additional Protocol (AP), 16, 33, 210, 243–44, 272–74, 277, 287
Adeniji, Oluyemi, 214
Adler, Emanuel, 7, 236, 239
African NWFZ Treaty, 206, 209, 211, 213–14, 216, 218–21, 224–25
African Union, 209, 211, 213–14
Agreed Framework with North Korea, 303
Ahmadinejad, Mahmoud, 276, 279, 281, 287
Alatas, Ali, 213
Alfonsin, Raul, 232–33, 239–40, 242, 245–46
Algeria, 199
al Kibar, Israeli airstrike on, 131
Al-Qaeda, 98, 273
Alvim, Carlos Feu, 238
Andreeva Bay, 101–2
Antarctica, 208, 212–13, 217, 225; Antarctic NWFZ Treaty, 206, 208, 214, 217, 219, 221
ANZUS Treaty, 215
Apartheid Regime, 209, 212, 214
Aquino, Corazon, 216
Arak nuclear facility, 272, 275, 277
Aramar uranium enrichment facility, 233, 245
Archangelskiy, Nikolai, 56
Argentina, 2, 211–13, 215–16, 218, 220, 229–47 passim, 302–3, 308; ballistic missile program, 36; ICSANT and, 166–67; as motivation for export controls, 26; as PSI participant, 123; reactor conversion by, 51, 53, 62
Argentine Physics Association (AFA), 234–35
Argonne National Lab, 48, 52–53, 55–57, 60–61, 63–64, 66, 302
Armenia, 88
Arms Control Association, 194
Arms Trade Treaty, 28
ASEAN, 25, 153–54, 209, 216, 259, 263–65; ASEAN-U.S. Joint Declaration for Cooperation to Combat International Terrorism, 263; Convention on Counter Terrorism, 255, 258, 262, 265; Political-Security Community Blueprint, 265; Regional Forum, 154, 263
Aum Shinrikyo, sarin gas attack by, 126, 165
Australia, 103, 116–17, 119, 121, 123–26, 128–29, 169–70, 174, 207, 209, 212–13, 215
Australia Group (AG), 23–24, 27–28, 36, 38–39, 43n15, 122
Austria, 32
Axelrod, Robert, 8
Ayewah, Isaac, 214

Bali, Naren, 235
Bali bombing, 126, 263–64
Bangkok NWFZ Treaty. See Southeast Asian NWFZ Treaty
Bangladesh, 164, 224
BBC China, 128, 131
Beijing Convention (Convention on the Suppression of Unlawful Acts Relating to International Civil Aviation), 132, 134
Belarus, 72, 74–75, 79, 87–88, 92
Belfer Center at Harvard University, 184
Belgium, 54, 103, 297
Belize, 131
Bharatiya Janata Party (BJP), 129
Biden, Joe, 99
biological weapons, 1, 4, 11, 23, 97, 114n30, 163, 262, 294, 297; bio-security, 104–5, 109, 308; as focus of Australia Group, 27, 43n15, 122; as focus of CTR program, 72, 93n9; U.K. nonproliferation work regarding, 106; UNSCR 1540 and, 141–46, 149
Biological Weapons Convention (BWC), 1, 4, 18, 25, 142, 294, 297, 314
biotechnology, 39
Board of Governors (BOG) of the IAEA, 88, 273–77, 281, 283–85, 287

Bolton, John, 98, 116, 118, 120–22, 155–56, 300
border controls, 72, 142, 145–46, 261, 311;
    enhanced border monitoring for detection of nuclear and radiological materials, 105
Border Monitoring Working Group, 102
Bratislava Bush-Putin Summit, 78
Brazil, 2, 26, 36–37, 199, 211–13, 215–16, 218, 220, 229–47 passim, 255, 280, 286, 296, 302, 303, 308
Brazilian-Argentine Agency for Accounting and Control of Nuclear Materials. *See* ABACC
Brazilian Physics Society (SBF), 216, 234, 245
Brazilian Society for the Advancement of Science (SBPC), 235, 239
brokering provisions, 32, 37, 142, 146
Bunn, Matthew, 82
Burr amendment, 55
Bush, George H. W., 74
Bush, George W.: Global Partnership program and, 97–100, 112; ICSANT and, 165, 167; impact of 2004 reelection, 184, 275, 282; international criticism of, 155–56, 158, 185, 295, 301; preference for informal mechanisms, 312; PSI and, 2, 17, 116–18, 120–23, 128, 303; Putin and, 57, 78, 169; relations with France, 261; relations with Iran, 272–73; support for UNSCR 1540, 141
buy American provision, 77, 80, 89, 304

Cairo Declaration, 213
Cambodia, 117, 209, 255, 262
Canada, 56, 102–3, 280, 298; as founder of NSG, 26; ICSANT and GICNT and, 168–69, 175–77; as medical isotope producer, 54–55, 62, 194; Ministry of Foreign Affairs, 62; PSI and, 123; scientist redirection programs and, 88, 106; as sponsor of Global Partnership program, 97–99, 106–7, 109, 111, 177, 301
capabilities as explanatory factor, 14, 29, 72, 90, 125, 130, 141, 151, 156–57, 171, 173–74, 177, 266, 299, 304, 310
capacity-building, 3, 142, 148, 151–52, 154, 158, 169, 174, 186, 191, 198–99, 201–2, 310
Castro regime, 215
catch-all provisions, 32, 37
Center for Nonproliferation Studies (CNS), 216

Center for Policy Studies in Russia (PIR Center), 78
Centers of Excellence (COEs), 109, 192, 194, 198–201
Central Asian NWFZ Treaty, 206, 210–12, 214, 216–17, 219–21, 224–25, 299
Cheban, Alexander, 76
chemical weapons, 1, 4, 11, 23, 120, 122, 163, 165, 262, 294, 297; chemical security, 109, 308, 310–11, 313; dismantlement, 12, 72, 76, 93n9; 97–105, 109–12, 296, 302; elimination in Syria, 305; as focus of UNSCR 1540, 141–46; use in Iran-Iraq War, 27
Chemical Weapons Convention (CWC), 1, 4, 12, 18, 25, 43n15, 101, 294, 297, 314
China: espionage by, 81; GICNT and, 169, 171–72, 178, 300; NSG and, 31–33, 35; Nuclear Security Summits and, 194, 199; as nuclear weapon state, 207, 224, 255, 262; NWFZ treaties and, 219; P5+1 talks and, 271, 275–82, 284–86, 289; PSI and, 120–21, 125, 127, 132, 141, 171, 295; RERTR program and, 57, 63, 65, 302; UNSCR 1540 and, 127, 134, 141, 155, 157; U.S. sanctions on, 120
Chirac, Jacques, 262, 277, 282
Christmas Island, 212
civil society, 141, 207, 210, 215–16, 218, 220, 222–24
Clinton administration, 62, 120
closed cities, Russian, 78, 86–87, 91
coalitions of the willing, 136n3, 155, 164, 173, 188, 201, 306
coercion, 3, 10, 46–47, 52–55, 57, 60–61, 64–66, 304
Coll, Jorge, 238
collaboration, 8–12, 18, 251–52, 296–97, 302, 314; in Global Partnership program, 101, 104; involving Argentina and Brazil, 238–39, 244, 296; in MECRs, 23–25, 29, 31, 39–40, 297; in PSI, 124, 132, 135, 296; in UNSCR 1540, 141, 297
collective security, 183, 189, 191, 196, 259
Collor de Mello, Fernando, 233–34, 239, 243, 246
Commerce, U.S. Department of, 72
Common System of Accounting and Control (SCCC), 233, 237
communication: face-to-face, 8; institutions as

INDEX [323]

promoters of, 256; involving scientists, 235, 237, 240, 244; suasive, 14
Comprehensive Test Ban Treaty (CTBT), 1, 4, 206, 221, 297
conferral, 153, 158
Congo, 143
Congress, U.S., 53, 55, 65, 74, 77, 87, 89, 91, 99, 129, 168, 184, 304; House of Representatives, 74, 167, 176. *See also* Senate, U.S.
constructivism, social, 6–7, 13, 314
Contact Expert Group, 101
control lists, 23–25, 28, 30–31, 33, 35–37, 39–40, 144, 146, 297
Convention on the Physical Protection of Nuclear Materials (CPPNM), 163–65, 167, 171–72, 187–89, 192, 198
Convention on the Suppression of Unlawful Acts Relating to International Civil Aviation (Beijing Convention), 132, 134
cooperation, building of, 3, 18, 314–15
Cooperation Theory, 4, 6, 12–13, 18. *See also* international regimes, theories of
Cooperative Agreement for the Development and Application of the Peaceful Uses of Nuclear Energy, 232
Cooperative Threat Reduction (CTR), 2, 15, 17, 72–92 passim, 97, 103, 111–12, 184, 295–96, 298, 300–305, 307, 309; Soviet Nuclear Threat Reduction Act of 1991, 74
Coordinating Committee on Multilateral Export Controls (COCOM), 25–26, 28–30, 39
coordination, 8–11, 18, 230, 252, 296–97, 304–5, 312, 314; in ABACC case, 233, 246; in ASEAN, 263; in GICNT, 169, 172; in Global Partnership program, 100–102, 108–9; involving Nuclear Security Summits, 194, 196, 198–99, 201; involving UNSCR 1540, 140, 142, 148–49, 151, 154, 157–58; in MECRs, 23, 25, 29, 33, 35, 41; in PSI, 118, 124
Core Group, PSI, 120–23, 125–26, 131
counterterrorism, 17, 97, 140, 145, 148–49, 153–55, 157, 168, 171, 263, 265
Cox Report, 81
Crimea, 110, 143, 281, 295. *See also* Ukraine: crisis
Cuban Missile Crisis, 208, 212, 255, 266, 299

Cupitt, Richard, 29
Cyprus, 36
Czechoslovakia, 208

Daase, Christopher, 2, 10
Daniels, Paul, 213
defection, 6, 8, 32
Defense, U.S. Department of (DOD), 72, 78, 81
de Klerk, Frederick, 214
de Klerk, Piet, 35
Democratic People's Republic of Korea (DPRK), 23, 36–37, 61, 72, 117, 119–20, 124–27, 129, 131–32, 166, 223–24, 261, 273, 306, 308; Agreed Framework, 303; nuclear tests by, 126, 129; Six-Party Talks, 2
Denmark, 123
denuclearization, 72, 79, 207, 208, 210, 213, 217, 223
Deudney, Dan, 207
developing countries, 27, 47, 65, 140, 147, 150–52, 157, 191, 193, 241, 304, 310–12
development, economic, 27, 42n13, 128, 150, 152, 156–57, 160n34, 310–11
Dhanapala, Jayantha, 214
dialogue, 142, 149, 154, 189, 202, 222, 225, 230, 237, 244, 311, 314
diplomacy, 47, 61–63, 65, 67, 116, 127, 224, 262, 273, 275, 282–83
dirty weapons. *See* radiological materials, weapons, or attacks
disarmament, 4, 12, 97, 156, 158, 184, 186, 188–89, 193, 210, 214, 243, 260, 297, 312–13
dismantlement, 72, 75, 92, 98, 100–101, 103–5, 109
diversion, 51, 62, 74, 82, 92, 189
domestic politics, 6–8, 14–15, 99, 189, 282, 299, 304, 306; impact on CTR, 73, 77, 81, 89–91; impact on ICSANT, 167–68, 176; impact on PSI, 125, 128–29, 131, 135; impact on RERTR program, 54, 65; impact on UNSCR 1540, 155, 157; role in ABACC case, 240, 242; role in NWFZ negotiations, 207, 211, 215, 218, 222–23
donor-recipient model, 78, 183, 189, 191, 196, 198, 201, 310–11
dual use, 23, 25–27, 39, 45, 105, 125, 259

Eastern Europe, 25, 130
Egypt, 36, 125, 132, 166, 210; Cairo, 156, 213–14

Eisenhower, Dwight D., 213
ElBaradei, Mohamed, 278
Elimination of Weapons-Grade Plutonium Production Program, 103
Energy, U.S. Department of (DOE), 46, 50, 58, 62, 65, 72, 75–77, 80–81, 83, 85–88
enlargement, 11, 30, 117, 123, 135, 177, 301
enrichment, uranium: in Argentina and Brazil, 233, 238–39, 243, 245; in Iran, 271–72, 276–81, 287–88; reduced in German reactors, 65; relation to ability to produce nuclear weapons, 26, 48; in Soviet-supplied reactors, 50, 56–57, 61; URENCO as producer, 193; USEC management in United States, 85. *See also* enrichment and reprocessing technology; highly enriched uranium; low-enriched uranium
enrichment and reprocessing technology (ENR), 26, 30, 31, 33, 35, 42n12, 273–75, 277–78, 285–87
environmental concerns, 25, 29, 31, 41, 75–76, 82, 91, 99, 105, 126–27, 165, 198, 220, 222, 231
epistemic communities, 7, 13, 17, 55, 64, 66, 81, 132, 134–35, 196, 210, 215–16, 223, 229–47 passim, 302–3
Epstein, William, 211, 213
Esfandiary, Dina, 288
E3 (European Three; also discussed as EU-3), 17, 271–79, 282–89, 301, 309
European Bank for Reconstruction and Development (EBRD), 102
European Strategy Against the Proliferation of Weapons of Mass Destruction (EU WMD Strategy), 254–55, 258–62
European Union (EU), 23, 28, 88, 97, 143, 152, 170, 182, 199, 259–61, 273, 280–82; commission, 36; Common Military List, 39; Dual-Use Control List, 39; membership, 36, 39, 102, 282
Exclusive Economic Zones (EEZs), 209, 219
export controls, 23–41 passim, 105, 141, 151, 297; regimes, 9, 17, 23–41 passim, 295–96, 306, 309, 312
Ezeiza nuclear facility, 233, 245

Fernandez-Moreno, Sonia, 237–38
Figueiredo, João Baptista de Oliveira, 232, 242
Fiji, 209, 317

Finland, 99, 105, 170
fissile material, 4, 51, 79, 80–82, 85, 97–98, 104, 106, 108–9, 112, 182–84, 187, 192, 196–97
Fissile Material Cutoff Treaty (FMCT), 4, 297
Fitzpatrick, Mark, 288
Former Soviet Union (FSU), 2, 72–92 passim, 98–100, 103–4, 106, 110, 112, 164–65, 210, 214
Foz de Iguaçu Joint Declaration (1985), 232, 234
Foz de Iguaçu Joint Declaration (1990), 216, 233, 237
Framework Agreement on a Multilateral Nuclear Environmental Program (2003), 76
France, 58, 155, 169, 199, 207; as NSG member, 26; nuclear fuel fabrication in, 64, 66, 280, 297; nuclear reactors in, 54, 63; nuclear testing by, 219–20; participation in Global Partnership, 97, 106; participation in PSI, 116, 120–23, 261; as part of E3, 271, 273, 282; as part of P5+1, 277–80; role in EU WMD strategy, 258–62
free-rider problem, 191, 257, 310
fuel cycle, nuclear, 26, 56, 80, 170, 229, 271, 273–77
Fukushima disaster, 197

Gaddafi, Muammar, 131
Gahlaut, Seema, 28
G8. *See* Group of Eight (G8)/Group of Seven (G7)
Georgia, Republic of, 88, 106, 279
Germany, 208, 259–60; coalition government in, 57; connection to A. Q. Khan, 128, 131; diplomatic interaction with United States over reactor fuel, 58, 62; nuclear fuel development by, 66; nuclear reactors in, 54, 57–58, 62–63, 65, 67, 68n31; as part of E3 and P5+1, 2, 271, 273, 277–78, 282; as part of NSG, 26; role in GICNT, 169; role in Global Partnership program, 106–8; role in PSI, 116, 120–21, 123, 131
Gerstl, Alfred, 265
gift baskets, 194, 196, 198–99, 200–201, 297
Gil, Vicente Espeche, 235, 237
Global Cleanout, 184. *See also* Global Lockdown
Global Initiatives for Proliferation Prevention, 87–88

Global Initiative to Combat Nuclear Terrorism (GICNT), 134–35, 163–65, 169–79, 186–88, 190, 300–301; Plenary, 169; Statement of Principles, 169
Global Lockdown, 183–85, 189, 196
Global Partnership Against the Spread of Weapons of Mass Destruction (GP), 17, 97–113 passim, 172, 175, 177, 187, 192, 295, 301–2, 304–5
Global South. *See* developing countries
Global Threat Reduction Initiative (GTRI), 46, 66
Goh, Chok Tong, 264
Goldblat, Jozef, 216
Goldemberg, Jose, 239
Gorbachev, Mikhail, 73
Gosatomnadzor, 77, 80
Graduated Reciprocation in Tension Reduction (GRIT), 8, 14
Graham, Thomas, Jr., 218
Greece, 123
Gremiikha, Russia, 101
Grenoble, 54, 58
Gridlock, 295–96
Grillot, Suzette R., 29
Group of Eight (G8) / Group of Seven (G7), 17, 26, 31, 97–102, 104–13, 143, 152, 171, 175, 177, 187, 192, 295, 305
Guadalajara Agreement of 18 July 1991, 232–33
Gulf War (1991), 260

Haas, Peter, 7, 230–31, 234, 236, 239
Hague Code of Conduct (HCOC), 28
Hague Gift Basket on Strengthening Nuclear Security Implementation, 194, 197–98, 200
Hague Summit. *See* Nuclear Security Summits
Halperin, Morton, 224
Harvard University, 73–74, 184
haves versus have-nots, 189–91, 311–12
Hawke, Robert, 213
Hayden, Bill, 213
hegemony: cooperative hegemony, 257; hegemonic actor, role of, 7, 13–14, 175, 207, 214, 301; hegemonic regimes, 251, 253; regional hegemons, 229, 265; U.S. hegemonic position, 89, 125, 150, 155, 157, 265–66, 282
highly enriched uranium (HEU): as focus of Nuclear Security Summits, 186–87, 192–94;

HEU Purchase Agreement, 76, 79, 84–85, 90; reducing use as reactor fuel, 17, 46–67, 105, 193, 297, 301, 304; Soviet stocks of, 79–80; use in medical isotope production, 50–51, 53–55, 62–63, 194, 280
Hoehn, William E., 104
Holmes, James, 127, 129
Holmes, John, 308
Holy See, 125, 130
Hormuz, Strait of, 281
house gifts, 186, 189, 194, 200, 297
House of Representatives, U.S., 74, 167, 176. *See also* Congress, U.S.
Hungary, 110
Hurrell, Andrew, 266
Hussein, Saddam, 260

ideas and ideational factors, 7, 13, 98, 111, 125, 174, 177, 230, 237–40, 246, 266, 298–99, 302, 305, 314
identity, role of, 13, 34, 36, 89, 98, 110–11, 125, 129–30, 168, 193, 195, 221, 241, 257, 299
illicit trafficking, 116–19, 124, 133–34, 141–42, 170, 173, 187, 193, 298–99, 308. *See also* smuggling, nuclear
Implementation and Assessment Group (IAG) of the GICNT, 169–70, 190
Implementation Support Unit, Biological Weapons Convention, 142
incentives, 7, 14, 29, 84, 254, 303–4; offered to Iran, 273, 276–77, 279, 285; in PSI, 129–30, 133; in relation to NWFZs, 222–24; in RERTR program, 60–61, 65
Independent and Nuclear Free Pacific Movement, 215
India, 27, 224; Indian Ocean, 125, 129; ISCANT and GICNT and, 167, 171, 178; NSG waiver for, 32; Nuclear Security Summits and, 182, 194, 199; nuclear test (1974), 1, 26, 298; nuclear tests (1998), 129; PSI and, 125, 127, 129, 132; seeks NSG membership, 33, 35–36, 129, 295, 300; U.S.-India nuclear deal, 30, 32, 129
Indonesia, 62, 125, 128–29, 131–32, 213, 216, 255, 258–59, 262–65, 295
Information Circular (INFCIRC) 225, 187, 197–98, 204n41, 309
Information Circular (INFCIRC) 254, 27

information sharing, 29–30, 32, 37, 40, 64, 130, 133, 168, 173, 237, 244, 256
Initiatives for Proliferation Prevention (IPP), 76, 79, 86–88
institutionalization, 27, 135, 154, 200, 232, 234, 240, 242, 257, 306–7
intelligence, 10, 37, 117–19, 123, 131, 260, 263–64, 279, 287, 296
interdependence, 57, 257, 266
interdiction, 10, 116–24, 126, 128, 130–36, 262, 296, 308
interests. *See* self-interest
Inter-Laboratory Board, 87
International Atomic Energy Agency (IAEA), 1, 9, 102, 142, 148, 152, 210; ABACC and, 232–33, 237, 242–43; director-general (DG), 277, 283; Iran and, 272–74, 277–78, 280–81, 283–85, 287; NSG and, 27; nuclear security and, 102–4, 108, 113, 170, 172, 176, 182, 186–90, 192–94, 196, 198–201, 220, 305, 309, 311; Nuclear Security Training and Support Centre Network, 199–200; RERTR program and, 55, 57, 65, 67, 302; safeguards, 26, 33, 61, 189, 206, 210, 220, 229, 239, 246; statute, 283, 285
International Code of Conduct, 28
International Convention for the Suppression of Acts of Nuclear Terrorism (ICSANT), 17, 163–69, 171–73, 175–78, 187–89, 192, 295
International Convention on International Terrorism, 166
International Court of Justice, 167
International Geophysical Year (1957–58), 208
international law, 116, 118, 122, 124, 126–27, 141, 150, 153, 167
International Maritime Organization, 134, 152
International Network for Nuclear Security Training and Support Centers, 199
international regimes, theories of, 6–7, 18, 24, 29–31, 33–36, 41, 150, 231, 251, 253, 266, 306, 313
International Relations (IR), 4, 250, 317
International Science and Technology Center (ISTC), 76, 79, 86, 88–89, 106
Interpol, 152, 170, 193
Ipero Joint Declaration on Nuclear Policy (1988), 232–33

Ipero nuclear complex, 233, 245
Iran, 166, 210, 223, 261; interdiction efforts toward, 120, 127, 131; Iranian Revolutionary Guard Corps, 278; missile programs, 36; nuclear negotiations with, 2, 15, 17, 271–89, 301, 305–6, 308–9; UN Security Council resolutions concerning, 23, 37, 271–89; U.S. 2007 National Intelligence Estimate (NIE) on, 279, 286
Iran-Iraq War, 27
Iraq War, 119–20, 155, 261, 276; U.S.-led invasion, 273, 283–84
Ireland, 32
Ishiguri, Tsutomu, 211, 214
Israel, 36, 210, 308
Italy, 102, 106, 116, 121, 123, 131, 166, 169, 199

Jalili, Saeed, 278
Japan, 26, 66, 88, 99, 103, 105–6, 169, 194, 199, 211, 224, 280; Fukushima disaster, 197; PSI and, 116, 119, 121, 123, 126, 129
Jenkins, Bonnie, 174
Job, Brian L., 263
Joint Declaration on the Denuclearization of the Korean Peninsula, 223
Joint Plan of Action, 281
Joint Working Group on Nuclear Affairs (JWG), 25, 232–34, 236–40, 242–44
Joyner, Christopher, 172–73

Kananaskis Summit (2002), 97–98, 104–7, 109, 112
Kansas City Plant, 87
Karimov, Islam, 214
Karp, Aaron, 37
Kazakhstan, 72, 74–75, 79, 87–89, 92, 99, 108
Kelly, James, 263
Keohane, Robert, 8, 253
Kerry, John, 184
Khan, A. Q., 2, 36, 128, 131, 193, 298
Korean Peninsula, 124, 126–27, 197, 210, 223
Kusuma-Atmadja, Mochtar, 213
Kyrgyzstan, 88, 210

laboratory-to-laboratory relations, 64, 80–82, 90, 303
Lange, David, 213
Laos, 209

INDEX [327]

Larijani, Ali, 278
Latin American NWFZ Treaty, 206, 208–9, 211, 216–20, 223–24, 229, 233, 236, 241–42, 255, 299; LANWFZ Protocol 2, 219
leadership, 7, 14, 89, 140, 158, 168, 173, 194, 225; in CTR, 89; in Global Partnership program, 98, 109, 111; ICSANT and GICNT and, 164, 175; in MECRS, 34, 41; not necessary in talks with Iran, 282, 289; Nuclear Security Summits and, 183, 185, 195, 197, 201; in PSI, 125, 135, 140; by regional actors, 207, 214–15, 222, 253–55, 258–59, 262–64, 266, 301; in RERTR program, 46, 52, 57, 64; Russian, 171, 177, 301; in UNSCR 1540, 150, 155–57; U.S., 13, 208, 251, 261, 299–301
learning, 10, 13, 299, 302; in ABACC case, 231, 240; in Global Partnership program, 98, 102, 111, 302; in NWFZS, 222; in Nuclear Security Summits, 183, 195, 201; in P5+1, 282, 289; promoted by GICNT, 176; in RERTR program, 57, 64, 302; role in MECRS, 24, 32, 34–36, 40–41, 302; role in PSI case, 120, 125, 128, 132; in UNSCR 1540, 140, 149, 151, 157–58
Lee, Myung-bak, 129, 192–93
Lesotho, 143
Liberia, 143
Libya, 106, 128, 131, 212
Lichtenstein, 125
Lipson, Michael, 28
London, 26, 235, 277; 2005 terrorist attack in, 261
London Club, 26
loose nukes, 165, 298
low-enriched uranium (LEU), 47–63, 65–67, 80, 84–85, 105, 192, 194, 280, 297, 301–2, 304, 308; silicide fuel, 56–57; ultra-high-density, 58, 66
Lugar, Richard, 74, 89, 98, 184, 301
Luongo, Kenneth, 104

Malacca, Strait of, 124–25, 128
Malawi, 143
Malaysia, 128, 216, 264, 281
Marshall Islands, 212
Martin, Lisa, 14
Marzo, Marco, 235–36, 238, 240, 243
Maslin, Evgenii, 77

Material Protection, Control, and Accounting (MPC&A), 75–76, 79–83, 90, 170, 303
Matos, James, 55, 59
Mauzy, Diane K., 263
medical isotopes, 50–51, 53–55, 59, 63, 65, 194, 280
Megatons to Megawatts Program, 76, 84; HEU Purchase Agreement, 76, 79, 84–85, 90
Meier, Oliver, 2, 10
Menem, Carlos, 233–34, 243, 246
Mexico, 56, 170, 213, 215, 224, 255; Mexico City, 170
Middle East, 170, 223, 287
Middle East WMD-free zone (WMDFZ), 207, 210, 223, 225
missiles: antiaircraft, 280; ballistic, 27, 36, 76, 214, 261; SCUD, 117; S-300, 280
Missile Technology Control Regime (MTCR), 23–24, 27–28, 36–39, 122
mistrust. See trust
mixed oxide (MOX) fuel, 83–84
Modi, Narendra, 129
Moritán, Roberto Garcia, 237, 239
Morocco, 169, 170, 174
Mousavian, Seyyed Hossein, 274
Müller, Harald, 2
multilateral export control regimes (MECRS), 17, 23–41 passim, 295, 297, 302, 306
Myanmar, 131, 209

Natalegawa, Marty, 213
Natanz nuclear facility, 272–73
national interests. See self-interest
National Security Council (NSC), U.S., 118, 212
National Security Strategy, U.S. (2010), 135
NATO, 208, 260
negative security assurances, 208, 211, 219, 221–23
neoliberalism, 4–7, 13
neorealism, 6–7, 13, 250
Netherlands, 54, 62, 116, 121, 123–24, 170, 182, 192–93, 197; HFR-Petten reactor, 54. See also Nuclear Security Summits
New Guinea, 209
New Lines for Action to Combat the Proliferation of Weapons of Mass Destruction and Their Means of Delivery, 258, 261

New York, 147
New Zealand, 32, 123, 152, 166, 168, 176–77, 209, 213, 215
9/11 attacks, 2, 17, 125–26, 163–65, 198, 272, 294, 296, 298; effects on CTR program, 78; European security and, 260–61; impact on RERTR program, 46; as impetus for Global Partnership, 97–98, 100, 111–12; as impetus for UNSCR 1540, 141, 150; Southeast Asia and, 262, 264
Non-Aligned Movement (NAM), 155, 167, 194, 276–77, 284–86, 312–13
nongovernmental organizations (NGOs), 54, 143, 152, 154, 157, 195, 210, 215, 305–6
noninterference norm, 153, 158
nonproliferation principle, 31–32
non-state actors, 3, 17, 40, 72, 79, 85, 116, 122, 125–26, 131, 140–42, 147–48, 154, 163, 296, 298
Nordion, 54, 62
norms, 2, 6–7, 13, 234, 252–53, 266–67, 298–99, 301–2, 308–9, 312–14; in CTR case, 89; in Global Partnership case, 98, 111; in ICSANT and GICNT cases, 164, 168, 173, 175–76; as motivation for E3, 282, 289, 301; nonproliferation, 10, 18, 129–30, 133, 207, 218, 222, 313; promoted by Nuclear Security Summits, 183, 185, 195, 201; in PSI case, 125, 129–30, 133–36, 306; in relation to NWFZ treaties, 207, 211, 217–18, 222, 225, 302; in relation to UNSCR 1540, 148, 150, 152–53, 157–58; in RERTR case, 47, 52, 57–60, 63, 65–66, 301; role of, in MECRS, 24, 29–31, 34–37, 40–41
Northeast Asia, 125, 207, 210, 223–24
North Korea. *See* Democratic People's Republic of Korea (DPRK)
North-South Dynamic, 155–56, 189, 223
Norway, 88, 99, 102–3, 105, 123
no undercut provision, 39–40
nuclear and WMD materials: loose nukes, 165, 298; verifying inventories in Argentina and Brazil, 237, 239, 243. *See also* Cooperative Threat Reduction; fissile material; Global Partnership; Nuclear Security Summits
—efforts to secure, 2–3, 9, 11, 17, 255–59, 262, 264, 294, 296–97, 299, 303–5, 308–9, 311–13; through CPPNM and ICSANT, 163–67, 172–73; through CTR program, 72, 74–76, 79–85, 89–90, 92; through GICNT, 170–73, 175–76; through Global Partnership, 97–99, 101–6, 108–9, 112; through interdiction, 116–23, 127–28, 131–34; through Nuclear Security Summits, 182–202 passim; through UNSCR 1540, 140–41, 144–45, 148–49
Nuclear Cities Initiative (NCI), 76, 79, 85–88
Nuclear Control Institute, 65
nuclear cooperation agreements, 61, 232–33, 242, 246
nuclear energy, 27, 32–33, 76, 84, 156, 174, 182, 186, 188, 193, 220, 232, 234, 256, 262, 287. *See also* reactors, nuclear
Nuclear Exporters Committee (Zangger Committee), 26–27
Nuclear-Free Philippines Coalition, 216
nuclear fuel, 26, 35, 101, 170, 229, 271, 275; mixed oxide, 83–84; spent, 26, 56, 60, 62, 65, 86, 100–102, 286
Nuclear Non-Proliferation Treaty (NPT), 1, 3, 16, 18, 25–27, 118, 166, 175, 206–7, 219, 223, 272, 288, 294, 297, 299, 306, 311, 314; Article III, 26; Article IV (peaceful-use provision), 13, 27, 33, 274, 276; Article VI, 190; as case of coordination not collaboration, 4, 9–10, 252; enforcement, 17, 271, 283–84; nonparties and states joining late, 2, 26, 32–33, 36, 126–27, 167, 178, 182, 214, 218, 229, 232–33, 236, 241–42, 246, 300; relation to PSI, 133; Review Conferences, 184, 210, 224; three pillars, 156, 158, 186, 188, 264, 312–13
Nuclear Posture Review, 184
Nuclear Regulatory Commission, U.S. (NRC), 50, 52–53, 61, 63
nuclear security. *See* nuclear and WMD materials: efforts to secure; Nuclear Security Summits
Nuclear Security Fund (NSF), 102–3
Nuclear Security Summits (NSS), 2, 17, 84, 103, 105, 134, 168, 172–73, 176, 180, 182–202 passim, 297, 303–5, 309, 311
Nuclear Suppliers Group (NSG), 1, 23–28, 30–33, 35–36, 38–39, 122, 129, 206, 229, 233, 242, 244, 295, 298, 300; *Guidelines*

INDEX [329]

for Transfers of Nuclear-Related Dual-Use Equipment, Material and Related Technology, 27
nuclear terrorism. *See* terrorism: nuclear
nuclear testing. *See* testing, nuclear
Nuclear Threat Initiative (NTI), 99
nuclear-weapon-free zones (NWFZs), 17, 206–25 passim, 229, 254–55, 262, 265–66, 295, 299, 301–2, 305, 308
Nunn, Sam, 73–74, 89, 188, 301
Nunn-Lugar Cooperative Threat Reduction Program. *See* Cooperative Threat Reduction (CTR)

Oak Ridge National Laboratory, 56
Obama, Barack: administration of, 16, 83–84, 165; CTR and, 103–4, 184; efforts to improve U.S. international image, 155–56, 158, 185, 195, 301; Iran and, 279, 281–82, 286; Nuclear Security Summits and, 2, 17, 173, 182–86, 192–93, 195, 197, 201, 303–4; NWFZ protocol ratification and, 219, 221; PSI and, 128, 132, 135, 175
Ochirbatthe, Punsalmaagin, 214
OPANAL, 208, 223
operational activities, 18, 116, 133, 135, 240, 246, 302, 314
Operational Experts Group (OEG) of the PSI, 117, 123, 126, 128, 130, 132, 135
operational level, 101, 104, 113
Organization for the Prohibition of Chemical Weapons (OPCW), 1, 43n15, 142, 148, 152
Organization of African Unity (OAU). *See* African Union
Orlov, Vladimir, 76
Osgood, Charles, 8

Pacific Island Countries, 150, 209
Pacific Security Fund, 152
Pakistan, 36, 57, 61, 125, 127–29, 166, 182, 194, 224, 261
Papua New Guinea, 209
peaceful use, 27, 156, 158, 186, 188, 232, 312–13. *See also* Nuclear Non-Proliferation Treaty: Article IV
Pedersen, Thomas, 257
Pelindaba Treaty. *See* African NWFZ Treaty
Perkovich, George, 288

Permanent Committee on Nuclear Affairs (PCNA), 232–40, 242–44
persuasion, 3, 14, 29, 157, 183, 186, 195, 201, 282, 299, 303–4
P5, 120, 124–25, 141, 271–89 passim, 309, 312
P5+1, 2, 15, 17, 271–72, 275, 277–89, 301, 305, 308–9
Philippines, 110, 207, 209, 213, 215–16, 263
Phleger, Herman, 213
piggybacking, 100, 102–4, 113
Pilcaniyeu uranium enrichment facility, 233, 239, 245
Piot, Peter, 222
PIR Center (Center for Policy Studies in Russia), 78
plutonium, 26, 76, 79–80, 82–84, 103, 105–6, 186–87, 194, 202, 271–72, 274, 298
Plutonium Management and Disposition Agreement (PMDA), 76, 79, 83–84, 91, 105
Poland, 116, 121, 123, 130, 132, 208
Pomper, Miles, 176
Portugal, 116, 121, 123
positive incentives. *See* incentives
Potter, William, 216
Prague speech, by Obama in 2009, 139, 175, 182–86, 195
Preparatory Commission for the Denuclearization of Latin America, 208
Prisoner's Dilemma (PD), 6, 8
Proliferation Security Initiative (PSI), 2–3, 10–11, 17, 116–36 passim, 172, 175, 188, 206, 295–96, 300, 303, 306, 308–9; China and, 120, 125, 127, 132, 141, 171, 178, 295, 300; Core Group, 120–23, 125–26, 131; France and, 116, 120–23, 261–62; Interdiction Principles, 116, 122–23, 262
proposal-making, 30, 117, 119, 135
Protocol to the Convention for the Suppression of Unlawful Acts Against the Safety of Maritime Navigation (SUA Protocol; 2005), 132, 134
psychology, 6–8, 75, 90
Putin, Vladimir, 57, 78, 169
Putnam, Robert, 8

Quadripartite Safeguards Agreement, 232–33, 236, 242, 244

radioactive fallout, 212, 215, 221
radioactive material, 102, 165–66, 172–73, 187, 202, 217
radiological materials, weapons, or attacks, 97, 104–5, 108–9, 165, 170, 172, 174, 184, 193–95, 197
Rafsanjani, Akbar Hashemi, 276
Rammell, Bill, 279
Rao, Nirupama, 171
Rapacki, Adam, 208
Rapacki Plan, 208, 224
Rarotonga NFZ Treaty. *See* South Pacific Nuclear-Free Zone Treaty
Razak, Datuk Seri Najib Tun, 128
reactors, nuclear, 9, 17, 26, 83, 297; Advanced Neutron Source, 58; barge-mounted "floating," 60; conversions from HEU to LEU fuel in relation to nuclear security summits, 192–93; FRG-1, 57, 63, 65; FRJ-2, 54; FRM-II, 54, 58, 62, 65, 67; heavy water for Iranian, 272, 275, 277, 287; HFR-Petten, 54; India's use of plutonium from, 26, 298; low- or zero-power, 53; naval propulsion, 165; Orphee, 54; ORR, 56; PARR, 57; pulsed, 51, 66; research, 46–67, 105, 275–76, 287, 298; RHF-Grenoble, 54; Tarapur, 35; Tehran Research, 280; TRIGA research, 56; University of Michigan Ford, 56
Redick, John, 215, 216, 218, 241
Red Sea, 124
Reduced Enrichment for Research and Test Reactors (RERTR), 17, 46–67 passim, 301–2, 304–5, 308
relative gains, 4, 6
reprocessing, 26, 33, 238, 274–75, 277–78, 285–87
Republic of Korea (ROK; South Korea), 170, 199, 207, 224, 280; ballistic missile test (1978), 27; contributions to threat reduction programs, 88, 103; PSI and, 120, 123–24, 126, 129; Seoul nuclear security summit, 172, 176, 182, 192–94, 197, 199–200, 297
Resende-Santos, Joao, 239
Rice, Condoleezza, 131, 275
Rice, Susan, 156
Robles, Alfonso Garcia, 213, 217

Roh, Moo-Hyun, 129
Russia, 35, 155, 184, 192, 194, 197, 206–7, 209–10, 212–14, 219, 255; CTR and, 72–92 passim, 300, 305; downturn in relations with West, 17, 73, 76, 92, 110, 143, 195, 279, 281, 295, 305; Duma, 84; Global Partnership program and, 97–114 passim, 305; Ministry of Atomic Energy, 77, 80; Ministry of Defense, 76–77; Navy, 82–83, 90, 303; as part of P5+1, 271, 275–82, 284–86, 289, 305; PSI and, 120–21, 123–24, 126, 131, 300, 303–4, 306; RERTR program and, 50–52, 54, 57, 59–67, 302; as sponsor of ICSANT and GICNT, 164, 167, 169–71, 173–76, 178, 301

safeguards, 2, 16, 26–27, 31–33, 61, 79, 189, 206, 210, 220, 229, 232–40, 243–46, 272–73, 276, 283–85, 289
Sagan, Scott, 3
Sarkozy, Nicolas, 261–62, 277, 279, 282
Sarney, Jose, 232–33, 239, 242, 245–46
Sarov, 86
Saudi Arabia, 124, 126, 273
Schumer, Charles E., 52
Schumer Amendment, 54–55, 62
Science and Technology Center Ukraine (STCU), 88, 106
scientist "redirect" efforts, 72, 75–76, 92, 97, 103–4, 106, 108–9, 112, 307
scientists, Russian, 72, 86–88, 92, 97–99
security, nuclear and radiological materials. *See* nuclear and WMD materials: efforts to secure
self-interest, 7, 13–14, 41, 298–301, 307, 313; heterogeneity of interests in relation to MECRS, 25, 33–36, 39; interests of regional powers, 251, 253, 257, 259, 265; as not always favorable to cooperation, 5, 7, 34, 89, 126–28, 190, 241, 276, 282, 289, 299–300; as potentially aligned with common interest, 150; role in ABACC case, 236, 240–42; role in CTR case, 82, 89; role in Global Partnership, 98–100, 111; role in ICSANT and GICNT cases, 164, 174–75, 177; role in NWFZ cases, 211–12, 221, 223; role in Nuclear Security Summits, 183, 190, 192–93, 195–96, 201; role in P5+1 case, 282,

INDEX [331]

289; role in PSI case, 125–31, 135; role in RERTR case, 46–47, 57; role in USNCR 1540, 150–51, 155, 157
Semipalatinsk NWFZ Treaty. *See* Central Asian NWFZ Treaty
Senate, U.S., 74, 98, 167–68, 184, 219, 221
September 11, 2001, terrorist attack. *See* 9/11 attacks
Serrano, Monica, 215
Shanghai Cooperation Organization, 280
Shchuch'ye, 102–3
significant quantity (SQ), 286–87
Singapore, 123–24, 258–59, 263–65
Singh, Manmohan, 130
Six-Party Talks, 2
smuggling, nuclear, 72, 134, 164, 182, 192. *See also* illicit trafficking
Snezhinsk, 86
Solana, Javier, 273, 276–78
So San, 117–18
South Africa, 36, 128, 193, 209, 212, 214, 220
South China Sea, 120, 127
Southeast Asia, 17, 125, 153, 174, 212–13, 215–16, 218, 221–22, 224, 255, 258, 262–66. *See also* ASEAN
Southeast Asian NWFZ Treaty, 206, 209, 216, 219, 224–25, 255, 262, 265
South Korea. *See* Republic of Korea
South Pacific, 152, 154, 209, 212–13, 215, 218, 220–22, 225, 299
South Pacific Nuclear-Free Zone Treaty, 206, 209, 213, 215, 218–22, 225, 299
South Sudan, 143, 226
Soviet Union, 25–27, 184, 208–9, 212, 216, 231, 254, 262, 266; collapse of, 1, 28, 72–74, 78, 85, 90, 185, 210, 298; nuclear fuel and reactor exports, 47, 50–51, 53, 56–57, 63; nuclear material accounting practices, 82. *See also* Former Soviet Union; Russia
space, 27, 30, 37, 54
Spain, 110, 116–18, 121–23, 169, 174; 2004 Madrid terrorist attack, 261
State Department, U.S., 53, 58, 61–63, 65, 67, 71, 76–77, 84, 106, 131, 169, 173–74, 176, 182
Stein, Arthur, 8–9, 41
Strait of Hormuz, 281
Strait of Malacca, 124–25, 128

Strategic Arms Reduction Treaty (START), 72, 79, 92, 184
Straw, Jack, 141
SUA Protocol (Protocol to the Convention for the Suppression of Unlawful Acts Against the Safety of Maritime Navigation; 2005), 132, 134
submarines: Brazilian program, 243; dismantlement, 72, 97–98, 100–101, 103–5, 109, 112, 307; nuclear propulsion of, 165, 195
Suez Canal, 125
Sweden, 99, 102, 105
Syria, 131–32, 166, 305, 308

taboo, nuclear, 217
Taiwan, 36, 207
Tajikistan, 210
technology transfer, 26–27, 31–33, 36, 57, 261; intangible, 31, 37, 146
Tehran Agreement of October 2003, 274–75, 287
Tenex, 85
10+10 over 10 program, 97–98
terrorism, 2, 5, 16, 23, 117, 126, 141, 254–65, 299, 301–2, 308–11; as focus of Global Partnership program, 97–100, 105, 109, 111–12, 153–55; as focus of Nuclear Security Summits, 163–78, 181–87, 189–91, 193, 195, 197, 201; as focus of UNSCR 1540, 140–42, 147, 150, 157–58; nuclear, 3, 15, 31, 72, 255, 261–62, 264, 295; radiological, 165, 193–95; RERTR program reduces risks of, 46, 49, 66; WMD, 13, 17–18, 133, 298. *See also* 9/11 attacks
testing, nuclear, 208–9, 212, 215, 219–21, 224, 286–87, 299; India's, 1, 129, 298; North Korea's, 126, 129
tit-for-tat, 6, 8, 14
Tlatelolco Treaty. *See* Latin American NWFZ Treaty
Tokyo subway attack, 126, 165
Tonga monarchy, 215
Touval, Saadia, 8
transit controls, 37, 146
transparency, 28, 64, 102, 143, 238, 277
transshipment, 36–37, 45–46, 151, 193
Travelli, Armando, 56, 58–59, 61, 64

trigger lists, 9, 26–27, 31, 39
trust, 10, 158, 221; mistrust, 232, 245, 250; in PSI case, 132, 134–35; trust and mistrust in threat reduction programs in Russia, 73–74, 77–78, 80–82, 90–91, 101–2, 104, 305; trust-building, 222, 230–31, 244–45
Turkey, 123, 169, 280–81, 286; Istanbul, Obama speech in, 156
Turkmenistan, 210
Turpen, Libby, 175

Ukraine, 17, 72–75, 79, 87, 92, 99, 108, 110, 194; crisis, 17, 73, 92, 98, 110, 143, 204n36, 281, 286, 295, 305; Science and Technology Center, 88, 106
UN Charter, 140, 153, 163, 217, 278, 284–85; Article 40, 278; Article 41, 278; Chapter VI, 190, 284; Chapter VII, 190, 284
UN Convention on the Law of the Sea (UNCLOS), 118, 124
UN General Assembly, 141, 152, 164, 166, 210, 224, 284, 302; Resolution 50/53, 164; Resolution 51/210, 164, 166
United Arab Emirates, 128
United Kingdom, 206–7, 259; as drafter of UNSCR 1540, 155, 301; GICNT and, 169; Global Partnership program and, 102–3, 106–7, 109–10; as NSG founder, 26; Nuclear Security Summits and, 194, 199; as part of E3 and P5+1, 271, 273, 277–80, 282; PSI and, 116–17, 119, 121, 123, 125, 129
United Nations (UN), 156, 208–9, 216; Disarmament Commission (UNDC), 208, 211, 219; Institute for Disarmament Research (UNIDIR), 216; Office of Disarmament Affairs, 148, 214; Office on Drugs and Crime, 148, 170; Regional Centre for Peace and Disarmament in Asia and the Pacific, 211, 214; secretary-general, 164, 211; Trust Fund for Global and Regional Disarmament Activities, 143
University of Rhode Island, 63
UNSCR 1540, 2–3, 15, 17, 140–58 passim, 163, 169, 173, 177, 188, 190, 262, 295–97, 301–2, 304, 307, 310–11; export control regimes as foundation for, 23, 37; Global Partnership support for, 109–11, 143; as involving coordination, 9, 296; relation to PSI, 127, 132–34, 141; support provided by Nuclear Security Summits, 187, 192, 198
UN Security Council, 120, 122, 127, 151, 188, 220, 289, 297, 312; expanded role reflected in UNSCR 1540, 140–42, 152–55, 157–58, 190, 302; Iran nuclear program and, 2, 271, 273–80, 283–86, 309
UN Security Council Resolutions (UNSCR): Resolution 1267, 143, 149; Resolution 1373, 143, 149, 153, 163, 165, 169, 177; Resolution 1673, 141; Resolution 1696, 277, 285; Resolution 1747, 278, 286; Resolution 1803, 279, 286; Resolution 1810, 141; Resolution 1929, 280, 285–86; Resolution 1977, 141, 149. See also UNSCR 1540
uranium, 47–50, 56–57, 76, 193, 233, 243, 245, 271–73, 276, 280–81, 286; U-235, 47–49; U-238, 49. See also enrichment, uranium; highly enriched uranium (HEU); low-enriched uranium (LEU)
URENCO, 193
U.S. Enrichment Corporation (USEC), 76, 85, 91
U.S. Export-Import Bank, 62
U.S. Industry Coalition (USIC), 87
USSR. See Soviet Union
Uzbekistan, 210, 214

Vajpayee, Atal Behari, 129
VERTIC, 152
Videla, Jorge Rafael, 232, 242
Vietnam, Cam Ranh Bay and Da Nang ports, 216
Vietnam War, 209, 255
Villagra-Delgado, Pedro, 236

War on Terror, 155, 263–64
Warsaw Pact, 208
Washington Summit, 2010. See Nuclear Security Summits
Wassenaar Arrangement (WA), 23–25, 28–29, 38–39
Winner, Andrew, 308
WMD materials. See nuclear and WMD materials
working-level relationships, 4, 10–11, 14, 18, 302–3, 305, 307, 313–15; in ABACC case, 235,

238, 240, 245–46; in CTR, 73, 79, 81, 90; in Global Partnership program, 102, 112; in ICSANT and GICNT, 164, 175; in MECRS, 41; minor role in P5+1, 282; in Nuclear Security Summits, 183, 196, 202; in PSI, 116–17, 121–22, 124, 132–35; in relation to NWFZS, 214, 221; in RERTR program, 55–56; in UNSCR 1540, 154, 157
World Institute for Nuclear Security (WINS), 305
World War II, 25
Wrobel, Paulo, 216, 235, 237, 245
Wuchte, Tom, 154, 157
Wunderlich, Carmen, 2

Yemen, 117
Yinhe, 120

Zaborsky, Victor, 28
Zangger Committee, 26–27; Zangger list, 26
Zartman, William I., 8
Zheleznogorsk, 86
Zone of Peace, Freedom, and Neutrality, 209, 213